# nebraska symposium on motivation

## 1969

WILLIAM J. ARNOLD and DAVID LEVINE, Editors

**Dalbir Bindra** — Professor of Psychology, *McGill University*

**Edward L. Wike** — Professor of Psychology, *University of Kansas*

**Roger W. Black** — Professor of Psychology, *University of South Carolina*

**Elliot Aronson** — Professor of Psychology, *University of Texas at Austin*

**Stuart W. Cook** — Professor of Psychology, *University of Colorado*

**Philip G. Zimbardo** — Professor of Psychology, *Stanford University*

university of nebraska press
lincoln
1969

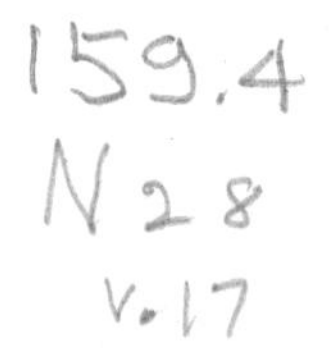


Publishers on the Plains
UNP


*Standard Book Number 8032–5617–5*
*Library of Congress Catalog Card Number 53–11655*
*Manufactured in the United States of America*

# Contents

Introduction, by William J. Arnold and David Levine vii

THE INTERRELATED MECHANISMS OF REINFORCEMENT AND MOTIVATION, AND THE NATURE OF THEIR INFLUENCE ON RESPONSE: Dalbir Bindra 1

SECONDARY REINFORCEMENT: SOME RESEARCH AND THEORETICAL ISSUES: Edward L. Wike 39

INCENTIVE MOTIVATION AND THE PARAMETERS OF REWARD IN INSTRUMENTAL CONDITIONING: Roger W. Black 85

SOME ANTECEDENTS OF INTERPERSONAL ATTRACTION: Elliot Aronson 143

MOTIVES IN A CONCEPTUAL ANALYSIS OF ATTITUDE-RELATED BEHAVIOR: Stuart W. Cook 179

THE HUMAN CHOICE: INDIVIDUATION, REASON, AND ORDER VERSUS DEINDIVIDUATION, IMPULSE, AND CHAOS: Philip G. Zimbardo 237

The Nebraska Symposium on Motivation: An Overview, by Ruben Ardila 309

Chronological List of Contents of the Nebraska Symposia on Motivation 313

Alphabetical List of Contents of the Nebraska Symposia on Motivation by Author 319

Subject Index 327

Author Index 332

# Introduction

This volume is the seventeenth in the series of the Nebraska Symposium on Motivation. For the first time the symposium was arranged by two people. We have found this arrangement to be particularly satisfactory because, as it has been in previous years, the symposium was held in two separate sessions. The first session, experimental in orientation, was primarily arranged by one of us (W. J. Arnold), and the second session, social-personality in orientation, by the other (David Levine).

We would like to point out features appearing in the Symposium series for the first time in this volume. These are the lists of contents of all the volumes and the review of the papers which have appeared in the symposium since its beginning in 1953. They were written by Mr. Ruben Ardila of Bogota, Colombia, who is now working toward his doctorate here at Nebraska. We are pleased that he has had the interest and enthusiasm to produce these useful additions to the series.

Before commenting more specifically on the papers in this volume, we would like to mention two things we regret. First, in our introduction to last year's symposium, we indicated our intention to continue a policy of extending invitations to potential contributors from overseas. Unfortunately, international economics—the balance-of-payments problem—has intervened so that a continuation of the policy appears presently infeasible. We have hopes for the future. Our second regret is that, for unavoidable reasons, we cannot include the paper on the behavior of newborn kittens which Lehrman and Rosenblatt gave in 1967.

The three papers of the first session of the symposium were focused on the notions of incentive motivation and secondary reinforcement. In his paper Dr. Bindra proposes the hypothesis that the effects on behavior produced by "reinforcement" and "motivation" arise from a common set of neurophysiological mechanisms, and that the principle of reinforcement is a special case of the more fundamental principle of motivation. He presents evidence to support a well-organized argument that the so-called backward-acting response-reinforcement influence of reinforcing events is illusory, and that reinforcing events, like motivating events, create central motive states that influence subsequent behavior. The specificity of this influence on a particular instrumental response is explained in terms of the assumption that the generation of a central motive state and the related conditioned incentive stimuli depends upon the incentive object in relation to which the response is defined.

The main focus of Dr. Wike's paper is secondary reinforcement, and particularly positive reinforcement deriving from the association of stimuli with rewards that reduce appetitional drives. In the first section of his paper, he reviews several of the important theoretical treatments of secondary reinforcement in connection with the motivational concepts of fractional antedating goal reaction ($r_g$) and frustration. The second section of his paper is devoted to a consideration of the more recent developments in secondary reinforcement research and theory. He examines several issues and presents some operant research on conditioned reinforcement, which he believes forces a reconsideration of the conception of secondary reinforcement. Then he proposes what he calls a simple hypothesis that he believes will integrate a considerable amount of the research on secondary reinforcement and suggests a number of new directions for research in this area. According to this hypothesis, which he calls the "reconditioning hypothesis," a secondary reinforcer will be strong and durable if, and only if, it has its reward value reconditioned from time to time by its being reassociated with primary reinforcements. In closing, he points out that for about 40 years much of the research on secondary reinforcement has been guided by an assumption that stimuli paired with primary reinforcement can become functionally autonomous sources of reward. He says that he believes that this assumption is a false one, that a secondary reinforcer retains its reward value only when it is renewed by reconditioning.

Dr. Black's paper deals with the notion of incentive motivation and its relation to parameters of reward in instrumental conditioning. He deliberately limited his analysis and concentrated on a very specific type of experimental situation, instrumental and differential appetitive conditioning. A careful consideration of several lines of research and theorizing dealing with this situation leads him to suggest several hypotheses in the context of instrumental appetitive conditioning, but he also points out that an extension of these notions to other types of situations is, in many cases, rather obvious. Some of the hypotheses he suggests are, first, that a primary "mechanism of reinforcement" seems to be incentive motivational, and in consequence he suggests a hypothetical incentive-motivation variable which depends on the quality or quantity of reward, but the strength of which is not always directly reflected in instrumental performance. In his opinion, the most plausible hypothesis regarding incentive motivation is that it is the result of the classical conditioning of components of the subject's response to the rewarding stimulus. It seems almost certain that this mechanism must be central in locus rather than consisting of peripheral anticipatory responses, such as licking, salivating, etc. It is quite possible, of course, that the strength of the hypothetical central state assumed to underlie incentive motivation may itself reflect characteristics of consummatory activity.

The second suggestion which he makes is that the apparent reinforcement value of the reward appears to depend not only on its magnitude or the amount of consummatory degree it evokes, but upon the consistency with which such behavior occurs. In short, he suggests a "two-factor" interpretation of reinforcement in instrumental appetitive conditioning: Increasing reward magnitude or the amount of consummatory activity facilitates performance. Decreasing the consistency of consummatory activity, or, conversely, increasing the amount of nonconsummatory activity, depresses performance and the apparent reinforcement value of the reward. Finally, he suggests the notion that "the sources of reward" appear to be multiple. He believes that while the efforts to reduce the number of *sufficient* characteristics of rewarding stimuli to a single *necessary* one have often been heroic, such attempts have typically failed to prove convincing. He points out, in closing, that there may be a multiplicity of stimuli which would "innately" serve as rewards and which must be identified empirically.

In the second session of the symposium, Dr. Eliot Aronson presented a paper dealing with some antecedents of interpersonal attraction. In simple language, as he puts it, his aim is to understand what makes people like one another. He points out that a look at the research literature reveals several important antecedents which presumably affect interpersonal attraction. Some of these antecedents are propinquity, similarity of values and beliefs, similarity of personality traits, complementarity of need systems, high ability, pleasant or agreeable characteristics or behavior, and being liked—we like people who like us. Then he observes that all of these antecedents can be loosely summarized under a general reward cost or exchange kind of theory, that is, we like people who bring us maximum gratification at minimum expense, or, more generally, we like people most whose overall behavior is most rewarding.

He then goes on to say that although the simplicity of the reward theory is appealing, its usefulness is diminished to the extent that it is difficult to specify the events and situations which are, in fact, rewarding. Then he describes the strategy by which one might specify these events in advance and which he has been successfully pursuing in his research for the past few years. Although this strategy is a useful one and has led to some interesting findings, he doesn't feel that it is very efficient. A more efficient approach entails the development of different "mini-theories" of attraction. This could lead to a greater understanding of the antecedents of attraction by helping define the limitations of a general reward theory. In recent years he has been working on such a "mini-theory" which he calls a gain-loss theory. Simply stated, it is: Increases in rewarding behavior from another person have more impact on an individual than constant invariant reward from a person. Thus, a person whose esteem for us increases over a period of time will be liked better than one who has always liked us, and a person whose esteem for us decreases over a period of time will be disliked more than someone who has always disliked us. Finally, he describes a number of intriguing experiments which yield evidence supporting his "mini-theory."

In his paper presented during the second session of the symposium, Dr. Cook gives a conceptual analysis for the study of behavior toward members of disliked groups. He says that by behavior toward disliked groups, he means what is ordinarily meant by such terms as *prejudiced behavior*, *discrimination*, *segregation*, *outgroup hostility*, *intergroup relations*, and so on. This is the attitude-related behavior to which the title refers.

Prior to presenting his analysis, Dr. Cook places it in perspective with respect tc theoretical strategy in social psychology. He points out that most social psychological theories, which are called process theories, focus on a single explanatory process and utilize this process in the explanation of any instance of social behavior to which it appears relevant. On the other hand, the second strategy—event theory, as he calls it—focuses not on a key explanatory concept or process but on a recurring pattern of events. The recurring pattern of events with which he is concerned is that which centers around unintended contact or personal experience with members of a disliked group and the reaction to this experience. More specifically, his concern is with unintended racial contact in desegregation situations. From an examination of "field" studies of his own and others, he abstracts five characteristics of unintended racial contact which favor friendly social behavior and favorable attitude change. Then he describes an experimental situation which he devised to investigate these five factors or characteristics under conditions offering more adequate opportunities for controlled observation.

With this background, Dr. Cook proceeds to present his conceptual analysis of the problem area which he described. In this conceptual scheme, he presents a useful analysis of the factors involved into the general categories of situational variables, person variables, and outcome variables. A fourth category is that of interaction variables, those variables which arise from neither the person nor the situation, but from an interaction of the person with others in the situation.

He elaborates, in a systematic way, the component factors within each of these categories, and finally relates his conceptual analysis to motivation. In summing up, he says that motives and motivelike constructs enter a conceptual analysis of attitude-related behavior both as 1) explanatory processes and as 2) subject attributes in which individual differences may be observed. As subject attributes, they range from motives and needs to such motivelike constructs as attitude, personality trait, and value. Both as explanatory processes and as subject attributes, their influence may be observed in relation not only to that part of the environment focal to the attitudinal object but also to that part consisting of contextual features. They contribute to understanding the subject's behavior at each of several time stages as this behavior unfolds in the pattern of events with which his analysis is concerned.

In the last paper of the second session, Dr. Zimbardo indicates that he is more interested in dealing with "messy" social behavior which is important in the present everyday world than with less important but "cleaner" behavior which may be more easily investigated under well-controlled conditions. He presents a heuristic model involving the concepts of *individuation* and *deindividuation.* "Volition, commitment, and responsibility fuse to form the core of one goal of the basic human choice. The act of freely making a commitment, for which one assumes responsibility, individuates the decision maker." He points out that the study of deindividuation links social psychology not only to the other social sciences but to basic themes in Western literature, mythology, and religion. Mythically, deindividuation is the ageless life force, the cycle of nature, the blood ties, the tribe, the female principle, the irrational, the impulsive, the anonymous chorus, the vengeful Furies. To be singular, to stand apart from other men, to aspire to Godhead, to honor social contracts and man-made commitments above family bonds is to be individuated. Then he goes on to relate these notions to current social problems and disturbances. He points out that conditions which foster deindividuation make each of us a potential assassin. He says that what is wrong with our society is that there are no institutionalized forms of release of antisocial impulses within a prescribed time period and other boundary conditions. Individuals who normally live controlled lives need such revels so that they can experience both the pleasure derived directly from such expression, and the greater pleasure of becoming reindividuated following a period of abandon or running amok.

In closing, he says "in the eternal struggle between order and chaos, we openly hope for individuation to triumph, but secretly plot mutiny with the forces within, drawn by the irresistible lure of deindividuation."

We wish again to express our gratitude to the National Institute of Mental Health and to the University of Nebraska for supporting this series.

W. J. Arnold
David Levine
*Professors of Psychology*

# The Interrelated Mechanisms of Reinforcement and Motivation, and the Nature of Their Influence on Response[1]

DALBIR BINDRA

*McGill University*

The hypothesis I want to propose in this paper is that the effects on behavior produced by reinforcement and motivation arise from a common set of neuropsychological mechanisms, and that the principle of reinforcement is a special case of the more fundamental principle of motivation.

Reinforcing events that follow a response influence the subsequent probability of occurrence of that response in that situation; this is the principle of reinforcement. The probability of occurrence of the response can also be influenced by motivating events present at the time of testing; this is the principle of motivation. It is customary to say that reinforcing events affect (increase or decrease) future response probability by the process of *response reinforcement*, that is, the strengthening or weakening of specific response tendencies, and that motivating events affect future response probability by the process of *response instigation*, that is, the activation or energizing of existing response tendencies. Is only one of these two hypothetical explanatory ideas, response reinforcement or response instigation, adequate to deal with the types of influences on response

1. The preparation of this paper was supported by Grant MH–03238–08 from the United States Public Health Service (National Institute of Mental Health) and Grant APT–74 from the National Research Council of Canada. I thank J. F. Campbell, M. Corcoran, C. Malsbury, Jane Stewart, and I. Szabó for their critical comments on earlier drafts of this paper.

probability traditionally considered under the two separate headings of reinforcement and motivation?

There is a conceptual difficulty in approaching this question. The difficulty arises from the common assumption that the process of response reinforcement works "backward" on responses that precede the reinforcing event, and that the process of response instigation works "forward" on responses that are to follow the motivating event. It should be noted, however, that in both cases the test of a change in response probability involves a before-and-after comparison. As shown in Table 1, what is actually observed in both cases

TABLE 1

EXPERIMENTAL PARADIGMS FOR DETERMINING REINFORCEMENT AND MOTIVATIONAL EFFECTS ON RESPONSE PROBABILITY

| *Antecedent Behavior* | *Experimental Event* | *Subsequent Behavior* |
|---|---|---|
| A: Response X | Motivating Event | B: Test Response [a] |
| Trial 1: Response X | Reinforcing Event | Trial 2: Test Response [b] |

[a] Comparison of A and B yields the motivational effect.
[b] Comparison of Trial 1 and Trial 2 yields the reinforcement effect.

is that the behavior following the experimental event (reinforcing or motivating) is different from the behavior preceding the experimental event. The fact that in the reinforcement paradigm the investigator specifies a particular response-reinforcement contingency, and may call the successive observation period a trial, is of no consequence so far as the logic of before-and-after comparison is concerned. Both the reinforcement and the motivational effects on response probability are *observed after* the reinforcing and motivating events respectively. Thus, while it remains possible that the response-reinforcement process works backward and the response-instigation process works forward, this may not in fact be so. Both may work forward or backward. My point is that there exists no necessary backward-vs.-forward distinction between reinforcement and motivational effects; the procedures employed by the investigator are different but the comparisons that define the two effects are the same.

Thus there is no a priori reason for considering reinforcing and motivational processes to be intrinsically different. However, the argument that they are fundamentally one and the same thing requires a close examination of several questions. I have grouped what appear to me to be the critical questions into three categories: Questions concerning Reinforcement, Questions concerning Motivation, and Questions concerning Response Determination.

## Questions concerning Reinforcement

In this discussion, the term *reinforcing event* refers to the manipulation (e.g., presentation, removal) of an *incentive object*, such as food, sexual partner, an electrified grid, or a threatening opponent; and *reinforcement* refers to the arrangement that a reinforcing event is contingent upon the occurrence of a specified response. The phrase *response reinforcement* is used here to denote a particular hypothesis about the process by which reinforcement affects response probability—the hypothesis that the change in response probability is caused by the process of direct, backward "strengthening" or "weakening" of particular response tendencies or stimulus-response associations.

### *Do Changes in Response Probability Reflect Response Reinforcement?*

According to the response-reinforcement hypothesis a reinforcement-induced change in the probability of occurrence of any specified instrumental response should not be possible without the actual occurrence of that response. But instrumental learning without performance of the response during the reinforced trials is possible. Experiments on "response substitution" (Lashley & McCarthy, 1926; Macfarlane, 1930; quoted by Munn, 1950) and "learning without responding" (e.g., Dodwell & Bessant, 1960; Solomon & Turner, 1962) have clearly demonstrated this. In these experiments, the probability of occurrence of a specified instrumental response is increased, but the increase cannot be attributed to the strengthening of that response, because the response is not allowed to occur during the training trials. But since such learning without responding does require the reinforcing event, the increase in response probability must be attributed to some influence of the reinforcing event other than response reinforcement. One possibility is that the reinforcing event creates a motivational influence which facilitates the subsequent emergence of certain types of instrumental responses. Such a motivational influence would be more general and would allow for the observed lack of response-specificity in what the animal learns.

*Is Response Reinforcement the Basis of "Motivational Excitement"?*

A view held commonly since the publication of Hull's (1943) general behavior theory is that motivational excitement—the "interest" and "arousal" that accompany goal-directed, instrumental behavior—does not represent a primary motivational process but is dependent upon response reinforcement. According to this view, the responses that are said to constitute motivational excitement are the responses that have been strengthened by prior reinforcement in the situation. Thus, if the principles of motivation and reinforcement appear to be alike, it is because the motivational characteristics of behavior are themselves produced by prior response reinforcement. Reinforcement is the primary factor; motivation is derivative.

This view is untenable. The responses displayed in the presence of an incentive object are seldom the same as the responses that are said to comprise motivational excitement. In a hungry rat, food elicits sniffing, biting, and swallowing, but the typical signs of anticipating food are exploration and searching, consisting of rearing, circling, scratching obstacles, etc. Similarly, the responses elicited by an electrified grid are prancing, jumping, squealing, and the like, but responses that usually indicate anticipation of electric shock are freezing and crouching. These common observations suggest that the responses usually considered as indicators of motivational excitement are so different from the responses elicited by the incentives themselves that it is unlikely that the basis of the excitement lies in the increased probability of occurrence of responses elicited by incentive stimuli.

However, these casual observations do not rule out the possibility of response reinforcement of the variety of actions that might precede the presentation of the reinforcing event (i.e., incentive presentation). In order to examine this possibility, Bindra and Palfai (1967) exposed thirsty rats to paired presentations of a conditioned stimulus (metronome) and an incentive (water) while the animals were held in restraining cages. After several conditioning sessions, they measured the effects of the conditioned stimulus on the exploratory activity of the rats in another situation. The types of responses that contributed to exploration scores (e.g., rearing, walking) were such that they could not have been performed in the restraining cages—during conditioning. Nevertheless, in the test situation the animals explored more in the presence of the conditioned stimulus than in its absence. Further, the acts displayed by the rats in the restraining cages were quite different from those that occurred on the presentation of the conditioned stimulus in the test situation. Thus, even if certain acts were conditioned in the restraining cages, they were not the acts that comprised motivational excitement in the test situation.

Clearly, the motivational excitement that may arise as a consequence of experience with an incentive is not crucially dependent upon the strengthening of the specific responses preceding or accompanying the incentive presentation. The motivational factor rather seems to be a general motivational state, not specifically linked to any particular responses. The actual actions displayed in the test situation would appear to arise from an interaction of the motivational state with the total stimulus characteristics of the test situation, and not depend on what the animal did just before or during the presentation of the incentive during conditioning. This points to the conclusion that the critical role of a reinforcing event (i.e., incentive manipulation) is to create a certain motivational state, and that while the motivational excitement is dependent upon the prior occurrence of the reinforcing event, it is not dependent upon response reinforcement.

### *Do All Reinforcing Events Produce Motivation?*

Before we can confidently conclude that the primary function of reinforcing events (manipulation of incentives) is not response reinforcement but the creation of a motivational state, we should be reasonably sure that all events said to be reinforcing are also motivating. Casual observation, of course, suggests that this is so. It is a common trick in training hungry animals to "prime" them by giving them an "appetizer" pellet of food *before* the training session. And a simple everyday success or failure may change a man's mood and outlook on life for several hours to come.

Campbell and I (Bindra & Campbell, 1967) have experimentally investigated whether events that are known to be positive reinforcers (that is, which increase response probability) have any measurable (motivational) effects on behavior immediately *following* the (reinforcing) event. In order not to confound any intrinsic motivational effects with the presumed effects of response reinforcement, it was necessary to create an experimental arrangement in which the reinforcing event could not be said to reinforce any responses. We achieved this by using intracranial electrical stimulation in lateral hypothalamic "reward sites" as the reinforcing event and by stimulating only when the animal was motionless. Since this type of reinforcing event requires no consummatory responses (e.g., eating in the case of food reinforcement), no response could be said to be consistently associated with the reinforcing event. We examined the changes in spontaneous behavior of the rat following intracranial stimulation. The results are shown in Fig. 1. In the left part of the figure, the speckled columns represent the prestimulation level of general activity. At the end of the prestimulation observation period, a 0.5 sec. intracranial stimulation was given. Even the first, momentary, response-independent stimulation produced a marked increase in exploratory activity (striped column), which generally lasted for as long as two minutes or more. Since this effect on exploration could have been caused by the novelty of electrical stimulation per se, we tried to condition whatever motivational state might have been created by the intracranial stimulation. A conditioned stimulus (metronome) was turned on for 15 sec. before the onset of a series of pulses of intracranial stimulation lasting for 30 sec. After several trials of conditioning, the animals started being active as soon as the tone was turned on. If we regard this increase in exploratory activity as motivational arousal, it is clear that the type of reinforcing event employed in this experiment has intrinsic motivating properties, not dependent upon response reinforcement.

But the question still remains whether *all* reinforcing events have motivating properties. Of course, it is not possible to prove that they do, for a proof would require showing that no reinforcing event, existing or imaginable, lacks motivational properties. What must serve in place of decisive proof is the demonstration that every reinforcing event that has been examined in this connection has been found to possess motivating properties. And this does appear to be the case; the successful conditioning of motivational states under curare (e.g., Solomon & Turner, 1962) is pertinent here. It is hard to imagine any incentive manipulation that can alter response probability but would not have motivating effects. In this connection it is interesting to note that it has not been possible to distinguish between brain sites involved in reinforcement and the sites involved in motivation; the same neural systems seem to underlie both (Christopher & Butter, 1968; Glickman & Schiff, 1967; Milner, in press).

### *Conclusion*

Four summarizing statements can be made on the basis of the above discussion. 1) While reinforcing events obviously are capable of altering response probability, the change in response probability is not produced by "response reinforcement"—the direct strengthening or weakening influence of the reinforcing event on specific preceding responses. 2) Response reinforcement is not the basis of motivational excitement that accompanies goal-directed, instrumental actions. 3) All reinforcing events (that is, incentive manipulations) that alter response probability also have intrinsic motivating properties not dependent upon response reinforcement. 4) It appears reasonable to proceed on the assumption that the primary effect of a reinforcing event is not response reinforcement, but the creation of a motivational state that influences a wide variety of subsequent behavior of the animal.

## Questions concerning Motivation

The concept of motivation refers to the fact that animals display particular types of goal-directed actions, such as feeding, copulating, and escaping, at certain times but not at others. Typically such actions involve searching or *exploratory responses*, approach-withdrawal or *instrumental responses*, and consummatory or *incentive-related responses*. When habit (i.e., learning or practice) is held

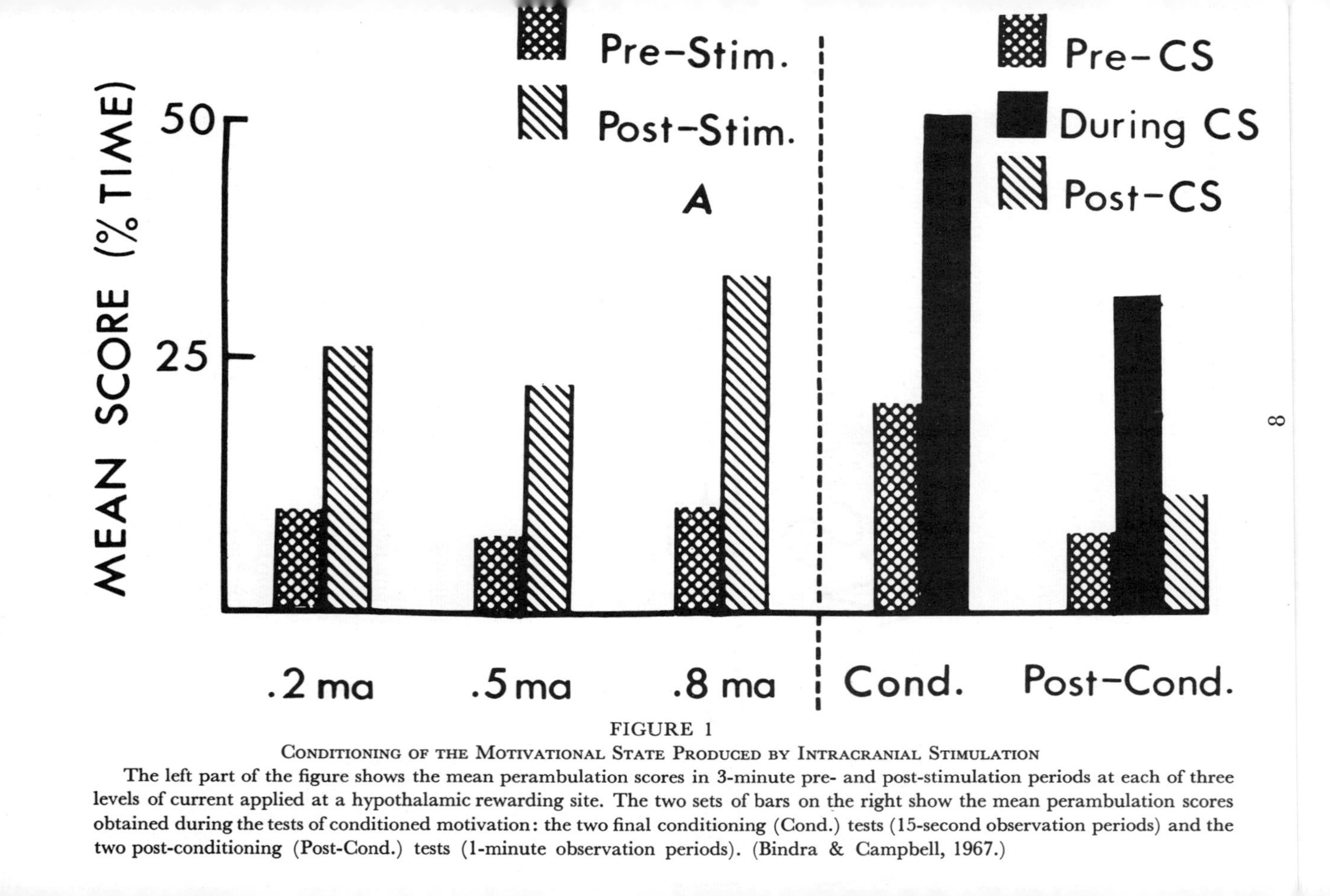


FIGURE 1

Conditioning of the Motivational State Produced by Intracranial Stimulation

The left part of the figure shows the mean perambulation scores in 3-minute pre- and post-stimulation periods at each of three levels of current applied at a hypothalamic rewarding site. The two sets of bars on the right show the mean perambulation scores obtained during the tests of conditioned motivation: the two final conditioning (Cond.) tests (15-second observation periods) and the two post-conditioning (Post-Cond.) tests (1-minute observation periods). (Bindra & Campbell, 1967.)

constant and the investigator manipulates variables related to incentives, or to bodily changes (e.g., those arising from food deprivation, fatigue, hormonal variations, or drugs), or both, the resulting changes in behavior are usually described as "motivational effects."

*Is Motivation Equivalent to Drive?*

Traditionally, motivational effects have been explained mainly with reference to the concept of *drive*, which was introduced into psychology around 1920 (e.g., Richter, 1922; Woodworth, 1918). The drive view of motivation, summarized in Fig. 2, holds that particular drive manipulations (e.g., food deprivation, induction of estrus, exposure to painful stimuli) induce particular physiological processes or "drives" that directly increase the level of general activity of the animal and facilitate the occurrence of particular instrumental and incentive-related responses. Thus, food deprivation is said to produce certain physiological processes, which in turn are thought to make the animal more active and to facilitate the occurrence of food-approach and eating.

For several years the drives were regarded as the primary motivational factors. However, now the developing consensus seems to be that the drive concept in the sense of the physiological consequences of certain drive manipulations, is inadequate for dealing with motivational effects. Some of the reasons are as follows:

1) When precautions are taken to remove from the test situation incentive objects, as well as incentive-related stimuli, drive manipulations do not instigate responses that could be described as searching or investigatory. In other words, drive per se, in the absence of incentive stimulation, is not sufficient to produce (goal-directed) exploratory responses. The increase in general activity produced by drives lacks the features of excitement and systematic investigation of the environment that characterize exploratory responses. These points have been documented recently by several authors (e.g., Bindra, 1968; Bolles, 1967).

2) The facilitation of instrumental responses by drive manipulations has traditionally been attributed to drive. However, the experiments on which this view was based confounded drive with incentive stimulation. Now it appears that drive per se, in the

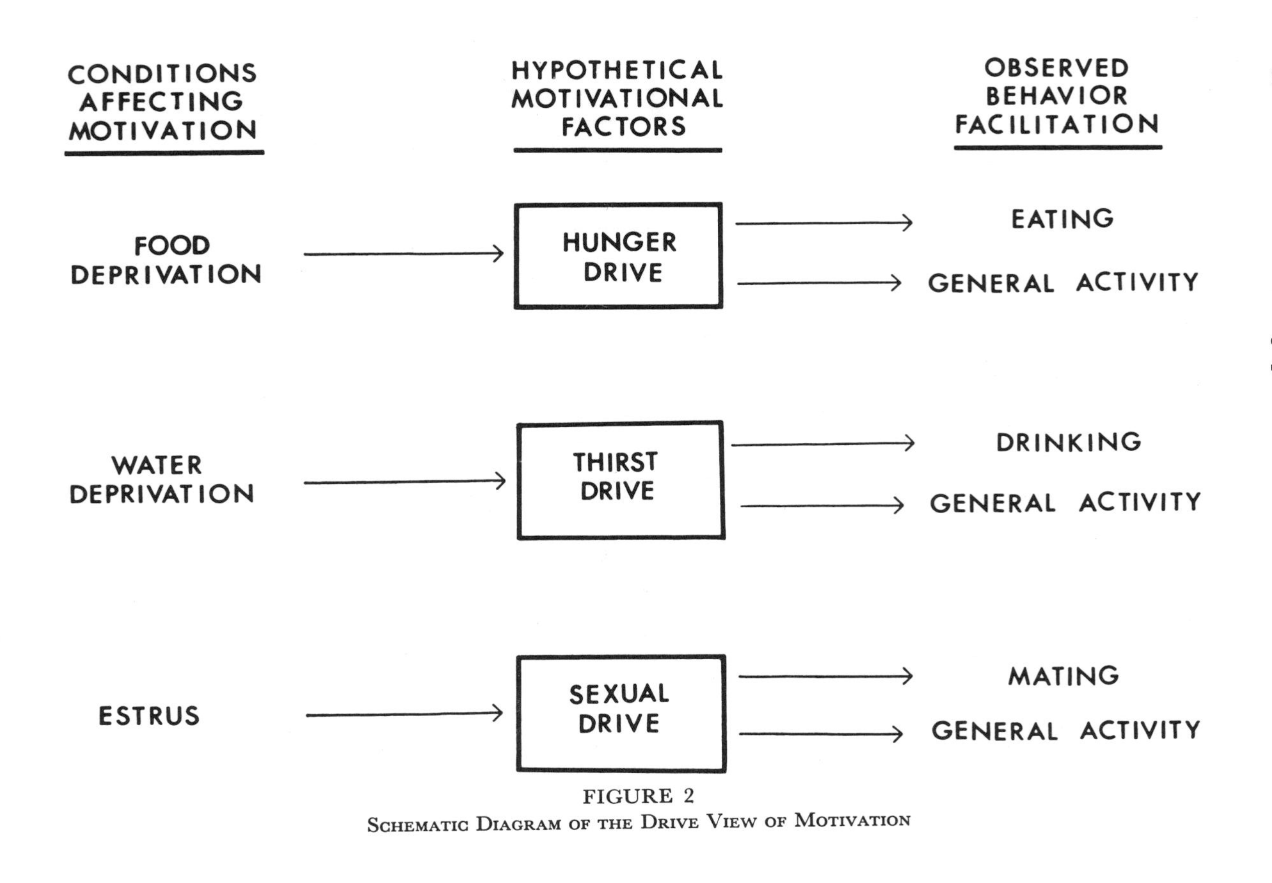


FIGURE 2
SCHEMATIC DIAGRAM OF THE DRIVE VIEW OF MOTIVATION

absence of incentive stimulation, is incapable of facilitating instrumental responses (Bindra, 1968). This conclusion can be supported both on the basis of argument (e.g., Black, 1965), and on the results of experiments which separate the effects of drive from those of drive plus incentive stimulation (e.g., Mendelson, 1966).

3) The fact that drive facilitates the occurrence of incentive-related (e.g., consummatory) responses cannot be taken as evidence that drive per se is the source of the facilitation, for a test of incentive-related responses cannot be made in the absence of incentive stimulation. However, evidence that, for example, given a certain level of hunger, the readiness with which an animal will eat depends on the palatability of food and other incentive properties (e.g., Young, 1948) indicates that the facilitation of consummatory responses produced by manipulating drive is not independent of incentive stimulation.

4) The concept of drive, as a special physiological process, is not applicable to a wide variety of motivational effects. For example, a normally satiated animal will readily eat a preferred (e.g., sweet) food, and highly novel objects will provoke withdrawal responses without requiring any specific physiological condition. It appears that many goal-directed actions of animals (e.g., grooming, exploring, playing) occur under a wide range of organismic states and do not require any highly specific physiological conditions of the type associated with hunger, thirst, estrus, or pain (Nissen, 1954). Thus, the answer to the question, Is motivation equivalent to drive? is no.

*What, Then, Is Motivation?*

Another view of motivation has been gradually emerging over the past couple of decades. Its early beginnings in the concept of "incentive motivation" (Hull, 1950; Seward, 1951; Spence, 1956) have now led to somewhat clearer formulations that regard environmental incentive stimuli to be a critical factor in goal-directed actions (e.g., Bindra & Palfai, 1967; Bolles, 1967; Black, 1965; Logan, 1960; Sheffield, 1966). The general idea is that motivational processes—that produce the observed motivational effects—are generated by a combination of physiological conditions and incentive stimulation. Within this broad framework, I (Bindra, 1968, 1969) have developed a specific model of motivation (Fig. 3). My view is that the processes that produce the observed motivational influences on behavior arise from an interaction between the neural consequences of the prevailing organismic state and the neural consequences of certain types of environmental incentive stimulation. The particular set of neural processes that arise from any such interaction may be described, following Morgan (1943), as a "central motive state," or cms. The organismic state, which is one of the interacting factors, may be a general state (e.g., being awake, sleepy, or sick) or a more specific physiological condition of the type traditionally called a drive (e.g., conditions produced by food deprivation, drug injection, or fatigue). The incentive stimulation, which is the other interacting factor, may consist of any stimuli arising from environmental objects that we usually describe as possessing affective properties and label "incentives," "reinforcers," or "emotional stimuli." The *central motive state*, then, is a functional neural change which is generated by an interaction of the neural representations of organismic state and incentive object, and which, once generated, persists for some time. The reasons for considering the motivational factor as a primary central factor, rather than as dependent upon sensory feedback from visceral or skeletal responses, as suggested by some (e.g., Mowrer, 1947, 1960; Spence, 1956, 1960), have been elaborated elsewhere (e.g., Bindra, 1968; Rescorla & Solomon, 1967).

The generation and persistence of a central motive state is necessary for goal-directed actions: exploratory, instrumental, and incentive-linked. While a central motive state persists, it facilitates the occurrence of a certain class of incentive-linked actions (e.g., eating, drinking, copulating); thus central motive states may be classified in terms of the type of incentive objects to which the animal's responses are addressed. Note that the concept of central motive state should not be identified either with organismic state alone or with incentive stimulation alone. It is their interaction that generates the central motive state. Thus, neither hunger nor food can by itself produce a food-directed central motive state, but when the neural consequences of hunger interact with the neural consequences of food-related stimuli (e.g., the smell and sight of food),

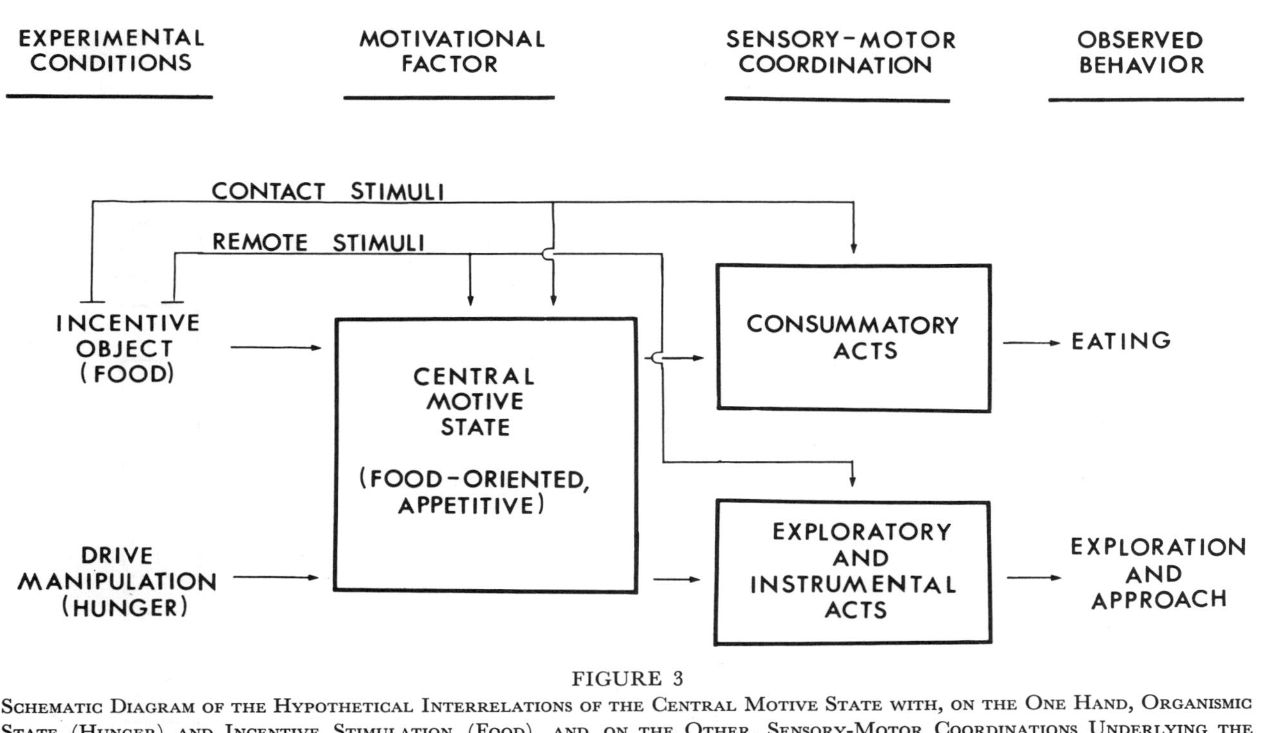


FIGURE 3

Schematic Diagram of the Hypothetical Interrelations of the Central Motive State with, on the One Hand, Organismic State (Hunger) and Incentive Stimulation (Food), and, on the Other, Sensory-Motor Coordinations Underlying the Observed Behavior

the central motive state is created and food-oriented behavior ensues.

One advantage of this formulation is that it allows a unified approach to the phenomena of motivation and emotion. The actions we associate with words such as fear, anger, love, joy, and depression are usually said to be "emotional" actions, and the actions we associate with the words such as hunger, thirst, sex, and motherhood are generally called "motivational" actions. My view (Bindra, 1969) is that each of such species-typical actions, whether called emotional or motivational, is crucially dependent on a central motive state, which in turn arises from an interaction of a certain organismic state and a certain class of environmental incentive object. Customarily, we think of emotional actions to be elicited by environmental stimuli and motivational actions to be instigated by internal organismic conditions. But in fact an interaction of internal organismic conditions and environmental factors is involved in both types of actions. While normally emotional actions do appear to be elicitable within a wide range of organismic conditions, it can be demonstrated that, holding environmental conditions constant, organismic conditions do play a part in emotional behavior. Premenstrual depressions, androgen-induced aggression, and the use of tranquilizers for reducing anxiety clearly show the role of organismic conditions in emotional behavior. Similarly, while normally motivational actions appear to be instigated in the presence of a wide range of incentive objects, so long as the appropriate organismic state is present, it can be demonstrated that, holding organismic conditions constant, the nature of environmental objects can affect the occurrence of motivational actions. An animal satiated on one food will readily resume eating when offered a preferred food, and a male rat, after copulation with one female, will prefer to copulate with another female than to copulate with the same one (Beach & Ransom, 1967). Even when a species-typical action (e.g., eating or attack) is produced by electrical stimulation of the appropriate hypothalamic site, the precise characteristics of the available incentive object determine the probability that the animal will display the action (Levison & Flynn, 1965; Tenen & Miller, 1964; Roberts et al., 1967).

*What Is Secondary or Learned Motivation?*

Scores of experiments inspired by the two-process theory of learning have shown that initially neutral stimuli can, through the procedure of classical conditioning, acquire conditioned incentive-motivational properties that resemble some of the properties possessed by the unconditioned (incentive) stimulus. For example, if a hungry animal is exposed to pairings of a tone and food, the tone will acquire some of the motivating properties of hunger-food. These motivating properties can be demonstrated by using the tone to modify a variety of responses in other situations (for recent examinations of this evidence, see Bacon & Bindra, 1967; Bindra, 1968; Bolles, 1967; Rescorla & Solomon, 1967). In terms of the model of motivation presented above, we can say that central motive states are conditionable.

What is the nature of such conditioning of a central motive state? Since a central motive state arises from an interaction of an organismic state and a certain type of incentive stimulation, it is reasonable to ask, What precisely is conditioned? Does the conditioned stimulus—metronome tone, light, etc.—become a conditioned stimulus (or substitute) for the organismic state or for the incentive or for both? Is the basis of secondary or learned motivation the conditioning of the neural consequences of the organismic state or of the neural consequences of the incentive stimulation, or both?

The early concepts of "secondary drive" and "secondary reinforcement," advocated in the writings of Hull (1943), Dollard and Miller (1950), and Miller (1951), implied that both organismic state ("drive") and incentive stimulation could be conditioned individually and separately. However, the evidence for the conditioning of organismic state was by no means conclusive. The difficulty, of course, is that of experimentally separating the conditioning of organismic state from the conditioning of incentive stimulation. In the absence of any critical experiments, attempts have been made to settle the issue on the basis of argument. Thus, Brown (1953) has set forth a variety of reasons why the idea of conditioning of an organismic state per se—of "secondary drive"—is untenable.

One of the results of the Bindra and Palfai (1967) experiment described above supports this conclusion. They found that the efficacy of a conditioned incentive-motivational stimulus depends on the actual existence of the appropriate organismic state. They measured the increase in exploratory perambulation produced at various levels of thirst by a conditioned stimulus that had previously been paired with water. As seen in Fig. 4, the increase in perambulation produced by the conditioned incentive stimulus was negligible when the animals were not thirsty, but was quite substantial when the animals were thirsty. This means that the efficacy of the conditioned (incentive-motivational) stimulus depended on the existence of a state of thirst. Clearly, if thirst was needed at the time of testing with the conditioned stimulus, then the conditioned stimulus could not have reinstated thirst. Since the actual incentive object (water) was not required at the time of test to produce the increase in perambulation, the conditioned stimulus must have assumed certain properties of the incentive. Thus, the conditioning of a motivational state rests on the conditioning of incentive properties. The conditioned stimuli that can create a central motive state should, therefore, be called *conditioned incentive stimuli.*

### *Conclusion*

The above discussion permits three conclusions. 1) Drive, defined as the direct physiological consequences of certain "drive" (metabolic) manipulations, is by itself not sufficient for explaining motivational effects on exploratory, instrumental, and consummatory responses. 2) The concept of *central motive state*, defined as a functional neural change which is generated by an interaction of the neural representations of organismic state (including "drive") and incentive object, appears more suitable for dealing both with naturally occurring species-typical actions and experimentally produced motivational effects. 3) When a central motive state is conditioned to an initially neutral stimulus, the latter serves as a substitute for incentive stimulation, not for organismic state; thus, the basis of secondary or learned motivation is secondary or conditioned incentives, and not secondary or conditioned organismic states (or "drives").

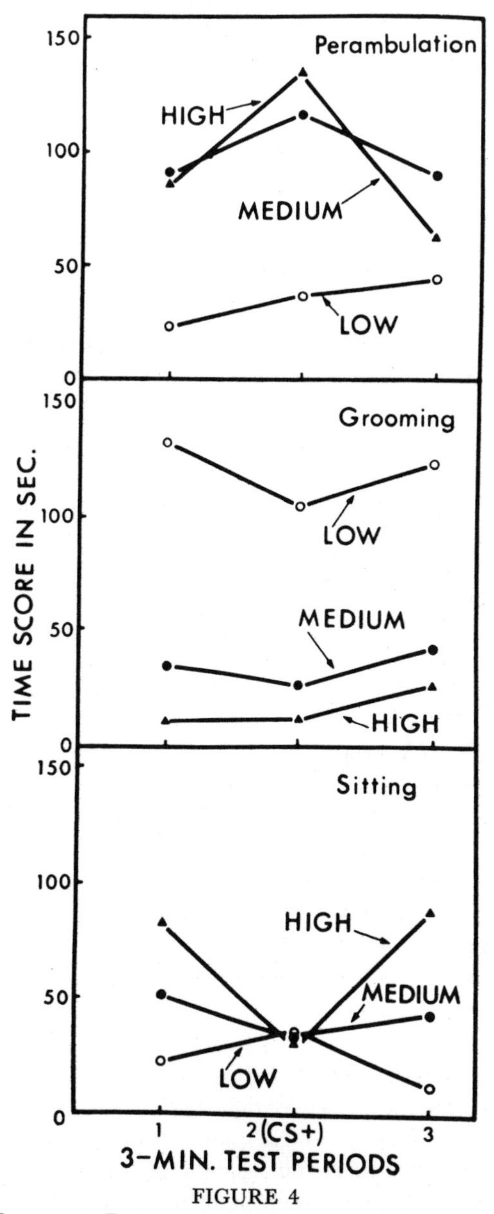


FIGURE 4

MEAN TIME SCORES FOR EACH OF THREE CATEGORIES OF ACTS OBTAINED BY THE HIGH-, MEDIUM-, AND LOW-DRIVE GROUPS DURING THE THREE SUCCESSIVE TEST PERIODS

The conditioned incentive stimulus (CS+) was presented during the middle test period. (Bindra & Palfai, 1967.)

## Questions concerning Response Determination

The traditional view has been that the motivational factor influences behavior merely by making a response more or less likely to occur, without directly determining *which* response would occur. For example, in Hull's (1943) behavior theory, the motivational factor ("drive") was postulated to explain when or how readily a response would occur, not which one would occur; motivation determines *response occurrence*, not the selection of response. *Response selection* was thought to be determined by the stimuli to which the animal is exposed at the moment and the relative strengths of their associations with different responses in the animal's repertoire. In general, the theorists (e.g., Miller, 1963; Mowrer, 1947; Rescorla & Solomon, 1967; Seward, 1956; Spence, 1956) who have followed the broad framework of Hullian response reinforcement theory have tended not to implicate the motivational factor in response selection.

A different way of conceptualizing the influence of the motivational factor on behavior is to suggest that it determines, in part, both response selection and response occurrence. This is the view taken by Mowrer (1960) in his latest theory, according to which successive acts in a response sequence are determined by moment-to-moment variations in the motivational factor. This appears to me to be a better approach, though Mowrer has made no attempt to outline the exact way in which the motivational factor may contribute to response determination (response selection and response occurrence). In this lack of specification of possible mechanisms, Mowrer's account has the same shortcoming as Tolman's (1948), who failed to specify the type of mechanisms by which cognitive factors ("expectancy," "cognition," etc.) may determine response.

This section is addressed to the broad question of the way in which the influence of the motivational factor on behavior may be conceptualized. Note that the discussion is not intended to be a full discussion of response determination, but only of the way in which the motivational factor, central motive state, may contribute to response determination. A full account of response determination would also have to include the role of cognitive factors, and this is beyond the scope of this paper.

*How Does the Central Motive State Influence Behavior?*

The technique of electrical stimulation of hypothalamic sites involved in various species-typical actions is at present the best way of studying the efferent influences of central motive states. The electrical stimulation of such "hypothalamic motive sites" produces, not specific motor patterns, but broad response tendencies which, in conjunction with environmental stimuli, determine the exact course of action. For example, the electrical stimulation of hypothalamic "feeding sites" leads to eating or drinking actions only in the presence of appropriate environmental incentive objects —food or water. Similarly, the stimulation of "aggression sites" leads to an attacking action only when an attackable incentive object is present in the environment. Thus, such hypothalamic sites are not motor centers, but appear to be parts of a system closely related to the loci at which particular central motive states are generated. It seems reasonable to suppose that the electrical stimulation of, say, a feeding site produces a central motive (feeding) state by bypassing the processes (hunger state and food stimulation) that are normally involved in generating that central motive state. This means that while studies involving electrical stimulation of hypothalamic motive sites cannot tell us anything about the mechanisms by which central motive states are normally produced, they may nevertheless elucidate the way in which central motive states, once generated, influence behavior. Consider some of the results of experiments that have made use of this method.

The first result to note is that though a satiated animal does not display a consummatory response (e.g., eating) in the presence of an incentive object (i.e., food), it begins to display it soon after the electrical stimulation of the appropriate (feeding) site is started. In other words, while in a normally satiated animal the stimulus characteristics of the food incentive are not in themselves sufficient to elicit the response of eating, the electrically induced central motive state renders the food more attractive, leading to appropriate approach and consummatory responses. Thus, it may be said that the central motive state alters the incentive value (attractiveness, repulsiveness) of incentive objects.

The second result of importance is that the electrical stimulation of a hypothalamic motive site is capable of producing exploratory responses even in the absence of any particular incentive object. That is, a stimulation-induced central motive state can render more effective the stimulus characteristics of the experimental chamber, so that they again become capable of eliciting the exploratory responses that presumably had been habituated before. This is consistent with the above suggestion that central motive states alter the incentive value of environmental objects and events.

The third result of interest here is that a stimulation-induced central motive state can be conditioned to an initially neutral stimulus. Thus, a tone paired with electrical stimulation of the hypothalamic feeding site would acquire the capacity of generating the feeding central motive state. But this does not mean that the animal will start to make eating movements on the presentation of the tone alone. The actual responses displayed by the animal will depend on the exact characteristics of the stimulus situation and the strength of the central motive state generated by the conditioned stimulus. In the absence of food, the animal will probably merely explore. If some food-related stimulus objects (e.g., food-delivery tray) are present, the animal is likely, at the presentation of the tone, to display instrumental approach responses to the location of the food-related objects. Finally, if food is present, the animal may, at the onset of the tone, start to eat but (in the absence of electrical stimulation) is not likely to continue to eat. In some observations made in this laboratory (A. Hilton, E. Lewicki, & D. Bindra, unpublished experiments), we have found that while conditioned stimuli in the absence of electrical stimulation and food will make the animals (rats) explore and make instrumental approach responses toward the usual location of food, the animals almost never actually eat. Thus the reliable and continuous elicitation of consummatory responses requires the presence of a continuing and strong central motive state, and the central motive states produced by conditioned stimuli (in "satiated" animals) are not persistent or strong enough to cause animals to display consummatory responses. This is consistent with the observations of Mendelson (1966), and Roberts and Kiess (1964) that while instrumental (approach) responses can be elicited by conditioned incentive stimuli (e.g., alley cues or the sight of a lever in a lever-pressing situation), the actual occurrence of the consummatory responses usually requires both the presence of the incentive object and electrical stimulation. It appears that normally an appropriate organismic state (drive) is required to produce a strong enough central motive state to instigate consummatory behavior. The above analysis also suggests that conditioned stimuli cannot reinstate organismic states, and that while conditioned stimuli acquire some of the properties of remote incentive stimuli (e.g., the smell and sight of food), which attract (or repel) the animal, they do not acquire the properties of contact incentive stimuli, which elicit consummatory responses.

A model that is consistent with the above observations on the way in which a central motive state influences behavior is shown in Fig. 5. The basic feature of this model is that it portrays the stimuli arising from the incentive object as having two separate routes to the sensory-motor coordination sites: a direct sensory-motor route and an indirect sensory-motivational-motor route. The fibers in the former, Route X, form direct connections with a variety of efferent coordination systems. The fibers in the latter, Route Y, form connections with central motive sites, where an interaction of the prevailing organismic state and incentive stimulation takes place and a central motive state is generated. The central motive state then selectively modulates (facilitates or inhibits) particular sensory-motor coordinations. The sensory stimulation arising from the other, nonincentive parts of the environment is capable of becoming conditioned stimulation (Route C) for producing the central motive state.

*How is a Response Determined?*

Assuming that the general mechanism of motivational influence on behavior is one of selective facilitation and inhibition of particular sensory-motor coordinations, we may next ask precisely how the sensory-motor coordinations corresponding to a particular response are "selected" and "activated"? My general approach to this question is that both so-called response selection and response occurrence are aspects of a single set of mechanisms of *response determination*. A response is not first selected and then made to occur;

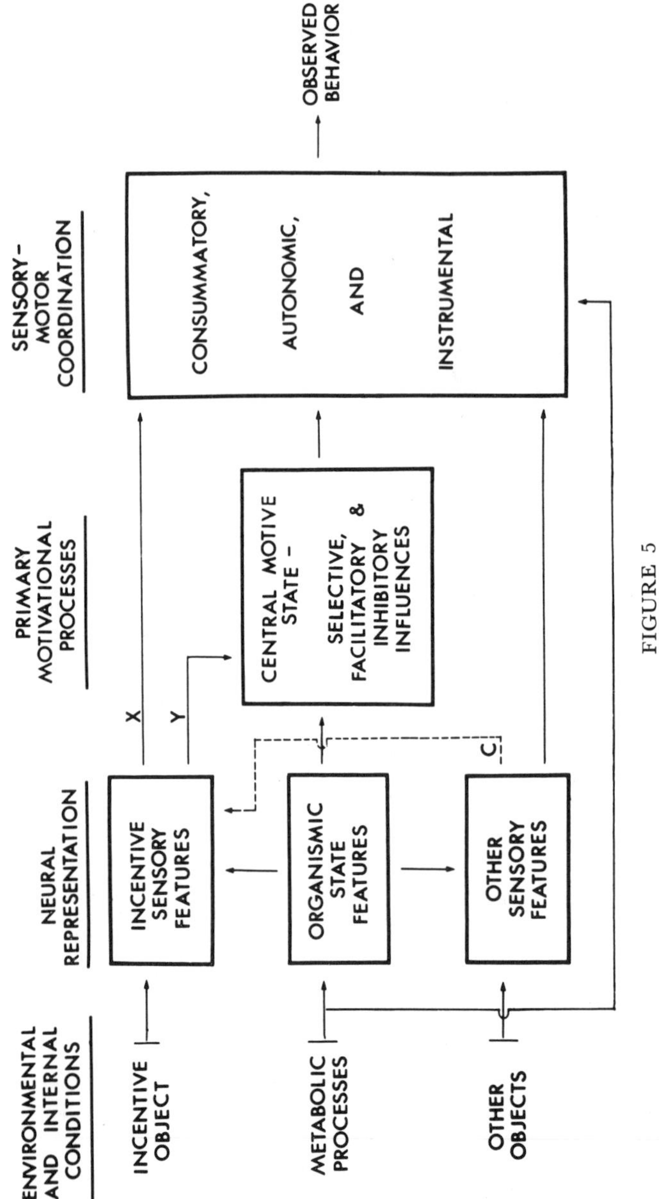


FIGURE 5

A Hypothetical Model of Motivation

Showing 1) how the central motive state is generated by an interaction of neural representations of organismic-state features and incentive-stimulation features (Route Y), and 2) how the environmental (incentive and nonincentive) stimuli, together with the central motive state, influence response determination by selective effects (facilitation or inhibition) on sensory-motor coordinations. The stimulation arising from nonincentive environmental stimulation can, through conditioning (Route C) acquire the same properties as Route Y.

"selection" and "occurrence" go hand in hand. A response does not exist prior to its occurrence; it attains a reality only by occurrence. Any defined response is organized afresh each time it occurs. From this point of view, the problem of response determination is simply that of the organized excitation of a sequence of sensory-motor coordinations that corresponds to the behavioral definition of the response.

Following Schneirla (1959), I assume that there exist largely innate sensory-motor coordinations that make animals move toward certain (appetitive) incentive objects and away from other (aversive) incentive objects. The incentive value of the stimuli from incentive objects depends upon the central motive state created by an interaction of the prevailing organismic state and the remote (olfactory, visual, auditory) stimuli arising from the incentive objects. Inasmuch as certain nonincentive stimuli occur in close temporal and spatial contiguity with the incentive object, they—the initially neutral stimuli—acquire some of the properties of remote incentive stimuli. Thus, goal-directed instrumental approach and withdrawal responses may be attributed to the direct excitation by conditioned and remote incentive stimuli of certain sensory-motor coordinations, which are selectively facilitated by the influence of central motive states. While this formulation is readily applicable to instrumental responses that involve direct approach or withdrawal, its application to the more complicated instrumental responses (e.g., lever pressing) is not obvious. A discussion of the whole problem of "response shaping" and other aspects of instrumental learning lies outside the scope of this paper.

Note that, according to this view, the occurrence of the successive acts comprising approach or withdrawal does not depend on the sensory feedback from visceral or other "emotional" responses produced by incentive stimuli—a proposition suggested by Mowrer (1960). As Miller (1963) has pointed out, the dependence of each successive act on sensory feedback would make the response completion much slower than it usually is. According to the present view the excitation of the appropriate sensory-motor coordinations, facilitated by the central motive state, is achieved directly by incentive stimuli, remote or conditioned. The exact neural mechanisms that link particular classes of incentive stimuli to certain sensory-motor coordinations representing approach and withdrawal emerges as an important problem for investigation (Milner, in press, Chap. 19; Schneirla, 1965).

*How Do Reinforcement and Motivation Affect the Probability of Particular Responses?*

As we have seen, the role of reinforcing events (incentive manipulations) is not the strengthening or weakening of preceding responses but the creation of central motive states that affect the subsequent behavior of the animal. This means that the effects on response probability of both reinforcing and motivating events arise from a common source—the central motive state. If the central motive state constitutes a fairly general facilitatory or inhibitory influence not specifically linked to any response, how can we explain the specificity of the influence on response probability obtained in experiments with reinforcement and motivation paradigms?

It should be noted in passing that this question of the specificity of the influences of reinforcing and motivating factors on response probability has not received the attention it deserves. Hullian theorists (e.g., Hull, 1943; Spence, 1956), arguing that reinforcement affects the strength of specific stimulus-response connections (${}_{S}H_{R}$), had no difficulty accounting for the specificity of the effects of reinforcing events, but they could not adequately explain the effects of motivating events (e.g., drive). For example, if drive is increased, why does it affect the probability of occurrence of a given response more than of all the other responses in the animal's repertoire that could occur in the given situation? In other words, why does drive interact with a specific habit (${}_{S}H_{R}$) tendency and not with other habit tendencies in the animal's repertoire? Two-process theorists (e.g., Mowrer, 1947, 1960; Rescorla & Solomon, 1967), who have demonstrated the importance of a learned incentive-motivational factor in determining response probability, have also so far not directed their attention to the problem of how the motivational factor affects the occurrence of any particular instrumental response. In fact, they seem to have so completely separated the motivational factor from the (instrumental) response that it is difficult to foresee how they would conceive of an interaction of these two. In general, the difficulty with all these theoretical formulations, with the possible exception of Mowrer's (1960), is that the motivational factor is regarded primarily as a contributor to response occurrence (Fig. 6, A & B) rather than to response selection.

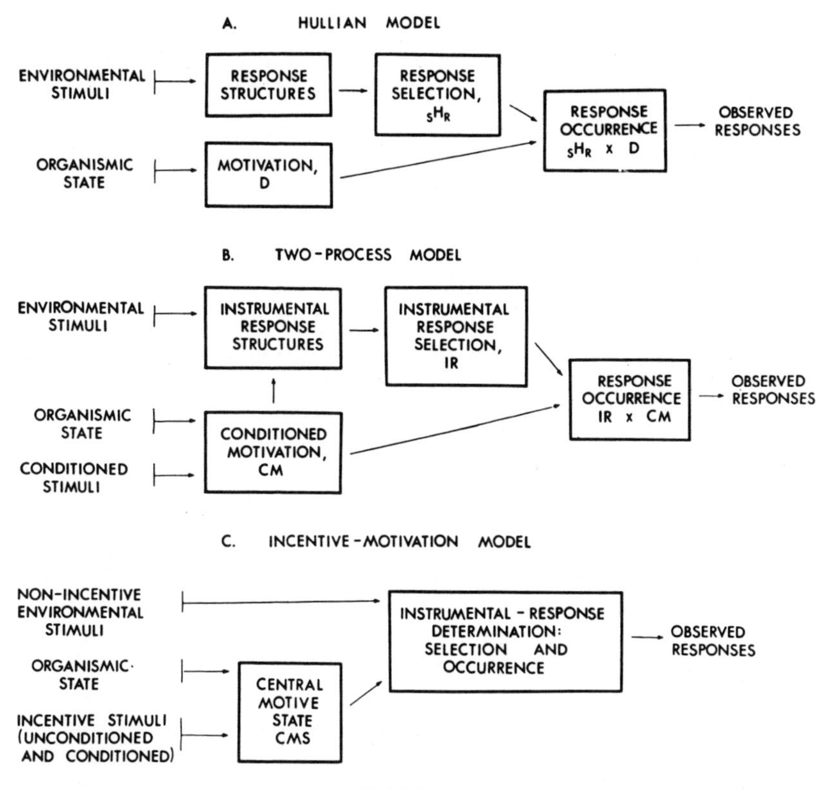


FIGURE 6

SCHEMATIC REPRESENTATION OF CERTAIN MODELS OF MOTIVATION-RESPONSE INTERACTION

The Hullian model regarded the motivational factor not to be involved in response selection but to contribute only to response occurrence. The current two-process model appears to regard the motivational factor as contributing something to response selection but to be primarily concerned with response occurrence. The incentive-motivation model suggests that response selection and occurrence are two aspects of a single process of response determination, which involves an interaction of influences from the central motive state and unconditioned and conditioned incentive stimuli, as well as nonincentive stimuli.

The general approach I have outlined above regards response selection and response occurrence to be the two aspects of the same process of excitation of particular sensory-motor coordinations by the joint action of environmental stimuli and the prevailing central motive state (Fig. 6C). The neural events by which the motivational factor influences behavior (i.e., affects response occurrence) are an inherent part of the process of response selection as well. Within this framework, then, there is no special problem of the interaction of response tendencies with the motivational factor, for the motivational factor itself determines the particular response tendencies that will be excited.

Consider now the details of the way in which the probability of a particular instrumental response is altered by the procedure of reinforcement. Imagine the training of a hungry rat to traverse a runway from a start box to a goal box containing food. After the rat, through exploration, has discovered and eaten food in the goal box, the stimulus features of the goal box, and later of the runway and the start box, would become conditioned stimuli and capable of creating the (feeding) central motive state. This central motive state and conditioned incentive stimuli would then jointly produce response tendencies of approaching the conditioned incentive stimuli. As the animal approaches one conditioned incentive stimulus after another (in the different parts of the runway), it will get closer and closer to the goal box and food. With repeated trials, the level of conditioning, that is, the acquired incentive characteristics of the conditioned stimuli, would increase, as would the strength of the central motive state. These developments, together with the habituation of initial exploratory responses, would make the rat approach the goal box faster, and the usual measures of "response strength," such as starting speed, running speed, and the probability of occurrence of the response (within a given time interval) would show improvement. As the response is performed repeatedly, its successive motor components would become organized into long chains, thereby making the response less dependent on the presence of runway incentive stimuli; at this stage, blinding the animal or any other sensory interference is not likely to disrupt the response completely (DeFeudis, 1968). Thus, while initially the response is "guided" in the sense that each successive approach component is elicited by a particular conditioned incentive stimulus in the runway, the final response is "ballistic" in the sense that once initiated it can be completed with a minimum of dependence on environmental stimuli.

The above account of the acquisition of an instrumental approach response clearly does not attribute any response-strengthening role to reinforcement, but rests on the assumption that a central motive state, together with the related incentive stimuli, guides the animal to the incentive object. The conditioned incentive stimuli, since their incentive properties depend on their proximity to the incentive object, increase the probability of occurrence of those very acts which the experimenter has chosen to "reinforce" (i.e., the acts on which the incentive is contingent). Thus, though the influence of a central motive state and incentive stimuli is, in principle, nonspecific, the influence will be specific to the reinforced response so long as the experimental arrangements remain unaltered (that is, so long as the location of the incentive object in the experimental environment remains the same). A similar interpretation of instrumental behavior has been proposed by Grastyán, Czopf, Ángyán, and Szabó (1965) on the basis of their neurophysiological experiments.

The general analysis of the reinforcement paradigm that I have outlined above indicates a way of accounting for several experimental findings that otherwise require ad hoc explanations. Consider two of these.

1. In demonstrating the acquisition of an instrumental response, it is customary to make the reward—say, water—contingent upon the response—say, lever pressing—*and* to create the appropriate organismic state, that is, thirst. At the time of training, the animal is thirsty and each lever press delivers a few drops of water, which the animal quickly drinks. If, as I have suggested, the increase in response probability is dependent upon the motivational factor and the motivational factor is dependent upon an interaction of organismic state and incentive stimulation, then it should also be possible to train animals by manipulating organismic state rather than incentive. That is, the probability of occurrence of a response could be increased by making the organismic state (thirst) contingent upon the response and making the reward (water) available all the time.

In other words, a nonthirsty animal, with water continuously available, should be able to learn to press a lever that would make it thirsty and make it drink water. This kind of experiment is difficult to do, for organismic states cannot be changed quickly enough to make them contingent upon a response. But by the use of electrical stimulation of the drinking hypothalamic motive site, it is possible to make the drinking central motive state contingent upon lever pressing. Mendelson (1967) has done this very experiment, and has found that, indeed, a nonthirsty rat will learn to press a lever that would electrically generate the drinking central motive state and make the animal drink for the duration of the stimulation. While this finding completely contradicts the Hullian drive-reduction hypothesis of instrumental learning, it can be readily accounted for in terms of the incentive-motivational view of learning. What probably happens is this. The electrical stimulation leads to drinking (for water is continuously available), and this provides the conditions for the environmental stimuli (lever, water receptacle) to acquire some of the properties of the incentive (water). In the absence of the electrical stimulation, these conditioned incentive stimuli would generate a weak central motive state which would be sufficient for eliciting the (approach) instrumental response, but not for the consummatory response of drinking. However, as soon as the instrumental response (lever press) leads to electrical stimulation, the central motive state would become strong enough to induce drinking (for the duration of the electrical stimulation), thereby providing the conditions for the association of the environmental stimuli with the (unconditioned) incentive object (water). Thus, while a nonthirsty animal would not drink the available water, the conditioned environmental stimuli would become capable of instigating the instrumental response—and this in turn would create the conditions (electrical stimulation) for drinking.

2. If the above account of response determination in terms of unconditioned and conditioned incentive stimuli is correct, it should be possible to obtain increases in the probability of certain approach and withdrawal responses even if these responses are not specifically reinforced in an instrumental reinforcement paradigm. That is, so long as the defined "instrumental" response involves only approach or withdrawal (rather than any complicated refined

sequences of acts requiring special "response shaping"), a *classical* conditioning procedure may be sufficient for increasing the probability of occurrence of the instrumental response. That this is so is shown by the phenomenon of "auto-shaping," recently described by Brown and Jenkins (1968). They showed that a pigeon would reliably increase its rate of key pecking following a classical conditioning procedure, which consisted of momentarily illuminating a key (conditioned stimulus) followed by presentation of food (unconditioned incentive stimulation). According to the incentive-motivational view of response probability, the illuminated key, which is followed by food, would acquire conditioned incentive-motivational properties of the same type as are possessed by the food tray and other remote food-associated stimuli. These conditioned incentive stimuli would then elicit approach responses in the bird, one of the approach components being pecking. It should be noted that this type of response-independent training would increase the probability of occurrence of only those responses that form a part of the general approach pattern of the species. Also, the fact that in the Brown and Jenkins experiment the food tray was located directly below the key may have contributed to the concentration of the approach responses in the general key-tray area.[2]

*Conclusion*

Five working assumptions appear to be justified on the basis of the discussion in this section. 1) In general, the central motive state influences behavior by facilitating and inhibiting a certain set of sensory-motor coordinations. 2) The strength of the central motive state required for the occurrence of exploratory and instrumental responses is less than the strength required for the occurrence of consummatory responses. 3) The processes of response selection and response occurrence are aspects of the common set of mechanisms of *response determination;* the organized excitation of a certain set of sensory-motor coordinations is the basis of response determination. 4) The organized excitation of sensory-motor coordinations corresponding to a particular response depends upon the stability of the

2. After sending this paper to press I learned that B. R. Moore of the Department of Psychology, Dalhousie University, Halifax, N.S., has independently developed a similar interpretation of auto-shaping, and has extended this kind of incentive interpretation to a wide variety of other learning phenomena.

spatial arrangement of the incentive stimuli (unconditioned and conditioned) in relation to the incentive object. 5) A change in the probability of occurrence of a particular instrumental response is possible with a reinforcement paradigm because the generation of a central motive state and the related conditioned incentive stimuli depends upon the incentive object in relation to which the response is defined (that is, the acts elicited by the incentive stimuli comprise the defined instrumental response).

## Summary

The probability of occurrence of a response can be altered by linking it to a reinforcing event (principle of reinforcement) or by manipulating the prevailing incentive and organismic conditions (principle of motivation). It is customary to attribute these two means of altering response probability to the hypothetical processes of "response reinforcement" and "response instigation," respectively. This paper presents evidence and argument in support of the hypothesis that response reinforcement and response instigation arise from a common set of neuropsychological mechanisms, and that the principle of reinforcement is a special case of the more primary principle of motivation. Three sets of questions are discussed, and the main conclusions are enumerated at the end of each of the three main sections of this paper.

A reinforcing event is essentially the manipulation of an incentive object in the presence of an appropriate organismic state (e.g., "drive"). An interaction of incentive stimuli with the relevant organismic state is also the condition for generating motivation. Both reinforcing events and motivating events are regarded here as events that create "central motive states," that selectively influence a certain set of sensory-motor coordinations. A particular response is organized through an interaction of the prevailing central motive state with unconditioned and conditioned incentive stimuli and other, nonincentive stimuli.

It is argued that the so-called backward-acting response-reinforcement influence of reinforcing events is illusory, and that reinforcing events, like motivating events, create central motive states that influence subsequent behavior. The specificity of this influence on a *particular* instrumental response is explained in terms of the assumption that the generation of a central motive state and the related conditioned incentive stimuli depends upon the incentive object in relation to which the response is defined.

## REFERENCES

Bacon, W. E., & Bindra, D. The generality of the incentive-motivational effects of classically conditioned stimuli in instrumental learning. *Acta biol. exp.* (Warsaw), 1967, **27**, 185–197.

Beach, F. A., & Ransom, T. W. Effects of environmental variation on ejaculatory frequency in male rats. *J. comp. physiol. Psych.*, 1967, **64**, 384–387.

Bindra, D. Neuropsychological interpretation of the effects of drive and incentive-motivation on general activity and instrumental behavior. *Psychol. Rev.*, 1968, **75**, 1–22.

Bindra, D. A unified interpretation of emotion and motivation. *Ann. N.Y. Acad. Sci.*, 1969, **159**, 1071–1083.

Bindra, D., & Campbell, J. F. Motivational effects of rewarding intracranial stimulation. *Nature*, 1967, **215**, 375–376.

Bindra, D., & Palfai, T. Nature of positive and negative incentive-motivational effects on general activity. *J. comp. physiol. Psychol.*, 1967, **63**, 288–297.

Black, R. W. On the combination of drive and incentive motivation. *Psychol. Rev.*, 1965, **72**, 310–317.

Bolles, R. C. *Theory of motivation.* New York: Harper & Row, 1967.

Brown, J. S. Problems presented by the concept of acquired drives. In *Current theory and research in motivation.* Lincoln: University of Nebraska Press, 1953. Pp. 1–21.

Brown, P. L., & Jenkins, H. M. Auto-shaping of the pigeon's key-peck. *J. exp. Anal. Behav.*, 1968, **11**, 1–8.

Christopher, Sister Mary, & Butter, C. M. Consummatory behaviors and locomotor exploration evoked from self-stimulation sites in rats. *J. comp. physiol. Psychol.*, 1968, **66** (2), 335–339.

DeFeudis, P. A. The role of sensory factors in the organization of the instrumental response. Unpublished M.A. thesis, McGill University, 1968.

Dodwell, P. C., & Bessant, D. E. Learning without swimming in a water maze. *J. comp. physiol. Psychol.*, 1960, **53** (5), 422–425.

Dollard, J., & Miller, N. E. *Personality and psychotherapy.* New York: McGraw-Hill, 1950.

Glickman, S. E., & Schiff, B. B. A biological theory of reinforcement. *Psychol. Rev.*, 1967, **74**, 81–109.

Grastyán, E., Czopf, J., Ángyán, L., & Szabó, I. The significance of subcortical motivational mechanisms in the organization of conditional connections. *Acta Physiol. Acad. Scien.* (Hungary), 1965, **26**, 9–46.

Hull, C. L. *Principles of behavior.* New York: Appleton-Century-Crofts, 1943.

Hull, C. L. Behavior postulates and corollaries. *Psychol. Rev.*, 1950, **57**, 173–180.

Lashley, K. S., & McCarthy, D. A. The survival of the maze habit after cerebellar injuries. *J. comp. Psychol.*, 1926, **6**, 423–433.

Levison, P. K., & Flynn, J. P. The objects attacked by cats during stimulation of the hypothalamus. *Animal Behav.*, 1965, **13**, 217–220.

Logan, F. A. *Incentive.* New Haven: Yale Univ. Press, 1960.

Macfarlane, D. A. The role of kinaesthesis in maze learning. *Univer. Calif. Pub. Psychol.*, 1930, **4**, 277–305.

Mendelson, J. Role of hunger in T-maze learning for food by rats. *J. comp. physiol. Psychol.*, 1966, **62**, 341–349.

Mendelson, J. Lateral hypothalamic stimulation in satiated rats: the rewarding effects of self-induced drinking. *Science*, 1967, **157**, 1077–1079.

Miller, N. E. Learnable drives and rewards. In S. S. Stevens (Ed.), *Handbook of experimental psychology*. New York: Wiley, 1951. Pp. 435–472.

Miller, N. E. Some reflections on the law of effect produce a new alternative to drive reduction. *Nebraska Symposium on Motivation*, 1963, 65–112.

Milner, P. M. *Physiological psychology*. New York: Holt, Rinehart & Winston, in press.

Morgan, C. T. *Physiological psychology*. New York: McGraw-Hill, 1943.

Mowrer, O. H. On the dual nature of learning—a re-interpretation of "conditioning" and "problem-solving." *Harvard Educat. Rev.*, 1947, **17**, 102–148.

Mowrer, O. H. *Learning theory and behavior*. New York: Wiley, 1960.

Munn, N. L. *Handbook of psychological research on the rat.* Boston: Houghton Mifflin Co., 1950.

Nissen, H. W. The nature of the drive as innate determinant of behavioral organization. *Nebraska Symposium on Motivation*, 1954, 281–321.

Rescorla, R. A., & Solomon, R. L. Two-process learning theory: relationships between Pavlovian conditioning and instrumental learning. *Psychol. Rev.*, 1967, **74**, 151–182.

Richter, C. P. A behavioristic study of the activity of the rat. *Comp. psychol. Monogr.*, 1922, **1**, 2.

Roberts, W. W., & Kiess, H. O. Motivational properties of hypothalamic aggression in cats. *J. comp. physiol. Psychol.*, 1964, **58**, 187–193.

Roberts, W. W., Steinberg, M. L., & Means, L. W. Hypothalamic mechanisms for sexual, aggressive, and other motivational behaviors in the opossum, Didelphis Virginiana. *J. comp. physiol. Psychol.*, 1967, **64**, 1–15.

Schneirla, T. C. An evolutionary and developmental theory of biphasic processes underlying approach and withdrawal. In *Current theory and research on motivation.* University of Nebraska Press, 1959, **7**, 1–42.

Seward, J. P. Experimental evidence for the motivating function of reward. *Psychol. Bull.*, 1951, **48**, 130–149.

Seward, J. P. Drive, incentive, and reinforcement. *Psychol. Rev.*, 1956, **63**, 195–203.

Sheffield, F. D. New evidence on the drive-reduction theory of reinforcement. In R. N. Haber (Ed.), *Current research in motivation.* New York: Holt, Rinehart, & Winston, 1966. Pp. 111–122.

Solomon, R. L., & Turner, L. H. Discriminative classical conditioning in dogs paralyzed by Curare can later control discriminative avoidance responses in the normal state. *Psychol. Rev.*, 1962, **69**, 202–219.

Spence, K. W. *Behavior theory and conditioning*. New Haven: Yale Univ. Press, 1956.

Spence, K. W. *Behavior theory and learning*. Englewood Cliffs, N.J.: Prentice-Hall, 1960.

Tenen, S. S., & Miller, N. E. Strength of electrical stimulation of lateral hypothalamus, food deprivation, and tolerance for quinine in food. *J. comp. physiol. Psychol.*, 1964, **58**, 55–62.

Tolman, E. C. Cognitive maps in rats and men. *Psychol. Rev.*, 1948, **55**, 189–208.

Woodworth, R. S. *Dynamic psychology*. New York: Columbia Univ. Press, 1918.

Young, P. T. Studies of food preference, appetite and dietary habit. VIII. Food-seeking drives, palatability and the law of effect. *J. comp. physiol. Psychol.*, 1948, **41**, 269–300.

## COMMENTS

*Edward L. Wike*

Dr. Bindra has left us all spellbound by his erudite analysis of some major motivational issues. He is attempting to create a broad-ranging theory whose roots appear to be in ethology, neurophysiology, epistemic behavior, classical and instrumental conditioning, etc. I must confess that I feel quite overwhelmed by the originality, logic, and theoretical breadth of his paper. A wise man would end his comments at this point—accordingly I will continue.

The first part of Dr. Bindra's paper is devoted to a careful consideration of two principles, *reinforcement* and *motivation.* (These correspond to what Dr. Black termed "mechanisms" of reinforcement.) The principle of reinforcement is that a response which is followed by an incentive will have the probability of its occurrence increased. Motivation, on the other hand, attributes the increased probability of a response to an energizing of the response tendency. The idea that reinforcement acts "backward" and motivation "forward" is skillfully demolished; a test of both processes requires a before-and-after comparison. Dr. Bindra contends that motivation is the more basic process and that reinforcement is a derivative.

A central notion is that incentive manipulations have motivational consequences. He says: "It appears reasonable to proceed on the assumption that the primary effect of a reinforcing event is not response reinforcement, but the creation of a motivational state that influences a wide variety of subsequent behavior of the animal." Part of the evidence for this assumption comes from studies of "learning without performance." However, the fact that such learning can occur does not lead me to conclude that learning never involves the strengthening of S-R connections.

The proposition that reinforcement produces a motivational state strikes me as too global. While I could imagine that giving a hungry rat a 45-milligram food pellet might increase his motivation, suppose he is rewarded with a 15-gram pellet? In short, we need more precise propositions that specify, for example, how much reward produces what kinds of motivational effects.

Let us try to make Dr. Bindra's theory more explicit by reference to a hungry rat's performance in a runway. Does the rat run faster on successive trials because of increased habit strength? Dr. Bindra thinks not. Rather he believes that the improvement in performance represents the interaction of a "largely innate" approach response and heightened motivation. There are several proposed sources of motivation: a) drive, produced by deprivation, etc.; b) remote stimuli from incentives; and c) conditioned incentive stimuli. The physiological summation of these motivational sources occurs in the CNS and, particularly, in the hypothalamus. Accordingly, Dr. Bindra incorporates Morgan's concept (1943) of a central motive state into his theory.

The conditioned incentive stimuli are stimuli that are close, temporally and spatially, to the incentive. They are, in other words, $S^r$'s. As the number of runway trials increases, the incentive value of these conditioned incentive stimuli becomes greater and the strength of the central motive state grows. "These developments, together with the habituation of initial exploratory responses, would make the rat approach the goal box faster. . . ." Not only do the conditioned incentive stimuli increase motivation but they also elicit successive elements of the approach response. Furthermore, with continued training, the components of the approach response become chained together so that the response is less dependent upon the conditioned incentive stimuli. Thus, we can see how faster running with increased trials is accounted for without recourse to a reinforcement interpretation of incentive. An interesting question is: How can one explain the acquisition of a *slow* running response with this theory?

Dr. Bindra's theory bears some similarity to Mowrer's viewpoint (1960). In effect, Mowrer says that organisms have built-in responses and what has to be learned is "wanting" to make them. As in the case of Mowrer's theory, Dr. Bindra, it seems to me, faces the same problems of response selection and initiation. While he has avoided some of the difficulties inherent in Mowrer's feedback mechanism by having conditioned incentive stimuli that are exteroceptive in nature, I still contend that theories that ascribe heavy weights to motivational factors encounter problems in response selection and imitation. You will note that Dr. Bindra begins by postulating innate approach and withdrawal responses, and that he indicates that when his theory is more fully developed it will include cognitive factors.

Does a habit-reinforcement theory obviate these difficulties? Dr. Bindra believes not. But there are some mechanisms in reinforcement theory that have possibilities. These are: 1) the habit-family hierarchy; 2) the drive stimulus mechanism, $S_D$; and 3) Hull's competing reaction rule. According to the latter: "When the reaction potentials to two or more incompatible reactions occur in an organism at the same time, only the reaction whose momentary effective reaction potential is the greatest will be evoked" (Hull, 1943, p. 344). However, I would certainly agree with Dr. Bindra that these matters have not received the attention they deserve. Finally, it might be suggested that a compromise theory of reinforcement in which incentives strengthen connections *and* have motivational effects might be entertained. Such a viewpoint might alleviate the problems of response selection in a motivation theory and the "sluggishness" of a habit-reinforcement theory. As Dr. Black pointed out, Hull's final theory was something of a compromise.

Both Dr. Bindra and I have stressed the importance of conditioned incentive stimuli, or $S^r$'s. He has been interested in the presentation of such stimuli *prior* to a response, while I focused upon their presentation *after* a response. He has offered an energizing interpretation of their effects, while I favored an empirical reinforcement interpretation. His conclusion, that conditioned incentive stimuli can be developed with primary appetitional drives but that secondary drives cannot, is in accord with Logan's summary (1968). I found it most interesting that the studies of Dr. Bindra and his coworkers, using ICS, have led to the same conclusion. And the fact that learned drives were not conditionable with ICS is evidence against the proposition by Mowrer (1960) and others that the failure to condition hunger and thirst is the result of not being able to "turn on" these drives suddenly.

In closing, let me mention that the three speakers appeared to agree on at least two points: first, that motivation is not a matter of drive alone but involves a consideration of drive and reward together; and second, all of us for various reasons have rejected $r_G$-$s_G$ theory.

## REFERENCES

Hull, C. L. *Principles of behavior.* New York: Appleton-Century-Crofts, 1943.

Logan, F. A. Incentive theory and changes in reward. In K. W. Spence & Janet T. Spence (Eds.), *The psychology of learning and motivation.* Vol. II. New York: Academic Press, 1968.

Morgan, C. L. *Physiological psychology.* New York: McGraw-Hill, 1943.

Mowrer, O. H. *Learning theory and behavior.* New York: Wiley, 1960.

# Secondary Reinforcement: Some Research and Theoretical Issues

EDWARD L. WIKE

*University of Kansas*

Most psychologists agree that behavior cannot be explained in terms of primary drives and rewards alone. One approach to this problem is to expand the list of primary drives and rewards. For example, Robert White (1959) introduced effectance motivation with a feeling of efficacy as its source of satisfaction, and Harlow (1953) added curiosity, exploration, and manipulation to the list of primary drives. Another approach is to enlarge the list of primary drives and rewards by adding secondary drives and rewards. Long ago, for example, Murray proposed a lengthy list of psychogenic needs which he said "are presumably dependent upon and derived from the primary needs" (1938, p. 80).

Behaviorists of diverse theoretical persuasions have also augmented the array of drives and rewards by introducing a variety of learned sources of motivation. Like Murray they believe that learned drives are dependent upon primary drives, and furthermore that learned rewards are developed by the association of stimuli with primary rewards. They have, however, not been content to merely postulate such acquired entities, but have taken these problems to the laboratory. The laboratory is an arena with its own moments of truth. The research worker must do battle with a host of troublesome questions such as, What is the nature of the association between a stimulus and a reward that endows the stimulus with reward value? How does one know whether a stimulus is rewarding a response or eliciting it? How can stimuli be developed that have strong and durable rewards effects? Under what conditions do stimuli have drivelike consequences? What are the criteria for a learned drive? And so on.

Not only have behaviorists committed themselves to the experimental investigation of learned sources of drive and reward, but they have also weighted these concepts heavily in their explanations of behavior. Hull said: "But the fact that the type of reinforcement here under consideration is secondary, in no way suggests that it is unimportant. Actually the great mass of our everyday acts are initiated by secondary drives, and the most of civilized human learning is apparently effected through secondary reinforcement" (1951, p. 28). In the same vein, Keller and Schoenfeld have remarked: "When added to the other functions of stimuli, it [the principle of secondary reinforcement] gives us a powerful and indispensable tool for the solution of many vexing and absorbing problems of human action" (1950, p. 260). In brief, then, behaviorists have regarded learned drives and rewards as problems that *demand* experimental study and have treated the concepts in question as crucial ones.

The main focus of the present paper is upon secondary reinforcement ($S^r$), and particularly upon positive $S^r$ deriving from the association of stimuli with rewards that reduce appetitional drives. If various behavior theories are analyzed, it is apparent that $S^r$ is frequently closely related to two other motivational mechanisms, the fractional antedating goal reaction ($r_G$) and frustration. In the first section of this paper, we will briefly consider the linkages among these three factors in the theories of Hull, Spence and Amsel, Sheffield, Mowrer, and Skinner. To round out this section, we will analyze in more detail the recent papers by Lott (1967) and Longstreth (1966), who have contended that $S^r$ and frustration are operationally identical.

The second section of the paper will be devoted to some developments in $S^r$ research and theory. First we will examine several issues posed by Bolles (1967) in his thoughtful summary and evaluation of $S^r$. Second, we will present some operant research on $S^r$ which we believe forces a reconsideration of our conception of $S^r$. Third, we will propose a simple hypothesis that appears to integrate a considerable part of the research upon $S^r$ and suggests some new directions of research. Finally, we will briefly describe a few of these suggested lines of research upon $S^r$.

## Secondary Reinforcement, Fractional Antedating Goal Reaction, and Frustration

### *Hull*

Four important motivational factors in Hull's system may be summarized in a 2 × 2 table (see Fig. 1A). Logan (1968) has

| A | Drives | Rewards |
|---|---|---|
| Primary | | |
| Secondary | | |

| B | Secondary Drives | Secondary Rewards |
|---|---|---|
| Appetitional | a | b |
| Aversive | c | d |

FIGURE 1

(A) Summary of Four of Hull's Motivational Factors

(B) Division of Secondary Drives and Rewards in Terms of Their Conditioning with Primary Appetitional and Aversive Drives

cogently pointed out that secondary drives and rewards may be arranged in another 2 × 2 table (see Fig. 1B) depending upon whether the stimulus in question has been associated with primary appetitional drives or primary aversive drives. Our chief concern, as indicated above, is with secondary rewards ($S^r$) based upon the pairing of a stimulus with the reduction of an appetitional drive like hunger. That is to say, we are interested in the upper right-hand cell (b) of Logan's 2 × 2 table. As Logan has noted, the experimental results in the four cells reveal an asymmetric pattern. There is substantial evidence for secondary rewards based upon appetitional drive reduction (cell b) and secondary drives based on aversive drive onset (cell c), but little or no evidence for the learned motivational entities in the remaining cells (a and d). These handy schemata are complicated by the fact that Hull had another learned motivational variable, the fractional antedating goal reaction, that was intimately related to $S^r$. Therefore, we need to explore this relationship in greater depth.

The $r_G$ mechanism occupied a central position in Hull's theorizing during the 1930s. For example, in Hull's 1936 APA presidential address the mark of a reinforcing state of affairs was said to be $S_G \rightarrow R_G$ in which $R_G$ was "the reaction associated with the goal" (1937, p. 17). Hull described $r_G$ as a "minor component" of $R_G$ that could occur without reward ($S_G$). He specified the various linkages among drives ($S_D$), the fractional goal stimulus ($s_G$), and responses, and incorporated the $r_G$-$s_G$ mechanism in a number of derivations. Parenthetically, it might be pointed out that in this miniature system Hull defined experimental extinction as "the weakening of a conditioned excitatory tendency resulting from frustration or the failure of reinforcement" (1937, p. 17). Although he mentioned frustration and the failure of reinforcement in the same context, it seems reasonably clear from his remarks that at this time he regarded frustration as the *blocking* of a response.

Hull's influential *Principles of Behavior* (1943) departed radically from the earlier miniature system. The new mark of reinforcement was drive reduction, extinction was explained by means of work-inhibition theory, and $r_G$ disappeared. The learned reward mechanism was now what Hull referred to as the "extremely important principle" of secondary reinforcement and to which he devoted a chapter. However, in the notes on this chapter $r_G$ reappeared:

> These considerations suggest rather strongly that the first secondary reinforcing stimulus acquires its power of reinforcement by virtue of having conditioned to it some fractional component of the need reduction process of the goal situation (*G*) *whose occurrence, wherever it takes place, has a specific power of reinforcement in a degree proportionate to the intensity of that occurrence.* [1943, p. 100; cf. Mowrer, 1960, pp. 104f.]

In short, Hull proposed that $S^r$ works because $S^r$ elicits $r_G$ and the vigor of $r_G$ determines the effectiveness of $S^r$.

Hull's proposition (1943, pp. 94f.) that $S^r$ develops as a consequence of the repeated and consistent association of a stimulus with a primary or secondary reinforcing state of affairs was largely unchanged in *Essentials of Behavior* (1951, p. 28). But now he proposed that, in addition to drive reduction, the rapid reduction of $s_G$ was reinforcing. A year later Hull (1952) asserted in a corollary (XV) that habits could be formed when S and R were followed by $r_G$-$s_G$, as a consequence of the secondary reinforcing value of $s_G$. It is evident that $r_G$ and $S^r$ were closely related in Hull's thinking. The question, of course, arises, Why do we need both concepts?

We have already observed that Hull included frustration in his miniature system to refer to the blocking of a response. From 1943 on, the work-inhibition theory was employed to account for extinction and related phenomena. Occasionally (Hull, Livingston, Rouse, & Barker, 1951; Hull, 1952, pp. 115, 133f.) frustration was introduced as an emotion resulting from the nonfulfillment of an anticipation (that is, $r_G$-$s_G$ occurs without $S_G$), but work inhibition was the predominant theme. Spence (1960, p. 96) has related his long-standing disagreement with Hull over work-inhibition theory.

The question of the relationship between $S^r$ and frustration has relatively little meaning in Hull's system. While Hull included $S^r$ and linked it to $r_G$ (1943) and later (1951; 1952) attributed the effectiveness of $r_G$ to the $S^r$ value of $s_G$, frustration played a very minor part in Hull's theorizing since he retained the work-inhibition theory until the end.

*Spence-Amsel*

In 1943, Hull hypothesized that the gradient of reinforcement consisted of a short primary reinforcement gradient of 30 to 60 seconds or less and a longer goal gradient. The latter gradient was attributed to the action of $S^r$. Spence (1947), on the other hand, proposed that there was no primary gradient but that all learning under the condition of delayed reinforcement could be interpreted in terms of immediate $S^r$. Moreover, he directed his students (e.g., Perkins, 1947; Grice, 1948) to investigate the effects of $S^r$ upon the gradient of reinforcement. Thus, it can be seen that $S^r$ played an important role in Spence's early thinking.

When Spence offered his own version of behavior theory, he (1956, pp. 33f.) defined four subclasses of reinforcing events: 1) primary appetitional reinforcers (e.g., food); 2) secondary appetitional reinforcers; 3) primary aversive reinforcers (e.g., shock reduction); and 4) secondary aversive reinforcers. For our purposes, it is important to note that secondary appetitional reinforcers are "stimulus cues which in the past experience of the organism have regularly accompanied the consumption of such needed objects [i.e., primary appetitional reinforcers]" (1956, p. 34). Having thus defined $S^r$, Spence promptly forgot about it. He focused instead upon the development of $r_G$-$s_G$ theory as the mechanism behind incentive motivation, K. While Hull clung to a feeble drive-reduction theory in which some unspecified minimum of drive reduction was required for learning, Spence moved to a contiguity interpretation of instrumental conditioning. For classical conditioning, the paradigm for the development of $r_G$, Spence retained drive reduction. Since K was the reflection of a classically conditioned $r_G$, the magnitude of K was hypothesized to be a function of: 1) the number of goal box conditioning trials, 2) the similarity of the goal box and alley cues, and 3) "any property of the goal object that produces unconditioned consummatory responses of different intensity or vigor" (1956, pp. 135f.). Thus, with the usual clarity that distinguished Spence's theorizing, he brought $r_G$ into the domain of testability. The results of subsequent experiments by Stein (1957), Swift and Wike (1958), Gonzalez and Diamond (1960), and others were largely negative with respect to Spence's theory. However, recent studies by Senkowski, Porter, and Madison (1968) and Patten (1968) have produced positive findings by measuring response speeds in segments other than the start box. In view of the earlier negative results, the replicability of these studies needs to be assessed.

If $r_G$ is a classically conditioned component of $R_G$, then studies involving concurrent classical and instrumental conditioning (e.g., Kintsch & Witte, 1962; cf. Shapiro & Miller, 1965; Rescorla & Solomon, 1967) would appear to bear upon $R_G$ theory. Also studies (e.g., Kraeling, 1961; Deaux & Patten, 1964) in which consummatory behavior is measured in an instrumental conditioning paradigm would appear to be relevant to the theory. The concurrent classical and instrumental studies have not yielded a simple yes-no interpretation. For example, Kintsch and Witte observed a parallelism between salivation and bar presses early in the transition from continuous to fixed-interval reinforcement, but later in training the parallelism began to break down. Regarding $r_G$ these authors concluded:

> In so far as salivation is considered to be an important component of the fractional anticipatory goal response, the present data do not suggest an "$r_G$" type mechanism. To fulfill the function of an $r_G$, salivation would have to consistently precede, or at least be simultaneous with, bar pressing. Furthermore, during the shift from continuous to FI reinforcement, salivation does not move backward from the point of reinforcement and in general it does not develop as rapidly as bar pressing. [Kintsch & Witte, 1962, p. 968]

On the other hand, Shapiro (1962), using a differential reinforcement of low rates (DRL) schedule, observed that salivation regularly preceded the instrumental response. After surveying these and other investigations, Rescorla and Solomon concluded: "It thus appears that although salivation and operant behavior may bear a gross relation to each other in typical instrumental training situations, the details of this relation are not constant . . . salivation must neither precede nor consistently follow operant behavior in order for that behavior to be maintained" (1967, p. 165).

In the Kraeling runway study there was a positive relationship between consummatory behavior and running speed, especially early in training. Running speeds continued to increase, however, after licking behavior had attained stable asymptotes. Kraeling concluded that

> Instrumental behavior was affected by concentration of sucrose solution in ways which could not be predicted merely from the observed strength of the consummatory response. Therefore, a simple view that the strength of the consummatory response is critical in reward in relation to instrumental behavior is not consistent with the results. [1961, p. 565]

One of the most fascinating studies in this area has been reported by Deaux and Patten (1964) who attempted to measure directly anticipatory and consummatory licking during runway training. A brass tube fitted into the rat's mouth enabled the *E*s to record licks and deliver the goal box reward. In support of Spence's theory, it was found that the lick rates increased as *S* locomoted to the goal box and that the increase in rate was a negatively accelerated function of training. Regarding the corresponding instrumental performance, the only data reported were for the second foot-long segment of the five-foot runway. These speeds increased over the course of training. One wonders how speeds in the other segments of the runway were related to the lick rates. This ingenious study needs to be followed up.

Let us now return to the question of what happened to $S^r$ in Spence's theory. As Lawrence (1958) has correctly noted, $S^r$ was superseded by $r_G$-$s_G$. So-called $S^r$'s serve to elicit $r_G$-$s_G$. The occurrence of $r_G$-$s_G$, in turn, is motivating in either of two ways: 1) $r_G$'s produce conflict and "heightened tension or excitement" that elevate the general drive level, D; or 2) the intensity of $s_G$ has a stimulus intensity dynamism effect like Hull's V. Since both D and V are multipliers of H, increased reaction potential (E) would result from either factor. In summary, $S^r$'s act as motivators in Spence's system by means of their elicitation of $r_G$-$s_G$ and its subsequent energizing effect.

The set of classically conditioned implicit responses, consisting of fractional anticipatory reward ($r_R$-$s_R$) and fractional anticipatory punishment or fear ($r_p$-$s_p$), was expanded by Amsel (1958) to include fractional anticipatory frustration ($r_F$-$s_F$). After a number of rewards an organism anticipates reward, that is, it makes $r_R$-$s_R$'s. Then, if the reward is absent or delayed, primary frustration (F), an aversive motivational state, results. As in the case of $r_R$, $r_F$ becomes classically conditioned to the apparatus stimuli. The instrumental response *leading to* reinforcement is extinguished by the presence of competing responses elicited by $s_F$. Amsel states: "If F is an aversive condition, $s_F$ should be associated with avoidant response tendencies which . . . would compete with locomotion toward the previously rewarding goal region" (1958, p. 108). Thus, the foregoing account provides for a frustration-inhibition explanation of extinction.

Another aspect of Amsel's theory concerns the frustration effect, that is, that responses made *after* frustration should be invigorated as a consequence of greater D stemming from frustration. This implication was verified in a dramatic fashion in the Amsel-Roussel double-alley study (1952). But, in general, our main interest is in Amsel's frustration-inhibition theory of extinction rather than in the frustration effect.

Although Spence (1956) displayed some interest in a Guthrie-type interference theory of extinction, for a long time he (Spence, 1936) had been intrigued by frustration theory and he had never adopted Hull's work-inhibition interpretation. In 1960 he (Spence, 1960) acknowledged his acceptance of Amsel's frustration theory and proceeded to extend the theory with respect to acquisition performance under partial reinforcement. He proposed that "the conditioned emotional response, $r_F$, should add substantially to the general drive level, D, of the partial group with the consequence that after a considerable amount of training, its performance should eventually be higher than that of the continuous group" (1960, p. 100). While some studies (e.g., Goodrich, 1959; Weinstock, 1958) supported Spence's prediction, the results have not been entirely consistent (Wike & Remple, 1960). A further problem (Hill, 1968) is that when partial groups do run faster in training, they often do so in the starting rather than in the goal section of the runway where frustration should be greater.

On a gross observational level, competing responses drop out during partially reinforced training. Amsel (1958, p. 109) reasoned that locomoting to the goal box is rewarded more than avoiding it because running leads to removal of the animal from a frustrating situation on nonreinforced trials and to reward on reinforced trials. Thus, the locomotor response becomes conditioned to $s_F$. Bower (Hilgard & Bower, 1966, p. 490) has questioned the evidence for the assumption that $s_F$ is conditioned to approach responses, and Wilton (1967) has tried to account for the partial reinforcement effect by introducing a generalization-decrement factor into frustration theory to supplement or replace the conditioning of approach responses to $s_F$. A further question suggested by Spence's modification of frustration theory is, How can frustration produce greater D without at the same time producing competing responses? Just how the various factors of $r_G$-$s_G$, $r_F$-$s_F$, approach, avoidance, competing responses, and D fit together to produce the results that have been observed in acquisition and extinction under partial and continuous reinforcement is not completely clear. Hill (1968) has attempted to solve some of these problems. Finally, before leaving the problem of the connection between $r_G$ and $r_F$ in the theories of Spence and Amsel, two diverse comments can be made. 1) It would seem that the frustrative events of delay or omission of reward, proposed by Amsel, should be expanded to include other reward variations such as decreases in the amount and quality of reward, increases in delay of rewards, etc. 2) It needs to be noted that in one recent statement Amsel (1967, p. 4) has limited the scope of his partial-reinforcement theory to widely distributed discrete-trial arrangements, and willed massed-trial problems to Capaldi (1966, 1967), whose modified generalization-decrement theory is primarily concerned with *sequences* of various rewarding events.

We have already indicated how $S^r$ was essential to Spence's 1947 reinterpretation of the gradient of reinforcement. By 1956, $S^r$ was replaced by $r_G$ and Spence contended (1956, p. 151) that in long response chains the vigor of $r_G$ varied with the similarity of the cues at the start and termination of a response chain, so that $r_G$ at the start would be weaker than $r_G$ closer to the goal. Since $S^r$ was swallowed up by $r_G$-$s_G$, the question of the relation of $S^r$ to $r_F$ reduces to the previously described linkages between $r_G$ and $r_F$.

*Sheffield*

A theory that bears a strong resemblance to Spence's has been offered by Fred Sheffield (1966a, b). Like Spence, he has proposed that the consummatory response becomes conditioned classically to neutral cues accompanying $R_G$. Unlike Spence, and in accord with his Guthrie background and the results of his "studies in sex and saccharine," he has argued that this conditioning takes place by contiguity. In this respect Sheffield's remarks about consummatory behavior warrant a closer look. He says: "In the present formulation the important thing about consummatory behavior is that *it brings striving to an end;* it removes the internal or external stimuli for excitement and brings about the stimulation that the animal 'does nothing to avoid, often doing such as to maintain' in Thorndike's (1911) definition of a reward" (1966a, p. 99). Accordingly, it would seem that the difference between this position and drive reduction is a fine one. In any event, Sheffield's second key concept is frustration. He says: "I will use it to mean a circumstance in which the animal is in a drive state and in which the consummatory response is stimulated but is prevented from occurring for one reason or another" (1966a, p. 99). The consequence of frustration is general excitement which "gets channeled into whatever skeletal response happens to be under way at the time the increase in excitement occurs" (1966a, p. 102).

Although Sheffield did not offer a fully explicit statement on $S^r$, the following passage suggests his approach to this problem:

> It [drive-induction theory] simplifies acquired drive and acquired reward by reducing them to the same thing, namely, cue patterns that elicit the consummatory response by way of conditioning. These patterns function as reward does when it is presented and has not quite been used yet, that is, they arouse the consummatory response. [1966a, p. 103]

Our interpretation of this statement is that $S^r$'s are cues which evoke consummatory responses which, upon being frustrated, generate excitement.

Sheffield has described an interesting laboratory "defeat" in which the salivary responses of dogs were investigated. A five-second tone preceded the delivery of liverwurst. The dogs displayed conditioned salivation to the tone and to food in the mouth. With continued training, however, the anticipatory salivation to the tone dropped out. It could only be maintained by highly variable training conditions, for example, different CS durations, irregular intertrial intervals, etc. And, as in the case of the Kintsch-Witte study, the expected correlation of salivary and instrumental responses was not evident. Sheffield states:

> A more important surprise, however, was the fact that the skeletal and instrumental behavior of the dogs did not follow the same history as the salivary behavior. Regardless of what the salivary response did, the dogs tended to orient to the food bowl and get set to eat when the CS started. This behavioral response to tone appeared before the first salivary response, persisted as an anticipatory response through training and was more resistant to extinction than was conditioned salivation. [1966b, p. 120]

The conclusion from this investigation and those cited earlier seems inescapable: the relation between salivary responding and instrumental performance is not a simple one.

The outcome of the Kraeling study, done at Yale, apparently surprised Sheffield. He suggested that Kraeling's observed lack of a simple relationship between running speeds and consummatory behavior might reflect the fact that the rats had reached their ceiling of tongue-lapping. He further proposed "the possibility that strength of *consummatory activation*, at the level of the CNS, can continue to increase" (1966b, p. 122). However, Sheffield's latter suggestion reminds one of Skinner's warning (1950) that the pursuit of constructs may lead us far from behavior.

Although Sheffield advocates a contiguity position on classical conditioning, in general there is a strong resemblance between his viewpoint and Spence's. But Sheffield's theory has not been developed as fully as the Spence-Amsel viewpoint and is less specific. For example, the major hypothesis of Sheffield's drive-induction theory is that frustration-produced excitement gets channeled into whatever response is occurring. He states: "If the excitement does not interfere with the ongoing behavior, or if it is not elicited by a stimulus for incompatible behavior, there is no place for it to show up except in an increased vigor of executing the behavior already under way" (1966a, p. 102). This ambiguous statement permits the post-diction of any outcome and prompts one to ask, Under what specific conditions does excitement interfere with or facilitate ongoing behavior? A further question concerns Sheffield's definition of frustration: Precisely what kinds of events are frustrating?

*Mowrer*

The most elaborate set of learned motivational mechanisms has been devised by Mowrer. Most germane is *hope* ($r_h$), the conditional portion of the consummatory response ($R_R$), which becomes attached to the stimuli produced by the instrumental response ($R_I$). The fact that $r_h$ is connected to movement-produced stimuli (1960, p. 256) rather than to external cues, as in the case of the previous theories, leaves Mowrer firmly impaled by a horn of a dilemma created by his view that habit *is* secondary reinforcement. Mowrer is confronted by a critical problem of explaining response selection and initiation (1960, p. 251; cf. Miller, 1963, pp. 85f.; Logan, 1968, pp. 7f.). If responses are facilitated by $r_h$ which is elicited by response-produced stimuli, what initiates $R_I$ and why does one $R_I$ occur rather than another? It should also be mentioned that Mowrer has asserted that $r_h$ may be indexed "among other ways, by salivation" (1960, p. 59). If habit is hope and hope may be measured by salivation, then why is the relationship between salivation and instrumental performance not a closer one?

The similarity of hope ($r_h$) to Spence's $r_G$ and Amsel's $r_R$ is obvious. The counterpart of frustration in Mowrer's theory is *anger*. He has proposed that "when hope is not confirmed (as in so-called extinction), the subject not only does not get positively reinforced (by food or the like) but, in addition, experiences the distinctive negative emotion of anger, which tends to countercondition the hope reaction" (1960, p. 418). And more generally Mowrer has contended that "all *un*learning of emotional reactions involves counterconditioning, and not simply the withdrawal or absence of the conditions of reinforcement which have previously prevailed" (1960, p. 419). He characterized Amsel's frustration-inhibition theory of extinction as one with "generality and power." Mowrer's proposal (1960, p. 469), that partially reinforced training produces better resistance to extinction because this type of training "neutralizes" anger in extinction, has much in common with Amsel's view.

While Mowrer often fails to bring his theory down to the level of specificity encountered in Spence and Amsel, he has presented a more elaborate set of learned motivational entities in an effort to deal with a wider range of phenomena. To consider but one example, just as the counterpart of hope is anger, the counterpart of fear is relief. "When a danger signal terminates without the customary reinforcement (noxious stimulation), the organism, as we well know, experiences *relief*, which is a form of secondary decremental reinforcement and ought, therefore, to be capable of counterconditioning fear itself" (1960, p. 419). Mowrer's theory can be charged for its lack of specificity and informality, but it cannot be faulted for its attempt at breadth.

Despite terminological differences, all of the viewpoints surveyed so far share a common concept, the fractional antedating goal reaction. We have shown that in general the evidence bearing upon Spence's $r_G$ theory and upon $r_G$ as an explicit response, for example, salivation, has not been confirmatory. Faced with this state of affairs some theorists like Logan (1968) have abandoned $r_G$ in favor of a learned incentive factor, while others like Sheffield have relegated $r_G$ to some unspecified locus in the CNS. Has the $r_G$ era come to an end?

*Skinner*

Interest in $S^r$ or conditioned reinforcement can be dated from Skinner's *Behavior of Organisms* (1938).[1] He (1938, pp. 245f.) proposed that an operant response could be reinforced by making a CS or a discriminative stimulus ($S^D$) contingent upon its occurrence. He also described the application of what currently are termed conditioned aversive stimuli "as when a tone which has preceded a shock is produced by an operant and the operant declines in strength" (1938, p. 246). Lastly, he anticipated future developments by pointing out that $S^r$ was intimately connected with the chaining of reflexes. Skinner's early work on $S^r$ was extended by Keller and Schoenfeld (1950), and we may say with confidence that today conditioned reinforcement is a major concept in the Skinner viewpoint and a problem area of active interest (e.g., Kelleher & Gollub, 1962; Kelleher, 1966a; Verhave, 1966).

We may quickly dispose of the matter of the relationship between $S^r$ and $r_G$ in Skinner's system. The notion of explaining $S^r$ in terms of $r_G$ is quite alien to this system. The chief reason for this position is that the Skinner group does not want to talk about unobservables. It also entails the question, Why do reinforcers reinforce? Such questions lead to theories, and Skinner (1950) has argued vigorously that research can be done without theories and that their use may have deleterious effects upon the development of a science of behavior. Usually the explanations offered by the Skinner group assume the form of what Hempel (1966) has called "reduction to the familiar" and a marked aversion has been shown toward the deductive-nomological type of explanation.

The question of the role of frustration in Skinner's system and its connection to conditioned reinforcement is a more complex one. In 1938, Skinner included "the restraint of a response . . . [and] the interruption of a chain of reflexes through the removal of a rein-

1. I wish to thank Professor Don Baer for his helpful comments on this section.

forcing stimulus" as members of his class of emotional operations. At a later point (1938, p. 76) he attributed the commonly observed cyclic fluctuations in extinction to an "emotional effect," resulting from the breaking of a normal ingestive chain, which temporarily lowers the rate of responding.

More than a decade later, in discussing rates of responding during extinction, Skinner mentioned two factors, stimulus-generalization decrement and emotion. He believed that the former factor was more important. Regarding emotion he said:

> When we fail to reinforce a response that has previously been reinforced, we not only initiate a process of extinction, we set up an emotional response—perhaps what is often meant by frustration. The pigeon coos in an identifiable pattern, moves rapidly about the cage, defecates or flaps its wings rapidly in a squatting position that suggests treading (mating) behavior. This competes with the response of striking a key and is perhaps enough to account for the decline in rate in early extinction. [1950, pp. 203f.; cf. Keller & Schoenfeld, 1950, p. 345; Skinner, 1953, p. 164]

Furthermore, Skinner stressed that the effects of frustration tend to adapt out. "Repeated extinction curves become smoother, and in some of the schedules [of reinforcement] . . . there is little or no evidence of an emotional modification of rate" (1950, p. 204).

After this interpretation of extinction, it might have been anticipated that: 1) frustration would become an important concept in the Skinner system; and 2) great interest would be displayed in Amsel's work. However if one examines recent summaries of the work of the Skinner group (e.g., Honig, 1966) and the issues of the *Journal of the Experimental Analysis of Behavior* over the last several years, it is clear that neither of these anticipations has been realized. Instead, frustration and frustration phenomena are, to a considerable degree, being reduced to familiar and presumed more basic processes. For example, Notterman and Mintz (1965) have asked why response magnitude (i.e., force) increases in extinction. While they mention Amsel's theory and the Skinner emotional view, they offer two learning explanations—one by Schoenfeld (1950) and another by Notterman and Block (1960). Schoenfeld held that various suprathreshold response magnitudes are reinforced especially early in acquisition and that each of these subclasses of responses must be extinguished separately. The Notterman-Block hypothesis, on the other hand, stressed "that biological organisms are exposed from birth to reinforcement contingencies in which successively more vigorous responding tends to produce reinforcement" (Notterman & Mintz, 1965, p. 104). Thus we can see that a phenomenon which Amsel might attribute to greater D as a consequence of frustration is being reduced to the past reinforcement history of the organism.

There is another movement within the Skinner group to treat extinction as an aversive event which is functionally similar to punishment. For example, Azrin and his co-workers have demonstrated in a number of species that the application of various aversive stimuli such as shock to the feet or tail or intense heat will elicit attack. They have reasoned that if extinction is also an aversive event, then attack should follow. Azrin, Hutchinson, and Hake (1966) have shown that pigeons reared in social isolation will, at the outset of extinction, attack another pigeon confined nearby or a stuffed model.

Another way to view extinction is to regard it as one member of a class of time-out operations in which organisms undergo a withdrawal of positive reinforcement or are denied the opportunity to obtain positive reinforcement. Other members of this class would be the presentation of a negative discriminative stimulus ($S^{\Delta}$) in discrimination training and intervals between reinforcement in different reinforcement schedules (Leitenberg, 1965). The question can then be asked whether or not such time-out operations are aversive events. This matter is far from simple, but under some conditions a tentative affirmative conclusion has been drawn (Leitenberg, 1965; cf. Azrin & Holz, 1966). For our purposes, if time-out operations are aversive, then cues signaling the onset of such operations should become conditioned aversive stimuli. Such stimuli should: 1) punish behavior which produces them; 2) maintain responses which postpone them; and 3) reinforce responses that terminate them. Accordingly, this line of development points up a linkage between operations, which Amsel would probably say produce frustration, and conditioned aversive stimuli.

Before leaving this topic, we might point out several parallels between the views of the Skinner group and previously described systems. For example, the conditioned aversive stimuli that signal nonreinforcement correspond to "danger" signals, a form of secondary punishment in Mowrer's theory (1960, p. 165). And working in the Spence-Amsel framework, Wagner (1963) has shown that the cessation of cues associated with frustration can serve as reinforcement for a hurdle-crossing response. In another study Brown and Wagner (1964; cf. Wagner, 1966) contrasted the extinction and punishment test performance in a runway of a group (N) of rats with partial reinforcement training, a group (C) with 100 percent reinforcement, and a group (P) that was trained like N except that food and shock were administered on the trials in which group N was nonreinforced. Groups N and P displayed enhanced resistance to extinction, and N was slowed less by punishment in test and P was less affected by nonreward than the C group. Brown and Wagner therefore concluded that fear and conditioned frustration have something in common. These outcomes are in accord with Azrin's idea above that the absence of reward is aversive.

So much for a brief look at some relationships among $S^r$, $r_G$, and frustration as they appear in a number of behavior theories. Let us now turn to a more detailed examination of the question of the relationship between $S^r$ and frustration that has been raised in a note by Lott (1967) and in a monograph by Longstreth (1966).

### *Lott and Longstreth*

In 1967, Lott described what he called a "conceptual paradox" existing between $S^r$ and frustration. More specifically, Lott argued: 1) that the basic test operation—the omission of reinforcement—is identical for frustration and $S^r$, and 2) that the operational identity of these two concepts had gone unnoticed. Since Amsel (1968) has already challenged Lott's second point, let us consider Lott's first argument. Lott attempted to document his position by comparing the early well-known $S^r$ study of Bugelski (1938) with an experiment by Lambert and Solomon (1952) in which groups of rats after training were blocked at different distances from a runway goal box. Rats blocked closer to the goal showed better resistance to extinction; this greater persistence was attributed by the authors to a greater frustration drive. If we grant that blocking *S* close to the goal vs. farther away is analogous to presenting the click or omitting it in Bugelski's experiment, then we agree with Lott that the operations are somewhat similar. However, it should be noted that extinction tests of $S^r$ like Bugelski's are open to a stimulus-generalization interpretation (Melching, 1954; Wike, 1966, p. 32) as, of course, is the Lambert-Solomon study. Furthermore, an extinction test of $S^r$ is only one of many paradigms for $S^r$.

Lott's claim of operational identity seems less defensible in his next two examples, Saltzman's $S^r$ experiment (1949) and the Amsel-Roussel double-alley demonstration (1952) of the frustration effect. The Saltzman study, involving a between-groups type of design, investigated the effects of making a formerly rewarded but now empty goal box contingent upon a new response by placing it at one end of a U maze. Even this description is oversimplified because a run in the opposite direction led, in different groups, to either a "novel" goal box or to one previously associated with nonreward. Accordingly, it is not clear to what extent Saltzman's rats were running *to* the $S^r$ box and to what extent they were running *away from* the other goal box or *both*. In the Amsel-Roussel study, on the other hand, the empty goal box was presented to a single group of rats on alternate trials prior to the measured response in the second alley. Thus, the Saltzman and Amsel-Roussel studies differed in at least three important respects: 1) the response measure—choice of new responses vs. speed of executing an old response; 2) type of design—between vs. within; and 3) cue presentation—cue after vs. before a response. In view of these gross differences, one might inquire how the two studies are "operationally identical." While we might concede that extinction tests of $S^r$ are similar to one frustration arrangement, the similarity breaks down when new learning tests of $S^r$ are compared to frustration effect studies. And although the new learning paradigm of $S^r$ usually embodies tests without primary reward, it is quite possible to present primary rewards during the test trials as some investigators have done (Greene, 1953; Powell & Perkins, 1957; Reynolds, Pavlik, Schwartz, & Besch, 1963). These studies serve to question the adequacy of Lott's presumed basic operation for $S^r$ as the omission of primary reinforcement. Then, too, as Lott himself admits in a footnote, the study of $S^r$ by chained schedules, in which primary reinforcement is present, constitutes an exception to his argument. There are, of course, still other techniques for studying $S^r$, like concurrent arrangements, which include primary reinforcement (cf. Kelleher & Gollub, 1962). In conclusion, we would challenge Lott's assumption that the test operation, omission of primary reinforcement, is identical for $S^r$ and frustration. Such a description does not do justice to the complexity of the operations for either concept. The critical operation in case of $S^r$ is that a stimulus which has previously been associated with a reinforcer is made contingent upon a response; this operation may be imposed either with or without primary reinforcement.

The issue of the similarity between frustration and $S^r$ has also been raised by Longstreth (1966). At the beginning of his monograph Longstreth stated:

> The basic definition of a secondary reinforcer ($S^r$) is well known: it is a stimulus configuration, which, through association with a reinforcer, acquires the capacity to influence preceding behavior in a way similar to that of the original reinforcer itself. In other words, *responses followed* by $S^r$ are strengthened (learned) or at least maintained at a higher level than responses followed by neutral stimuli not previously paired with reinforcement. [1966, p. 1, emphasis added]

We would agree completely with this statement. And, in accord with the remarks made regarding Lott's paper, we would stress that a very significant phrase in Longstreth's definition is "responses followed by $S^r$."

After reviewing several theories concerned with the sufficient conditions for the establishment of $S^r$, Longstreth posed his major issue:

> It is to be noted that all these elaborations share the two operations of the pairing to be $S^r$ with an established reinforcer and then presenting it alone. Of primary importance to the current discussion is the fact that a current theory of frustration specifies exactly the same operations as necessary for creating a *frustrating* situation. Reference is made here to Amsel's well-known frustration theory. [1966, p. 2]

Once again, let us emphasize that the operation of presenting the $S^r$ in test after the response and without the primary reinforcement is a valid description for only two paradigms of $S^r$, extinction tests and new learning tests without primary reinforcement. Nevertheless, it was Longstreth's intention to arrange crucial experiments in which the $S^r$ and frustration theories generate differential predictions.

Before a consideration of two of these experiments, we should mention that Longstreth presented a number of precautions to be employed before experiments can be legitimately interpreted in terms of $S^r$. One of these, termed the elicitation precaution, was described as follows: "According to this requirement, it must be insured that the $S^r$ does not *elicit* the response it is assumed to *strengthen*" (1966, p. 25). Immediately after distinguishing between *direct* elicitation, e.g., Bugelski's proposal (1956) that the click in his study could have evoked rather than strengthened bar pressing, and *indirect* elicitation, e.g., the proposal by Wyckoff, Sidowski, and Chambliss (1958) that the click might elicit approach to the food magazine and thereby increase the chances of responding, Longstreth asserted: "In either case, secondary reinforcing processes are clearly not required: a simple cueing effect accounts for the data" (1966, p. 25). As we have suggested elsewhere (Wike, 1966), the possibility of such elicitation interpretations would appear to be diminished by the use of widely distributed test trials and new learning tests of $S^r$ rather than extinction tests. Also, studies in which yoked-controls were included (Crowder, Morris, & McDaniel, 1959; Crowder, Gill, Hodge, & Nash, 1959; Crowder, Gay, Bright, & Lee, 1959; Crowder, Gay, Fleming, & Hurst, 1959; Egger & Miller, 1962), have demonstrated that elicitation is inadequate to account for all of the observed $S^r$ effect.

Let us now turn to Longstreth's research.[2] In Experiment I, 66 second- and third-grade children received successive discrimination training in which S+ was one light intensity (e.g., 20 ftc.) and S− was another (e.g., 0.3 ftc.). The correct instrumental response to S+ was moving a joystick in one direction (e.g., right 30°). When *S* made a correct response, S+ was immediately terminated, two seconds later the reward, a marble, was delivered, preceded by the noise of a solenoid, and two seconds later the next stimulus, either S+ or S−, was presented. The appropriate response to S− was moving the stick in the opposite direction (e.g., left 30°). If *S*

2. Longstreth's monograph includes three experiments. We shall consider only the first two.

responded appropriately to S –, that light was terminated, and four seconds later the next illumination was presented. The children were told that when the marbles reached a marker on the exposed marble tube, they could exchange them for a prize. Since 36 training trials were given (18 S+ and 18 S –), the *S*s had 18 marbles and 2 more marbles were needed when extinction, unannounced, began. There were three extinction conditions. For the S+ group only the illumination corresponding to S+ was presented. In the S + n group the S+ stimulus was presented and two seconds after the correct response the solenoid noise was delivered. In the S – condition only the S – was presented.

The response measures were: 1) response amplitude, 2) response speed, and 3) number of responses to extinction (the criteria were either a 10-second latency, the child's saying that he wished to stop, or 150 extinction trials). By the end of training the *S*s responded more vigorously to the S+ than to S –. In extinction there was no difference in response amplitude between S+ and S + n, but these groups combined had greater amplitude than S –. This large difference, which was consistent throughout extinction, was apparently not statistically significant. The *S*s responded faster to S+ than to S – in training. Groups S+ and S + n displayed a significant drop in speed from trial 1 to 2 in extinction, but on extinction trials 2 to 6 the three groups did not differ significantly. In addition, the response speeds were more variable during extinction for S+ and S + n than for S –. The *S*s in both S+ and S – made significantly more responses in extinction than S + n, but S+ and S – did not differ from one another.

Longstreth concluded that the data on the number of responses in extinction did not support $S^r$ theory since the opposite ranking of the groups would be expected. According to frustration theory, he reasoned, the anticipation of reward should be the strongest for S + n and the absence of reward in extinction should, therefore, produce maximum frustration and the least resistance to extinction. He also expected that S+ would produce greater frustration and faster extinction than in the case of S –. This expectation was not confirmed statistically. Other evidence that Longstreth stressed as supportive of frustration theory was the increased variability of the response speeds for S+ and S + n and the drops in speed from trial 1 to trial 2 in extinction. The former finding he interpreted as indicative of conflict. Finally, it should be noted that the failure of S+ and S + n to extinguish faster than S−, when extinction was indexed by amplitude and speed measures, would not appear to be in accord with frustration theory.

Longstreth's second experiment was designed to study further two of the extinction conditions, S+ and S−. The study differed in many respects from Experiment I: 1) 34 mental retardates were the *S*s; 2) greater force was required to move the response stick; 3) half of the *S*s had intertrial intervals of two seconds and a reinforcement interval of one second, while the other half had intervals of four and two seconds, respectively, as in Experiment I; 4) all *S*s had 120 pretraining trials (60 with the bright light and 60 with the dim) without reward; 5) instead of simply seeing marbles in a tube, the *S*s removed the steel marble rewards from a reward box and placed them in a container; 6) the *S*s were told that they could have a reward of either a bag of M & M's or a nickel when the container was filled with 30 marbles; and 7) each *S*'s preferred reward was placed beside the container. After 36 training trials (18 S+ and 18 S−), extinction began without any interruption. Half of the *S*s received only S− and, in another procedural change from Experiment I, the other half of the *S*s, termed S+, had the stimulus sequence of S+, S+, S−, S−, S+.

The *S*s in S+ extinguished faster than those in S−. Again, a significant drop in response speed occurred from trial 1 to trial 2 in S+, and S+'s speed scores were more variable in contrast to S−. Overall in the first 19 extinction trials, the trend in the S+ group was essentially linear, while the S− group for some curious reason displayed *shorter* latencies as extinction progressed. Response amplitude in the S+ group showed an increment from extinction trial 1 (S+) to trial 2 (S+), decrements on trial 3 (S−) and trial 4 (S−), a large increment on trial 5 (S+), followed by a gradual decline on the following trials. The decremental trend for the S− group was gradual throughout extinction, and the curves for the S+ and S− groups had essentially the same slope from trial 5 to trial 19 and the same average amplitudes.

We have already indicated that Longstreth expected greater resistance to extinction under S− than under S+ because of greater frustration under the S+ condition. Other predictions offered by Longstreth were: "Compared to S−, the S+ condition would be expected to (a) produce a greater decrement in starting speeds after the first extinction trial; (b) produce greater speed variability on early extinction trials; and (c) produce an *increment* in response amplitude, followed by a decrement on later extinction trials" (1966, p. 9). Two of these predictions, a and c, seem to be contradictory. Why should frustration produce an early decrease in speed but an increase in amplitude?

Let us now examine some features of the two experiments. The rationale of the studies was to provide conditions in which frustration theory predicted one set of outcomes and $S^r$ theory another. We would contend that: 1) the conditions may not have been favorable for the development of $S^r$; and 2) in every extinction condition, except possibly for S + n in Experiment I, no conventional test of $S^r$ was performed.

Regarding the first point, it was assumed by Longstreth that S+ was a $S^r$. Two complicating features of $S^r$ training were that the response turned off S+, and then the marble was not delivered until either one or two seconds later. Moreover, the marble was a something like a token reward; the children were not permitted to keep the tokens, all they had was *E*'s promise that if enough tokens were accumulated they would receive a prize. Unlike regular token rewards, these marbles did not have a history in which *E* had in fact exchanged them for rewards. Thus, the $S^r$ training operations asked the question, Can a stimulus (S+) which set the occasion for a response that terminated the stimulus and was followed one or two seconds later by a quasi-token become a $S^r$? Suppose that before these training conditions, the *S*s had experiences in which *E* had rewarded them with marbles and then permitted the *S*s to exchange them for candy or toys. Then if the marbles were given *without delay* upon *S*'s making the stick response and S+ stayed on until the marble was delivered, the chances of S+'s becoming a $S^r$ might have been enhanced.

So much for the contention that the training conditions used by Longstreth might not have been favorable for the development of $S^r$. Let us now consider the second contention that the experimental conditions did not constitute a conventional test for $S^r$. For the purposes of argument, let us assume that S+ was a $S^r$. How was this stimulus applied? Certainly not as Longstreth himself says (1966, p. 1) in his definition of $S^r$. Rather than $S^r$'s being made contingent upon a response, it was presented before the response as a $S^D$. Thus, Longstreth arranged conditions which were contrary to his "elicitation precaution." Furthermore, so-called $S^r$ theory is concerned with the effect of presenting a $S^r$ after an old response, as in an extinction test, or after a new response, as in a new learning test. The predictions from the theory are clear; in contrast to appropriate control conditions, a group with $S^r$ should resist extinction longer or display better conditioning of a new response. An empirical interpretation of $S^r$ yields no prediction about the consequences of presenting a $S^r$ before a response.

As stated above, the only possible exception to this criticism was the S + n condition in Experiment I, in which the solenoid noise (n) might be considered to be a $S^r$ by virtue of its pairing with the marble. Again, however, there is the problem that this noise was associated with what we have termed a quasi-token. If we contrast the performance of S + n with that of S+, then the situation would be more similar to a conventional extinction test of $S^r$. Longstreth would predict that S + n should extinguish faster—which it did—because of greater primary frustration and consequent $r_F$ conditioning and interfering responses on the ensuing trials. This deduction brings us to the *real* conceptual paradox existing between $S^r$ and frustration. This paradox has been succinctly described by Bower as follows: "Conventional tests for secondary reinforcement are also theoretically optimal conditions for the production of aversive frustration. Hence, positive demonstrations of secondary reinforcement create a paradox for frustration theory" (1963, p. 359). If Longstreth believes that $S^r$ test conditions are optimal for the production of frustration and frustration produces faster extinction, then how can he account for the results of the many previous $S^r$ studies using extinction or new learning tests, in which extinction was slower and new learning was better with $S^r$?

Spence and others (e.g., Bergum, 1960) have tried to assimilate these $S^r$ results by treating $S^r$'s as elicitors of $r_G$, which results in either greater D due to conflict or greater V due to an intensified $s_G$. Bergum says:

> Secondary reinforcement is the association of $r_G$'s with stimuli proximate to the primary reinforcer by a process of classical conditioning. Elicitation of these fractional responses results in heightened tension, which contributes to the general drive level. [1960, p. 52]

The difficulty with this theoretical interpretation of $S^r$ is that greater frustration should also result and thereby produce more inhibitory responses and faster extinction.

Let us now move to the second major topic of this paper, some developments in secondary reinforcement. We will begin by looking at several issues raised recently by Bolles (1967) in a thoughtful summary and evaluation of $S^r$. Next we will consider some recent research on $S^r$ using different paradigms. Finally, we shall suggest a hypothesis regarding durable $S^r$ and indicate how it might be tested.

## Developments in Secondary Reinforcement

### *Bolles*

We will consider only a few ideas regarding $S^r$ based on appetitive drives from the Bolles chapter (1967) on $S^r$. Bolles begins on a provocative note:

> There is no concept in all of psychology that is in such a state of theoretical disarray as the concept of secondary reinforcement. We know that there are secondary reinforcers because we know that the bulk of human behavior is learned by means of socially instilled rewards and punishments. But we know essentially nothing about how this instilling is done. The attempts to conduct systematic laboratory investigations to disclose how secondary reinforcers are established have as often as not failed to obtain any effects at all, much less show how they depend upon experimental parameters. [1967, p. 13]

Next Bolles documents the shortcomings of laboratory studies of $S^r$ by reference to three pioneer experiments by Frolov (Pavlov, 1927), Williams (1929), and Grindley (1929) and to later investigations (e.g., D'Amato, 1955; Miles, 1956), which disclosed $S^r$ effects that were small in magnitude and of short temporal duration. On the other hand, he is impressed by the striking $S^r$ effects that were obtained in the early token-reward studies of Wolfe (1936) and

Cowles (1937). He says: "These studies with token rewards demonstrate that laboratory-controlled secondary reinforcement can have the sort of durability and persistence that are necessary to explain social learning and motivation" (1967, p. 370). Three possibilities are suggested as to why these token rewards were effective: 1) that chimpanzees or humans are more capable of using tokens; 2) that the possession of tokens by *S* constitutes a $S^D$ for responding; and 3) "that the token reward serves as a subgoal, or as an invariant link between the instrumental behavior and the ultimate primary reinforcement" (1967, p. 371).

The fact that token rewards have been demonstrated with dogs (Ellson, 1937) and cats (Smith, 1939) led Bolles to reject the first possibility, types of *S*, as the sole cause for the greater effectiveness of tokens. Since the publication of Bolles's book, Malagodi (1967a, b, c) has shown that rats can acquire bar pressing with token rewards of a rubber ball or marbles. Following this initial training, the delivery of the tokens was programmed according to fixed-ratio (FR) and variable-interval (VI) schedules, and the resulting performance was comparable to that observed under similar schedules of unconditioned reinforcement. In follow-up studies, Malagodi (1967b, c) investigated FR and VI schedules of token reinforcement when more than one token was required before the tokens could be exchanged for food. VI performance was disrupted when two tokens were required for exchange. With FR token schedules the rates of bar pressing decreased as the number of tokens which were required before exchange increased. This work would appear to be of great significance and demands further investigation.

Bolles's other two suggestions, that $S^r$'s are $S^D$'s and that $S^r$'s are links in a chain terminating in primary reinforcement, form the basis for his *associative* theory of $S^r$. The basic idea is that "secondary reinforcers are merely stimuli that hold together chains of behavior" (1967, p. 372). According to this theory, $S^r$ is a stimulus which is conditioned by primary reward to an approach or withdrawal response. Bolles then elaborates on this theme:

> Stimuli present at the time of primary reinforcement will acquire secondary reinforcing powers to the extent that they have acquired associative control over the response. Thus, the organism will acquire a response by secondary reinforcement if that response produces stimuli

> which elicit another previously learned response. . . . The strength and durability of secondary reinforcement therefore depend upon the reliability of the eliciting power of the secondary reinforcer and this can be enhanced by discriminative training, and by prior conditioning of the response to possibly interfering concurrent stimuli, such as those arising from frustration. [1967, p. 414]

Bolles's $S^r$ theory can best be explicated by contrasting it with other viewpoints. To begin with, it is a variant of elicitation theory in which $S^r$ acts as a $S^D$ to elicit a response rather than as a $S^r$ to strengthen a response. As was indicated earlier, Wyckoff *et al.* (1958) and Bugelski (1956) have proposed elicitation theories of $S^r$. Wyckoff *et al.* suggested that $S^r$ might act as a cue 1) to bring the *S* to the vicinity of the magazine, and 2) to energize the *S* so that the probability would increase that a response (e.g., a bar press) might occur. Thus, $S^r$ might indirectly operate as a cue to facilitate bar presses. Although Bugelski (1938) originally interpreted his $S^r$ study in terms of the click's acting as a subgoal, he later (1956) offered a different view. His remarks have been interpreted by a number of writers (e.g., Crowder, Morris, & McDaniel, 1959; Kelleher & Gollub, 1962; Wike, 1966; Longstreth, 1966) to mean that $S^r$ evokes bar pressing. For example, Kelleher and Gollub have said: "According to Bugelski's analysis, the click is a conditioned stimulus that elicits lever-pressing. Thus, animals that receive the click in extinction will respond more frequently than animals that do not receive it" (1962, p. 581). However, the nearest that Bugelski comes to such a statement is in the following passage: "The click is part of the stimulation that is associated with approaching the food cup which automatically puts the animal in position for pressing the bar" (1956, p. 271). Thus, it is apparent that Bugelski does not believe that the click directly produces the bar press. In fact, if one examines Bugelski's $S^r$ theory in detail (1956, pp. 91–93), it is obvious that it is similar in many respects to Bolles's theory.

Both Bugelski and Bolles draw heavily upon a study by White (1953; cf. Bugelski, 1956) to support their interpretation of $S^r$. After Skinner box training, White gave half of his rats 30 pre-extinction trials in which a click was periodically sounded but no primary reward followed, and during these trials the bar was removed from the box. These *S*s made fewer bar presses and fewer trips to the food cup in regular extinction tests than control *S*s without such pre-extinction trials. According to Bugelski and Bolles, extinction occurred faster for the *S*s with pre-extinction trials because the last link of the chain, stimulus-bar press–click–going to food cup, was broken by the pre-extinction procedures. However, an empirical interpretation of $S^r$ would predict the same experimental outcome because presenting the click without food during the pre-extinction trials should reduce the acquired reward value of the stimulus. One interesting empirical question here is, In a Bugelski-type extinction study, without pre-extinction trials, do the *S*s with a click make more trips to the food cup during extinction than *S*s without a click?

While the Bugelski-Bolles associative theory offers a plausible interpretation in the case of extinction tests for $S^r$, how about new learning tests? At this point it would seem that Bugelski and Bolles have parted company. Bugelski, in discussing the Saltzman $S^r$ experiment (1949), said of the $S^r$ goal box:

> The size, shape, and decor of a goal box are stimulus features associated with eating and arouse appropriate eating responses which are frustrated by removal from the box as well as nonpresence of food. They probably serve to "strengthen" (that is, added to the stimulus pattern) food-approach responses if these are permitted. If the animal is immediately replaced on the starting leg of the T-maze, it may be more strongly "motivated" to choose the "good" goal box rather than the other. [1956, p. 271]

Thus, we can see that the simple associative theory of $S^r$ has now become complicated by the addition of a somewhat vague frustration factor. One also wonders why frustration should occur in new learning tests but was not mentioned by Bugelski in extinction tests.

Bolles regards new learning tests as a possible line of evidence against his associative theory of $S^r$. He admits that learning does occur in these situations (e.g., Saltzman, 1949; Klein, 1959) but terms it as "fragile." According to an empirical interpretation of $S^r$, the impermanence of the learning is explained by the postulation that $S^r$ extinguishes rapidly. Bolles says: "To apply the elicitation hypothesis, it is only necessary to add that secondary reinforcement extinguishes rapidly to the extent that the chain which gives the goal box its secondary reinforcing effect is disrupted" (1967, p. 383).

This statement accounts for the extinction of the learning, but why does the rat turn to the $S^r$ goal box?

We may ask, What direction is imparted to research by the Bolles associative theory of $S^r$? The most obvious and intriguing implication is that the stronger the conditioning of $S^r$ to a final response in the chain, such as approaching the food cup, the more effective $S^r$ ought to be as a reward. Thus, one might try different variables, for example, schedules of primary reward, etc., in magazine training with a click as the $S^D$ for approach to the magazine, and then see which schedule produced the most magazine responses during extinction when the click was presented. It would then be anticipated with a new group of rats that this particular schedule of magazine training might endow the click with the best $S^r$ for the acquisition of a new response such as bar pressing. In this context Bolles says: "Zimmerman (1957), who has gotten perhaps the most vivid evidence of response acquisition based on secondary reinforcement, has emphasized that there must be a very strong association between the buzzer and the next response (turning to the food cup) if the buzzer is to reinforce a new response" (1967, p. 380). But it should be noted that a magazine training regimen that conditions the *S*s to approach the food magazine and remain there can actually interfere with the learning of another response like bar pressing or key pecking. Accordingly, Ferster and Skinner (1957, p. 31) have usually employed three stages in the magazine training of pigeons: 1) getting the bird to eat from the magazine, 2) getting the bird to approach the magazine only when the magazine stimuli are activated, and 3) preventing the bird from hovering about the magazine by reinforcing its approach in the presence of the magazine stimuli from all sectors of the box. Nevertheless, the main research direction that the Bolles theory suggests is to investigate procedures for strengthening the final link which is evoked by $S^r$. Again, this approach is dictated by the assumption that a $S^r$ rewards *because* it elicits the final response.

One further thought on associative and reinforcing interpretations of $S^r$ is this: perhaps both factors are involved. That is, it seems possible that a $S^r$ strengthens or maintains the response that produces it and then acts as a $S^D$ for a subsequent response in a chain. After an examination of much of the same literature as Bolles used

(Wike, 1966), a different approach to the durability of $S^r$ suggested itself. To set the stage for this proposed direction in research, we need to examine other studies of $S^r$. In some of these paradigms it is often difficult or it may be impossible to separate the two stimulus functions—reinforcing and discriminative—of $S^r$. Furthermore, the view that these functions must be separated may seem relatively unimportant.

Lastly, we must not overlook the important concluding statement in Bolles's chapter: "Such explanations [in terms of secondary reinforcement] put upon the theorist and the researcher the very healthy responsibility of having to indicate precisely what stimuli, responses, and reinforcers are involved in the behavior being explained" (1967, p. 415).

*Other Paradigms for Secondary Reinforcement*

In this section we shall look at several experiments that exemplify some paradigms for $S^r$ which differ from the classic extinction and new learning techniques. More particularly, we shall examine a few studies of 1) token rewards, 2) chained schedules of reinforcement, 3) the concurrent technique developed by Joseph Zimmerman, and 4) what Kelleher has called "brief exteroceptive stimulus changes." These methods represent a selection from a larger group of methods which have been considered in greater detail by Kelleher and Gollub (1962) and Kelleher (1966a).

The token reward studies of Wolfe (1936), Cowles (1937), and Malagodi (1967a, b, c) were mentioned above. Let us now consider a series of investigations by Kelleher using two chimpanzees as *S*s. In Experiment I, Kelleher (1957a) put the chimps through three training stages. First, lever pressing was shaped, established with continuous food reinforcement, and then the *S*s had 180 hours of exposure to a five-minute fixed-interval schedule, FI 5. In the second stage, the chimps were trained to insert poker chips in a slot in exchange for food when the food window was illuminated by a red light. Third, after 500 chip-food exchanges, the *S*s were returned to lever pressing under a FI 5 schedule of token rewards.[3] Following

3. It should be noted that the procedures of this experiment differ greatly from those of Malagodi, described earlier, who developed the tokens as $S^r$'s and then used them to condition a new response.

an accumulation of 12 poker chips (one hour), a ten-minute exchange for food was permitted. While lever pressing for tokens was sustained at low rates initially, the rates soon diminished, and by the fourteenth hour extinction was complete.

In Experiment II the time that *S* had to wait before the chips could be exchanged was gradually lengthened by increasing the number of chips required for exchange from two to eight. While behavior was maintained for over 200 hours of tests, the rates of responding were low (range of 2.16 to 8.27 responses per minute for one *S* and .07 to 3.54 for the other *S*), and after the fifth session (three hours per session), in which eight chips were required, the rates dropped to below one per minute for both *S*s. It was also observed that rates were very low after a token exchange, but increased as the exchange time neared. Kelleher concluded: "The results of both experiments indicate that poker chips are not strong reinforcers for lever-pressing behavior when delivered on a FI 5 schedule" (1957a, p. 574). This conclusion appears to be a conservative one when we remember that the behavior was maintained for over 200 hours in Experiment II.

Next Kelleher (1957b, Experiment I), using the same two *S*s, achieved much longer delays before the exchanges of chips for food by imposing a multiple schedule of token reinforcement for lever pressing. When the lever was illuminated by an orange light, a FI 5 schedule was in effect; when a green light was on, a FR 20 schedule was in effect. These schedules were presented randomly. The first response that completed each schedule was followed by a token, and the time *S*s had to wait before exchanging the chips was gradually lengthened from 35 minutes to a maximum of 200 to 270 minutes. Some indication as to the efficacy of the multiple token schedule is shown by the fact that during the four sessions in which *S*s had to wait for the maximum period before token exchange one *S* averaged 5.33 responses per minute and the other *S* averaged 6.03. Thus, responding was sustained for over 200 minutes in these sessions without any primary reward until the end of the session.

In the following experiment Kelleher (1958) studied the effects of FR schedules of tokens upon lever pressing. After 30 sessions (60 poker chips per session) at FR 30, the number of responses required for a token was gradually increased to FR 100. Later a FR 125 schedule was enforced, and *S*s had to acquire 50 poker chips before exchange. These higher ratios produced lengthy pauses at the start of the sessions. Kelleher found that these pauses could be largely eliminated by giving the *S*s 50 chips at the start of a session and then requiring that the *S*s work for 50 more chips under FR 125. With these ratio schedules of token reinforcement very high rates of lever pressing were observed, for example, three responses per second. Since the handout of 50 poker chips greatly reduced the pauses at the start of the sessions, Kelleher concluded that the tokens not only reinforced pressing, but also acted as a $S^D$ for responding.

The literature on chained schedules has been summarized by Kelleher and Gollub (1962), who describe an operant chain as follows: "In an operant chain, responses occur in the presence of a discriminative stimulus and produce the discriminative stimuli for the other responses" (1962, p. 544). Chains are classed as homogeneous or heterogeneous, the criterial attribute being whether or not the responses are alike in their topography. A chained schedule of reinforcement is one in which responding in the presence of one $S^D(S_2)$ produces another $S^D(S_1)$, and responding in the presence of the latter stimulus terminates the chain with primary reinforcement. Since our purpose is merely to describe some different techniques of investigating $S^r$, one experimental example from Ferster and Skinner (1957, p. 667) will suffice:

> Pigeons were first exposed to a multiple schedule, *mult ext* FR 50. In the *ext* component, an orange stimulus was presented on a VI 1 schedule. . . . At the end of this time, $S_2$ was turned off, and $S_1$, a blue light, appeared. When the bird made 50 pecks under $S_1$, it was reinforced with food. The cycle was then repeated by presenting the orange light again. This multiple schedule was continued for 10 experimental sessions, during which three of the four birds displayed rapid responding in the presence of the blue light and almost no responding under the orange light. The fourth bird differed from the others by making a number of responses to the orange stimulus at the start of the sessions but extinguished later in the sessions.
>
> The schedule was then changed to a chained schedule, *chain* VI 1 FR 50. The first response after the particular interval in effect, e.g., 1 min., terminated the $S_2$, and turned on $S_1$. Fifty responses under $S_1$ resulted in primary reinforcement. Presumably, during the multiple

schedule $S_1$ had become a conditioned reinforcer as a consequence of its association with the primary reinforcer. Thus, it would be expected that the presentation of $S_1$ in the *chain* schedule would produce increments in responding within the first component of the schedule. The results were in accord with this expectation; the birds now responded at a stable intermediate rate during the $S_2$ segment in contrast with their earlier near-zero rate of responding. [Wike, 1966, pp. 39f.]

We shall not discuss the control procedures for this design. The important point is that stable responding in the first link was achieved by the chained schedule and, furthermore, this behavior could be maintained in what Kelleher and Gollub term "a stable and chronic situation."

Other instances of sustained behavior under $S^r$ have been reported by Joseph Zimmerman. Zimmerman's concurrent method of studying $S^r$ differs from chained schedules, he asserts, because the response that produces $S^r$ is not part of an explicit chain with the response that produces primary reinforcement. In his first experiment (1963) pigeons were confronted by two keys. Pecking the left-hand key led to a four-second exposure of grain on a VI 3 (minute) schedule. The feeding was accompanied by solenoid noise, a magazine light, and turning off of the key and house lights. On the other hand, pecking the right-hand key produced a one-half-second access to the magazine, which was too brief for the *S*s to get food, and the same set of stimulus changes that normally accompanied feeding. These events were programmed according to an independent VI 3 schedule. Thus, responding to one key produced food and the attendant stimuli, while responding to the other key produced only the stimuli. Under these conditions the behavior, "which could be maintained indefinitely," consisted of responding at a rate of one and a half to two responses per second on the food key and about one-tenth of these rates on the conditioned reinforcer key.

A later study (Zimmerman & Hanford, 1966) used a single response key and the presentation of food was not contingent upon *S*'s making any response. In the first phase the *S*s, three pigeons from the 1963 experiment and one naïve bird, were confronted by a key which was illuminated by a blue light, and pecks were rewarded secondarily by a half second of stimulus changes according to a FI 1 or FI 3 (minute) schedule. Concurrently, a three-second feeding plus the stimulus changes occurred according to a VI 3 schedule, provided that no key peck had taken place for a period of at least six seconds. Regarding this delay, the authors say: "This no-response contingency was programmed in order to (a) eliminate the possibility of accidental unconditioned reinforcement of key-pecking and (b) actually 'load against' the maintenance of response-contingent conditioned reinforcement" (1966, p. 394).

The second phase of the study investigated other causal factors in the situation by programming the key according to five two-component multiple schedules. In each schedule *S* was exposed during every session to a blue key light for 24 minutes, then to a yellow key light for 24 minutes, and then this schedule was repeated once. The five schedules were: 1) baseline of $S^r$ on both components; 2) neutral stimuli on blue, $S^r$ on yellow; 3) $S^r$ on blue, neutral stimuli on yellow; 4) extinction for $S^r$ on blue, $S^r$ on yellow; 5) $S^r$ on blue, extinction for $S^r$ on yellow. The stimuli, neutral or $S^r$, were presented for one-half second according to a FI 1 schedule. The neutral stimuli consisted of a 400-cps tone and a flashing house light and key light, none of which had ever been paired with food. Each of the schedules was continued until performance was stable over four sessions, and food was given throughout according to a VI 3 schedule with the six-second no-response contingency.

The results were as one would expect: 1) when no stimuli were contingent on key pecking (*ext*), the rate of pecking was very low; 2) likewise, neutral stimuli produced very low rates of key pecking; 3) higher rates of responding were produced by $S^r$; and 4) although three out of four birds responded at a higher rate to blue, the baselines of $S^r$ were recoverable. Regarding the stability of the behavior, Zimmerman and Hanford reported: "Under these conditions, responding was maintained indefinitely (up to 6 months) at rates which ranged from 3.0 to 8.0 responses per minute" (1966, p. 394). Zimmerman and his collaborators have replicated and extended their findings in later studies.

Lastly, let us turn to two studies that demonstrate the effects of briefly presented exteroceptive stimuli. Kelleher (1966a, b) has introduced the name second-order schedule for a schedule of a schedule. That is, the behavior resulting from one schedule, for example, FI 2, is treated as one response, and this response can be reinforced according to a schedule. Thus, FR 30 (FI 2) means that the *S* has to complete 30 FI 2 segments before reinforcement would be forthcoming. The experimental question which Kelleher asked was, What are the behavioral consequences in such a schedule of marking the completion of each FI 2 segment by a brief stimulus which is occasionally associated with primary reinforcement? Three pigeons with long experimental histories were trained to peck a key that was illuminated by a blue light. When the bird made the response that completed a FI 2 segment, a seven-tenths of a second white light was presented. When 30 FI 2 segments were so completed, the *S* received primary reinforcement consisting of 10 successive three-second presentations of food. During these food deliveries, the hopper was illuminated by two white lights and these lights reflected on the key, which was not illuminated. Thus, the second-order schedule was FR 30 (FI 2:W) in which W signifies the briefly presented white key light. After 37 sessions (three completions of the schedule per session), the *S*s had 6 sessions without the brief white key light, that is, FR 30 (FI 2). Following this, the *S*s were returned to FR 30 (FI 2:W) for 22 sessions. The effects of the brief white key light upon another second-order schedule were also investigated: FR 15 (FI 4:W) vs. FR 15 (FI 4).

When the fixed intervals were divided into quarters and the data were examined for the last five sessions on the four schedules, it was found that: 1) with the brief white key lights the average rates of responding increased over successive quarters of the fixed interval, and 2) without the light the rates were relatively constant over the successive quarters of the fixed interval. Thus, with the brief white key lights the *S*s displayed positively accelerated responding which resembled the typical pattern of responding shown on FI schedules of primary reinforcement. In another variation the key turned dark upon completion of the FI—a stimulus change that had not been associated with unconditioned reinforcement. This procedure FR 14 (FI 4:D) led to lower response rates and less positively accelerated responding than during the brief white key lights, FR 15 (FI 4:W). Therefore, it was not simply a stimulus change after completing each interval that was important; the stimulus which had been paired with primary reinforcement produced much larger effects.

A year earlier, Findley and Brady (1965) did a similar study with a second-order schedule involving a large FR schedule. A chimpanzee with a long history of training on ratio schedules was conditioned to press a button. After 4,000 responses (FR 4000), the *S* was rewarded with 20 two-thirds of a gram food pellets, one at a time in a hopper illuminated by a flashing light. This FR 4000 schedule was in effect when the response button was illuminated by a red light. When a green light was present, a second-order schedule was in effect: FR 10 (FR 400: L). That is, after each 400 responses the final response was followed by flashes of the hopper light for half a second. And after the tenth FR 400 segment, the primary reward was given. These two schedules, FR 4000 and FR 10 (FR 400: L), were alternated over a 31-day period during which *S* lived in the experimental space and received all his food there. The brief flashes of the hopper light had powerful effects upon pause lengths and the time spent working; the modal values in minutes for these indices were, respectively, about 23 and 19 for FR 4000 and 2 and 17 for FR 10 (FR 400: L).[4] In addition, in the case of each measure *S* displayed far less variability under the second-order schedule with brief light flashes.

We may summarize the foregoing studies by saying that in contrast to the weak and evanescent effects of $S^r$ found in extinction and new learning tests, profound and highly durable effects may be produced in such $S^r$ paradigms as token rewards, chained schedules, concurrent arrangements, and with briefly presented exteroceptive stimuli.

*The Reconditioning Hypothesis*

Many writers have dismissed $S^r$ as a useful explanatory concept because laboratory demonstrations have disclosed effects which were small in magnitude and transitory. Others, for example, Mowrer (1960), have assumed that the $S^r$ durability problem could be solved by the discovery of the proper $S^r$ training and test conditions. In fact, Mowrer (1960, pp. 113f.) regarded the durability problem as solved by D. W. Zimmerman's finding (1957) that a combination

4. Time spent working was defined as the time required to complete the schedule once *S* started responding.

of partial primary reinforcement during $S^r$ conditioning and partial $S^r$ in a new learning test produced substantial responding. Another example of this type of thinking is the implication drawn from Bolles's association theory of $S^r$, that the stronger the connection between $S^r$ and a final response, the stronger the $S^r$ would be. Despite the innumerable investigations of $S^r$ using extinction and new learning tests and involving many variables, convincing demonstrations of $S^r$ have not been evident. At the same time, it is obvious in everyday life that secondary reinforcers, like grades, money, and the like, appear to have long-term and powerful effects upon behavior. How can we reconcile the unimpressive results of $S^r$ experiments, employing extinction and new learning paradigms, with these everyday observations?

The key that unlocks this puzzle can be found, we believe, in the studies on token rewards, chained schedules, and so on, which we have just reviewed. In these experiments powerful and durable $S^r$ effects were seen. If we compare the $S^r$ studies using extinction and new learning with these recent studies of the Skinner group, a hypothesis and some different directions in $S^r$ research are suggested. This hypothesis, which we will call the *reconditioning hypothesis*, is not a novel proposition, since it is a basic assumption underlying the work on conditioned reinforcement by the Skinner group. It is also a notion that is virtually an empirical generalization. Nevertheless, we think it may be valuable to label it, so as to direct attention to it and its implications. *According to the reconditioning hypothesis, a $S^r$ will be strong and durable if, and only if, it has its reward value reconditioned from time to time by its being re-associated with primary reinforcement.* Thus, in token reward studies, the token exchange is critical in the maintenance of the reward value of the tokens. In chained schedules, it is the association of $S_1$ with primary reinforcement that sustains the $S^r$ value of $S_1$. In Zimmerman's concurrent situation and in the case of briefly presented exteroceptive stimuli, it is the constant but sporadic recoupling of the $S^r$ stimuli and primary reinforcement that endows the stimuli with durable acquired reward value. By way of contrast, the $S^r$'s from conventional extinction and new learning paradigms wither away because these stimuli are generally associated with primary reward *only* during $S^r$ training.

So much for the reconditioning hypothesis itself; does it do any more than account for what we already know? We believe it suggests some new lines of research. For example, it suggests that 1) token reward studies and 2) the investigation of chains should receive far more attention. It further implies that the token exchange aspects of token-reward studies should be explored in greater detail. Two aspects of token exchange must be distinguished: 1) the *token exchange training* in which the *S* is conditioned to trade tokens for primary rewards; and 2) the *token exchange procedure* in which the tokens, which have been presented as rewards for the *S*'s making some response, are exchanged. Kelleher's research (1957a) tells us that a large number of pairings of a token with primary reinforcement during token exchange training do not automatically endow the tokens with strong acquired reward value. Kelleher exposed his chimpanzees to 500 poker chip–food pairings, but when these tokens were administered on a FI 5 schedule, they did not sustain lever pressing too well. Nevertheless, we need to investigate token exchange training more fully. For example, suppose that instead of a token's always yielding food, the exchange was put on an intermittent schedule. This same question can be asked in the case of the token exchange procedure. For example, in the studies we examined, when the proper stimulus was present, inserting a token always led to primary reward. Suppose the token exchange procedure were put on an intermittent schedule? And, of course, various combinations of schedules in token exchange training and procedure could be studied.

Second, we indicated that chains should have a high priority as a research problem. Chains are held together by $S^r$'s and terminate in primary reinforcement. How can long chains be established and maintained? If we can answer this question, we will learn some significant facts about $S^r$.

The studies we reviewed on token rewards, chained schedules, etc., generally had two things in common: 1) usually the *S*s had long experimental histories, and 2) the experimental arrangements involved free responding. Are either or both of these conditions essential to obtain lasting $S^r$ effects? The answer to the first issue can readily be found by testing some naïve *S*s. The latter problem serves to raise a basic question and to suggest some further investigations. The basic question is this: Is a free-responding arrangement a "good model" for the kinds of behavior that we are seeking to explain? This is, of course, an empirical question, and can be translated into a further question: Do the principles established in free-responding arrangements hold for discrete-trial situations and vice versa? Therefore, we must find out whether or not the durable $S^r$ effects, which have been demonstrated in free-responding arrangements incorporating $S^r$ reconditioning, can be produced in discrete-trial situations. For example, could the performance in new learning tests of $S^r$ be enhanced and made more lasting by including $S^r$ reconditioning trials during the tests? More concretely, instead of the traditional two-stage $S^r$ experiments involving $S^r$ training (e.g., traversing a runway to food in a distinctive goal box) and $S^r$ testing (e.g., trials in a T-maze with the empty goal box as a $S^r$), rewarded runway trials would be imposed during the second stage. When should this $S^r$ reconditioning be given and how? Thus, the focus of this research would not be upon the role of the $S^r$ training conditions in endowing a stimulus with durable learned reward value, but upon $S^r$ reconditioning in the maintenance of reward value.

For about 40 years much of the research on $S^r$ has been guided by an assumption that stimuli paired with primary reinforcement can become functionally autonomous sources of reward. We believe that this assumption is a false one. A $S^r$ retains its reward value only when it is renewed by reconditioning.

## REFERENCES

Amsel, A. The role of frustrative nonreward in noncontinuous reward situations. *Psychol. Bull.*, 1958, **55**, 102–119.

Amsel, A. Partial reinforcement effects on vigor and persistence: Advances in frustration theory derived from a variety of within-subjects experiments. In K. W. Spence & Janet T. Spence (Eds.), *The psychology of learning and motivation.* Vol. 1. New York: Academic Press, 1967.

Amsel, A. Secondary reinforcement and frustration. *Psychol. Bull.*, 1968, **69**, 278.

Amsel, A., & Roussel, Jacqueline. Motivational properties of frustration: I. Effect on a running response of the addition of frustration to the motivational complex. *J. exp. Psychol.*, 1952, **43**, 363–368.

Azrin, N. H., & Holz, W. C. Punishment. In W. K. Honig (Ed.), *Operant behavior: Areas of research and application.* New York: Appleton-Century-Crofts, 1966.

Azrin, N. H., Hutchinson, R. R., & Hake, D. F. Extinction-induced aggression. *J. exp. Anal. Behav.*, 1966, **9**, 191–204.

Bergum, B. O. Gradients of generalization in secondary reinforcement. *J. exp. Psychol.*, 1960, **59**, 47–53.

Bolles, R. C. *Theory of motivation.* New York: Harper & Row, 1967.

Bower, G. H. Secondary reinforcement and frustration. *Psychol. Rep.*, 1963, **12**, 359–362.

Brown, R. T., & Wagner, A. R. Resistance to punishment and extinction following training with shock or nonreinforcement. *J. exp. Psychol.*, 1964, **68**, 503–507.

Bugelski, R. Extinction with and without subgoal reinforcement. *J. comp. Psychol.*, 1938, **26**, 121–134.

Bugelski, B. R. *The psychology of learning.* New York: Holt, 1956.

Capaldi, E. J. Partial reinforcement: An hypothesis of sequential effects. *Psychol. Rev.*, 1966, **73**, 459–477.

Capaldi, E. J. A sequential hypothesis of instrumental learning. In K. W. Spence & Janet T. Spence (Eds.), *The psychology of learning and motivation.* Vol. 1. New York: Academic Press, 1967.

Cowles, J. T. Food-tokens as incentives for learning by chimpanzees. *Comp. Psychol. Monogr.*, 1937, **14**, no. 5.

Crowder, W. F., Morris, J. B., & McDaniel, M. H. Secondary reinforcement or response facilitation?: I. Resistance to extinction. *J. Psychol.*, 1959, **48**, 299–302.

Crowder, W. F., Gill, K., Hodge, C. C., & Nash, F. A. Secondary reinforcement or response facilitation?: II. Response acquisition. *J. Psychol.*, 1959, **48**, 303–306.

Crowder, W. F., Gay, B. R., Bright, M. G., & Lee, M. F. Secondary reinforcement or response facilitation?: III Reconditioning. *J. Psychol.*, 1959, **48**, 307–310.

Crowder, W. F., Gay, B. R., Fleming, W. C., & Hurst, R. W. Secondary reinforcement or response facilitation?: IV. The retention method. *J. Psychol.*, 1959, **48**, 311–314.

D'Amato, M. R. Transfer of secondary reinforcement across the hunger and thirst drives. *J. exp. Psychol.*, 1955, **49**, 352–356.

Deaux, E. B., & Patten, R. L. Measurement of the anticipatory goal response in instrumental runway conditioning. *Psychon. Sci.*, 1964, **1**, 357–358.

Egger, M. D., & Miller, N. E. Secondary reinforcement in rats as a function of information value and reliability of the stimulus. *J. exp. Psychol.*, 1962, **64**, 97–104.

Ellson, D. G. Acquisition of a token-reward habit in dogs. *J. comp. Psychol.*, 1937, **24**, 505–522.

Ferster, C. B., & Skinner, B. F. *Schedules of reinforcement.* New York: Appleton-Century-Crofts, 1957.

Findley, J. D., & Brady, J. V. Facilitation of large ratio performance by use of conditioned reinforcement. *J. exp. Anal. Behav.*, 1965, **8**, 125–129.

Gonzalez, R. C., & Diamond, L. A test of Spence's theory of incentive motivation. *Amer. J. Psychol.*, 1960, **73**, 396–403.

Goodrich, K. P. Performance in different segments of an instrumental response chain as a function of reinforcement schedule. *J. exp. Psychol.*, 1959, **57**, 57–63.

Greene, J. E. Magnitude of reward and acquisition of a black-white discrimination habit. *J. exp. Psychol.*, 1953, **46**, 113–119.

Grice, G. R. The relation of secondary reinforcement to delayed reward in visual discrimination learning. *J. exp. Psychol.*, 1948, **38**, 1–16.

Grindley, G. C. Experiments on the influence of the amount of reward on learning in young chickens. *Brit. J. Psychol.*, 1929, **20**, 173–180.

Harlow, H. F. Mice, monkeys, men, and motives. *Psychol. Rev.*, 1953, **60**, 23–32.

Hempel, C. G. *Philosophy of natural science.* Englewood Cliffs, N.J.: Prentice-Hall, 1966.

Hilgard, E. R., & Bower, G. H. *Theories of learning.* 3d ed. New York: Appleton-Century-Crofts, 1966.

Hill, W. F. An attempted clarification of frustration theory. *Psychol. Rev.*, 1968, **75**, 173–176.

Honig, W. K. (Ed.). *Operant behavior: Areas of research and application.* New York: Appleton-Century-Crofts, 1966.

Hull, C. L. Mind, mechanism, and adaptive behavior. *Psychol. Rev.*, 1937, **44**, 1–32.

Hull, C. L. *Principles of behavior.* New York: Appleton-Century-Crofts, 1943.

Hull, C. L. *Essentials of behavior.* New Haven: Yale Univ. Press, 1951.

Hull, C. L. *A behavior system.* New Haven: Yale Univ. Press, 1952.

Hull, C. L., Livingston, J. R., Rouse, R. O., & Barker, A. N. True, sham and esophageal feeding as reinforcements. *J. of comp. physiol. Psychol.*, 1951, **44**, 236–245.

Kelleher, R. T. Conditioned reinforcement in chimpanzees. *J. comp. physiol. Psychol.*, 1957a, **50**, 571–575.

Kelleher, R. T. A multiple schedule of conditioned reinforcement with chimpanzees. *Psychol. Rep.*, 1957b, **3**, 485–491.

Kelleher, R. T. Fixed ratio schedules of conditioned reinforcement with chimpanzees. *J. exp. Anal. Behav.*, 1958, **1**, 281–289.

Kelleher, R. T. Chaining and conditioned reinforcement. In W. K. Honig (Ed.), *Operant behavior: Areas of research and application.* New York: Appleton-Century-Crofts, 1966a.

Kelleher, R. T. Conditioned reinforcement in second-order schedules. *J. exp. Anal. Behav.*, 1966b, **9**, 475–485.

Kelleher, R. T., & Gollub, L. R. A review of positive conditioned reinforcement. *J. exp. Anal. Behav.*, 1962, **5**, 543–597.

Keller, F. S., & Schoenfeld, W. N. *Principles of psychology.* New York: Appleton-Century-Crofts, 1950.

Kintsch, W., & Witte, R. S. Concurrent conditioning of bar press and salivation responses. *J. comp. physiol. Psychol.*, 1962, **55**, 963–968.

Klein, R. M. Intermittent primary reinforcement as a parameter of secondary reinforcement. *J. exp. Psychol.*, 1959, **58**, 423–427.

Kraeling, Doris. Analysis of amount of reward as a variable in learning. *J. comp. physiol. Psychol.*, 1961, **54**, 560–565.

Lambert, W. W., & Solomon, R. L. Extinction of a running response as a function of distance of block point from the goal. *J. comp. physiol. Psychol.*, 1952, **45**, 269–279.

Lawrence, D. H. Learning. In P. R. Farnsworth & Q. McNemar (Eds.), *Annual review of psychology*. Palo Alto: Annual Reviews, 1958.

Leitenberg, H. Is time-out from positive reinforcement an aversive event? A review of the experimental evidence. *Psychol. Bull.*, 1965, **64**, 428–441.

Logan, F. A. Incentive theory and changes in reward. In K. W. Spence & Janet T. Spence (Eds.), *The psychology of learning and motivation.* Vol. 2. New York: Academic Press, 1968.

Longstreth, L. E. Frustration and secondary reinforcement concepts as applied to human conditioning and extinction. *Psychol. Monogr.*, 1966, **80**, no. 11 (whole no. 619).

Lott, D. F. Secondary reinforcement and frustration: A conceptual paradox. *Psychol. Bull.*, 1967, **67**, 197–198.

Malagodi, E. F. Acquisition of the token-reward habit in the rat. *Psychol. Rep.*, 1967a, **20**, 1335–1342.

Malagodi, E. F. Fixed-ratio schedules of token reinforcement. *Psychon. Sci.*, 1967b, **8**, 469–470.

Malagodi, E. F. Variable-interval schedules of token reinforcement. *Psychon. Sci.*, 1967c, **8**, 471–472.

Melching, W. H. The acquired reward value of an intermittently presented stimulus. *J. comp. physiol. Psychol.*, 1954, **47**, 370–374.

Miles, R. C. The relative effectiveness of secondary reinforcers throughout deprivation and habit-strength parameters. *J. comp. physiol. Psychol.*, 1956, **49**, 126–130.

Miller, N. E. Some reflections on the law of effect produce a new alternative to drive reduction. In M. R. Jones (Ed.), *Nebraska symposium on motivation.* Lincoln: Univ. of Nebraska Press, 1963.

Mowrer, O. H. *Learning theory and behavior*. New York: Wiley, 1960.

Murray, H. A. *Explorations in personality*. New York: Oxford Univ. Press, 1938.

Notterman, J. M., & Block, A. H. Response differentiation during a simple discrimination. *J. exp. Anal. Behav.*, 1960, **3**, 289–291.

Notterman, J. M., & Mintz, D. E. *Dynamics of response.* New York: Wiley, 1965.

Patten, R. L. A straight-runway application of the incentive-motivation behavior-guidance theory. *Psychol. Rep.*, 1968, **23**, 1287–1294.

Pavlov, I. P. *Conditioned reflexes*. London: Oxford Univ. Press, 1927.

Perkins C. C. The relation of secondary reward to gradients of reinforcement. *J. exp. Psychol.*, 1947, **37**, 377–391.

Powell, D. R., & Perkins, C. C. Strength of secondary reinforcement as a determiner of the effects of duration of goal response on learning. *J. exp. Psychol.*, 1957, **53**, 106–112.

Rescorla, R. A., & Solomon, R. L. Two-process learning theory: Relationships between Pavlovian conditioning and instrumental learning. *Psychol. Rev.*, 1967, **74**, 151–182.

Reynolds, W. F., Pavlik, W. B., Schwartz, M. M., & Besch, Norma F. Maze learning by secondary reinforcement without discrimination training. *Psychol. Rep.*, 1963, **12**, 775–781.

Saltzman, I. J. Maze learning in the absence of primary reinforcement: A study of secondary reinforcement. *J. comp. physiol. Psychol.*, 1949, **42**, 161–173.

Schoenfeld, W. N. On the difference in resistance to extinction following regular and periodic reinforcement. *Notes, Conference on the Experimental Analysis of Behavior.* Indiana Univ., 1950, no. 20.

Senkowski, P. C., Porter, J. J., & Madison, H. L. Goal gradient effect of incentive motivation (K) manipulated through prior goal box placements. *Psychon. Sci.*, 1968, **11**, 29–30.

Shapiro, M. M. Temporal relationship between salivation and lever pressing with differential reinforcement of low rates. *J. comp. physiol. Psychol.*, 1962, **55**, 567–571.

Shapiro, M. M., & Miller, T. M. On the relationship between conditioned and discriminative stimuli and between instrumental and consummatory responses. In W. F. Prokasy (Ed.), *Classical conditioning: A symposium.* New York: Appleton-Century-Crofts, 1965.

Sheffield, F. D. A drive-induction theory of reinforcement. In R. N. Haber (Ed.), *Current research in motivation.* New York: Holt, Rinehart, & Winston, 1966a.

Sheffield, F. D. New evidence on the drive-induction theory of reinforcement. In R. N. Haber (Ed.), *Current research in motivation.* New York: Holt, Rinehart, & Winston, 1966b.

Skinner, B. F. *The behavior of organisms.* New York: Appleton-Century-Crofts, 1938.

Skinner, B. F. Are theories of learning necessary? *Psychol. Rev.*, 1950, **57**, 193–216.

Skinner, B. F. *Science and human behavior.* New York: Macmillan, 1953.

Smith, M. F. The establishment and extinction of the token-reward habit in the cat. *J. gen. Psychol.*, 1939, **20**, 475–486.

Spence, K. W. The nature of discrimination learning in animals. *Psychol. Rev.*, 1936, **43**, 427–449.

Spence, K. W. The role of secondary reinforcement in delayed reward training. *Psychol. Rev.*, 1947, **54**, 1–8.

Spence, K. W. *Behavior theory and conditioning.* New Haven: Yale Univ. Press, 1956.

Spence, K. W. *Behavior theory and learning: Selected papers.* Englewood Cliffs, N.J.: Prentice-Hall, 1960.

Stein, L. The classical conditioning of the consummatory response as a determinant of instrumental performance. *J. comp. physiol. Psychol.*, 1957, **50**, 269–278.

Swift, Carolyn F., & Wike, E. L. A test of Spence's theory of incentive motivation. *Psychol. Record*, 1958, **8**, 21–25.

Thorndike, E. L. *Animal intelligence.* New York: Macmillan, 1911.

Verhave, T. *The experimental analysis of behavior.* New York: Appleton-Century-Crofts, 1966.

Wagner, A. R. Conditioned frustration as a learned drive. *J. exp. Psychol.*, 1963, **66**, 142–148.

Wagner, A. R. Frustration and punishment. In R. N. Haber (Ed.), *Current research in motivation.* New York: Holt, Rinehart, & Winston, 1966.

Weinstock, S. Acquisition and extinction of a partially reinforced running response at a 24-hour intertrial interval. *J. exp. Psychol.*, 1958, **56**, 151–158.

White, R. T. Analysis of the function of a secondary reinforcing stimulus in a serial learning situation. Unpublished Ph.D. dissertation, Univ. of Buffalo, 1953. Cited by Bugelski (1956).

White, R. W. Motivation reconsidered: The concept of competence. *Psychol. Rev.*, 1959, **66**, 297–333.

Wike, E. L. *Secondary reinforcement: Selected experiments.* New York: Harper & Row, 1966.

Wike, E. L., & Remple, R. Runway performance as a function of reinforcement schedule and alley length. *J. exp. Psychol.*, 1960, **59**, 277–278.

Williams, Katherine A. The reward value of a conditioned stimulus. *Univ. Calif. Pub. Psychol.*, 1929, **4**, 31–55.

Wilton, R. On frustration and the PRE. *Psychol. Rev.*, 1967, **74**, 149–150.

Wolfe, J. B. Effectiveness of token rewards for chimpanzees. *Comp. Psychol. Monogr.*, 1936, **12**, no. 60.

Wyckoff, L. B., Sidowski, J., & Chambliss, D. J. An experimental study of the relationship between secondary reinforcing and cue effects of a stimulus. *J. comp. physiol. Psychol.*, 1958, **51**, 103–109.

Zimmerman, D. W. Durable secondary reinforcement: Method and theory. *Psychol. Rev.*, 1957, **64**, 373–383.

Zimmerman, J. Technique for sustaining behavior with conditioned reinforcement. *Science*, 1963, **142**, 682–684.

Zimmerman, J., & Hanford, P. V. Sustaining behavior with conditioned reinforcement as the only response-produced consequence. *Psychol. Rep.*, 1966, **19**, 391–401.

## COMMENTS

*Dalbir Bindra*

In his paper on secondary reinforcement, Professor Wike has addressed himself to an important problem: What is the basis of the observed durability of the effectiveness of certain secondary reinforcers? The problem poses two separate questions: 1) What are the conditions that determine the duration for which the effectiveness of a secondary reinforcer will last without any further association with a primary reinforcer? 2) Is the mechanism underlying secondary reinforcing effects an instigational or eliciting one, or is it a response-reinforcing one?

Professor Wike's detailed analysis of a variety of secondary reinforcement experiments leaves little doubt that the main condition for obtaining durable secondary reinforcing effects is *periodic* reconditioning or re-association of the secondary reinforcing stimulus with a primary reinforcer. This "reconditioning hypothesis" constitutes a valid conclusion empirically, and is also consistent with the results of another body of data, namely, data from experiments on the partial reinforcement extinction effect. What Professor Wike's analysis shows is, in effect, that the partial reinforcement procedures (including reinforcement schedules of all types) that make a response persist in the face of nonreinforcement (extinction) also make the reinforcing properties of a secondary reinforcer persist in the absence of primary reinforcement. In other words, the concept of resistance to extinction is equally applicable to both extinction and secondary reinforcement experiments. The partial reinforcement schedules (during acquisition) increase the resistance to extinction of a response in the case of extinction experiments and of a secondary reinforcer in the case of secondary reinforcement experiments. Thus the problem of the durability of secondary reinforcing properties may be regarded as a special case of the general problem of the partial reinforcement extinction effect. The main clue to the basis of the partial reinforcement extinction effect appears to me to be the empirical generalization that the more varied the experimental conditions are, the greater will be the persistence of the acquired effects during extinction (e.g., Bacon & Bindra, 1965; Brown & Bass, 1958; Mackintosh, 1955).

Professor Wike's critical examination of the mechanism of secondary reinforcement is also most valuable. It clearly distinguishes between the "elicitation" (or discriminative stimulus, $S^D$) view, according to which secondary reinforcing stimuli elicit or facilitate an existing response tendency, and the reward or "response reinforcement" view, according to which secondary reinforcing stimuli strengthen (that is, increase the future probability of occurrence of) preceding responses. Professor Wike ends up by suggesting that both these functions are served by secondary reinforcers. He appears inclined to the view that the response reinforcement function is the more important if not the primary one, but is willing to admit that secondary reinforcers may play an eliciting role. My view, though closer to the elicitation view, is different from both the above. It is that secondary reinforcers are essentially conditioned incentive stimuli that influence behavior through motivational mechanisms; the apparent response reinforcing function of secondary reinforcing stimuli is a by-product of the motivational mechanisms. Thus, the obvious question for further examination is this: What evidence is there that makes it necessary to attribute to secondary reinforcers a response reinforcing function in addition to a motivational one? As I have argued in my paper, the fact that the response probability may be increased by secondary reinforcement is not compelling evidence for postulating a separate response-reinforcing function.

## REFERENCES

Bacon, W. E., & Bindra, D. Stimulus variation and resistance to extinction: Satiation or disinhibition? *Psychon. Sci.*, 1965, **2**, 119–120.

Brown, J. S., & Bass, B. The acquisition and extinction of an instrumental response under constant and variable stimulus conditions. *J. comp. physiol. Psychol.*, 1958, **51**, 449–504.

Mackintosh, Irene. The resistance to extinction of responses acquired under irregular conditions of learning. *J. comp. physiol. Psychol.*, 1955, **48**, 363–370.

# Incentive Motivation and the Parameters of Reward in Instrumental Conditioning

ROGER W. BLACK

*University of South Carolina*

The topic of this paper, as the title indicates, is the role of reward and reinforcement in simple learning situations. For a number of years the analysis of reinforcement in its various aspects has been one of the most prominent problems in behavior theory. Thus, a large number of experimental and theoretical analyses of the nature and functions of reinforcement have been proposed—and few of these, it seems, have been "officially" discarded. As a result, I have chosen to limit my remarks to what might be considered a very specific type of experimental situation—instrumental and differential appetitive conditioning. Thus, I shall ignore not only classical conditioning and the so-called higher forms of learning but also all forms of learning which involve primarily aversive drives and incentives.

## The Definitions of Reinforcement

A discussion of reinforcement can scarcely begin, and cannot productively proceed, without some initial attention to what might be called the basic reinforcement vocabulary. The selection of the particular words to be included in this vocabulary varies, of course, from one experimenter or theorist to the next. Nevertheless, we can recognize as frequent members of that vocabulary such terms as "drive," "incentive," "reward," "goal," "reinforcer," etc. Sometimes several of these terms are treated as though they were synonymous and can be used interchangeably, while at other times the same terms are treated as though they had importantly different meanings. For example, for one theorist, an "incentive," a "reward," a "reinforcer," and a "goal object" may all refer to the same object or event—for example, a pellet of food in the goal box of a runway. For another theorist, however, a "reward" may refer to an event which, if it follows a given response, tends to increase the strength with which that response will occur on subsequent occasions, while an "incentive" may refer to an event the anticipation of which facilitates an ongoing response. Unfortunately, it is often the case that a reader is unable to determine the precise meaning that these terms were intended to convey.

Perhaps the greatest ambiguity regarding terms associated with the concept of reinforcement is "reinforcement" itself. Thus, this term is sometimes used in reference to an *empirical principle* which is usually stated roughly as follows: There are certain stimuli or events such that if they closely follow a given response, the probability is increased that that response will occur on the next presentation of the same stimulus. Stimuli which have this effect of strengthening responses which they follow are called "reinforcers"; stimuli which do not have this effect are "nonreinforcers." A second way in which "reinforcement" is used is as a label for a *set of operations* performed by *E*. Typically, these operations consist of presenting, applying, or making available to *S* a stimulus which is a "reinforcer" as defined above. The term "reinforcement" seems to have this meaning when, for example, it is used as follows: "Each *S* was given 10 reinforcements a day." Note that when the concept of "a reinforcement" is so defined, the occurrence of "a reinforcement" depends solely on the behavior of *E* and not on that of the *S*. This probably creates little difficulty in most classical conditioning situations, since *E* can usually ensure that the reinforcer is effectively received by the *S* (e.g., food powder can be blown directly into the mouth; an airpuff can be delivered directly to the cornea; etc.). In instrumental conditioning, however, the matter is less simple. If we define "a reinforcement" in terms of the operations of the *E* (e.g., placing a food pellet in the goal box of a runway), some curious problems can arise. To put the matter bluntly, assume that the *E* has placed food in the goal box and that the animal traverses the runway and enters the goal box but fails to consume that food. Does this constitute "a reinforcement" of the locomotor response? By definition, of course, "a reinforcement" *has* occurred, since the appropriate operations have been performed. Nevertheless, I think that the difficulty to which I am alluding here is obvious.

A third way in which the term "reinforcement" is used is to refer to a *change in performance* which presumably can be attributed to the presentation or occurrence of a reinforcing stimulus. In this sense, "a reinforcement" is *that which results* from "a reinforcer." The term is apparently being used in this manner when one says, for example: "This stimulus is extremely reinforcing for this *S*." Presumably what this means is that the presentation of the stimulus in question produces large changes in *S*'s behavior. It is interesting to note that in the previous case "reinforcement" was defined in terms of the operations of *E*, while in the present instance it is defined in terms of changes in the performance of *S*. A fourth way in which "reinforcement" is used is to designate some hypothetical change within the organism. The best-known example of this usage is, perhaps, the equation of "reinforcement" with "drive reduction." This is sometimes called the "strong form" of the principle of reinforcement in that it asserts more than the fact that there are certain stimuli which tend to strengthen responses with which they are contiguous; it also specifies the type of stimulus which presumably has this reinforcing effect (i.e., drive-reducing stimuli). It is unfortunate that the notion that "reinforcement" is equivalent to "drive reduction" was once so vigorously championed that many psychologists still seem to have difficulty conceiving of the concept in other ways. In any case, it may be noted that of the four definitions of the term "reinforcement" described above, this final one is the only one which could be described as theoretical. Thus, although the first three definitions are different, they are nevertheless in each case unambiguously empirical.

For purposes of the present paper, the terms "reward" and "reinforcer" are considered interchangeable and refer to a stimulus or event which tends to strengthen or make more probable the occurrence of responses which it closely follows. (It might be noted that when "reinforcers" and "rewards" are defined in this manner, the empirical principle of reinforcement becomes nothing more than the assertion that such stimuli *do exist.*) The choice of a definition for "reinforcement" is more difficult. My initial preference was to define it as "a change in performance presumably attributable to the presentation of a reinforcer." For reasons which I hope will become clear later, I decided instead to define "a reinforcement" as the operations on the part of the *E* which are involved in presenting the *S* with a "reinforcer." It proved necessary, however, to retain the concept of "a change in performance attributable to the presentation of a reinforcer." This concept, designated "apparent reinforcement value (ARV)," is discussed later in this paper.

## Two Basic Problems regarding Rewards

While the concepts of reward and reinforcement can quickly lead to a variety of important empirical and theoretical problems, there are two such problems which seem of particular significance in terms of the present discussion. First is the problem of *identifying* those stimuli which do, in fact, have the characteristics of rewards or reinforcers. From a strictly empirical point of view such as that suggested by the present definition of a reward, the task is relatively simple. Thus, if a stimulus can experimentally be demonstrated to strengthen responses which are contiguous with it, then that stimulus is added to an ever increasing list or catalogue of "rewards." If a stimulus fails to strengthen preceding responses, it is not included in that catalogue. While there is clearly nothing "wrong" with this procedure in principle, it is also obvious that its repeated employment would eventually result in a list of rewards so extensive that it would quickly become cumbersome. Thus, one might hope that a careful examination of the various stimuli in the "catalogue of rewards" would reveal some common characteristic which is shared by those stimuli and which, presumably, is the "necessary condition" for reward. In this case, it would no longer be necessary to determine empirically whether a given stimulus is a reward or to maintain a lengthy list of rewards, since one would be able to identify as a reward any stimulus which possesses the "critical characteristic." (For example, for Hull, the ability to reduce drive or the intensity of drive stimuli was the common characteristic of all primary rewards and any stimulus which possessed this characteristic would be designated a reward.) Of course, it may very well be the case that there is no single necessary condition for reward. Rather, there may be several, or even many, different characteristics or properties *sufficient* to make a stimulus rewarding. In this event, the alternative to the "catalogue of rewards" becomes the specification of the several sufficient characteristics or properties which allow certain stimuli to act as rewards. Several hypotheses regarding the critical properties of rewarding stimuli are discussed later.

A second major problem in the analysis of reward is the specification of the mechanism or mechanisms by which rewards come to influence performance. The problem here is not that of identifying which stimuli will be rewarding, but rather that of indicating in some detail the events which presumably intervene between the presentation of a reward (reinforcement) and the subsequent strengthening or facilitation of performance. For example, one might ask, Do rewards affect "S-R connections," "drives," "expectancies," "habits," etc.? This will become the central problem of the present paper.

## Theories of Reward

At this point I should like to describe some of the better-known theoretical interpretations of the nature and effects of rewards. Before doing so, however, it is necessary to acknowledge the fact that one need not adopt a theoretical position with respect to rewards in order to make substantial contributions to the understanding of them. Skinner, for example, has made many extremely significant contributions to the understanding of the various parameters of reinforcement in instrumental (operant) conditioning, although his approach has been consistently and exclusively "empirical." Thus, he states: "A positive reinforcer is a stimulus which, when added to a situation, strengthens the probability of an operant response" (Skinner, 1953, p. 73). He specifically mentions food, water, and sexual contact as positive reinforcers, but these are presumably only three examples from a very large catalogue of empirically demonstrated reinforcers. Thus, Skinner apparently has no interest in seeking common critical features of these stimuli which would allow him to shorten or dispense with this empirical catalogue. Moreover, he seems uninterested in theoretical speculation about "inferred mechanisms" which might underlie the effects of rewards. Instead, he has been content with the discovery of functional relationships between performance and the parameters of reinforcement, and does not really address himself to the problems dealt with in the remainder of this paper.

*Sources of Reward*

I have already mentioned the problem of attempting to discover what it is about some stimuli which makes them rewarding. In the context of an empirical "catalogue of rewards" this is the equivalent of identifying the characteristics which are common to "rewarding stimuli" and which, therefore, might be considered the "basis" or "source" of their facilitory effect on performance. By a "source of reward," then, is meant that aspect of the reinforcement situation which is primarily responsible for the behavioral effects of reinforcement.

For purposes of exposition, consider the simple and familiar runway conditioning situation. Here the apparatus often consists of a straight alley divided into a start box, runway, and goal box. A typical training trial might consist of placing *S* in the start box, opening the start box door, and measuring the speed with which *S* runs through various segments of the alley. When *S* enters the goal box, a "retrace door" is closed to confine the animal to the goal box for some specified period. If there is no food, water, or other appropriate reward in the goal box, very little improvement in performance can be expected over successive trials. On the other hand, if *S* has been deprived, say, of food and if food is present in the goal box, performance will probably show progressive improvement over successive trials. Thus, according to the current definition, the food in the goal box constitutes a "reward" and *E*'s operation of placing it there constitutes a "reinforcement." In this context, one may ask, What *specifically* is the "source of reward" in this situation? Several solutions to this problem have been proposed.

1) *Stimulus Factors:* It may be that the sensory effects associated with, or produced by, the food used as reward constitute the crucial events or the "source of reward"—that is, there may be certain

stimuli which are "palatable," or rewarding per se. Some evidence for this view is provided by the fact that performance in instrumental conditioning does seem to vary with the "quality" (e.g., taste) of the rewarding stimulus as well as with its "quantity." For example, response strength has been shown to vary significantly with the "sweetness" of the rewarding solution in the Skinner box (e.g., Guttman, 1953), in a straight runway (Homzie & Ross, 1962), and in a Y-maze (Black, 1965b). Moreover, performance also varies with changes in sweetness even when the nutritional value of the solutions is equal (e.g., Sheffield, Roby, & Campbell, 1954). Similarly, it has been demonstrated that incomplete copulation is rewarding to male rats in spite of the termination of the act prior to its completion—that is, before ejaculation (e.g., Sheffield, Wulff, & Backer, 1951). Further, an apparently powerful reward effect resulting from certain types of intracranial stimulation has apparently been demonstrated (e.g., Olds & Milner, 1954). Finally, it appears that, under the appropriate circumstances, a stimulus need have no other property to be a reward other than that of being "novel" (Berlyne, 1950). Thus, the hypothesis that the stimulus itself (or, more correctly, the sensory consequences of the stimulus) may be the source of reward does have a certain plausibility.

2) *Response Factors:* When a hungry animal enters the goal box of a straight alley and there encounters familiar and palatable food, it is very likely that the animal will eat that food—that is, a vigorous "consummatory response" is likely to be elicited. It has been suggested (e.g., Sheffield, Roby, & Campbell, 1954) that it is such consummatory activity itself which is rewarding rather than the stimulus or sensory properties of the food or its nutritional effect on the organism. A detailed statement of this position requires, of course, the specification of the parameters of consummatory activity which are considered important (e.g., the duration, frequency, consistency, and vigor of the consummatory response, etc.). Thus, one implication of this position is that the strength of the instrumental response should show a strong positive correlation with the amount or vigor of consummatory activity, and with exceptions noted later, this relationship has typically been obtained (e.g., Sheffield, Roby, & Campbell, 1954). A further implication of this position is that if a vigorous consummatory response can be elicited, immediately

preceding responses should be strengthened, even though the consummatory response fails to result in drive reduction. This implication seems to be confirmed, for example, by the observations that incomplete copulation is apparently rewarding (Sheffield, Wulff, & Backer, 1951) and that animals with esophageal fistulas (which prevent swallowed food from reaching the stomach) learn new responses which allow them to engage in such "sham feeding."

3) *Difficulties with the Stimulus and Consummatory Response Views:* There seems to be little question that both stimulus and consummatory-response factors may contribute to the behavioral consequences of reinforcement. Unfortunately, in the case of much of this research the effects of the stimulus and those of consummatory activity tend to be almost completely confounded. Thus, when *E* varies the "amount of consummatory activity" by manipulating the amount of food presented, he often simultaneously varies the "amount of stimulation" as well. On the other hand, if he seeks to vary the "quality" or "palatability" of the rewarding stimulus, he may at the same time be increasing the vigor or consistency of consummatory activity. Thus, the apparently rewarding effect of incomplete copulation could be equally well attributed to the vigorous consummatory response (copulation) or to the stimulation associated with that response. In short, the relative contributions to reward of these two potential sources is difficult to assess, since a consummatory response is usually accompanied by considerable resulting stimulation, while the presentation of a palatable stimulus is likely to elicit consummatory activity.

Beyond the problem of distinguishing between stimulus and consummatory-response factors as sources of reward in instrumental conditioning, there is the question of whether either of these factors is a *necessary* condition for reward. Thus, for example, Miller and Kessen (1952) reported that rats with esophageal fistulas learned a spatial discrimination in which the reinforcement consisted of the direct injection of milk into the animal's stomach following a correct choice. If one assumes that this procedure involved neither consummatory activity nor gustatory and olfactory stimulation, then it might be concluded that "reward" had been demonstrated in the absence of both of these factors. One might wonder, however, to what extent the direct injection of milk into the stomach might be considered to simulate a portion of the normal "consummatory response" of the intact organism. In this connection, Glickman and Schiff (1967) have commented:

> Miller (1963) described several problems for Sheffield's theory which the formulation of a consummatory response theory might handle. He pointed out that the main difficulties with the earlier theory derive from the emphasis on the peripheral consummatory response. The present authors, however, have considered the neural activity in the motor paths to be the sufficient condition for the reinforcement of new responses. Accordingly, the data of Miller and Kessen (1952) and of Clark, Schuster and Brady (1961), which are demonstrations of learning in the absence of overt consummatory activity, present no necessary problem. We would conclude that the injection of foodstuffs directly into the stomach or bloodstream would differ from ordinary ingestion only in providing less facilitation of the motor pathways, and the demonstrated, and relatively weaker, reinforcing effects would be expected. [Glickman & Schiff, 1967, p. 101]

4) *Premack's Response Theory:* Premack (1961, 1962, 1965) has proposed an interpretation of reinforcement which might be described as a "response theory of reinforcement," although it is certainly not a "consummatory response theory." Premack, in fact, insists that no fundamental distinction should be made between consummatory responses and other responses so far as their potential reward value is concerned. Specifically, he states:

> For any pair of responses, the more probable one will reinforce the less probable one. . . . Reinforcement is a relative property. The most probable response of a set of responses will reinforce all members of the set; the least probable will reinforce no member of the set. However, responses of intermediate probability will reinforce those less probable than themselves but not those more probable than themselves. [Premack, 1965, p. 132]

Premack's theory has led to a variety of intriguing experimental results, some of which have apparently indicated that consummatory activity can actually be made to act as an instrumental response which is reinforced by other, nonconsummatory behaviors. From the point of view of the present paper, Premack's position is an attempt to specify the crucial characteristics which make a stimulus a reward. He is, as noted above, quite explicit on this point: a reinforcer is a response rather than a stimulus; it is a response the probability or operant level of which is greater than that of the response which it strengthens. Thus, Premack has clearly stated the criterion for identifying the "source of reward," but the mechanism by which such rewards affect performance remains uncertain.

5) *Drive-Reduction Factors:* It frequently has been argued that in appetitive conditioning it is neither the stimulus qualities of the rewarding stimulus nor the consummatory responses which that stimulus may elicit which is the primary source of reward, but rather the metabolic or motivational effects of that stimulus which constitute "reward." In its most familiar form, this view asserts that a reward is a stimulus which reduces the intensity of drive or of drive stimuli. The intuitive appeal of this hypothesis is obvious when one considers the fact that the great majority of investigations of appetitive conditioning with animals involve the establishment of a metabolic drive (e.g., hunger or thirst) and the selection of rewarding stimuli (food or water) which at least partially satiate that drive. In such investigations, performance is typically found to vary directly with both the level of drive and the degree of drive reduction presumably produced by the reward. Unfortunately, these experiments typically confound the "amount of drive reduction" with both the "amount of stimulation" and the "amount of consummatory activity." Thus, if the rewarding stimulus is a "large quantity of food," a "large amount of drive reduction" will normally result from its ingestion. A "large amount of consummatory activity" will, however, also be required to ingest that reward, which will result in a "large amount of stimulation." Thus, if a "large increment in performance" follows such a reinforcement, its source remains ambiguous. Nevertheless, there seem to be some situations, mentioned later, in which these factors become at least partially disentangled.

### *Mechanisms of Reinforcement*

I wish to turn now from the discussion of hypotheses regarding the characteristics essential to stimuli which have the property of strengthening responses which they closely follow (i.e., "sources of reward") to a consideration of the mechanisms by which the operations called "reinforcement" result in such strengthening of instrumental performance. Theories regarding the manner in which reinforcement affects performance may be divided into two general categories: "associative interpretations" which assume that reinforcement, in some manner, directly or indirectly, affects learning or conditioning per se; and "incentive interpretations" which assume that reinforcement affects only performance by contributing to *S*'s level of motivation, excitement, or arousal. Some representative instances of each of these points of view are presented below, although this discussion is not intended to be exhaustive.

*Associative Interpretations of Reinforcement:* Probably the earliest explicit associative interpretation of reinforcement was that proposed by Thorndike (1913, 1932), who assumed that the effect of a reward (or "satisfying state of affairs") was to directly strengthen the connection between a response and the stimulus which immediately preceded or was coincidental with it. Thus, Thorndike considered rewards to make a direct and positive contribution to learning by "cementing" the association between specific stimuli and responses.

Guthrie also interpreted the empirical effect of rewards in associative terms. Thus, he assumed that "a combination of stimuli which has accompanied a movement will on its occurrence tend to be followed by the same movement." Moreover, "a stimulus pattern gains its full associative strength on the occasion of its first pairing with a response" (Guthrie, 1942, p. 30). This is, of course, a so-called strict contiguity interpretation of learning. Nevertheless, Guthrie, like all other learning theorists, had to account for the empirical facts of reinforcement. To do so, he relied on the stimulus properties of the reward. Consider again the case of the rat traversing a straight runway: "What encountering the food does is not to intensify a previous item of behavior but to protect that item from being unlearned. The whole situation and action of the animal is so changed by the food that the pre-food situation is shielded from new associations" (Guthrie, 1940, p. 144). Thus, rewards do not contribute directly to "S-R connections" for Guthrie as they did for Thorndike. Instead, they affect performance indirectly by "protecting" an S-R association which has been previously learned solely on the basis of contiguity. Nevertheless, like Thorndike's, Guthrie's interpretation of reward was associative—that is, rewards affect S-R connections.

Guthrie (1935) also advanced an associative interpretation of the effect of reinforcement in instrumental appetitive conditioning. In its most general form, this position asserts that the behavior of *S* in the goal box may be dichotomized into "consummatory activity" and "nonconsummatory activity." Consummatory activity, of course, consists of such responses as eating or drinking the reward, etc., while nonconsummatory behaviors may involve grooming, exploration, remaining inactive, retracing toward the runway, etc. In any event, it is often assumed that both consummatory and nonconsummatory activities tend to become conditioned to the cues present in the goal box and to generalize to the runway and start box. Further, it might be assumed that conditioned or generalized consummatory responses, since they cannot genuinely occur in the absence of the rewarding stimulus, do not interfere with the instrumental (e.g., locomotor) response. On the other hand, nonconsummatory responses, such as grooming or exploring, can occur in the runway before entrance to the goal box and may, therefore, interfere with and depress the speed or vigor of the instrumental response. Thus, an important function of reinforcement may be the degree to which it "encourages" *S* to engage in consummatory activity and "discourages" it from engaging in nonconsummatory responses which have the potential of interfering with the instrumental response.

A final instance of an associative interpretation of the effect of reinforcement is found in Hull's 1943 version of his behavior theory. Hull assumed that reinforcement contributed to his primary associative variable, "habit strength ($_{s}H_{r}$)," in two ways. First, he assumed that habit strength theoretically increased only on those occasions when an S-R sequence was closely followed by reinforcement. Second, he assumed that the magnitude of reinforcement set the maximum or limit to which habit strength could grow. As a matter of fact, in his 1943 formulation, Hull proposed no construct other than habit strength to which reward was considered a direct contributor. Thus, at this point his interpretation of reinforcement, like that of Thorndike and Guthrie, was purely associative.

*Incentive Interpretations of Reinforcement:* While a variety of "incentive theories" of reinforcement have been proposed, they have in common the assumption that rewards, in one way or another, add to the *S*'s level of motivation or arousal. Hull (1952), for example, was led to modify his views in the direction of an incentive interpretation of reward as a result, at least in part, of experiments which involved shifts in the magnitude of reward. Thus, Crespi (1942) and Zeaman (1949) reported that shifts in the quantity of food reward administered to rats in a straight alley resulted in very rapid and "appropriate" changes in the speed with which *S*s ran in that alley. Of particular importance was the fact that decremental shifts in reward magnitude produced an almost immediate decline in performance. Since Hull (1943) had assumed that reward primarily affects habit strength, and since habit strength was considered to be a relatively permanent variable, this result was unexpected. To account for these rapid changes in performance following shifts in reward magnitude, Hull introduced a new construct, "incentive motivation (K)," the value of which was determined by the magnitude of reward and the function of which was, like D, to multiply $_{s}H_{r}$. On the other hand, Hull continued to insist that reinforcement influenced habit strength to the extent that at least some minimal amount of reinforcement must follow the occurrence of the instrumental response before any increment in $_{s}H_{r}$ for that response can occur. Thus, Hull's final (1952) position with respect to reward might be described as being both associative and motivational (i.e., incentive) in character.

In his modifications and extensions of Hull's position, Spence (1956) placed still more emphasis on the incentive-motivational aspects of reward. Thus, Spence discarded the assumption that reinforcement was a necessary determinant of the associative variable, H, in instrumental reward conditioning. Rather,

> according to Spence (1956) K is the molar theoretical variable that summarizes the motivational consequences of the $r_g$-$s_g$ mechanism which is assumed to consist of implicit components of the overt consummatory response ($R_g$) that become conditioned to the stimulus situation in which the instrumental response is appetitively reinforced. The strength of the $r_g$-$s_g$ mechanism depends, in turn, upon at least two variables. First, since it results from classical conditioning to goal box cues, the

strength of $r_g$-$s_g$ will be an increasing function of the frequency and duration with which $R_g$ has been elicited in the presence of those cues. Thus, K is assumed to be an increasing function of the number of rewarded trials and approaches an asymptote determined, in part, by the magnitude of reward. Second, since the strength of $r_g$-$s_g$ is assumed to reflect the vigor of the overt consummatory response ($R_g$) of which it is a component, any variable which contributes to the vigor of $R_g$ will also affect the theoretical value of K. [Black, 1965b, p. 310]

Although he emphasized the motivational (incentive) effects of reward, Spence's analysis of this variable also had associative components. Thus, the basis or source of K (i.e., $r_g$) was itself conceived of as a conditioned response subject to all the rules or laws governing other conditioned responses. Moreover, $r_g$ was assumed to result in distinctive internal cues, $s_g$, which presumably serve as part of the stimulus complex which evokes the instrumental response. In fact, at least in personal conversations, Spence repeatedly expressed the view that the motivational or facilitative effects of K would benefit only those responses which had previously become conditioned to $s_g$. Thus, Spence considered K, unlike D, not to be a general or nonspecific energizer of all response tendencies.

A similar interpretation of the mechanism of reward was also proposed by Sheffield and his associates. According to this view components of the consummatory response become conditioned to cues in the goal box and subsequently come to be evoked by similar cues before the goal box is reached. This anticipatory and incomplete arousal of the consummatory response is further assumed to create a state of "excitement" which is "channeled into whatever response is being performed at the moment" (Sheffield, Roby, & Campbell, 1954, p. 354). To emphasize the incentive-motivational nature of their position, Sheffield *et al.* (1954) describe it as a "drive-induction" theory of reinforcement. Seward (1950, 1951, 1956) has also proposed a "drive induction" interpretation of the effects of reward based on the notion of the conditioning and generalization of consummatory activity ($R_g$). Thus, he states:

When a response (R) is followed by a reward, $R_g$ is conditioned to concurrent stimuli. By generalization of this conditioning, stimuli accompanying R now serve to intensify $r_g$. . . . This intensification called tertiary motivation is endowed with the property of facilitating R, the activity in progress. [Seward, 1951, p. 130]

Miller (1963) has more recently suggested an interpretation of reinforcement which is essentially incentive-motivational in character, although he relates it more explicitly than prior theorists to hypothesized events in the CNS. Specifically, Miller assumes "that there are one or more 'go' or 'activating' mechanisms in the brain which act to intensify ongoing responses to cues and traces of immediately preceding activities, producing a stronger intensification the more strongly the 'go mechanism' is activated" (Miller, 1963, p. 95). He further assumes that this "go mechanism" can be activated in a variety of different ways, including "by the taste of food to a hungry animal, possibly by feedback from still more central effects of eating." He also states that the "go mechanism" will depend in large part on the strength of the UCR (presumably consummatory activity). Finally, he assumes that the "go mechanism" will be weakened or extinguished if it is repeatedly elicited without reinforcement from the UCS (e.g., food). With the exception of its emphasis on a central as opposed to a peripheral locus, Miller's "go mechanism" has, quite obviously, most of the properties of the conditionable components of consummatory behavior ($r_g$) as discussed by Spence, Sheffield, Seward, etc.

*Theories of Reinforcement: A Common Parameter*

I have attempted to classify and briefly describe some of the major hypotheses regarding two fundamental problems in the analysis of the effects of reinforcement on performance in instrumental, appetitive conditioning. With respect to the source of reward, these hypotheses have emphasized the potential importance of the sensory consequences of the stimulus characteristics of the reward, the properties of the consummatory response which the rewarding stimulus typically evokes, and the motivational or metabolic effects on the organism of the ingestion of the reward. While these factors are admittedly difficult to separate experimentally, they are, nevertheless, quite different in principle.

The problem of specifying the mechanism by which the operation termed reinforcement strengthens or otherwise affects performance has also resulted in a variety of alternative hypotheses. Perhaps arbitrarily, I have categorized these hypotheses as being *primarily* "associative" or *primarily* "motivational (incentive)" in character.

Within these categories, however, important differences exist. Thus, an associative interpretation of reinforcement may assume that rewards directly strengthen S-R connections, that they "protect" already established connections against unlearning, or that they reduce the likelihood of the learning of responses which subsequently interfere with the instrumental response. Similarly, while incentive interpretations of reward generally emphasize the importance of the conditioned or anticipated consummatory response, the details of the analysis vary considerably from one theorist to another.

In spite of these several and significant differences, there is at least one parameter of the general "reinforcement situation" which is critically important to any interpretation of the effect of reinforcement on the *normal, intact organism:* the behavior of *S* in relation to the reward. Thus, food, water, and other primary rewards will not be expected to strengthen performance unless *S* consumes them. This expectation would appear to follow from a "stimulus theory," a "consummatory response theory" or a "drive-reduction theory" of the source of reward. With respect to the mechanism of reinforcement, an available but nonconsumed reward would not be expected to fulfill any of the associative criteria of a "reward"—for example, "strengthening connections," "protecting S-R bonds," or "preventing the establishment of competing responses." Even more obviously, an incentive interpretation of reward would not predict an enhancement of performance as the result of a "reward" which failed to produce a consummatory response. In short, regardless of one's theoretical views regarding the sources and mechanisms of reward, it must be recognized that no set of operations on the part of the experimenter nor any physical characteristic of the rewarding stimulus can ensure an enhancement in the performance of *S* unless the behavior of *S* with respect to that reward is "appropriate."

## Some Recent Research on Reward

My interest in the mechanism by which reward affects performance in instrumental conditioning developed out of a concern with a related theoretical issue. Both Hull (1952) and Spence (1956) assumed that the motivation for performance in instrumental, appetitive conditioning arose from two distinct sources—drive (D) and incentive-motivation (K). Their assumptions regarding the manner in which these variables combined, however, differed. Thus, Hull assumed that the combination was multiplicative while Spence assumed it was additive. In the last decade a substantial body of experimental evidence regarding these alternative formulations has been reported. The typical experimental design has employed two or more levels of food or water deprivation combined factorially with two or more levels of reward magnitude. In such a design, if performance is plotted as a function of deprivation level with reward magnitude as the parameter, Hull's multiplicative assumption predicts divergence of the performance curves, while Spence's additive hypothesis predicts that the curves will be parallel. In statistical terms, Hull's view implies a significant interaction of "deprivation" and "reward magnitude," while Spence would predict no such interaction.

The majority of studies which have been conducted to test these alternative hypotheses regarding the combination of deprivation and reward magnitude have supported Spence's view—that is, no "deprivation" × "reward" interaction is reported (Black, 1965c). A notable exception, however, to this generalization was provided by a series of experiments reported by Seward and his associates. These studies were somewhat unusual in that they involved "extreme" levels of deprivation or reward magnitude. For example, in a runway conditioning situation, Seward, Shea, and Elkind (1958) factorially combined two levels of deprivation with two levels of reward magnitude (0 or 1.0 g. food). "High-drive" *S*s were trained under 23 hours' food deprivation, while "low-drive" *S*s were fed their entire daily ration almost immediately prior to their daily training trials. Thus, "small reward" involved *no reward*, while "low drive" presumably was also *very low* and probably approached a state of temporary satiation or "zero hunger." Under these conditions, Seward *et al.* reported that *S*s in both of the zero-reward groups, as well as those in the "zero"-hunger or -drive group, failed to show any reliable improvement in performance over conditioning trials. In fact, only *S*s in their "high-drive, large-reward" group showed any improvement over conditioning trials, thus producing a statistically reliable "deprivation" × "reward" interaction. In other words, the effect of reward magnitude was found to depend on the level of deprivation in a manner such that a significant main effect of "reward" was obtained only when *S* was "hungry" (i.e., "nonzero" deprivation). Similar results when extreme levels of deprivation and reward are employed were also reported by Seward and Proctor (1960) and Seward, Shea, and Davenport (1960). These *E*s interpreted their results to mean that Spence's additive assumption may hold for intermediate levels of drive and reward magnitude but that Hull's multiplicative assumption seems to better describe the data obtained with more extreme levels of these variables. This interpretation was based on the fact that no interaction of "deprivation" and "reward" was observed in any of their comparisons unless either "deprivation" or "reward" or both were reduced to "zero."

In 1965, I suggested that the apparent inconsistency between the results obtained by Seward and his associates and those generally obtained by other experimenters who employed "intermediate" levels of deprivation and reward magnitude might be reconciled by a more detailed analysis of Spence's assumptions regarding K. Recall that Spence treated K as an intervening variable which summarized the motivational consequences of the hypothetical $r_g$-$s_g$ mechanism. Specifically, the magnitude of K was assumed to reflect the vigor with which $r_g$ was elicited in the experimental situation, which, of course, depended on the vigor or frequency with which overt consummatory activity ($R_g$) had been evoked in the goal box. A fundamental prediction of this analysis is that no K will develop unless a reward is presented in the goal box which evokes consummatory responding there. Thus, if *S* has been prefed to a point approaching satiation and engages in little or no consummatory activity in the goal box, there will be no development of K for that *S* regardless of the nominal "reward magnitude" present in the goal box. In short, Spence's analysis of reinforcement defines K in terms of the amount and vigor of consummatory behavior, and experiments which involve manipulations of "magnitude of *nonconsumed* reward" simply violate the boundary conditions of the theory. This is, of course, one instance of the more general problem mentioned earlier: in the intact organism, the effect of reinforcement ultimately depends on the behavior of *S* with respect to the reward.

*Reward Magnitude, Consummatory Activity, and Satiation*

The basic assumption of the preceding analysis is that in instrumental conditioning satiated animals presumably eat very little of their nominal "reward" and, therefore, do not develop the level of K which would be produced by the same magnitude of reward for a hungry *S*. Thus, it is not surprising that a "deprivation" × "reward" interaction occurs in experiments which employ groups which are administered different quantities of "reward" when some of those groups are trained under near satiation throughout the course of the experiment. As in the Seward studies, such an interaction could easily arise from the fact that only those groups which are *both* hungry *and* rewarded with food will be expected to show improvement with training, since only for those groups will K develop. On the other hand, there is no theoretical reason to expect a "deprivation" × "reward magnitude" interaction—even when one level of deprivation approaches zero—as long as K has already been allowed to become differentially established by different magnitudes of reward. To test this hypothesis Black and Elstad (1964) trained two groups of rats to run a straight alley for different magnitudes of reward under the same level of food deprivation (8 g. lab chow per day). Specifically, *S*s in G10 received four daily training trials for 11 days with reward on each trial consisting of 10 seconds' access to a large dish of wet mash in the goal box. The *S*s in G30 were treated identically except that the reward on each trial consisted of 30 seconds' access to the dish of wet mash. Thus, G10 was the "small-reward" group and G30 was the "large-reward" group. The purpose of this phase of the experiment was to theoretically ensure the development of different levels of K for the groups under conditions of equal drive. Subsequently, both groups were to be shifted to a condition approaching "zero" hunger as the result of an elaborate satiation procedure to be administered before each day's training trials. Thus, it should have been possible to compare the difference between large reward vs. small reward under "high drive" with the difference between these reward magnitudes under "zero drive"—that is, to test the "deprivation" × "reward magnitude" interaction as a within-*S*s effect. Spence's position would

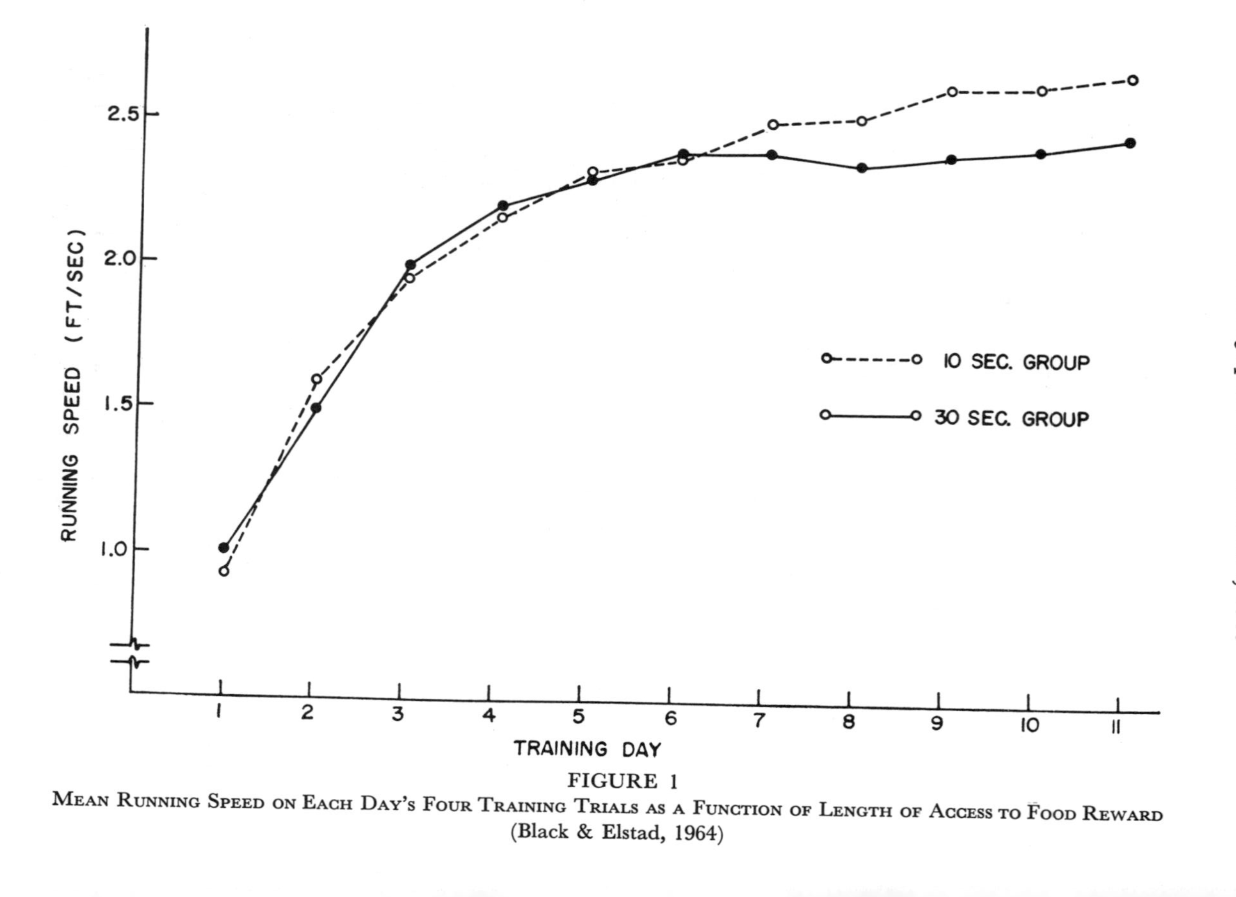


FIGURE 1

Mean Running Speed on Each Day's Four Training Trials as a Function of Length of Access to Food Reward (Black & Elstad, 1964)

presumably predict that no such interaction would be obtained, at least when the final trials of the first phase are compared with the initial trials of the second (Black, 1965).

This experiment, unfortunately, did not allow this hypothesis to be tested, since, during its initial phase, *S*s in the "small-reward" group were found to perform (run) at a higher level than those in the "large-reward" group. This result was, of course, unexpected, since a direct relationship between magnitude of reward and performance in instrumental conditioning seems well established in the psychological literature (e.g., Pubols, 1960). Thus, skeptical of these results, we replicated the experiment. In addition, we recorded the amount eaten by each *S* on each trial of the final three days of training. Again it was found that animals in the "small-reward" (10 seconds' food access) group came to run more rapidly than those in the "large-reward" (30 seconds) group. A third replication was conducted in which we recorded the amount of food consumed on all trials throughout the experiment. As in the previous cases, terminal running speed was greater for G10 than for G30.

Fig. 1 presents the mean running speed over the second 6 of the alley for the three replications combined (n = 25 per group). Inspection of this figure suggests that *S*s in the two groups ran at the same speed during the first six days (24 trials) of training, after which animals in G10 ran more rapidly than those in G30 for the final 20 trials. While slight, this superiority was nevertheless reliable. Fig. 2 indicates (for Replication 3) the "average eating rate" (grams of food per trial divided by the length of the reward period). Following the first day of training, *S*s in G10 were eating significantly more rapidly than those in G30. It should also be noted that, although *S*s in G10 were eating more rapidly, those in G30 nevertheless ate a greater average quantity of food as a result of their longer reward period (.31 g. per trial vs. .20 g. per trial). Thus, *S*s in G10 ran more quickly than those in G30 in spite of both the nominally "larger reward" presented the latter group (i.e., 30 seconds vs. 10 seconds access to food) and the greater amount of food actually consumed by those *S*s.

Two potential interpretations of these data seemed at least plausible. First, it may have been the case that the animals in G10, which ate at a higher average rate than those in G30, might have

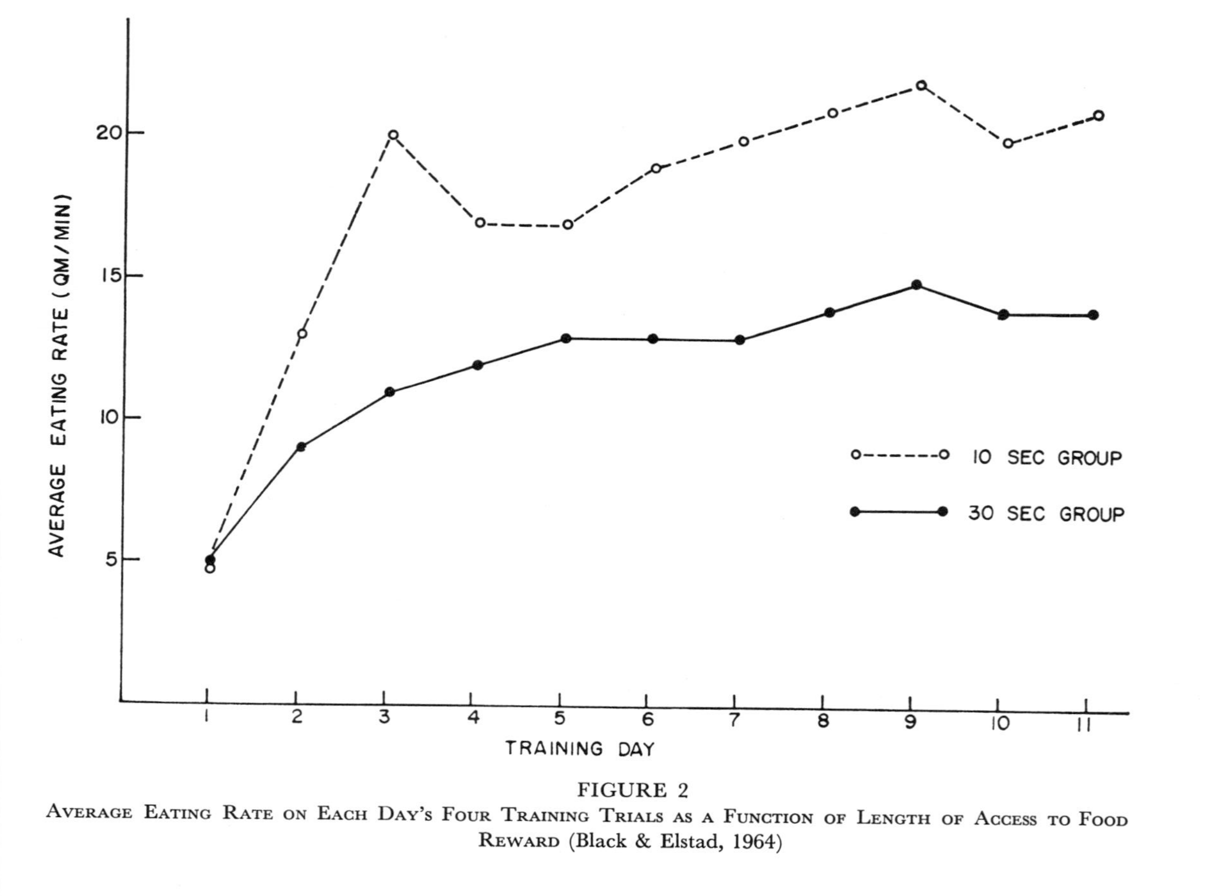


FIGURE 2

Average Eating Rate on Each Day's Four Training Trials as a Function of Length of Access to Food Reward (Black & Elstad, 1964)

engaged in more "vigorous" consummatory activity—that is, a more "vigorous" $R_g$ was occurring in the goal box and becoming conditioned to goal box cues. In this case, an incentive theory such as Spence's analysis of incentive motivation would predict that these *S*s would have developed a stronger $r_g$-$s_g$ mechanism which would result in a higher level of K and, therefore, more rapid performance. An alternative interpretation might assume that *S*s in G10 ate more "consistently" rather than more "vigorously" than those in G30. If this were indeed the case, then *S*s in the latter group would have had the greater opportunity to engage in *nonconsummatory activity*, which, in terms of an associative theory such as Guthrie's, could have led to "deconditioning" of the instrumental response.

In an attempt to experimentally test these alternative analyses of the preceding result, a series of exploratory experiments were conducted (Elstad & Black, 1965). Each study involved training food-deprived rats to run a straight alley with different groups receiving as reward different lengths of exposure to a large dish of wet mash. The runway had been modified to allow recording of the number of times the rat made contact with the food ("bites") and the length of time it stayed in physical contact with the dish ("contact-time"). In addition, the amount of food each animal consumed on each trial was recorded. From these records it was possible to compute several measures of consummatory activity: "average eating rate" (amount consumed divided by length of the reward period), "momentary eating rate" (amount consumed divided by the amount of time in contact with the food), "amount per bite" (amount eaten divided by the number of contacts with the food), and "consistency of eating" (time in contact with food divided by the length of the reward period).

According to one hypothesis regarding the $r_g$-$s_g$ mechanism proposed by Spence (1956), the value of K (and, thus, the strength of the instrumental response) should be a direct function of the "vigor" with which consummatory activity occurs. While the concept of the "vigor" of a consummatory response is ambiguous, we decided to assume that it would be most directly reflected in measures of "momentary eating rate" and "amount consumed per bite." On the other hand, "average eating rate" and "consistency of eating" were assumed to reflect the consistency with which the animal engaged in consummatory behavior as opposed to other activities. Thus, the expectation from an $r_g$-$s_g$ interpretation of reinforcement was that the strength of the instrumental response should be directly related to the "vigor" of the consummatory response. In fact, for reward periods varying from 5 to 60 seconds, running speed was again found to be to a slight but significant degree an *inverse* function of the length of the reward period. Moreover, as the length of the reward period increased, "average eating rate" and "consistency of eating" decreased. Thus, *S*s in the 5-second reward group spent an average of over 85 percent of their reward period in contact with the goal dish, while *S*s in the 60-second reward group spent slightly less than 40 percent of that period in contact with the goal dish. On the other hand, no relationship between running speed and measures of the "vigor" of consummatory activity was obtained. In fact, "momentary eating rate" and "amount consumed per bite" were almost identical for the different reward periods.

Subsequent investigations described later (e.g., Cammin, 1968; Hiers, 1968; Cilluffo, 1968) have provided further information regarding the relationship between the strength of the instrumental response and the consistency of consummatory behavior. Each of these *E*s observed that eating or drinking tends to occur in discrete "bursts." Thus, when the subject first enters the goal box there usually occurs a relatively brief period of consummatory activity, followed by a period of nonconsummatory activity (e.g., exploration, grooming, etc.), followed by another "burst" of consummatory responding, and so on. These observations are very similar to those reported by Stellar and Hill (1952), Goodrich (1960), Sidman and Stebbins (1954), and Premack (1965), etc., and point to an important methodological problem: as the quantity of reward increases in instrumental conditioning the length of time which *S* will require to consume that reward will also usually increase. Thus, with large rewards the opportunities for the occurrence of nonconsummatory responses will be greater than with smaller rewards. On the other hand, allowing *S* to consume a large reward will usually result in a greater amount of consummatory activity than a smaller reward. In short, when the quantity of reward is varied, at least three variables are usually confounded: the amount of reward per se, the amount or duration of consummatory activity, and, finally, the amount or duration of nonconsummatory responding. For example, if one varies the magnitude of reward between groups but confines *S*s in each group for the same duration in the goal box, then *S*s in the "small-reward" group will usually have not only a smaller quantity of reward but also a smaller amount and shorter duration of consummatory activity in the presence of goal box cues than *S*s in the "large-reward" group. Moreover, *S*s in the "small-reward" group will, in most cases, also have a greater opportunity to engage in nonconsummatory activities, since less of their goal box confinement time will be required to consume the reward. As an alternative, *E* might elect to remove *S* from the goal box "immediately" after it has completely consumed the available reward. In this event, it is likely that *S*s in the "large-reward" group not only will receive a larger reward but also will have a greater opportunity for "bursts" of both consummatory and nonconsummatory behaviors. Thus, if consistency of consummatory activity in the goal box is an important determinant of the behavioral effects of reinforcement, the rule according to which *S* is removed from the goal box is crucial. Unfortunately, there currently seems to be no rule for removing *S* from the goal box which is completely satisfactory, since none seems to adequately partition the effects of reward magnitude, consummatory activity, and nonconsummatory activity. An awareness of this problem, however, is necessary to understand the interpretation given the experiments about to be described.

In 1966 Elstad (see also Black & Black, 1967) again sought to test the hypothesis derived from Spence's additive assumption regarding the combination of D and K. According to this hypothesis, if two groups of subjects are trained with large vs. small reward under the same high level of drive and then both groups are shifted to very low or near zero drive, no "drive" × "reward magnitude" interaction should occur. Elstad's experiment consisted of two phases. In Phase I two groups of rats were trained to run a straight alley in which the reward was two 45-mg. Noyes pellets for G2 and ten such pellets on each trial for G10. A total of 54 acquisition trials were conducted, and on each trial *S*s were removed from the goal box as soon as *E* could determine that they had consumed their reward. In

Phase II each animal's daily training session was immediately preceded by a period of one hour's access to a large quantity of lab chow in the home cage, followed by 30 minutes' access to a large dish filled with a mash composed of ground lab chow, condensed milk, and sugar. During the intertrial interval in the carrying cage, *S*s had continuous access to a canister filled with Noyes pellets identical to those which they received in the goal box. The purpose of these procedures was, of course, to attempt to approximate a state of satiation, or "zero hunger." Except for these satiation procedures, *S*s received exactly the same treatment in Phase II as they had in Phase I, and testing in Phase II continued for five days.

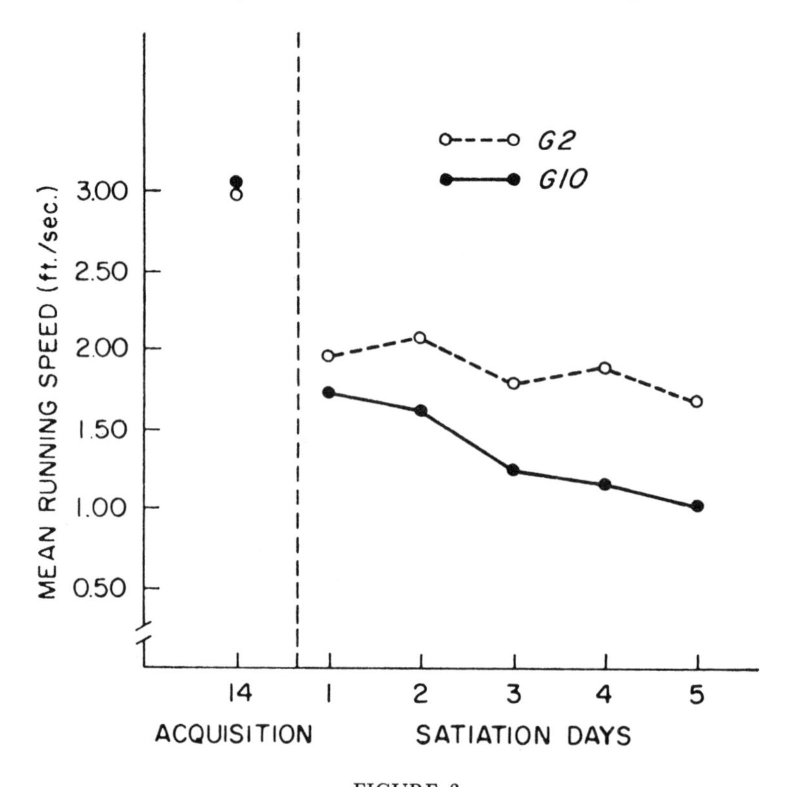


FIGURE 3
Terminal Acquisition Running Speed and Mean Running Speed on Five Days of Satiation (Elstad, 1966)

The results of this experiment are presented in Fig. 3 in terms of terminal mean running speeds in Phase I and daily mean speeds in Phase II. It is obvious that ten pellets did not produce faster terminal performance than two pellets. In fact, throughout the course of Phase I there was no difference whatsoever in the performance of G2 and G10. When the interaction between "reward" and "deprivation" was tested, using as the criterion scores the *S*s' performance on the final day of Phase I and the initial day of Phase II, the effect proved to be nonsignificant. Although this result was consistent with Spence's additive assumption regarding D and K, it was not a very convincing finding in view of the fact that no main effect of reward had been demonstrated during Phase I.

Aside from the primary intent of the experiment, several features of the Phase II results are of some interest. First, it may be noted that the satiation procedure resulted in an immediate decrement in performance in Phase II. Second, G2 performed at a higher level than G10 throughout this phase. Third, both groups showed a gradual decline in running speed which was greater for G10 than for G2 and thus produced the divergence of the curves which is apparent in this figure. These results are particularly interesting when compared with those represented in Fig. 4, which indicates the mean percentage of the available pellets consumed by *S*s in G2 and G10 on each of the five days of the satiation phase of the experiment. It is apparent that the curves in Fig. 4 closely parallel those in Fig. 3. Thus, *S*s in G10 ate a smaller average percentage of their available reward than those in G2 throughout the satiation phase; both groups showed a decline in the percentage consumed; and a divergence in the functions occurred.

An associative interpretation of reinforcement seems to handle these results rather well. Thus, it might be assumed that *S*s in both groups engaged in an initial "burst" of consummatory activity immediately upon entering the baited goal box. For G2 this initial eating would tend to be followed by rapid removal from the goal box, which would tend to "protect" the association of runway cues with the instrumental response as well as preventing the development of competing responses. For *S*s in G10, however, the initial burst of consummatory activity was presumably followed by a period of nonconsummatory activity followed by a return to eating, etc.

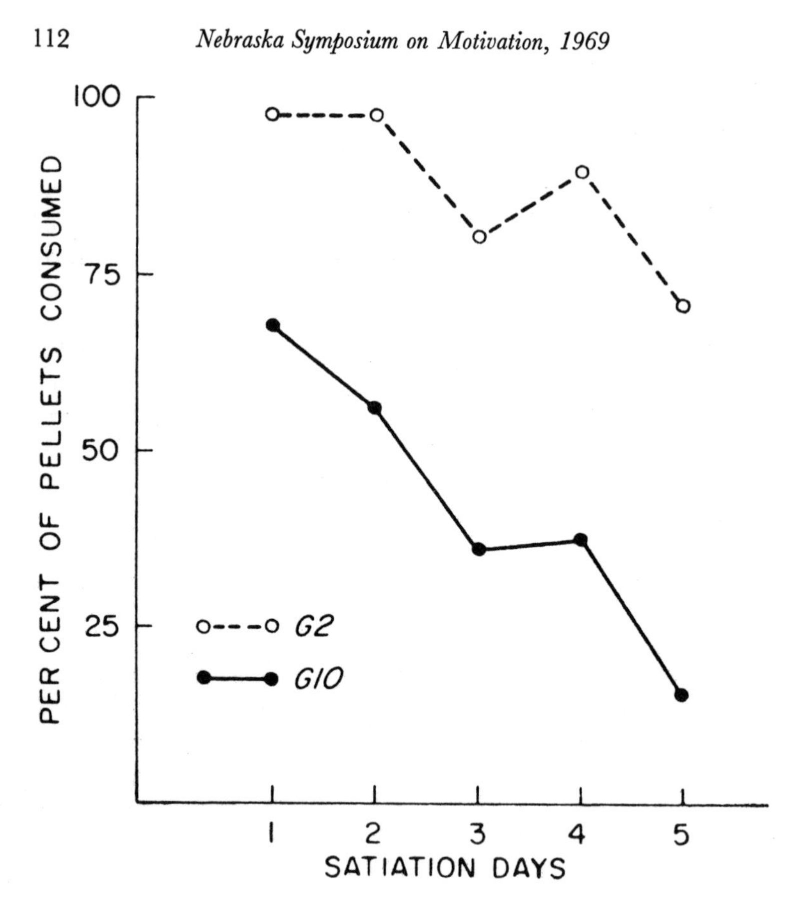


FIGURE 4

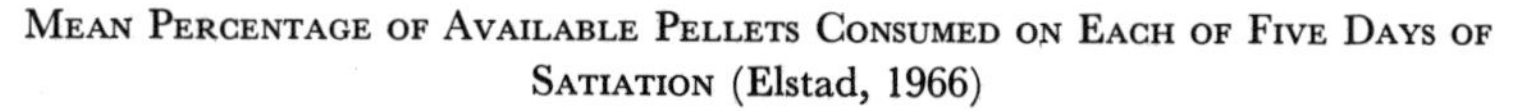

MEAN PERCENTAGE OF AVAILABLE PELLETS CONSUMED ON EACH OF FIVE DAYS OF SATIATION (Elstad, 1966)

Thus, these animals presumably had the opportunity to both "unlearn" the instrumental response and to learn other competing responses. This interpretation seems plausible in terms of the similarity between the running speed and percentage-consumed curves.

Elstad's (1966) results were generally confirmed by Gragg (1967; Gragg & Black, 1967), who trained rats to run a straight alley with rewards of one or ten 45-mg. Noyes pellets. Unlike the Elstad (1966) study, however, Gragg did find a significant (although small) effect of reward magnitude on performance during the initial acquisition trials under food deprivation. Nevertheless, during five days of satiation testing, Gragg found that animals which received the smaller reward (G1 in this case) ran more rapidly than *S*s in the larger reward group (G10). Although consistent with those obtained by Black and Elstad (1964) and by Elstad (1966) Gragg's results are contrary to the more general finding (e.g., Pubols, 1960) that the strength of an instrumental response is directly related to the magnitude of reward. Nevertheless, these data are not without precedent in psychological literature. Thus, for example, Guild (1960) trained two groups of rats on a spatial discrimination in a T-maze. One group was allowed to eat food powder in the "correct" arm of the maze for 15 minutes following each correct response, while *S*s in the second group were allowed only a 5-second eating period following correct responses. During initial training, all *S*s were maintained on 23 hours' food deprivation, while subsequently *S*s were satiated for food prior to test trials in the maze. Guild reported that, under conditions of food satiation, "the group trained under the 5-sec condition ran faster, turned to food more frequently, and ate more frequently than did the group trained under the 15-min condition" (1960, p. 357). In addition, during the phase of initial training under food deprivation the "small-reward" group (5 seconds' food access) performed at a higher level than the nominally "larger reward" group (15 minutes' food access). In short, the "apparent reinforcement value" of the former condition was greater than that of the latter. These results, of course, are analogous to those described above.

### *Shifts in Magnitude of Reward*

Considerable insight into the mechanisms of reinforcement has resulted from studies involving shifts in the magnitude of reward. The well-known experiments of Crespi (1942) and Zeaman (1949) were apparently the first to explore the effects of such shifts in reward magnitude in a simple runway conditioning situation. Basically, these *E*s reported that when they trained groups of rats to traverse a straight alley for a relatively large quantity of reward and then shifted those subjects to a smaller reward, performance (i.e., running speed) showed an almost immediate decline. In fact, they reported that the performance of *S*s for which reward was decreased actually fell to a lower level than that of those which had always received the smaller reward. Similarly, *S*s shifted from a small to a larger reward showed a rapid improvement in performance to a level superior to that of *S*s which had always received the larger reward. Crespi referred to this apparent "undershooting" and "overshooting" in postshift performance as an "elation effect" and a "depression effect," respectively. In the current literature similar phenomena are generally referred to as "contrast effects" (CE). More specifically, if an R to one reward is enhanced as a result of *S*'s experience with similar but smaller rewards, then a "positive contrast effect" (PCE) is said to have occurred. If the R to a particular reward is depressed as a result of experience with a larger reward, then a "negative contrast effect" (NCE) is said to have occurred (Black, 1968).

Most of the many recent runway conditioning studies of CE fall into one of two basic classes—those which employ a "successive-CE" design similar to that of Crespi (1942) and Zeaman (1949) and those which employ a "simultaneous-CE" design (e.g., Bower, 1961; Goldstein & Spence, 1963, etc.). Successive CEs are investigated in experiments in which *S*s are initially given consistent experience (training) with one level of reward and are subsequently shifted to a different reward in the same or a similar task. Simultaneous CEs are investigated in situations in which *S* receives two or more rewards in some intermixed order throughout training. For example, *S* may be given differential conditioning such that some trials are run in one alley (A1) and some in second alley (A2), with the reward in A1 being larger than that in A2. If it can be shown that *S*'s performance in A2 varies inversely as a function of the reward associated with A1, or vice versa, then a simultaneous CE is said to occur—that is, performance to one reward is affected by its "contrast" with a second reward. The demonstration of a successive PCE simply requires that *S*s shifted from a smaller to a larger reward perform at a higher level than *S*s which have consistently received the larger reward. Similarly, a successive NCE is demonstrated if *S*s shifted from a large to a smaller reward perform at a level which is inferior to that of control animals which have always received the smaller reward.

That shifts in reinforcement result in rapid and more or less "appropriate" shifts in performance in both instrumental and differential conditioning seems well established. Thus, in instrumental conditioning an upward shift in reward magnitude consistently results in an increment in the strength of the instrumental response (e.g., running speed). Similarly, in differential conditioning, *S*s typically respond more strongly or rapidly to the cue associated with the larger of two rewards (e.g., Matsumoto, 1965), the shorter of two delays of rewards (Fowler, 1963; Beery, 1968), or the higher of two probabilities of reward (e.g., Weiss, 1965). On the other hand, *contrast effects* seem to result reliably only from *downward* shifts in reward in both the successive and the simultaneous design—that is, NCE but not PCE seems to be the rule. Several attempts to account for this apparent asymmetry in the results of reward shifts have recently been proposed (Spear, 1967; Black, 1968; Capaldi, 1967).

In an attempt to assess the degree to which NCEs persist following a downward shift in reward and, further, to determine the effect of repeated decremental and incremental shifts, Hiers (1968) trained six groups of food-deprived rats each to run a straight alley with 45-mg. Noyes pellets serving as reward. The experiment consisted of four phases. During Phase I all *S*s received a total of 60 consistently reinforced acquisition trials, while Phases II, III, and IV each involved 30 additional training trials. Designated in terms of the number of food pellets received on each trial of the four phases of the experiment, the groups were: Group 1 (1-25-1-25), Group 2 (25-1-25-1), Group 3 (1-1-1-1), Group 4 (25-25-25-25), Group 5 (25-25-25-1), and Group 6 (25-1-1-1). It should be noted that Groups 3 and 4 did not experience a shift in reward magnitude during the experiment and, thus, constituted consistently "small-" and consistently "large-"reward control groups respectively. Groups 5 and 6 each received a single downward shift in reward, after either 60 or 120 trials with "large" reward, respectively. Groups 1 and 2, however, each received three successive shifts in magnitude of reward.

Hiers' results during Phase I are presented in Fig. 5, in which it may be observed that *S*s which received 25 pellets initially ran more

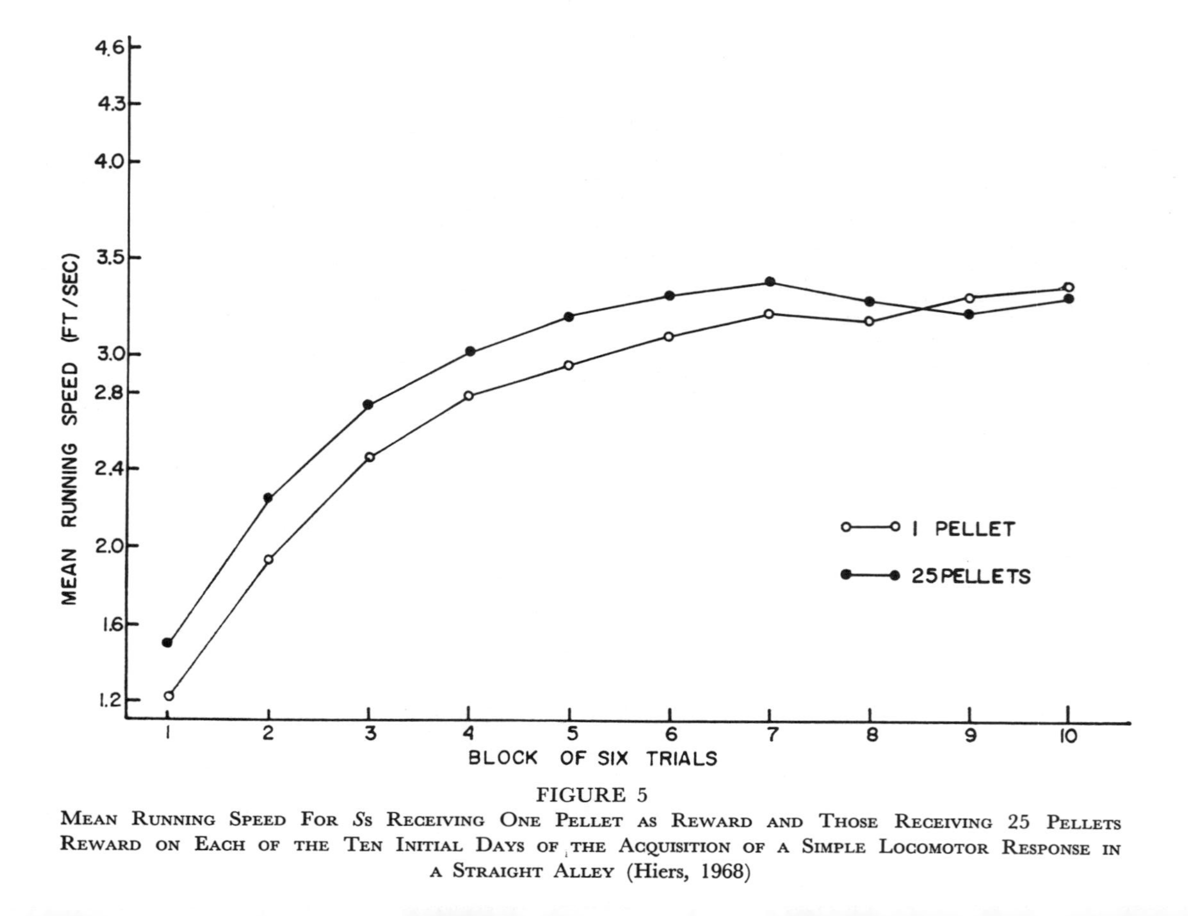


FIGURE 5

Mean Running Speed For *S*s Receiving One Pellet as Reward and Those Receiving 25 Pellets Reward on Each of the Ten Initial Days of the Acquisition of a Simple Locomotor Response in a Straight Alley (Hiers, 1968)

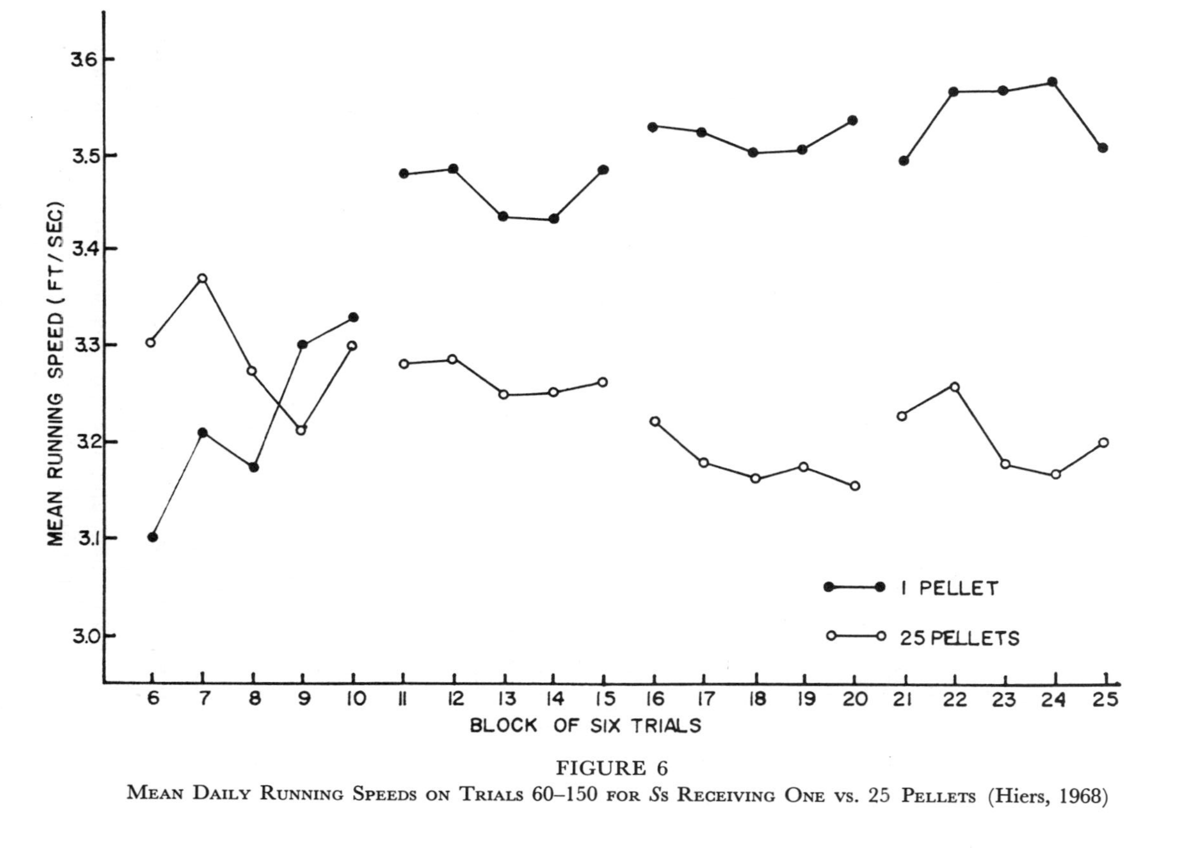


FIGURE 6

Mean Daily Running Speeds on Trials 60–150 for *Ss* Receiving One vs. 25 Pellets (Hiers, 1968)

rapidly than those which received a single pellet, but by the final two days of Phase I, the running speed for these groups had converged and, in fact, *S*s receiving one pellet were actually running slightly faster. Fig. 6 represents the performance of the nonshifted reward groups (Groups 3 and 4) on the last five days of Phase I and during each of the remaining phases of the study. It is apparent that *S*s in Group 3, which received the nominally smaller reward (one pellet), ran more quickly throughout the last three phases of the experiment than those in Group 4, for which the reward was 25 pellets. It is interesting to note that the rule according to which Hiers removed his *S*s from the goal box was similar to that employed by Elstad (1966), Gragg (1967), and others who have obtained such a "reversal" in the effects of magnitude of reward. Thus, Hiers states that he removed *S* from the goal box as soon as he could ascertain that it had completely consumed the available reward or at the end of one minute—whichever came earlier. Hiers further reported that animals in the one-pellet group tended to consume their reward immediately upon entering the goal box and were, therefore, rapidly returned to the carrying cage, while in the large-reward groups most *S*s failed to consume all of the available 25 pellets and, thus, remained in the goal box for the entire one minute. These *S*s were described as typically eating a few pellets immediately upon entering the goal box, then engaging in other, nonconsummatory behaviors which were followed by a resumption of eating, etc. Thus, running speed appeared to be more intimately connected with the consistency of consummatory activity than with the nominal magnitude of reward which the *E* made available.

Fig. 7 represents the performance of several other groups for which reward magnitude was shifted by Hiers. Of particular interest is the effect of the shift from 25 to one pellet during Phase IV for Group 5 (25-25-25-1), since during most of the first three phases this group ran more slowly than those which consistently received the smaller reward (e.g., Group 3: 1-1-1-1). In other words, the "apparent reinforcement value (ARV)" of one pellet was greater than that of 25 pellets, and it would, therefore, not seem unreasonable to expect that shifting *S*s from 25 pellets to one pellet (an apparently "more favorable reward") would result in an *improvement* in performance to a level similar to that of *S*s which received a

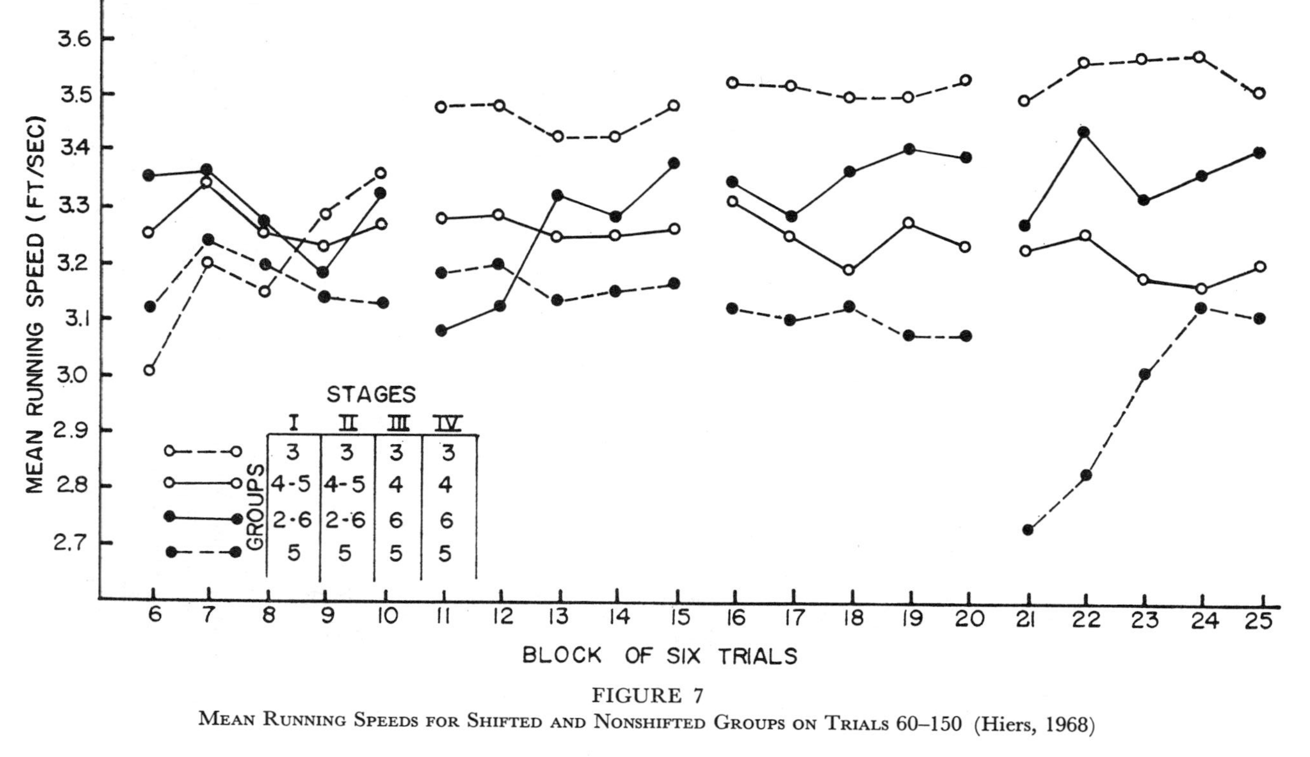


FIGURE 7
Mean Running Speeds for Shifted and Nonshifted Groups on Trials 60–150 (Hiers, 1968)

single pellet as reward. That this was not the case is clear from an inspection of Fig. 7, which indicates that the reduction from 25 pellets to one pellet resulted in a marked depression in performance of Group 5. A similar result attended the reduction in reward magnitude for Groups 2 and 6 at the beginning of Phase II. Thus, although a nominally "larger" reward resulted in a smaller ARV than a "smaller" reward, a reduction in the magnitude of that larger reward produced an almost immediate, and very substantial, decrement in performance.

In a related study of CE, Cammin (1968) trained rats to run a straight alley with sucrose solution as reward. The magnitude of reward was varied both "quantitatively" (volume of solution) and "qualitatively" (concentration of solution) and the experiment was conducted in two phases. In Phase I each *S* received three trials per day for 25 days, while during Phase II the magnitude of reward was reduced (quantitatively, qualitatively, or both) for one-half of the subjects, and Cammin reported that reliable "depression," or NCE, occurred with each type of decremental shift in reward.

Fig. 8 indicates Cammin's results during the preshift phase of the experiment. The top four curves in this figure represent groups which received either 16 percent or 32 percent sucrose in quantities of either 0.5 ml or 3 ml over the 75 trials of this phase of the experiment. The lowest two curves indicate performance for the groups which received the weakest sucrose concentration: Group I (4 percent—3 ml) and Group V (4 percent—0.5 ml). Although these groups received the same quality of reward (4 percent), Group I, which ran significantly more slowly, received the larger quantity of reward.

In Cammin's study, *S* was removed from the goal box as soon as *E* could ascertain that it had completely consumed its reward or after 60 seconds, whichever was earlier. Cammin reported that after the first few training trials, *S*s in the higher concentration groups (16 percent and 32 percent) tended to consume their reward quite rapidly and consistently after entering the goal box. The *S*s in the weak (4 percent) concentration groups, however, appeared to drink with much less consistency. Thus, these *S*s typically showed a burst of consummatory activity immediately upon entering the goal box which for rats in Group V (4 percent—0.5 ml) was often sufficient

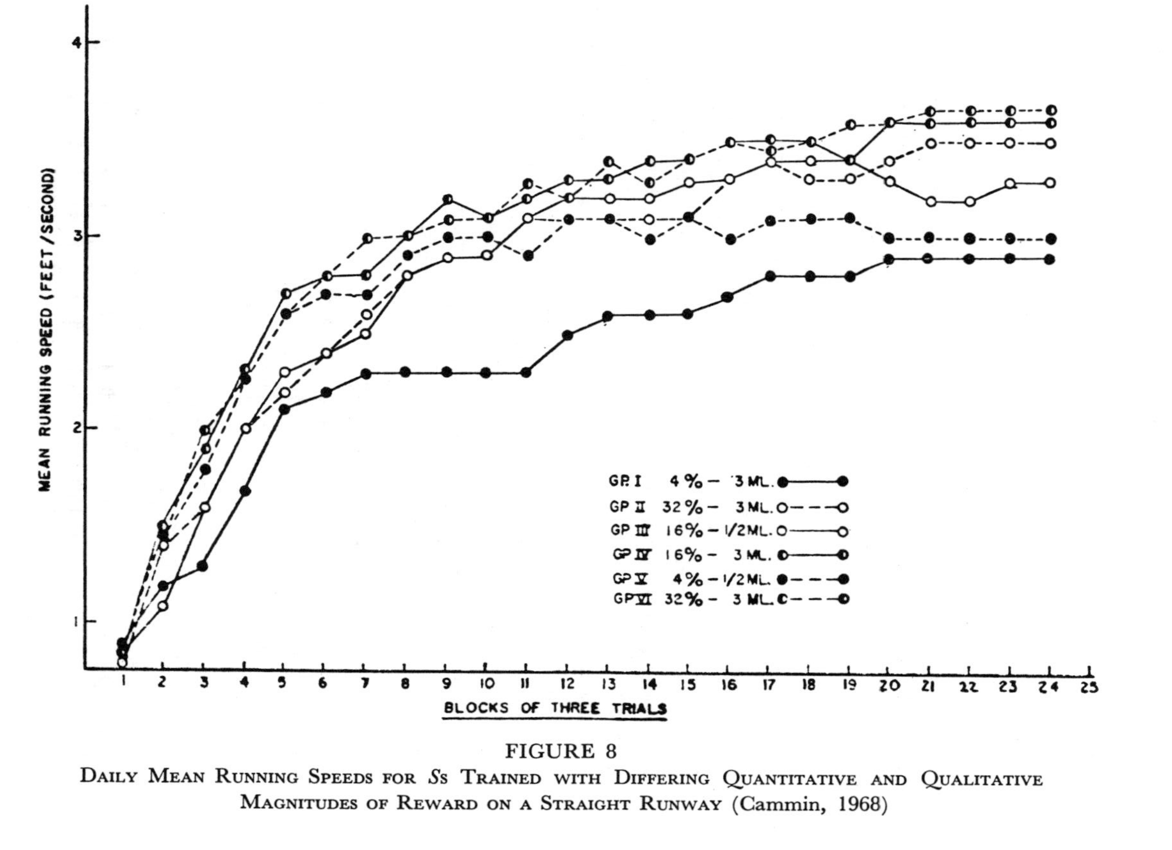


FIGURE 8

Daily Mean Running Speeds for *Ss* Trained with Differing Quantitative and Qualitative Magnitudes of Reward on a Straight Runway (Cammin, 1968)

to completely exhaust the available reward. Thus these *S*s were usually promptly removed from the goal box. The typical *S* in Group I (4 percent—3 ml), however, did not consume all of its available reward during the initial burst of drinking. Rather, it tended to leave the goal dish and engage in other, nonconsummatory responses prior to the resumption of drinking or removal from the runway. These observations are interesting in terms of the running speed data of Phase I of this experiment. Thus, there was very little "magnitude-of-reward effect" between the 16 percent and the 32 percent groups, both of which appeared to engage in consistent consummatory behavior. These groups were, however, superior to those trained with the weakest concentration (4 percent) and which appeared to show the least consistent drinking. Finally, of the two 4 percent groups, Group I (4 percent—3 ml), which had the greater opportunity for nonconsummatory activity, showed poorer instrumental performance (i.e., lower ARV) than Group V, although the latter received a smaller nominal magnitude of reward.

In a 1963 doctoral dissertation Fowler reported the results of a study concerned with the question of whether simultaneous CEs occur in a simple T-maze as the result of shifts or "contrasts" in magnitude of reward as well as the result of analogous shifts or contrasts in delay of reward. Fowler employed two sets of six groups of rats, with differential magnitude of reward (percent concentration of sucrose solution) serving as the discriminanda for one set and differential delay of reward serving as the discriminanda for the other set. Specifically, for one set of groups the discrimination involved either 8 percent vs. 16 percent or 16 percent vs. 32 percent sucrose solutions associated with the alternative arms of the maze under a delay of 1, 3, or 5 seconds in each of the arms. Similarly the other set of groups learned a spatial discrimination based on a delay of 1 vs. 3 seconds or 3 vs. 5 seconds in the alternative arms with either 8, 16, or 32 percent sucrose concentrations in each arm. This design allowed Fowler to test for the main effect of sucrose concentration on performance in the latter set of groups and the main effect of delay of reward in the former set. In addition, he was able to test for the occurrence of a simultaneous CE with respect to both magnitude and delay of reward. Thus, if *S*s ran faster to a 16 percent solution when that solution was the "positive" or stronger solution which they received (i.e., *S*s receiving 8 vs. 16 percent) than when 16 percent was the "negative" or weaker solution (16–32 percent groups), a CE with respect to reward magnitude could be said to have occurred. Similarly, if *S*s ran faster in an arm of the maze associated with a 3-second delay when that was the "positive" or shorter delay (3- vs. 5-second groups) than *S*s for which 3 seconds was the "negative" or longer delay (1-second vs. 3-second groups), then a simultaneous CE with respect to delay of reward would presumably have been demonstrated.

Fowler (1963) reported that with respect to both running speed and percent choice of the "positive arm," a significant CE did occur in contrasts of both reward magnitude and delay. His results regarding simultaneous CE with reward magnitude have been subsequently confirmed by Matsumoto (1965), while Beery (1968) confirmed the occurrence of simultaneous CE resulting from shifts in delay of reward. The main effect of delay which Fowler reported, however, was unexpected: both starting and running speeds increased as delay increased, with a 5-second delay thus resulting in better performance than a 1-second delay.

Fowler's rule for removal of *S* from the goal box was to wait until the animal had completely consumed the available solution and then to remove it immediately. His reward-dispensing device consisted of a goal dish or "fountain" into which the incentive was automatically introduced after the appropriate interval following *S*'s entry into the goal box. In commenting on his results regarding the effect of delay of reward on instrumental performance, he stated:

> Perhaps the best explanation to be offered of these results is in terms of the $r_g$-$s_g$ mechanism set forth by Spence (1956). The incentive motivational factor, K, has the $r_g$ mechanism as its basis. Thus, any experimental variables which determine the vigor or number of $r_g$'s will in turn affect K (and be reflected in response speed). From this it follows that "any property of the goal object that produces unconditioned consummatory responses of different intensity or vigor will presumably determine the value of K . . ." (Spence, 1956, pp. 136–137). In the present investigation, the typical response of *S* during the longest delay period was to lick the goal dish vigorously until, at last, the sucrose was delivered and consumed. Although these displaced consummatory

> responses might be more properly labeled "conditioned" consummatory responses, their number, and it seemed, their vigor was greatest in the five second group. This idea is in line with the various consummatory response theories of reinforcement. For example, licking without reinforcement is analogous to copulation without ejaculation (Sheffield, Wulff, and Backer, 1951), or thrusting without intromission (Kagan, 1955). Therefore, if response speed and vigor of consummatory activity are positively correlated, as has been shown (Sheffield, Roby, and Campbell, 1954), it is plausible that *S*s could run faster to longer delays under certain conditions. [Fowler, 1963, pp. 44–45]

Somewhat similar results were reported earlier by Wike and Barrientos (1957). These *E*s equated the quantity of reward (water) which their *S*s received in either arm of a T-maze. The reward, however, was obtained from a "large diameter" tube in one goal box, while the other goal box contained a "small diameter" tube which required considerably more consummatory activity in order to receive the same quantity of water. Under these conditions, *S*s learned to choose the goal box associated with the larger amount of consummatory activity, and this result was interpreted as being consistent with an $r_g$-$s_g$ (Spence, 1956) analysis of reward. Similar data have also been reported by Kling (1956).

## Recent Attempts to Control Experimentally the Parameters of Consummatory Activity

In much of the preceding research the primary interest was that of relating the strength of an instrumental response to the various parameters of consummatory activity, the most important of which seemed to be the length of time in the goal box, the proportion of that time spent in consummatory and nonconsummatory behavior, and the actual amount of reward which the *S* consumes. Unfortunately, in these experiments we were never able to place more than one of these variables simultaneously under the direct control of *E*. For example, one can vary the amount of reward which *S* consumes by making a specific amount of reward available in the goal box and leaving *S* there until it consumes all of it. This procedure (which is, of course, a very common one) "leaves it up to the subject" to determine how long it will remain in the goal box and what percentage of that time it spends in consummatory vs. other activities. The most common alternative to this reinforcement procedure is to allow *S* to remain in the goal box for some fixed period of time and to make available during this period an essentially limitless quantity of food. This procedure ensures that *S* will remain in the goal box for the appropriate or desired period of time, but it also makes the percentage of time spent in eating or drinking, and the amount of the reward consumed, dependent on the behavior of *S*. Thus, neither procedure gives *E* much direct control over the animal's behavior during the reward period. It is, of course, true that the investigator can exercise some *indirect* control over these variables. For example, if the length of time *S* has access to a very large reward is increased, the ratio of consummatory to nonconsummatory activities typically decreases. Similarly, with procedures which lead to satiation or to incentives possessing extremely low qualitative value, consummatory activity is depressed and becomes inconsistent. Nevertheless, these procedures obviously leave much to be desired in the degree to which *E* can precisely control the behavior of the animal in the goal box.

Recently we have attempted to design an apparatus and experimental procedure which will allow *E* to exert considerably more *direct* control over the events which occur in the goal box of a simple runway. The basic apparatus is a straight alley consisting of a 10-inch start box, a 3-foot runway, and a 12-inch goal box. The floor of the goal box is a stabilimeter which gives an indication of the rat's gross motor behavior. Activity is further monitored by a series of photocells spaced at two-and-one-half-inch distances along the length of the goal box which allow recording of the amount of time *S* spends in each segment. Reward is presented by a liquid dipper which periodically descends into a reservoir of water below the floor of the goal box and returns with a small quantity of water. Through the use of appropriate timing and counting circuits, it is possible to independently vary 1) the number of discrete rewards made available to *S*, 2) the quantity of water per reward, 3) the length of time between each reward, and 4) the proportion of the time between rewards during which the dipper is in the "down" position (reward cup unavailable) as opposed to "up" (cup available). Finally, 5) a "drinkometer" connected to the dipper makes it possible to record frequency, rate, and duration of consummatory activity (i.e., licking). The purpose of this apparatus is to allow the control of the rate and frequency with which reward becomes available to *S*, while at the same time monitoring the animal's consummatory and nonconsummatory behavior.

The first study to be completed which employed this apparatus was conducted by Cilluffo (1968) and consisted of four groups of ten rats each. Thus, two levels (2 and 10) of "number of discrete reinforcements per trial" were combined factorially with two levels (4 seconds or 10 seconds) of "inter-reinforcement interval." Designated in terms of the number of reinforcements per trial (n) and inter-reinforcement interval (I), the groups were: Group I: n2, I4; Group II: n2, I10; Group III: n10, I4; and Group IV: n10, I10. Each reinforcement consisted of 0.1 ml of tap water delivered by the liquid dipper. Thus, for example, when *S*s in Group III (n10, I4) entered the goal box, ten consecutive 4-second exposures of the filled dipper were presented; Group II (n2, I10) received two 10-second exposures to the dipper, etc. Cilluffo gave his *S*s three training trials per day with an average intertrial interval of about 20 minutes and the animals were removed from the goal box as soon as they had finished their last reinforcement. In this connection, it is important to note that the typical rat required 3–4 seconds of consistent licking to empty the dipper cup. Throughout the experiment, all *S*s were maintained on 23 hours' water deprivation.

The course of acquisition for the four groups in Cilluffo's study are presented in Fig. 9 in terms of mean daily running speed. Inspection of this figure indicates that Group I, which received the small number of reinforcements and the shortest total exposure to the goal box, ran faster than any of the other groups, at least following the fifth day of training. On the other hand, Group IV, which received the larger number of reinforcements as well as the longer exposure to goal box cues, ran the most slowly throughout training. Groups II and III, which received either the smaller number of reinforcements or the shorter duration, were intermediate.

Ignoring the "inter-reinforcement interval," the effect of the "number of reinforcements per trial" is presented in Fig. 10, in which the two 2-reinforcements groups (Groups I and II) are combined and compared with the 10-reinforcements groups (III and IV). It is apparent that the nominally smaller reward resulted in

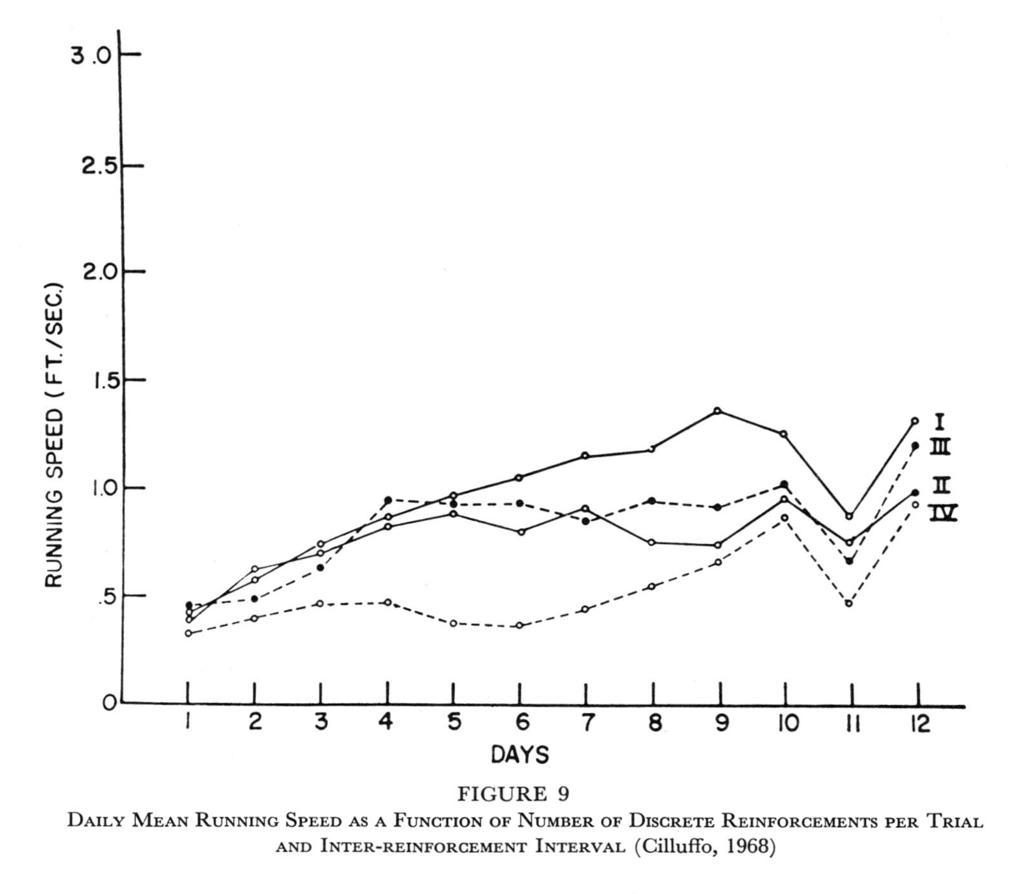


FIGURE 9

DAILY MEAN RUNNING SPEED AS A FUNCTION OF NUMBER OF DISCRETE REINFORCEMENTS PER TRIAL AND INTER-REINFORCEMENT INTERVAL (Cilluffo, 1968)

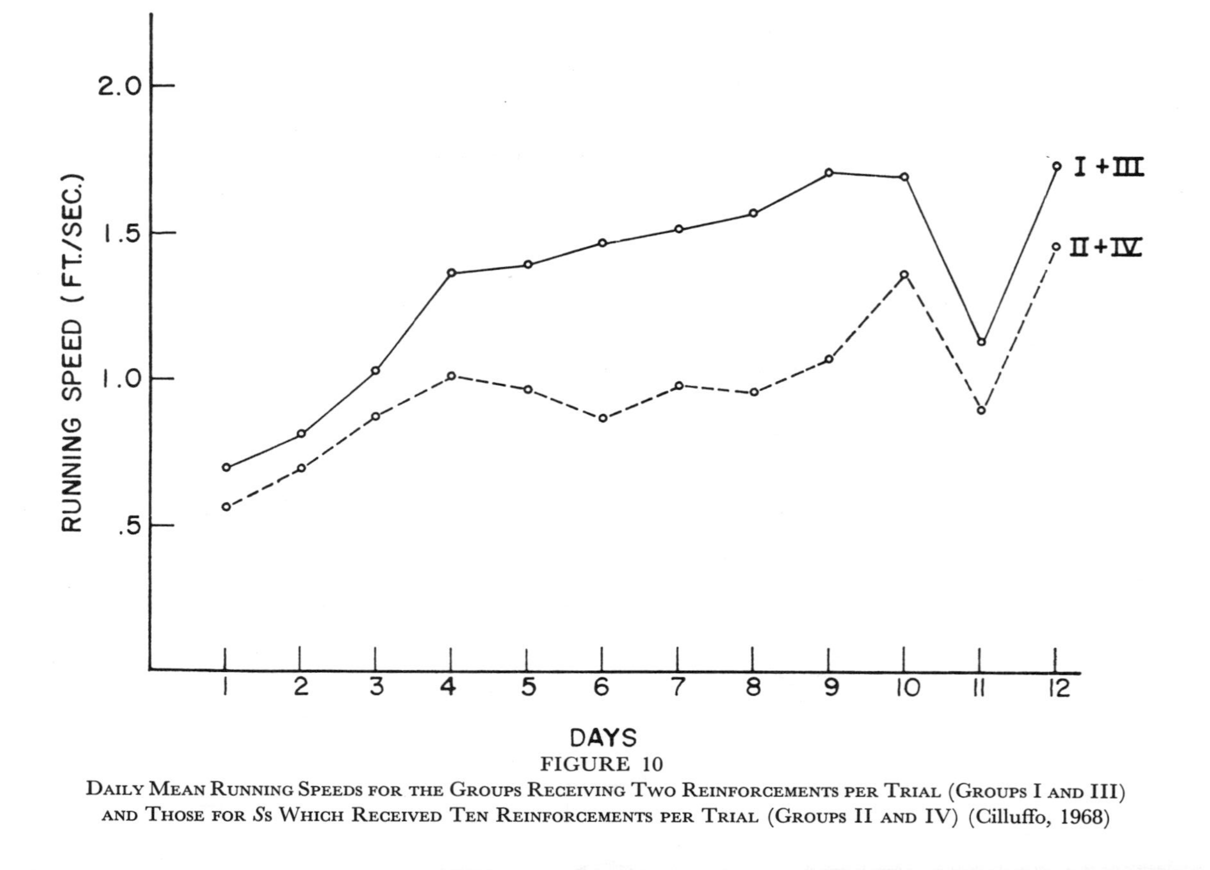


FIGURE 10

Daily Mean Running Speeds for the Groups Receiving Two Reinforcements per Trial (Groups I and III) and Those for *Ss* Which Received Ten Reinforcements per Trial (Groups II and IV) (Cilluffo, 1968)

better performance than the larger number of reinforcements. In Fig. 11, the performance of the two short-reinforcement interval groups (I and III) is combined for comparison with that of the longer-interval groups (Groups II and IV). A consistent difference was again observed. Thus, *S*s ran more rapidly when the reinforcements were presented at a fairly rapid rate than when they were presented more slowly. All of the above differences were statistically reliable.

With respect to the general behavior of the animals in the goal box, Cilluffo reported that animals in the short (4-second) reinforcement interval groups tended to maintain their orientation toward the liquid dipper throughout the period during which they were confined in the goal box. In fact, since 3–4 seconds seemed required to completely ingest the 0.1 ml of water, these *S*s spent nearly all of their time engaged in licking (consummatory) behavior. Those rats which received reinforcements at the longer (10-second) interval, however, tended to engage in a variety of nonconsummatory activities during the period after they had consumed one reinforcement and before the next became available. One such response commonly observed was that of leaving the dipper when it had been emptied and running to the retrace door at the opposite end of the goal box and there engaging in various vigorous manipulatory responses with respect to that door. In some *S*s this response tendency was so pronounced that it might almost be described as "superstitious behavior." In any event, the possibility that the response of running away from the goal box might have competed with the instrumental response of running toward the goal box clearly existed.

In a subsequent investigation, Fischman (1968) generally confirmed Cilluffo's (1968) results in an experimental design which involved a partial replication of the earlier experiment. Of particular interest in Fischman's study, however, was the finding that the level of gross motor activity per unit time in the goal box (as measured by the activity platform, which was the floor of the goal box) increased significantly with both the number of reinforcements per trial and the inter-reinforcement interval. Since *S*s in these groups also ran more slowly, an inverse relationship between the strength of the instrumental response and the amount of nonconsummatory activity

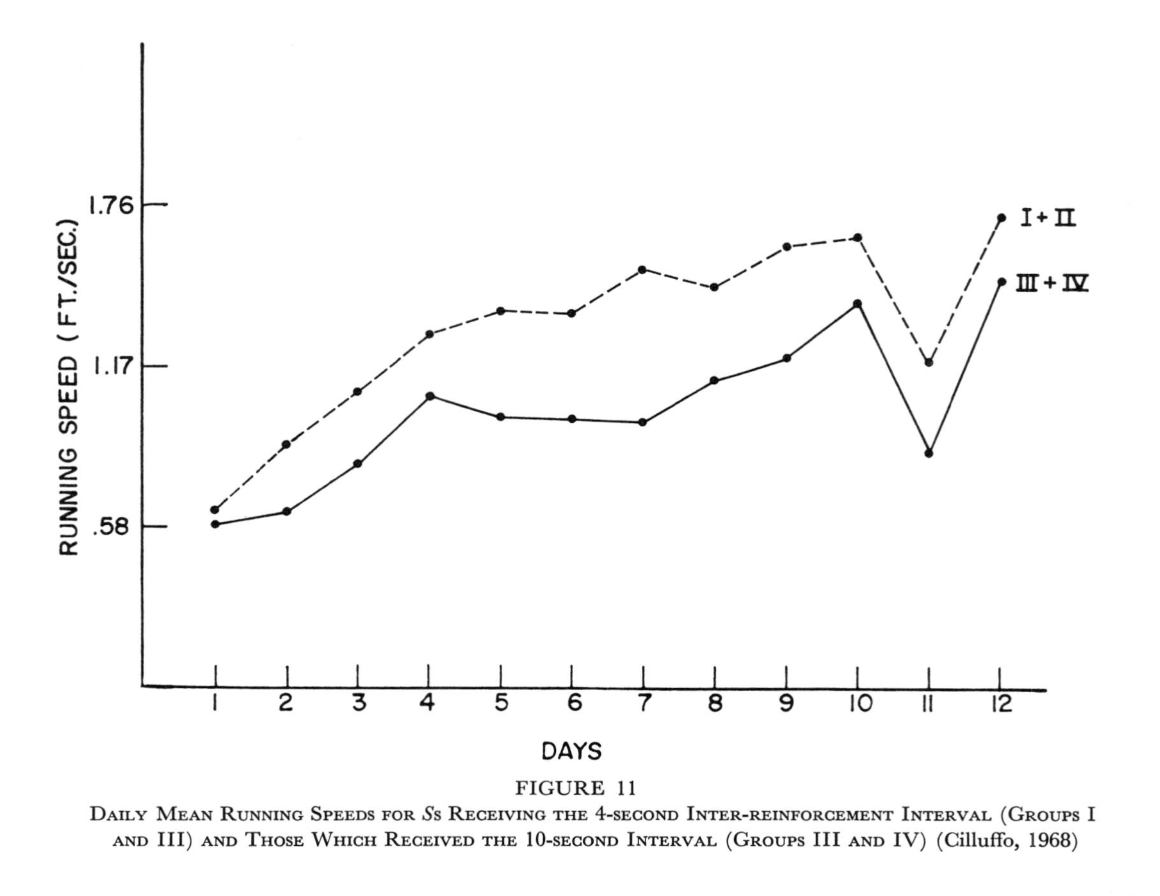


FIGURE 11

DAILY MEAN RUNNING SPEEDS FOR *S*s RECEIVING THE 4-SECOND INTER-REINFORCEMENT INTERVAL (GROUPS I AND III) AND THOSE WHICH RECEIVED THE 10-SECOND INTERVAL (GROUPS III AND IV) (Cilluffo, 1968)

was obtained. On the other hand, neither Cilluffo (1968) nor Fischman (1968) could detect any relationship between rate or vigor of consummatory responding and running speed. Thus, regardless of the group, when the animals licked, they licked at the same constant rate. This finding was, of course, in agreement with others described earlier.

## Summary and Conclusions

The outcomes of the various lines of research concerned with the function and nature of reinforcement which have been described above suggest several hypotheses which I wish to present in a rather general and tentative manner. While I have explicitly stated these hypotheses in the context of instrumental appetitive conditioning, the possibilities for extension to other types of learning situations are, in many cases, fairly obvious. Much of this summary, however, represents an extension, or even a reiteration, of views which have recently been expressed by others who are concerned with the general problem of reinforcement.

1) A primary "mechanism of reinforcement" seems to be incentive-motivational. Perhaps the most direct evidence in support of this statement is the fact that the effect of reward magnitude on performance is so rapidly reversible. Thus, both incremental and decremental shifts in reward magnitude have repeatedly been shown to result in "appropriate" adjustments in performance which are far more abrupt than would be expected if reward magnitude were assumed to directly strengthen "habits," "S-R connections," etc. Moreover, the incentive-motivational value of a given reward seems to depend on the magnitude of that reward even in experimental situations in which a "large reward" results in a lower ARV than a smaller reward. For example, in some of the studies described above a "small reward" resulted in greater ARV than a "larger reward." Nevertheless, when *S*s were shifted from the "large" (and apparently "poorer") reward to the "small" (and apparently "better") reward, an abrupt decrement in performance occurred. Similarly, although *S*s may, under some circumstances, run faster to "smaller" rewards than to "larger" ones, they nevertheless seem to "prefer" the latter in a discrimination learning situation. I am

suggesting, therefore, a hypothetical incentive-motivation variable which depends on the quality or quantity of reward but *the strength of which is not always directly reflected in instrumental performance.*

In my opinion, the most plausible hypothesis regarding incentive-motivation is that it is the result of the classical conditioning of components of the *S*s response to the rewarding stimulus. It seems almost certain that this mechanism must be central in locus rather than consisting of peripheral anticipatory responses such as licking, salivating, etc. It is quite possible, of course, that the strength of the hypothetical central state presumed to underlie incentive-motivation may itself reflect characteristics of consummatory activity. In this connection, I might make note of my very strong suspicion that the facilitatory effects of "drive" on instrumental performance result solely from the enhancement of consummatory activity or the conditionable central components of that activity. I have previously suggested a somewhat similar view (Black, 1965c) as has Bindra (1968) within the context of a physiological model of incentive-motivation.

2) The apparent reinforcement value of a reward appears to depend not only on its magnitude or the amount of consummatory behavior it evokes but upon the consistency with which such behavior occurs. Thus, measures of the strength of the instrumental response such as running speed, etc., are not always accurate or appropriate indices of the "incentive value" or the extent to which one reward is "preferred" over another. Nominally large rewards, if they tend to "encourage" the *S* to engage in inconsistent consummatory activity and thus to engage in other forms of responding, may produce considerable incentive-motivation and still have relatively low ARV. Similarly, small rewards which result in vigorous and consistent consummatory activity may have greater ARV than larger rewards, even though *S* "prefers" (i.e., will learn to choose) the latter. In short, I am suggesting a "two-factor" interpretation of reinforcement in instrumental appetitive conditioning. Increasing reward magnitude or the amount of consummatory activity facilitates performance. Decreasing the consistency of consummatory activity, or, conversely, increasing the amount of nonconsummatory activity, depresses performance and the ARV of the reward. This depression may result either from the development

of responses which interfere with the instrumental response or by virtue of the fact that an inconsistently consumed reward will provide little "protection" for the association between the test situation and the instrumental response. In either case, this depression in performance is sometimes sufficient to actually produce a reversal in the usual "magnitude-of-reward effect." In such circumstances, however, the greater "incentive value" associated with the larger reward can sometimes be demonstrated by allowing *S* a choice between large and small rewards or by shifting the magnitude of reward.

3) The "sources of reward" appear to be multiple. While the efforts to reduce the number of *sufficient* characteristics of rewarding stimuli to a single *necessary* one have often been heroic, such attempts have typically failed to prove convincing. Even theorists who have associated themselves with one of the molar positions regarding reward (e.g., drive-reduction, consummatory response, or stimulus theories) have been forced to acknowledge their inability to identify in an a priori way those specific stimuli which will prove to be rewarding. For example, Young, who has consistently maintained a "stimulus theory" of reward, has recently stated:

> The neurophysiology of pleasantness and unpleasantness is largely unknown and unexplored. The total evidence suggests that sensory stimulations produce primary evaluations, or appraisals, in terms of "good" or "bad" on the basis of innate neural mechanisms. The genetic basis of primary evaluation is found in untold eons of biological evolution. As a result of evolution there are built-in neural mechanisms that evaluate gustatory stimuli immediately in terms of acceptance-rejection and preference. [Young, 1966, pp. 83–84]

Similarly, Glickman and Schiff (1967), who emphasized the role of species-specific patterns of consummatory activity in reinforcement, stated:

> The thesis presented here is . . . that facilitation of motor patterns is considered the sufficient condition for reinforcement. . . . We visualize sets of parallel neural pathways regulating species-typical response patterns. It is the activation of these independent paths by whatever means which constitutes what is conventionally described as reinforcement. Those stimuli which are uniquely capable of reliably activating particular primitive approach or withdrawal sequences would be especially reinforcing agents. [Glickman & Schiff, 1967, p. 85]

Both of these passages, of course, suggest a multiplicity of stimuli which would "innately" serve as rewards and which must be identified empirically.

## REFERENCES


Beery, R. G. A negative contrast effect of reward delay in differential conditioning. *J. exp. Psychol.*, 1968, **77**, 429–434.

Berkun, M. M., Kessen, M. L., & Miller, N. E. Hunger reducing effects of food by stomach fistulas versus food by mouth measured by a consummatory response. *J. comp. physiol. Psychol.*, 1952, **45**, 550–554.

Berlyne, D. E. Novelty and curiosity as determinants of exploratory behavior. *Brit. J. Psychol.*, 1950, **41**, 68–80.

Bindra, D. Neuropsychological interpretation of the effects of drive and incentive motivation on general activity and instrumental behavior. *Psychol. Rev.*, 1968, **75**, 1–22.

Black, Patricia E., & Black, R. W. Interaction of drive and incentive motivation. *Psychon. Sci.*, 1967, **8**, 128–130.

Black R. W. Differential conditioning, extinction and secondary reinforcement. *J. exp. Psychol.*, 1965a, **69**, 67–74.

Black, R. W. Discrimination learning as a function of varying pairs of sucrose reward. *J. exp. Psychol.*, 1965b, **70**, 452–455.

Black R. W. On the combination of drive and incentive motivation. *Psychol. Rev.*, 1965c, **72**, 310–316.

Black, R. W. Shifts in magnitude of reward and contrast effects in instrumental and selective learning: a reinterpretation. *Psychol. Rev.*, 1968, **75**, 114–126.

Black, R. W., & Elstad, Patricia. Instrumental and consummatory behavior as a function of length of reward period. *Psychon. Sci.*, 1964, **1**, 301–302.

Bower, G. H. A contrast effect in differential conditioning. *J. exp. Psychol.*, 1961, **62**, 196–199.

Cammin, W. B. An investigation of contrast effects in reward magnitude employing sucrose solution as reward in instrumental conditioning. Unpublished Ph.D. dissertation, University of South Carolina, 1968.

Capaldi, E. J. A sequential hypothesis of instrumental learning. In: Spence, K. W., & Spence, J. T. (Eds.), *The psychology of learning and motivation*. Vol. 1. New York: Academic Press, 1967.

Cilluffo, A. F. Rate and frequency of discrete reinforcements as determinants of instrumental performance. Unpublished MS, University of South Carolina, 1968.

Clark, R., Schuster, C. R., & Brady, J. V. Instrumental conditioning of jugular self-infusion in the rhesus monkey. *Science*, 1961, **133**, 1829–1830.

Coppock, H. W., & Chambers, R. M. Reinforcement of position preference by automatic intravenous injection of glucose. *J. comp. physiol. Psychol.*, 1954, **47**, 355–357.

Crespi, L. P. Quantitative variation of incentive and performance in the white rat. *Am. J. Psychol.*, 1942, **55**, 467–517.

Elstad, Patricia A. Effects of reward magnitude upon performance under deprivation and satiation. Unpublished Master's thesis, University of Iowa, 1966.

Elstad, Patricia A., & Black, R. W. Running speed as a function of duration of reward and various parameters of consummatory activity. Unpublished MS, University of Iowa, 1965.

Fischman, Paul. Runway performance by rats as a function of consummatory and nonconsummatory activities. Unpublished Master's thesis, University of South Carolina, 1968.

Fowler, R. L. Magnitude and delay of reinforcement in spatial discrimination learning. Unpublished Ph.D. dissertation, University of Tennessee, 1963.

Glickman, S. E., & Schiff, B. B. A biological theory of reinforcement. *Psychol. Rev.*, 1967, **74**, 81–109.

Goldstein, H., & Spence, K. W. Performance in differential conditioning as a function of variation in magnitude of reward. *J. exp. Psychol.*, 1963, **65**, 86–93.

Goodrich, K. P. Running speed and drinking rate as functions of sucrose concentration and amount of consummatory activity. *J. comp. physiol. Psychol.*, 1960, **53**, 245–250.

Gragg, Linda. Performance in instrumental conditioning following shifts in drive and reward magnitude. Unpublished Master's thesis, University of South Carolina, 1967.

Gragg, Linda, & Black, R. W. Runway performance following shifts in drive and reward magnitude. *Psychon. Sci.*, 1967, **8**, 177–178.

Guild, R. E. Incentive motivation in satiated rats. *J. comp. physiol. Psychol.*, 1960, **53**, 351–358.

Guthrie, E. R. *The psychology of learning.* New York: Harper and Row, 1935.

Guthrie, E. R. Association and the law of effect. *Psychol. Rev.*, 1940, **47**, 127–148.

Guthrie, E. R. Conditioning: A theory of learning in terms of stimulus response and association. In Nat'l Soc. Stud. Educ., *The psychology of learning.* 41st yearbook, pt. 2, pp. 17–60.

Guttman, N. Operant conditioning, extinction, and periodic reinforcement in relation to concentration of sucrose used as reinforcing agent. *J. exp. Psychol.*, 1953, **46**, 213–224.

Hiers, J. M. An investigation of the persistence of contrast effects in reward magnitude in instrumental conditioning. Unpublished Ph.D. dissertation, University of South Carolina, 1968.

Homzie, M. J., & Ross, L. E. Runway performance following a reduction in the concentration of a liquid reward. *J. comp. physiol. Psychol.*, 1962, **55**, 1029–1033.

Hull, C. L. *Principles of behavior.* New York: Appleton-Century-Crofts, 1943.

Hull, C. L. *A behavior system.* New Haven: Yale University Press, 1952.

Hull, C. L., Livingston, J. R., Rouse, R. O., & Barker, A. N. True, sham and esophageal feeding as reinforcement. *J. comp. physiol. Psychol.*, 1951, **44**, 236–245.

Kagan, J. Differential reward value of incomplete and complete sexual behavior. *J. comp. physiol. Psychol.*, 1955, **48**, 59–64.

Kling, J. W. Speed of running as a function of goal box behavior. *J. comp. physiol. Psychol.*, 1956, **49**, 474–476.

Kraeling, Doris. Analysis of amount of reward as a variable in learning. *J. comp. physiol. Psychol.*, 1961, **54**, 560–565.

Matsumoto, R. Relative reward effects in differential conditioning. Unpublished Ph.D. dissertation, University of Iowa, 1965.

Miller, N. E. Some reflections on the law of effect produce a new alternative to drive reduction. In Jones, M. R. (Ed.), *Nebraska symposium on motivation.* Lincoln: University of Nebraska Press, 1963.

Miller, N. E., & Kessen, M. L. Reward effect of food via stomach fistula compared with those of food via mouth. *J. comp. physiol. Psychol.*, 1952, **45**, 555–564.

Olds, J., & Milner, P. Positive reinforcement produced by electrical stimulation of septal area and other regions of the rat brain. *J. comp. physiol. Psychol.*, 1954, **47**, 419–427.

Premack, D. Predicting instrumental performance from the independent rate of the contingent response. *J. exp. Psychol.*, 1961, **61**, 163–171.

Premack, D. Reversibility of the reinforcement relation. *Science*, 1962, **136**, 255–257.

Premack, E. Reinforcement theory. In Levine, D. (Ed.), *Nebraska symposium on motivation.* Lincoln: University of Nebraska Press, 1965.

Pubols, B. H. Incentive magnitude learning and performance in animals. *Psychol. Bull.*, 1960, **57**, 89–115.

Seward, J. P. Secondary reinforcement as tertiary motivation: a revision of Hull's revision. *Psychol. Rev.*, 1950, **57**, 362–374.

Seward, J. P. Experimental evidence for the motivating function of reward. *Psychol. Bull.*, 1951, **48**, 130–149.

Seward, J. P. Introduction to a theory of motivation in learning. *Psychol. Rev.*, 1952, **59**, 405–413.

Seward, J. P. Drive, incentive and reinforcement. *Psychol. Rev.*, 1956, **63**, 195–203.

Seward, J. P., & Proctor, D. M. Performance as a function of drive, reward and habit strength. *Am. J. Psychol.*, 1960, **73**, 448–453.

Seward, J. P., Shea, R. A., & Davenport, R. H. Further evidence for the interaction of drive and reward. *Am. J. Psychol.*, 1960, **73**, 370–379.

Seward, J. P., Shea, R. A., & Elkind, D. Evidence for the interaction of drive and reward. *Am. J. Psychol.*, 1958, **71**, 404–407.

Sheffield, F. D., & Roby, T. B. Reward value of a nonnutritive sweet taste. *J. comp. physiol. Psychol.*, 1950, **43**, 471–481.

Sheffield, F. D., Roby, T. B., & Campbell, B. A. Drive reduction versus consummatory behavior as determinants of reinforcement. *J. comp. physiol. Psychol.*, 1954, **47**, 349–354.

Sheffield, F. D., Wulff, J. J., & Backer, R. Reward value of copulation without sex drive reduction. *J. comp. physiol. Psychol.*, 1951, **44**, 3–8.

Sidman, M., & Stebbins, W. C. Satiation effects under fixed-ratio schedules of reinforcement. *J. comp. physiol. Psychol.*, 1954, **47**, 114–116.

Skinner, B. F. *Science and human behavior.* New York: MacMillan, 1953.

Spear, N. E. Retention of reinforcer magnitude. *Psychol. Rev.*, 1967, **74**, 216–234.

Spence, K. W. *Behavior theory and conditioning.* New Haven: Yale University Press, 1956.

Stellar, E., & Hill, J. H. The rat's rate of drinking as a function of water deprivation. *J. comp. physiol. Psychol.*, 1952, **45**, 96–102.

Strait, Judith. Negative contrast effects following decremental shifts in reward magnitude in instrumental conditioning. Unpublished Master's thesis, University of South Carolina, 1968.

Thorndike, E. L. *Educational psychology.* New York: Teachers College, Columbia University, 1913.

Thorndike, E. L. *The fundamentals of learning.* New York: Teachers College, Columbia University, 1932.

Weiss, G. Partial reinforcement in mixed-phase differential instrumental conditioning. Unpublished Ph.D. dissertation, University of Iowa, 1965.

Wike, E. L., & Barrientos, G. Selective learning as a function of differential consummatory activity. *Psychol. Rep.*, 1957, **3**, 255–258.

Young, P. T. Hedonic organization and regulation of behavior. *Psychol. Rev.*, 1966, **73**, 59–86.

Zeaman, D. Response latency as a function of the amount of reinforcement. *J. exp. Psychol.*, 1949, **39**, 466–483.

## COMMENTS

*Edward L. Wike*

Dr. Black has presented: 1) a most penetrating analysis of the concept of reinforcement, 2) the detailed results from an impressive array of experiments done in his laboratory, and 3) the implications of this research for the nature of reinforcement. Let us consider these topics in order. Because of the large amount of material covered by Dr. Black, we shall, of necessity, have to be selective in our comments.

1) *The Concept of Reinforcement.* Dr. Black has carefully limited the scope of his analysis to simple instrumental conditioning with discrete trials and appetitional drives and rewards. This strategy has my full support because the rigorous theoretical analysis of more complex situations becomes enormously complicated. He has drawn a distinction between *sources* and *mechanisms* of reward. To oversimplify this useful distinction, let us say that by source he means what makes X a reward. And by mechanisms he means what does X affect. Thus, under sources are included a) the stimulus properties of X (e.g., taste, etc.); b) response factors (e.g., the consummatory response or high rate responses in the manner of Premack); and c) drive reduction. In short, is X a reinforcer because it is palatable, evokes a vigorous response, or reduces a drive? As was repeatedly pointed out, grave difficulties are encountered when one tries experimentally to fractionate these sources of reward; a large reward takes longer to consume, looks larger, provides more drive reduction, and so on.

What rewards affect, or the mechanisms of reward, are divided into *associative* and *incentive* interpretations. Examples of associative interpretations are those of Thorndike, Guthrie, and Hull (1943), in which rewards directly or indirectly influence S-R connections. More recently, of course, incentive views (Hull, 1951; Spence, 1956), in which rewards act as motivators, have become prominent. All in all, this section of Dr. Black's talk is an excellent discourse on the nature of reinforcement.

2) *Research on Rewards.* The research, mainly upon amount of reward, developed from attempts to test the Hull vs. Spence posi-

tions (i.e., multiplicative vs. additive) on the relationship between D and K (Black, 1965). Dr. Black's position is that exceptions to an additive combination will only be observed when D or K is zero. This interpretation does a nice job of explaining the results of Seward's studies, but not the findings of Kintsch (1962). Before regarding this problem as closed, I would like to see more studies, incorporating wider variations of D and K.

The experiments by Black and his students have shown that rats run faster to small rewards than to large rewards. As study after study was presented, I felt as if I was a helpless observer of some great natural disaster. At last, a simple dissonance-resolving hypothesis suggested itself: all of Dr. Black's figures were mislabeled! Since Dr. Black assured us that the figures are correct, this fantasy solution was dropped. We are left with the question, Why do the rats run faster to small rewards?

As a result of much careful research, Dr. Black has come to believe that large rewards lead to inconsistent consummatory behavior with the attendant conditioning of responses that interfere with the locomotor response. Although this is an attractive hypothesis, I would like to offer an alternative one, namely, that as a consequence of the *S*s' undergoing more than one training trial per day, the high-reward *S*s became less motivated than the low-reward *S*s. Thus, perhaps what was being investigated was not small vs. large reward with drive constant, but small reward–high drive vs. large reward–low drive. To test this hypothesis I would be most interested in some replications of these studies done with a single training trial daily. A further implication of Dr. Black's major finding is that there may be two rules for amount of reward—one for single trial per day studies and another for multiple daily trials.

Two other comments may be offered on the role of nonconsummatory activity in reward studies. a) The question can be raised about the possibility of *direct* manipulation of such presumed competing responses. For example, suppose the runway performance of two control groups with rewards of one and two units of food, respectively, were contrasted with an experimental group that received one unit of food for running and then a unit of food for executing some competing response like jumping upward in the goal box. Would the latter group's runway performance be retarded? In short, it is being suggested that it might be fruitful to manipulate such competing responses experimentally rather than having them occur capriciously and then attempting to correlate them with instrumental performance. b) It should be noted that nonconsummatory activity in the goal box appears to be more closely related to instrumental performance than is consummatory activity. For example, Elstad and Black (1965) found that two indices of consummatory vigor, momentary eating rate and amount consumed, showed no relationship to running speed. This outcome obviously would not be anticipated from $r_G$-$s_G$ theory. A most interesting point, made by Dr. Black during the discussion, concerned the difficulty in explaining sudden changes in performance after shifts in reward by an $r_G$-$s_G$ theory, since $r_G$-$s_G$ is a learned mechanism. It was the suddenness in change that caused the problem for a habit theory. The $r_G$-$s_G$ mechanism, as a learned mechanism, is therefore faced with the same problem.

3) *Implications of Reward Research for Reinforcement.* Four provisional conclusions were suggested by Dr. Black: a) "The sources of reward appear to be multiple"; b) "a primary mechanism of reinforcement seems to be motivational"; c) "incentive motivation . . . is the result of classical conditioning of components of the subject's response to the rewarding stimulus [and] . . . this mechanism must be central in locus rather than peripheral anticipatory responses such as licking, salivating, etc."; and d) "the ARV of a stimulus depends not only on its magnitude of the amount of consummatory activity it evokes but upon the consistency with which such behavior occurs." I have no quarrel with the first and last views. However, some reservations may be voiced against b) and c). First, the emphasis upon incentive-motivational mechanism of reward seems somewhat surprising to me in view of the evidence on nonconsummatory activity found in Dr. Black's experiments and his Guthrie-like associative interpretation. In fairness to him, it should be noted that his concern at this point was in accounting for sudden shifts in performance following changes in reward magnitude. Second, while I would agree with Dr. Black's rejection of $r_G$-$s_G$ as a peripheral response like licking or salivating, I see no great gain in postulating it as a "central mechanism." This latter reservation stems from a bias on my part toward behavioral investigations. One of my

concerns is that unless one has an explicit, testable physiological theory, important problems may be buried in the nervous system.

Again, let me compliment Dr. Black on his most penetrating analysis of reinforcement. His presentation did two things to me that a good paper should do: first, it generated a lot of verbal responses (thinking, if you prefer); and second, it triggered an urge to do more research on reinforcement.

## REFERENCES

Black, R. W. On the combination of drive and incentive motivation. *Psychol. Rev.*, 1965, **72**, 310–316.

Elstad, Patricia A., & Black, R. W. Running speed as a function of duration of reward and various parameters of consummatory activity. Unpublished MS, University of Iowa, 1965.

Hull, C. L. *Principles of behavior*. New York: Appleton-Century-Crofts, 1943.

Hull, C. L. *Essentials of behavior*. New Haven: Yale University Press, 1951.

Kintsch, W. Runway performance as a function of drive strength and magnitude of reward. *J. comp. physiol. Psychol.*, 1962, **55**, 882–887.

Spence, K. W. *Behavior theory and conditioning*. New Haven: Yale University Press, 1956.

# Some Antecedents of Interpersonal Attraction[1]

ELLIOT ARONSON

*University of Texas at Austin*

During the past several years, my students and I have been busily and even happily engaged in an investigation of the antecedents of interpersonal attraction. In simple language, our aim is to understand what makes people like one another. Since man *is* a social animal, it seems reasonable to assume that being liked by his fellows would be important to him. Indeed, even a casual observation of human behavior suggests that most people much of the time act in a manner which can be interpreted to mean that they like to be liked. They seek friendships, they try to impress others with their abilities, they entertain guests, they smile a lot, they express pleasure when told someone is fond of them, they give presents, they seem unhappy when someone ignores them or acts unkindly to them, they turn a simple little book called *How to Win Friends and Influence People* into a phenomenal best seller.

What affects interpersonal attraction? If we look at the research literature, several important antecedents emerge:

1) Propinquity—we like people who are close to us better than people who are at a distance from us, all other things being equal (Festinger, Schachter, & Back, 1950; Kendall, 1960; Newcomb, 1961; Gullahorn, 1952).

2) Similarity of values and beliefs—we like people who agree with us better than people who disagree with us (Richardson, 1940; Precker, 1952; Schachter, 1951; Newcomb, 1961; Byrne, 1969).

1. Supported by a grant from the National Institute of Mental Health (MH 12357) to Elliot Aronson.

3) Similarity of personality traits—we like people who are like us (Shapiro, 1953; Secord & Backman, 1964).

4) Complementarity of need systems—under certain conditions we like people whose characteristics make it easy for them to satisfy our needs and whose needs are such that we can easily satisfy them (Winch, 1958).

5) High ability—we like able and competent people better than incompetent people (Stotland & Hillmer, 1962; Iverson, 1964).

6) Pleasant or agreeable characteristics or behavior—we like people who are "nice" or who do "nice things" (Bonney, 1944; Lemann & Solomon, 1952; Jackson, 1959).

7) Being liked—we like people who like us (Backman & Secord, 1959).

All of these antecedents can be loosely summarized under a general reward-cost or exchange kind of theory. It is tempting to encompass all of these phenomena under one blanket (see, for example, Homans, 1961): We like people who bring us maximum gratification at minimum expense; or, more succinctly, we like people most whose overall behavior is most rewarding. Briefly, to go through the list I have just presented, 1) propinquity is more rewarding, all other things being equal, because it costs less in terms of time and effort to receive a given amount of benefit from a person who is physically close to us than one who is at a distance (Thibaut & Kelley, 1959); 2) people with similar values reward each other through consensual validation (Byrne, 1969); 3) the same would be true for similarity of some personality traits, whereas 4) for some needs, complementarity would be most rewarding—for example, sadism-masochism or nurturance dependency; 5) people perhaps expect to gain more through association with highly competent people than with people of low or moderate competence. That is, in general, our past histories are such that we have usually been more rewarded by people who knew what they were about than by people who tended to blunder frequently. 6) Obviously, pleasant, agreeable behavior is more rewarding than unpleasant, disagreeable behavior; and 7) being liked can probably be considered a reward in and of itself—in addition, for most people it also entails a similarity of beliefs because most of us think rather highly of ourselves (Byrne & Ramey, 1965).[2]

While the data embodied in these statements are undoubtedly accurate and useful, one may legitimately question the extent to which one can generalize from them. It is tempting to postulate a general reward theory and let it go at that—but perhaps we should resist this temptation. I believe that the major problem with such a general theory is the difficulty of establishing an a priori definition of reward in a complex social situation. In simple situations we have little trouble: For a starving man, food is a clear-cut reward; therefore the person who provides food will probably be liked better than one who withholds food. For someone who is drowning, rescue is a clear-cut reward; therefore a drowning man will like a person who saves his life more than someone who allows him to drown. But many social situations are not that clear. As the situation becomes more complex, the context in which the "reward" is provided can change its meaning and, consequently, have a great effect upon whether or not the "rewarder's" attractiveness is increased. For example, if a person does a fine piece of work and his boss says, "Nice work, Joe," that phrase will function as a reward and Joe's liking for his boss will probably increase. But suppose Joe did a very poor job—and knew it. The boss comes along and emits the exact same phrase in exactly the same tone of voice. Will that phrase function as a reward in this new situation? I am not sure. Joe *may* interpret this statement as the boss's attempt to be encouraging and nice even in the face of a poor performance. Because of this display of considerateness, Joe may come to like the boss even more than in the case where he *had*, in fact, done a good job. On the other hand, Joe may interpret this behavior as being sarcastic, manipulative, dishonest, undiscriminating, patronizing, or stupid—any one of which could reduce Joe's liking for his boss.

2. It should be noted that these seven antecedents of liking do not quite encompass all of the research on attraction. There are some findings that cannot be easily squeezed under the rubric of reward theory. For example, it has been repeatedly shown that people like other people and things for which they have suffered (Aronson & Mills, 1959; Aronson, 1961; Gerard & Mathewson, 1966). These phenomena will not be discussed in this essay.

Let us look at a different situation: As previously mentioned, there are many studies indicating that agreement is more rewarding than disagreement and that we like people who hold similar views better than people who hold dissimilar views (see Schachter, 1951; Byrne, 1969). Is this always the case? Suppose you are an instructor lecturing to a class full of graduate students and presenting a theory that you are developing. In the rear of the classroom are two students. One of these fellows is nodding and smiling and looks as though he is in rapture. At the close of your presentation, he comes forward and tells you that he agrees with everything you said. The other fellow frowns and shakes his head occasionally during your presentation. Afterward he tells you that there are several aspects of your theory that he disagrees with—and explains why. That evening, while ruminating on what was said, you realize that the second person, while basically incorrect, made a few worthwhile points and forced you to rethink a few of your assumptions. This leads you to a minor modification of your theory. Which of these two people do you like better? I don't know. It seems like an empirical question. While agreement is clearly rewarding, disagreement which leads to improvement may carry its own rewards.

The first example, the one involving praise, leads me to suspect that a general reward theory of attraction runs the risk of circularity because social rewards, like praise, are not transituational—that is, they may function as a reward in some situations but may have no effect or even the opposite effect in other situations. The second example, that involving disagreement, suggests to me that there may be some aspects of apparently punitive behavior (e.g., disagreement) which may be rewarding (e.g., by allowing us to improve).

The simplicity of a reward theory of liking is appealing, but its usefulness is diminished to the extent that it is difficult to specify the events and situations which are, in fact, rewarding. How might one attempt to specify these events in advance? One reasonable but rather laborious strategy involves the refinement of a definition of reward and requires the following steps: a) searching the literature for instances where an event which would appear to be rewarding does not, indeed, lead to an increase in liking; b) trying to understand the dynamics of this apparent contradiction; and c) testing this interpretation empirically. Although this is a rather painstaking procedure, it can help to clarify what we mean by "reward" and, consequently, it can lead to a greater understanding of the antecedents of attraction. We have been pursuing this strategy for the past few years with some success. Since space is limited, I would like to illustrate this technique by focusing on one application of this procedure.

If we assume that able, competent people are more rewarding to us than incompetent people, shouldn't it follow that we would like people of extremely high ability and competence to a greater extent than people who are moderately or poorly endowed with competence and ability? This seems like a truism; yet, as obvious as this relationship may seem, there is some evidence which indicates that it is not always the case. For example, Hollander and Webb (1955) have demonstrated that group members who are considered the most able are not necessarily the best liked. Moreover, in their investigations of problem-solving groups, Bales and his associates have shown that people who initiate the most ideas and who are generally acknowledged to be the best idea men of the group are most often *not* the best-liked group members (Bales, 1953, 1955,1958; Bales & Slater, 1955). Now, there are several possible reasons why a person of high intellectual ability might be rejected by the people in his group. For example, Bales suggests that there may be an incompatibility between proficiency in an intellectual role with that of proficiency in a social role. That is, individuals of high intellectual ability may be brusque or unpleasant interpersonally, and it may be the socio-emotional leader who is preferred to the idea man who is weak in other aspects of social behavior. This is certainly conceivable. I would like to suggest another possibility: It may be that these data reflect a nonlinear relationship between ability and attractiveness. A great deal of ability, in and of itself, might make a person appear to be too good, unapproachable, distant, nonhuman. This could conceivably occur even if his social skills were the equal of those of his less intellectually gifted counterpart. If this were the case, then some manifestation of fallibility on his part might actually increase his attractiveness.

Some very tentative support for this notion can be mentioned in passing. According to a Gallup poll, John Kennedy's personal popularity increased immediately *after* the Bay of Pigs fiasco. Here is a situation in which a president commits one of history's truly great blunders (up until that time, that is) and, lo and behold, people like him more. Explanation? Perhaps President Kennedy was too perfect. He was young, handsome, bright, witty, a war hero, super wealthy, charming, athletic, a voracious reader, a master political strategist, an uncomplaining endurer of physical pain—with a perfect wife (who spoke several foreign languages), two cute kids (one boy, one girl), and a talented, close-knit extended family. Some evidence of fallibility (like the Bay of Pigs fiasco) could have served to make him more human, and hence more likable. But the real world is no place to test such a hypothesis. Kennedy's popularity could have increased for any number of reasons, including the selfless manner in which he accepted total responsibility for the blunder.

In order to test this proposition, an experiment was needed—and was performed (Aronson, Willerman, & Floyd, 1966). The intent of this experiment was to present subjects with one of four stimulus persons: 1) a near-perfect person, 2) a near-perfect person who commits a clumsy blunder, 3) a mediocre person, and 4) a mediocre person who commits a clumsy blunder. This was accomplished in the format of an investigation of social perception. Subjects listened to a tape recording of a stimulus person; they were told that they would be listening to a person who was a candidate for the College Quiz Bowl and that they would be asked to rate him in terms of what kind of an impression he made, how much they liked him, etc. The tape itself was an interview between the candidate, or stimulus person, and an interviewer. It consisted primarily of a set of extremely difficult questions posed by the interviewer; the questions were of the kind that are generally asked on the College Quiz Bowl. On one tape the stimulus person was of very high intellectual ability and seemed to be virtually perfect. He answered 92 percent of the questions correctly; furthermore, in the body of the interview, he admitted (modestly) that in high school he had been an honor student, yearbook editor, and member of the track team. On another tape (using the same voice) we presented the stimulus person as one of average ability. On this tape he answered only 30 percent of the questions correctly, and during the interview he admitted that he had received average grades in high school, that he had been a proofreader on the yearbook, and that he had tried out for the track team but failed to make it. In two additional conditions (one involving the superior person, one involving the average person) the stimulus person committed an embarrassing blunder. Specifically, near the end of the interview, he clumsily spilled a cup of coffee all over himself. On this tape this blunder was accompanied by a good deal of noise and clatter, the scraping of a chair, and the stimulus person's anguished statement, "Oh, my goodness, I've spilled coffee all over my new suit." The coffee-spilling incident was taped, duplicated, and spliced onto a copy of the superior-ability tape and onto a copy of the average-ability tape. Thus, to repeat, there were four conditions: A person of superior ability who either blundered or did not blunder, and a person of average ability who either blundered or did not blunder. After listening to the tape, the subject was interviewed by a person who was ignorant of the experimental condition. The interviewer asked for ratings of how much the subject liked the stimulus person, would he like him as a friend, was he pleasant, etc. The results were clear-cut: The most attractive stimulus person was the superior person who committed a blunder, while the least attractive was the person of average ability who also committed a blunder. The interaction between ability and blunder was highly significant. A contrast comparing the difference between the Blunder and the No Blunder conditions within the Superior Ability ($M_D = +9.4$) condition and with the Average Ability ($M_D = -20.3$) condition is highly significant in the predicted direction ($t = 3.18$, $p < .005$). Thus, there was nothing

TABLE 1

MEAN ATTRACTION SCORES

| | *Pratfall* | *No Pratfall* |
|---|---|---|
| Superior Ability | 30.2 | 20.8 |
| Average Ability | −2.5 | 17.8 |

(Adapted from Aronson, Willerman, & Floyd, 1966.)

charming about the blunder itself; it had the effect of increasing the attractiveness of the superior person and decreasing the attractiveness of the average person. Although a high degree of competence is probably rewarding and, therefore, attractive, some evidence of incompetence leads to *higher* ratings of attractiveness.

The strategy illustrated by this experiment is a useful one and has led us to some interesting findings, but it is not very efficient—it would be extremely tedious to attempt to map out a definition of reward and its relationship to attraction by employing a technique which is almost exclusively empirical. My inclination is not to produce an encyclopedia of antecedents of liking. A more efficient approach would entail the development and testing of different "mini-theories" of attraction. This could lead to a greater understanding of the antecedents of attraction by helping us to define the limitations of a general reward theory. I have been working on one such "mini-theory" in recent years, and I would like to describe it as well as some of the research it has led to. I call it the gain-loss theory, and I refer to it as a "mini-theory" in order to emphasize the fact that it is not intended to account for all of the data of attraction; rather, it is to be considered useful in helping us understand a small sub-set of such data. The simplest way to state it is as follows: Increases in rewarding behavior from another person (*P*) have more impact on an individual than constant, invariant reward from *P*. Thus, a person whose esteem for us increases over time will be liked better than one who has always liked us. This would be true even if the number of rewards were greater in the latter case. Similarly, losses in rewarding behavior have more impact than constant punitive behavior on *P*'s part. Thus, a person whose esteem for us decreases over time will be disliked more than someone who has always disliked us—even if the number of punishments were greater in the latter situation. The reasons behind this proposition will be clearer if discussed after a description of the definitional experiment.

Imagine yourself at a cocktail party having a conversation with a person whom you've never met before. After several minutes he excuses himself and drifts into a different conversational group. Later that evening, while standing out of sight behind a potted palm, you happen to overhear this person in conversation—talking about a person he met earlier in the evening; lo and behold, it's you that he's talking about! Suppose that you attend seven consecutive cocktail parties, have a conversation with the same person at each of these parties, and, as luck would have it, chance to overhear him talking about you each time.

There are four outcomes that I find particularly interesting: 1) you overhear the person saying exclusively positive things about you on all seven occasions; 2) you overhear him saying exclusively negative things about you on all seven occasions; 3) his first couple of evaluations are exclusively negative, but they gradually become increasingly positive; 4) his first couple of evaluations are exclusively positive, but they gradually become more negative. Which situation would render him most attractive to you? Our theory would predict that you'd like him best in the "gain" condition and least in the "loss" condition.

In order to test our theory, we needed an experimental analogue of the above situation—but for reasons of control we felt that it would be essential to collapse the above events into a single long session. Moreover, it was essential that, unlike our example, the subject be absolutely certain that his evaluator is totally unaware that he (the evaluator) is being overheard; this would eliminate the possibility of the subject's suspecting that he is being flattered when he is being evaluated positively.

The central problem involved in operationalizing this situation was this: How do we provide a credible situation where, in a relatively brief period of time, the subject a) interacts with a preprogrammed confederate, b) eavesdrops while the preprogrammed confederate evaluates him to a third party, c) engages in another conversation with the confederate, d) eavesdrops again, e) converses again, etc., through several pairs of trials. To provide a sensible cover story would indeed be difficult; to provide a sensible cover story which would prevent subjects from becoming suspicious would seem impossible. We (Aronson & Linder, 1965) solved our problem with the following scenario:

> When the subject arrived for the experiment, the experimenter greeted her and led her to an observation room which was connected to the main experimental room by a one-way window and an audio-amplification system. The experimenter told the subject that two girls were scheduled for this hour—one would be the subject and the other would help perform the experiment. He said that since she had arrived first, she would be the helper. The experimenter asked her to wait while he left the room to see if the other girl had arrived yet. A few minutes later,

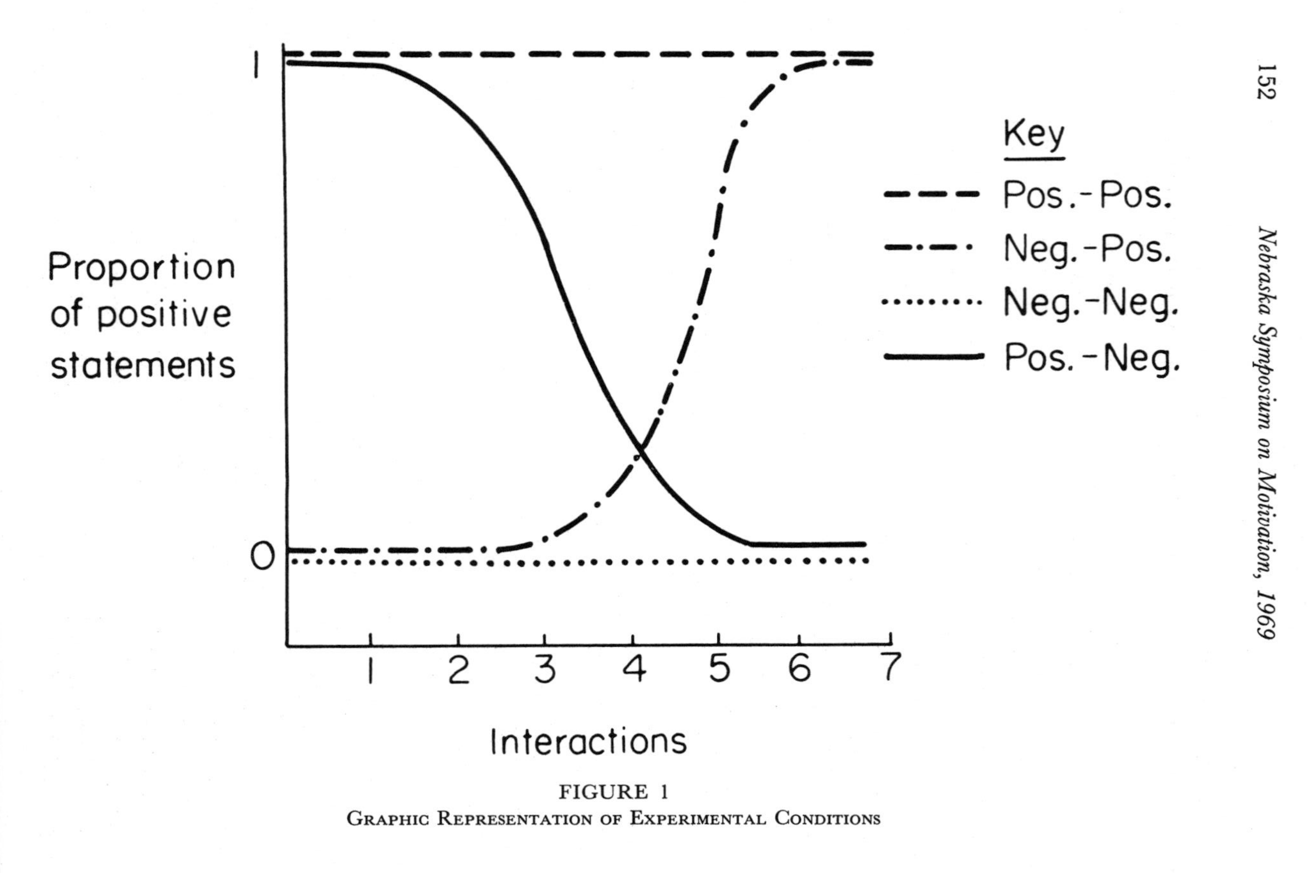


FIGURE 1
GRAPHIC REPRESENTATION OF EXPERIMENTAL CONDITIONS

through the one-way window, the subject was able to see the experimenter enter the experimental room with another female student (the paid confederate). The experimenter told the confederate to be seated for a moment and that he would return shortly to explain the experiment to her. He then returned to the observation room and began the instructions to the real subject. The experimenter told her that she was going to assist him in performing a verbal conditioning experiment on the other student. He explained verbal conditioning briefly and went on to say that his particular interest was in the possible generalization of conditioned verbal responses from the person giving the reward to a person who did not reward the operant response. He explained that he would condition the other girl to say plural nouns to him by rewarding her with an "mmm hmmm" every time she said a plural noun. He mentioned that this should increase the rate of plural nouns said to him by the other girl. The subject was then told that her tasks were: 1) to listen in and record the number of plural nouns used by the other girl, and 2) to engage her in a series of conversations (not rewarding plural nouns) so that the experimenter could listen and determine whether generalization occurred. The experimenter told the subject that they would alternate in talking to the girl (first the subject, then the experimenter, then the subject) until each had spent seven sessions with her.

The experimenter made it clear to the subject that the other girl must not know the purpose of the experiment lest the results be contaminated. He explained that, in order to accomplish this, some deception must be used. The experimenter said that as much as he regretted the use of deception, it would be necessary for him to tell the girl that the experiment was about interpersonal attraction. ("Don't laugh, some psychologists are actually interested in that stuff.") He said that the other girl would be told that she was to carry on a series of seven short conversations with the subject and that between each of these conversations both she and the subject would be interviewed, the other girl by the experimenter and the subject by an assistant in another room, to find out what impressions they had formed. The experimenter told the subject that this "cover story" would

> enable the experimenter and the subject to perform their experiment on verbal behavior since it provided the other girl with a credible explanation for the procedure they would follow.
>
> The independent variable was manipulated during the seven meetings that the experimenter had with the confederate. During their meetings the subject was in the observation room, listening to the conversation and dutifully counting the number of plural nouns used by the confederate. Since she had been led to believe that the confederate thought that the experiment involved impressions of people, it was quite natural for the experimenter to ask the confederate to express her feelings about the subject. Thus, without intending to, the subject heard herself evaluated by a fellow student on seven successive occasions.

Note how, by using a cover story that *contains* a cover story involving interpersonal attraction, we were able to accomplish our aim without arousing suspicion—only 4 of 84 subjects had to be discarded. Again, there were four major experimental conditions: 1) Positive—the successive evaluations of the subject made by the confederate were all highly positive; 2) Negative—the successive evaluations were all very negative; 3) Gain—the first few evaluations were negative but gradually became more positive, reaching an asymptote at a level equal to the level of the positive evaluations in the Positive condition 1; 4) Loss—the first few evaluations were positive but gradually became negative, leveling off at a point equal to the negative evaluations in the Negative condition 2. The results confirmed our theoretical position: The subjects in the Gain condition liked the confederate better than the subjects in the Positive condition. It should be noted that if one had simply summed the number of positive (rewarding) statements, one would have been led to the opposite prediction; i.e., the confederate handed out more rewards and fewer punishments in the Positive condition than in the Gain condition. By the same token, the subjects in the Loss condition had a tendency to dislike the confederate more than the subjects in the Negative condition. This latter result did not quite reach an acceptable level of statistical significance. Once again, a theory which merely summed rewards and punishments algebraically would have led to the opposite prediction. In sum, the results are in line with our general theoretical position: A gain has more impact on liking than

TABLE 2

MEANS AND STANDARD DEVIATIONS FOR LIKING OF THE CONFEDERATE

| *Experimental Condition* | *Mean* | *SD* |
|---|---|---|
| Gain | 7.67 | 1.51 |
| Positive | 6.42 | 1.42 |
| Negative | 2.52 | 3.16 |
| Loss | 0.87 | 3.32 |

(Adapted from Aronson & Linder, 1965)

a set of events that are all good, and a loss tends to have more impact on liking than a set of events that are all nasty. There are probably a great many possible explanations; I will discuss the most plausible ones:

1) *Anxiety reduction.* When a person expresses negative feelings toward us, we probably experience some negative affect—for example, anxiety, hurt, self-doubt, etc. If the person's behavior gradually becomes more positive, his behavior is not only more rewarding in and of itself, but it also serves to reduce the existing anxiety that he previously aroused. The total reward value of his positive behavior is, therefore, greater. Thus, paradoxically, we will like the person better *because* of his previous negative, punitive behavior. This reasoning is consistent with that of Walters & Ray (1960), who demonstrated that prior anxiety arousal increases the effectiveness of social reinforcement on children's performance. Our "mini-theory" goes a step further—the existence of prior anxiety increases the attractiveness of an individual who has both created and reduced this anxiety. The kind of relationship we have in mind was perhaps best expressed some 300 years ago by Spinoza in Proposition 44 of *The Ethics:*

> Hatred which is completely vanquished by love passes into love, and love is thereupon greater than if hatred had not preceded it. For he who begins to love a thing which he was wont to hate or regard with pain, from the very fact of loving, feels pleasure. To this pleasure involved in love is added the pleasure arising from aid given to the endeavor to remove the pain involved in hatred accompanied by the idea of the former object of hatred as cause.

The same kind of reasoning, in reverse, underlies the loss part of our theory. Here the person tends to like the confederate better when the latter's behavior was invariably negative than if his initial behavior had been positive and gradually became more negative. When negative behavior follows positive behavior, it is not only punishing in its own right, but it also eradicates the positive effect associated with the rewarding nature of the other person's earlier behavior. He showed us how good it could feel to be liked—and then he snatched it away from us. Therefore, we dislike this person more than the entirely negative person, not *in spite* of the fact that he had previously rewarded us, but precisely *because* of the fact that he had previously rewarded us.

2) *Competence.* A second reason for the gain-loss phenomenon may involve the feeling of competence or effectance (White, 1959). If a person succeeds in changing someone's opinion, he may feel effective. Since this is a positive feeling, it may generalize to its cause. Therefore, the person may like the evaluator better because of his success at converting him. By the same token, if the person likes us initially and then gradually comes to dislike us, we may feel a loss of effectance, and this negative feeling may generalize to the person who is the cause of it.

3) *Discernment.* The gain-loss phenomenon may also be due to the attributed discerning ability of the evaluator. By changing his opinion about us, *P* forces us to take his evaluation more seriously. If he had expressed a uniformly positive or uniformly negative feeling toward us, we could dismiss this behavior as being a function of his own style of response; that is, we could believe either that *P* likes everybody or that *P* dislikes everybody. But if he begins by evaluating us negatively and then becomes more positive, we must consider the possibility that his evaluations are a function of his perception of us, and not merely a function of his style of responding. Because of this, we are more apt to take his evaluations personally and seriously if he changed his opinion than if his opinion had been invariably positive or invariably negative. In short, *P*'s early negative evaluations force us to take his subsequent positive evaluation more seriously because he is displaying discernment and discrimination. It proves, if nothing else, that he's paying attention to us; that he's neither blind nor bland. This renders his subsequent positive evaluation all the more meaningful and valuable. By the same token, if *P*'s evaluation of us was entirely negative, we may be able to write him off as either a misanthrope or a fool. But if his initial evaluations were positive and then became negative, we are forced to conclude that he can discriminate among people. This adds

meaning (and sting) to his subsequent negative evaluation and, consequently, will decrease our liking for him.

4) *Contrast.* Another conceivable alternative explanation involves the phenomenon of contrast. After a succession of negative statements, a single positive statement may stand out and, therefore, may seem more positive than the same statement preceded by other positive statements. Similarly, a negative evaluation following closely behind several positive evaluations may appear to be more negative than one that forms part of a series of uniformly negative responses. I believe that this explanation is less likely because in our experiment a sharp contrast did not occur between adjacent sessions; rather, the shift from positive to negative and from negative to positive in the behavior of the confederate in this experiment was very gradual—that is, from extremely negative, to negative, to slightly negative, to neutral, to slightly positive, etc. Therefore, it seems unlikely that a contrast effect would be operating during such a gradual transition.

Although these explanations for the gain-loss phenomenon are not necessarily mutually exclusive, it would be helpful if we could determine which, if any, of the processes is involved—and if more than one is involved, which is most powerful. Some evidence concerning necessary preconditions occurs in the Aronson-Linder experiment itself. In this experiment we had a fifth experimental condition not previously described. In this condition, the confederate's initial evaluation of the subject was neutral rather than negative, and then became increasingly positive. Our reasoning behind this condition was that if some sort of anxiety or pain was unnecessary, then it might be the case that the results of the Neutral-Positive condition would be closer to those of the Gain condition than to those of the entirely Positive condition. If this had occurred, then one could conclude that pain or suffering is not necessary. However, in this condition the mean liking for the confederate was almost identical with the mean in the completely Positive condition. The difference between the Neutral-Positive and the Gain condition approaches statistical significance ($p < .07$, two-tailed). Thus, on the basis of these results, we certainly cannot eliminate anxiety reduction as a possible explanation. But, alas, we cannot easily eliminate any of the other explanations either.

Some additional but highly tentative data are available by dint of an internal analysis conducted on the results of this experiment. In pondering our data, we asked ourselves what we would have expected if the subjects in the Gain condition did not take the early negative evaluations personally. For these subjects there would be no anxiety to be reduced. Similarly, in the Loss condition, loss would not be experienced if the confederate's negative behavior, for some reason, were not taken personally by the subject. It should be noted that the existence of a negative drive state is not necessary for the existence of the other possible antecedents—discernment, contrast, or feelings of effectance. In the Aronson-Linder study, near the close of the session, the interviewer asked the subject if it had bothered, embarrassed, upset, or made her anxious to listen to herself being evaluated by the other girl. In the Positive condition none of the subjects were at all bothered, upset, embarrassed, or made anxious by the situation. This, of course, is not surprising. In the Gain condition, however, 11 of the 20 subjects admitted to having been somewhat upset when the other girl was evaluating them negatively. Similarly, 9 girls in the Negative condition and 9 in the Loss condition admitted that they had been upset by the negative evaluation. In these latter conditions, the subjects who claimed that they had *not* been upset by the negative evaluation tended to explain this by saying that the communication situation was so restricted that they lacked the freedom and relaxation to be themselves and make a good impression on the other girl. Typically, they felt that it was not so unreasonable for the other girl to think that they were dull, stupid, and uninteresting, but this had nothing to do with their own personalities; mainly it had to do with the fact that the situation was so restricted that it forced them to appear dull, uninteresting, and even stupid. In short, many of the girls simply refused to take the negative evaluation as a personal reflection on themselves and, consequently, they felt that the confederate would have liked them better if the situation had been freer and had allowed them to express their usual lovable personalities. For what it's worth, one can compare the results of those who were upset by the negative evaluation with the results of those who weren't upset by it in terms of how much they liked the confederate.

Let me issue a caveat regarding an internal analysis. It has been said—with what I'm afraid is more justification than jest—that the internal analysis is the last refuge of a scoundrel. To state it more prosaically, data based on an internal analysis are never conclusive, since they are not experimental in nature. That is, it may be that the kinds of people who are upset by a negative evaluation (or, strictly speaking, who admit to being upset by a negative evaluation) may differ in many ways from those who do not admit to being upset. Thus, the differences in their liking for the stimulus person may simply be the result of some of these individual differences rather than for the reasons relevant to the theory. But while not conclusive, these data can be suggestive; like good hypotheses, they can show us where to look. In our experiment, within the Gain condition, those subjects who were upset by the negative evaluations liked the confederate more than those who were not upset. This was highly significant. Similarly, within the Loss condition, those who were upset by the negative evaluation tended to like the confederate less than those who were not upset. These results suggest the possibility that some degree of upset might be necessary in order for the gain-loss phenomenon to occur.

In sum, the results of the Aronson-Linder experiment demonstrate that the gain-loss phenomenon exists, and it indicates that anxiety reduction may be an important aspect of the phenomenon, without eliminating any of the other possible explanations.

With these data in mind, we performed a separate experiment in order to ascertain the importance of prior anxiety as a determinant of attraction (Sigall & Aronson, 1969). We reasoned that if a person is aware that he is about to be evaluated, he will experience anxiety. All other things being equal, the more attractive the evaluator, the greater the anxiety. Thus, if a beautiful woman were to evaluate a male subject favorably, she would be liked better than a homely woman who evaluated him favorably; however, if a beautiful woman were to evaluate him unfavorably, she would be liked *less* than a homely woman who evaluated him unfavorably—because the beautiful woman is leaving him with more anxiety than the homely woman. Thus, our theory does not lead to the prediction that beautiful women are liked better than homely women; rather, our theory indicates that our liking for a beautiful woman depends on what she does—that being beautiful creates more anxiety in the evaluated person which the beautiful woman may either reduce or increase, depending upon the nature of her evaluations.

As an aside, I might mention that physical attractiveness is rarely investigated as an antecedent of liking—even though casual observation (even by us experimental social psychologists) would indicate that we seem to react differently to beautiful women than to homely women. It is difficult to be certain why the effects of physical beauty have not been studied more systematically. It may be that, at some level, we would hate to find evidence indicating that beautiful women are liked better than homely women—somehow this seems undemocratic. In a democracy we like to feel that with hard work and a good deal of motivation, a person can accomplish almost anything. But, alas (most of us believe), hard work cannot make an ugly woman beautiful. Because of this suspicion, perhaps most social psychologists implicitly would prefer to believe that beauty is, indeed, only skin deep—and avoid the investigation of its social impact for fear that they might learn otherwise.[3]

Another possible reason for steering clear of beauty as a variable might be methodological. At first glance it appears to be a sloppy independent variable because it seems as though one might need two confederates (one beautiful and one ugly) to perform an experiment. Using two confederates, of course, introduces a great deal of variance because the two would most certainly differ on many dimensions in addition to beauty. A few years ago Judson Mills and

3. I can't let this parenthetical discussion go by without mentioning one of my pet ideas—that our visual perception exercises a terribly conservative influence on our feelings and behavior. We are wedded to our eyes—especially as a means of determining physical attractiveness. Moreover, once we have categorized a person as pretty or homely, we tend to attribute other qualities to these people; i.e., pretty people are more likely to strike us as being warm, sexy, exciting, and delightful than homely people. Recently I have become involved in the encounter-group movement—for research purposes as well as for reasons which are more directly humanistic. One of the things we do occasionally in these groups is to "turn off our eyes" and become acquainted with people nonvisually—solely through the sense of touch. After participating in one of these exercises, group members typically report a dramatic diminution of their prior stereotypes. Basically, individuals find that there is no "homeliness" in a nonvisual situation. Moreover, participants are frequently overwhelmed to learn that, for example, the incredibly warm, gentle, and sensitive person that they had been having a nonvisual encounter with is, "in reality," the funny-looking guy with the pimples. After even one such nonvisual encounter, I somehow doubt that they can ever relate to him again as merely a funny-looking guy with pimples.

I (Mills & Aronson, 1965) solved this problem by demonstrating that we could get by with only one confederate. We accomplished this by the simple device of taking a naturally attractive young lady and making her up to look homely in one condition by dressing her in loose, ill-fitting clothing, making her hair look unkempt, making her complexion oily and unwholesome-looking, and even etching a trace of a mustache on her upper lip. Thus, while it may be the case that only God can make a woman truly beautiful, we demonstrated that all it takes is a couple of diabolical experimenters to make a beautiful woman look ugly.

In the experiment presently under discussion, Sigall and I used a technique of uglification similar to the one described above. In both the "beautiful" and the "ugly" conditions our confederate posed as a graduate student in clinical psychology who interviewed and tested the subject and then presented him with the results of her personal clinical judgment, which were either favorable or unfavorable. The results confirmed our predictions: There was a significant interaction—the beautiful-positive evaluator was liked best, the beautiful-negative evaluator was liked least.

While the results of this experiment support anxiety reduction, they do not eliminate the possibility that competence may have played a role. To some extent the two are confounded in this type of design. That is, while subjects experienced more anxiety at the prospect of being evaluated by a beautiful woman, they may have experienced greater feelings of effectance from impressing a beautiful woman than they got from impressing a plain woman. Indeed, very recently Sigall, Page, & Brown (1969, in preparation) completed a study in which they demonstrated that subjects work harder and perform better after a negative evaluation from a beautiful woman than after either a positive evaluation from a beautiful woman or a negative evaluation from a plain woman. If subjects work hard and succeed, one might guess that they feel more effective than if they don't work as hard to succeed.

One way to measure the effects of anxiety reduction relatively independent of any effects due to feelings of effectance would involve using more than one evaluator; that is, instead of the subject's trying to induce a person to change his mind, as in the Aronson-Linder and Sigall-Aronson experiments, one could confront a subject with several respondents of differing opinions—in a variety of sequences. Such a design has been employed both by Worchel & Schuster (1966) and by Stapert & Clore (1969). Instead of using evaluations of the subject as their manipulations, these investigators examined different sequences of attitudinal disagreement and agreement. They found that a person who agreed with the views of the subject was liked better when he was preceded by a different person who disagreed with the subject than when the agreer was preceded by a person who agreed with the subject. One can assume that disagreement arouses some anxiety; encountering an agreer reduces this anxiety without producing a great deal of effectance and, incidentally, without allowing much reason for the subject to attribute powers of discernment to the confederate.

Thus, it has been shown that anxiety *can* be manipulated without confounding it with effectance. It is more difficult to investigate effectance in the absence of anxiety. Harold Sigall has taken a very good stab at it: In his Ph.D. dissertation (1968), Sigall investigated what we have called the conversion effect. The question is, Does a missionary feel more kindly disposed toward someone whom he has converted to the faith than toward someone who has always been a loyal member of the flock? It's a fascinating question. As mentioned earlier, it has been shown that, generally, we prefer people who agree with us to people who disagree with us. According to Byrne (1969), this is due to consensual validation; people who agree with us on an issue, by so doing, provide us with evidence that our position is correct—since consensual validation is rewarding and since we like people who reward us, we like people who agree with us. Moreover, people who hold the same view as we do on one issue are more likely to be like us on other issues—for example, if a person agrees with us on Medicare, he is more likely to agree with us on racial integration (generalized similarity). Consider a person who disagrees with us initially, but who, after we present him with a cogent argument, comes to agree with us. Clearly, his initial lack of consensual validation is far from rewarding, but his eventual conversion may erase the negative feeling engendered by the early disagreement. Moreover, extrapolating from the results of the Aronson-Linder experiment, such a sequence may go beyond merely erasing this negative feeling and may provide us with a larger reward, due at least in part to a feeling of effectance. This might lead us to like him more than if he had agreed initially. At the same time, the initial disagreement might suggest that our "audience" might disagree with us on other, related issues—even if we convert him on this one issue; thus, we might like him *less* than the initial agreer.

It was to this problem that Sigall directed his attention. Sigall reasoned that agreement might be more effective than disagreement because of greater generalized similarity. But Sigall hypothesized that in a situation where the individual was concerned with doing a good job, the attractiveness of the initially disagreeing audience would be heightened (compared to the agreeing audience) because of the added importance of effectance.

Sigall went even further: He predicted that this would occur even if he compared an agreeing condition with a condition in which the audience showed a sizable change in the direction of the communicator's position but still remained in basic disagreement. This is complex—an illustration might help: Suppose you felt that marijuana should be made available to everyone, all the time, and you were presenting your argument to a person who believed that all marijuana and marijuana seeds should be destroyed. After hearing your argument, he now believes that marijuana could be used on Saturday nights under supervised conditions by people over 35. On a linear scale from $-10$ to $+10$, his position has moved from $-10$ to $-2$. In short, he is still on the "wrong" side of the zero point—he still disagrees with you—but you would have every right to feel proud and effective, especially if you were ego-involved in doing a good job.

In Sigall's experiment, the subject delivered a persuasive communication to a person who was either very close to his own opinion or very far from his opinion. Thus, if the communicator's own opinion was 27 on a 30-point scale, he gave his speech to a person whose initial position was either 23 or 8. After hearing the speech, the listener (actually a confederate) changed either from 23 to 24 or from 8 to 13. There was a third condition in which the listener began as a disagreer (13) but eventually swung to the agree side of the neutral point (18). In this condition there is effectance plus final agreement, whereas in the other conditions there is either a) general agreement without effectance, or b) effectance, but with the subject remaining in general disagreement.

In this experiment, "involvement" was manipulated in the following manner: In the Low Involvement condition the subject was given a prepared speech and was told to read it without dramatics since the experimenter was interested only in the effect of the content—not in the manner of delivery. In the High Involvement condition the subject was asked to organize an argument from several points that were suggested by the experimenter. The experimenter informed the subjects that in the past he had found that the manner in which the arguments were organized by different subjects had had a profound effect on the impact of the speech; some people were simply better than others in constructing persuasive arguments from these materials.

Sigall examined the interaction between degree of involvement in the Agreement/No Effectance versus Effectance/No Agreement conditions. When there was low involvement, the subjects liked the confederate better in the Agreement/No Effectance condition than in the Effectance/No Agreement condition. When there was high involvement, this relationship was reversed. Thus, people like similar people better than converts unless they are ego-involved with converting them. In the latter case they like the convert better.

As mentioned earlier, it is difficult to disentangle effectance from anxiety reduction because they tend to co-vary. It was to this purpose that Sigall inserted an additional set of conditions in which the audience began at a scale position of 13 and ended at a scale position of 18. That is, one can assume that greater initial disagreement arouses greater initial anxiety; the listener whose initial opinion was 8 probably elicited more anxiety than the one whose initial opinion was 13. Each was moved 5 scale points by the subject's communication, but it was our judgment that the one who moved from 13 to 18 created more effectance feelings because he crossed the middle of the scale from disagreement to agreement. Of course, he may be reducing anxiety also—but recall, he probably aroused less anxiety to begin with. With this in mind, it is interesting to note that the subject who produced the greatest feelings of effectance (i.e., the one who moved from 13 to 18 in the High Involvement condition) received the highest overall rating. Performing separate contrasts,

Sigall found that the confederate in this cell was liked significantly better than in any other condition. Thus, effectance as well as anxiety would seem to be an important antecedent of this phenomenon.

We have done several experiments on one other possible antecedent: the attribution of discernment to an evaluator who changes his evaluations. Thus far, all of our results have been negative—indicating that discernment is not involved. Typical of this work is a recent study by Landy & Aronson (1968). Subjects were allowed to observe the behavior of their partner (actually a confederate) on some task which appeared irrelevant but from which they could (and did) gather evidence allowing them to rate their partner as either high or low on discernment. Subsequently the subject and the confederate engaged in a meaningful interaction. The confederate then evaluated the subject positively or negatively. If discernment is an important aspect of the gain-loss effect, one would expect an interaction: The discerning confederate should be liked best when he evaluated the subject positively and liked least when he evaluated the subject negatively—this would parallel the results of the Aronson-Linder experiment. Instead, there were two main effects and no significant interaction. High-discerning partners were liked better than low-discerning partners; positive evaluators were liked better than negative evaluators. This pattern of results has occurred frequently enough in our research to convince me that there is no interaction between discernment and positivity, and, hence, that the attribution of discernment does not play a role in the gain-loss effect. I am led to believe that this is a rare phenomenon in social psychology —a theorist actually believing disconfirming evidence.

Let me summarize where we are so far. We have shown that we like a person better who increases his liking for us over time than one who likes us at an invariantly high level. We have shown a tendency to dislike someone whose liking for us *decreases* over time more than one who has invariantly held us in low esteem. We have presented some evidence supporting the contention that these phenomena are in part caused by anxiety reduction (and induction) and in part caused by feelings of competence (or incompetence). We have also *failed* to show any evidence supporting the view that an evaluator who changes his esteem for us is viewed as a more discerning, more discriminating person and, hence, that we like or dislike him because his evaluations have more impact on us. We have not as yet tested a possible explanation due to contrast.

Space limitations do not allow for a complete cataloguing of all of the investigations of the roots of the gain-loss phenomenon. But since I have characterized the gain-loss notion as a "mini-theory," it seems reasonable to explore at least one of the limitations of the conceptualization.

David Mettee, in his Ph.D. dissertation (1968), has made an interesting contribution toward this end by exploring the nature (global versus specific) of the evaluations involved in the gain-loss sequence. Mettee found that a globally positive evaluation, followed by a specific negative evaluation, did not produce a loss effect; that is, a subject could accept a negative evaluation which was highly specific—once he was assured that he was liked in general—without lowering his esteem for the evaluator. At the same time, he found that a sequence which went from specific-positive to global-negative produced a rather dramatic decrease in the attractiveness of the evaluator.

### *A Note on the Dependent Variable*

Most of the time social psychologists working in this area display a touching and primitive faith in the mightiness of paper-and-pencil measures of attraction. I think that this is a serious example of myopia. Of course, I am as guilty (and as primitive, touching, and myopic) as the next guy on this score. Most of us get stuck on these measures because it's so easy to collect data that way. The problem is that it's also easy for the subject to fill out a rating scale—too easy. Since no commitment and no work is required, there is danger that a subject who is merely required to circle a number reflecting how much he likes another person either may not bother to take it very seriously, or may try to answer in a way that makes him look good to the experimenter. This may not be a serious methodological problem in many kinds of experiments, but in my opinion, there is particular reason for concern when we are dealing with experiments that are not well camouflaged from subjects. If subjects can figure out the purpose of the experiment, they will behave in a way so as to make themselves look good—or to please the experimenter (see Sigall, Aronson, & Van Hoose, 1969, for an empirical demonstration of this phenomenon).

I should note that we are not completely wedded to this technique. Occasionally situations arise which make it necessary, reasonable, or convenient for us to deviate from total fidelity to our easygoing bedmate, the paper-and-pencil test. The results of these ventures are often comforting; the data reflect trends which are identical to less imaginative measures of attraction. For example, in one experiment (Sigall & Aronson, 1967) a confederate evaluated subjects in either a totally positive manner or in a gain manner (i.e., beginning negative and becoming positive). The confederate then delivered a persuasive communication favoring the abolition of cigarette advertising. As expected, we found that the gain confederate was far more effective (induced greater opinion change) than the totally positive confederate. In much the same vein, Aronson & Cope (1968) used, as a measure of attraction, the number of phone calls subjects volunteered to make on behalf of a confederate. The results supported the predictions.

Occasionally the results of such measures are not parallel to ratings of liking and, thus, they teach us something new. For example, the experiment involving the beautiful woman versus the ugly woman mentioned earlier found that subjects frequently committed themselves to spend time with someone they said they didn't like. Specifically, subjects reported dislike for a beautiful girl who evaluated them negatively. However, they showed a great desire to return and be in another experiment with the same person. Our interpretation is that although we *do* dislike a beautiful woman who dislikes us to a greater extent than a homely woman who dislikes us, simultaneously we want to see the beautiful woman again because we have a great desire to change her impression of us, whereas we don't care that much about the impression we've made on an ugly woman.

## Gain-Loss Theory, Marital Infidelity, and the Maintenance of Friendships

Our theorizing and research leads us to postulate what some of my students have dubbed "Aronson's law of marital infidelity." Let me describe it for you: One of the implications of gain-loss theory is that, in the words of the well-known ballad, "you always hurt the one you love." That is, once we have grown certain of the good will (rewarding behavior) of a person (e.g., a mother, a spouse, a close friend), that person may become less potent as a source of reward than a stranger. Since we have demonstrated that a gain in esteem is a more potent reward than the absolute level of the esteem, then it follows that a close friend (by definition) is operating near ceiling level and, therefore, cannot provide us with a gain. To put it another way, since we have learned to expect love, favors, and praise from a friend, such behavior is not likely to represent a gain in his esteem for us. On the other hand, the constant friend and rewarder has great potential as a punisher. The closer the friend, the greater the past history of invariant esteem and reward, the more devastating is its withdrawal. Such withdrawal, by definition, constitutes a loss of esteem. In effect, then, he has power to hurt the one he loves—but very little power to reward him.

An example may help clarify this point. After ten years of marriage, a doting husband and his wife are leaving their house for a cocktail party. He compliments her on her appearance—"Gee, honey, you look great." Her response might well be a yawn. She already knows that her husband thinks she's attractive. On the other hand, if the doting husband (who in the past was always full of compliments) were to tell his wife that he had decided that she was actually quite ugly, this would cause a great deal of pain since it represents a distinct loss of esteem.

But what about the stranger? Mr. and Mrs. Doting arrive at the cocktail party and a total stranger engages Mrs. Doting in conversation. After a while he says, with great sincerity, that he finds her very attractive. My guess is that she would not find this boring. It represents a distinct gain, makes her feel good, and increases the attractiveness of the stranger.

This reasoning is consistent with previous experimental findings. Harvey (1962) found a tendency for subjects to react more positively to a stranger than to a friend when they were listed as sources of a relatively positive evaluation of the subject. Moreover, subjects tended to react more negatively to a friend than to a stranger when they were listed as sources of negative evaluations of the subject.

Similarly, experiments with children indicate that strangers are more effective as agents of social reinforcement than parents, and that strangers are also more effective than more familiar people (Shallenberger & Zigler, 1961; Stevenson & Knights, 1962; Stevenson, Keen, & Knights, 1963). It is reasonable to assume that children are accustomed to receiving approval from parents and familiar people. Therefore, additional approval from them does not represent much of a gain. However, approval from a stranger *is* a gain and, according to gain-loss theory, should result in a greater improvement in performance.

More recent data have also lent support to these speculations. In a rather complex experiment, Jones, Bell, & Aronson (1969) produced some evidence confirming their prediction that a stimulus person whose attitudes are dissimilar to the subject's but who indicates that he likes the subject would be liked better by the subject than one whose attitudes are similar and likewise indicates that he likes the subject. Our reasoning here was that individuals expect similar people to like them (much like the wife expects the doting husband to find her attractive). On the other hand, being liked by a dissimilar person—because it is not as expected—does represent a gain which is reflected in greater liking for the stimulus person.

The above speculations and data suggest a rather dismal picture of the human condition—forever seeking favor in the eyes of strangers and being hurt by familiar people. Before we leap to this conclusion, let us discuss the impact that gain or loss of esteem has on the behavior of individuals—quite aside from its effect on the perceived attractiveness of the evaluator. We have already mentioned (obliquely) one finding (Sigall & Aronson, 1969) to the effect that not only does being negatively evaluated by a beautiful girl make her the most disliked of the four possible stimulus people in this 2 × 2 design—but it also makes her among the most sought after. That is, subjects didn't like her, but they really wanted to see her again.

Let us look at this finding more closely. The theory leads us to suspect that a loss of esteem from a wife or a close friend *does* hurt and *does* induce people to lower their evaluation of the person who caused this loss. But the Sigall-Aronson data suggest that it also might possibly increase *approach* behavior. Would this occur in an ongoing relationship? Some rather direct evidence comes out of an experiment by one of my former students, Joanne Floyd. As part of her Ph.D. dissertation (1964), Floyd paired young children who were either close friends or strangers. She then allowed one of them to earn several trinkets and instructed him to share these with his partner. She manipulated the perceived stinginess of the sharer. Some subjects were led to believe that the friend (or stranger) was treating them generously, others were led to believe that the friend (or stranger) was treating them in a stingy manner. She then allowed the subject to earn several trinkets of his own and instructed him to share them with his partner. She found, as predicted, that subjects showed the most generosity in the gain and loss conditions—i.e., toward a generous stranger and a stingy friend. In short, they were relatively stingy to the stingy stranger (why not, the stranger had behaved as they might have expected) and to the generous friend ("Ho-hum, so my friend likes me—what else is new?"). But when it looked as if they might be gaining a friend (the generous stranger), they reacted with generosity—and likewise, when it looked as if they might be losing a friend (the stingy friend), they also responded with generosity.

Personally, I find this last datum a touching aspect of the human condition. While it appears to be true, as the lyric goes, that "you always hurt the one you love," the hurt person is inspired to react kindly rather than in kind in order to reestablish the intensity of the relationship. This suggests the comforting possibility that individuals have some motivation toward the maintainance of stability in a dyad.

In this vein, one of my students, Tom Chase, has come up with an interesting insight relating this aspect of gain-loss theory to some of the data linking birth order to social and intellectual achievement and eminence (Sampson, 1965). Specifically, when a sibling is born, the first-born child, who had been the sole focus of his parent's love, inevitably experiences a significant loss in attention received. It could be that this early and dramatic loss causes the first-born to strive to regain his parent's attention and approval. The findings that first-borns show high achievement motivation and academically out-perform their younger siblings might reflect an attempt to regain what was lost. Having once been first and then falling into second place, the displaced first-born tries harder. This conclusion is lent weight by the data which show that first-borns will volunteer more frequently than later-borns (Dittes & Capra, 1962). We are currently designing some experiments to test this implication.

If you were listening carefully, you will notice that I have finally gotten around to using the word *motivation* at this Symposium —not only have I used it, but I have used it twice! I now feel that I can end this talk with a clear conscience.

## REFERENCES


Aronson, E. The effect of effort on the attractiveness of rewarded and unrewarded stimuli. *J. abnorm. soc. Psychol.*, 1961, **63**, 375–380.

Aronson, E., & Cope, V. My enemy's enemy is my friend. *J. Pers. soc. Psychol.*, 1968, **8**, 8–12.

Aronson, E., & Linder, D. Gain and loss of esteem as determinants of interpersonal attractiveness. *J. exp. soc. Psychol.*, 1965, **1**, 156–171.

Aronson, E., & Mills, J. The effect of severity of initiation on liking for a group. *J. abnorm. soc. Psychol.*, 1959, **59**, 177–181.

Aronson, E., Willerman, B., & Floyd, Joanne. The effect of a pratfall on increasing interpersonal attractiveness. *Psychonom. Sci.*, 1966, **4**, 227–228.

Backman, C. W., & Secord, P. F. The effect of perceived liking on interpersonal attraction. *Human Relations*, 1959, **12**, 379–384.

Bales, R. F. The equilibrium problem in small groups. In T. Parsons, R. F. Bales, & E. A. Shils, *Working papers in the theory of action*. Glencoe, Ill.: Free Press, 1953. Pp. 111–161.

Bales, R. F. How people interact in conferences. *Scientific American*, 1955, **192**, 31–35.

Bales, R. F. Task roles and social roles in problem solving groups. In Eleanor E. Maccoby, T. M. Newcomb, & E. L. Hartley (Eds.), *Readings in social psychology*. 3d Ed. New York: Holt, 1958. Pp. 437–447.

Bales, R. F., & Slater, P. E. Role differentiation in small decision-making groups. In T. Parsons, R. F. Bales, *et al.*, *The family, socialization, and interaction process*. New York: Free Press, 1955. Pp. 259–306.

Bonney, M. E. Relationships between social success, family size, socioeconomic home background, and intelligence among school children in grades III to V. *Sociometry*, 1944, **7**, 26–39.

Byrne, D. Attitudes and attraction. In L. Berkowitz (Ed.), *Advances in experimental social psychology*. Vol. 4. New York: Academic Press, 1969. (In press.)

Byrne, D., & Rhamey, R. Magnitude of positive and negative reinforcements as a determinant of attraction. *J. Pers. soc. Psychol.*, 1965, **2**, 884–889.

Dittes, J. E., & Capra, P. C. Affiliation: comparability or compatibility? *Am. Psychol.*, 1962, **17**, 329.

Festinger, L., Schachter, S., & Back, K. *Social pressures in informal groups: A study of human factors in housing*. New York: Harper, 1950.

Floyd, Joanne M. K. Effects of amount of reward and friendship status of the other on the frequency of sharing in children. Unpublished Ph.D. dissertation, Univ. of Minnesota, 1964.

Gerard, H. B., & Mathewson, G. C. The effects of severity of initiation on liking for a group: a replication. *J. exp. soc. Psychol.*, 1966, **2**, 278–287.

Gullahorn, J. T. Distance and friendship as factors in the gross interaction matrix. *Sociometry*, 1952, **15**, 123–134.

Harvey, O. J. Personality factors in resolution of conceptual incongruities. *Sociometry*, 1962, **25**, 336–352.

Hollander, E. P., & Webb, W. B. Leadership, followership, and friendship: an analysis of peer nominations. *J. abnorm. soc. Psychol.*, 1955, **50**, 163–167.

Homans, G. *Social behavior: its elementary forms*. New York: Harcourt, Brace & World, 1961.

Iverson, M. A. Personality impressions of punitive stimulus persons of differential status. *J. abnorm. soc. Psychol.*, 1964, **68**, 617–626.

Jackson, J. M. Reference group processes in a formal organization. *Sociometry*, 1959, **22**, 307–327.

Jones, E. E., Bell, Linda, & Aronson, E. The reciprocation of attraction from similar and dissimilar others: a study in person perception and evaluation. To appear in C. C. McClintock (Ed.), *Experimental social psychology* (tentative title). 1969. (In preparation.)

Kendall, Patricia. Medical education as social process. Abstract, American Sociological Association, 1960.

Landy, D., & Aronson, E. Liking for an evaluator as a function of his discernment. *J. pers. soc. Psychol.*, 1968, **9**, 133–141.

Lemann, T. B., & Solomon, R. L. Group characteristics as revealed in sociometric patterns and personality ratings. *Sociometry*, 1952, **15**, 7–90.

Mettee, D. R. Attraction for an evaluator as a function of the importance and sequence of positive and negative evaluations. Unpublished Ph.D. dissertation, Univ. of Texas, 1968.

Mills, J., & Aronson, E. Opinion change as a function of the communicator's attractiveness and desire to influence. *J. Pers. soc. Psychol.*, 1965, **1**, 173–177.

Newcomb, T. M. *The acquaintance process*. New York: Holt, Rinehart, & Winston, 1961.

Precker, J. A. Similarity of valuings as a factor in selection of peers and near-authority figures. *J. abnorm. soc. Psychol.*, 1952, **47**, 406–414.

Richardson, Helen M. Community of values as a factor in friendships of college and adult women. *J. soc. Psychol.*, 1940, **11**, 302–312.

Sampson, E. E. The study of ordinal position: antecedents and outcomes. In B. A. Maher (Ed.), *Progress in experimental personality research*. Vol. 2. New York: Academic Press, 1965. Pp. 175–228.

Schachter, S. Deviation, rejection and communication. *J. abnorm. soc. Psychol.*, 1951, **46**, 190–207.

Secord, P. F., & Backman, C. W. Interpersonal congruency, perceived similarity, and friendship. *Sociometry*, 1964, **27**, 115–127.

Shallenberger, Patricia, & Zigler, E. Rigidity, negative reaction tendencies and cosatiation affects in normal and feebleminded children. *J. abnorm. soc. Psychol.*, 1961, **63**, 20–26.

Shapiro, D. Psychological factors in friendship, choice, and rejection. Unpublished Ph.D. dissertation, Univ. of Michigan, 1953.

Sigall, H. The effects of competence and consensual validation on a communicator's liking for the audience. Unpublished Ph.D. dissertation, Univ. of Texas, 1968.

Sigall, H., & Aronson, E. Opinion change and the gain-loss model of interpersonal attraction. *J. exp. soc. Psychol.*, 1967, **3**, 178–188

Sigall, H., & Aronson, E. Liking for an evaluator as a function of her physical attractiveness and nature of the evaluations. *J. exp. soc. Psychol.*, 1969, **5**, 93–100.

Sigall, H., Aronson, E., & Van Hoose, T. The cooperative subject: myth or reality? *J. exp. soc. Psychol.*, 1969.

Sigall, H., Page, R., & Brown, Ann Carol. The effects of physical attractiveness and evaluation on effort expenditure and work output. 1969. (In preparation.)

Spinoza, B. *The Ethics.* Dover Press.

Stapert, J. C., & Clore, G. L. Attraction and disagreement-produced arousal. *J. Pers. soc. Psychol.*, 1969, **13**, 64–69.

Stevenson, H. W., Keen, Rachel, & Knights, R. M. Parents and strangers as reinforcing agents for children's performance. *J. abnorm. soc. Psychol.*, 1963, **67**, 183–185.

Stevenson, H. W., & Knights, R. M. Social reinforcement with normal and retarded children as a function of pretraining, sex of *E*, and sex of *S*. *Am. J. Mental Deficiency*, 1962, **66**, 866–871.

Stotland, E., & Hillmer, M. L., Jr. Identification, authoritarian defensiveness, and self-esteem. *J. abnorm. soc. Psychol.*, 1962, **64**, 334–342.

Thibaut, J., & Kelley, H. H. *The social psychology of groups.* New York: Wiley, 1959.

Walters, R. H., & Ray, E. Anxiety, social isolation, and reinforcer effectiveness. *J. Pers.*, 1960, **28**, 258–267.

White, R. W. Motivation reconsidered: the concept of competence. *Psychol. Rev.*, 1959, **66**, 297–334.

Winch, R. F. *Mate-selection: a study of complementary needs.* New York: Harper & Row, 1958.

Worchel, P., & Schuster, S. D. Attraction as a function of the drive state. *J. exp. Res. Pers.*, 1966, **1**, 277–281.

## COMMENTS

*Philip G. Zimbardo*

Elliot has done it again! He has turned the banality of interpersonal attraction ("people like people who like them or are like them, etc.") into a theoretically exciting venture with his mini-theory and his ingenious experimental paradigms. From two simple propositions he generates a host of intriguing, testable hypotheses about the determinants of perceptual, affective, and behavioral relationships between people. He forces us to reconsider the narrow conceptual focus in which we have traditionally viewed reinforcement. He demonstrates why future applications of any version of reinforcement theory to meaningful human behavior must be sensitive to the context of the reinforcement, to the agent of reinforcement, to expectancies, to the operation of past reinforcers, and to anticipated future consequences. The results of his systematic program of research also occasion a reevaluation of many of our tried and true homilies, as well as some "bubba" psychology. Does distance make the heart grow fonder, or is out of sight, out of mind? Is love at first sight lasting love, or do you always hurt the one you love? What do nice guys win when they lose ball games? Why should we tell our children never to attain perfection in all things?

There is yet another way in which this research is significant; it reflects a basic change evolving in our society, a change which has caught most psychologists unprepared. For decades psychology has been preoccupied with the consequences of negative motivational states induced by deprivation or noxious stimuli. But now in our everyday life and in the world around us we are becoming overwhelmed by conflict, aggression, anxiety, and all kinds of hostility and interpersonal ugliness. Touch. Trust. Tenderness. This is what the young people want and what they are seeking through drugs, sensitivity training, T-groups, "Free University" courses, and communal living. It is not surprising then, that Elliot Aronson is at the frontier of this social movement, being personally involved in leading such groups and theoretically involved in abstracting the relevant variables which may help us understand the dynamics of interpersonal attraction.

Among the many questions, speculations, and ideas for future research which this paper generates, only a portion will be outlined here:

1) If subjects in the initially disliked condition worked harder to get the evaluator to like them, then there is a confounding of effort and their "superstitious" interpretation of the relationship between this response and subsequent evaluation (which is actually not contingent on this effort). Thus in the always low evaluation condition, the expenditure of effort doesn't change the evaluation, but in the low-switched-to-high condition, the subject's attempts to get the evaluator to like him more are apparently reinforced. This effect could account for some of the obtained differences, and the experimental procedure should be modified to minimize this source of systematic variance.

2) The experimental technique of having the subject believe he is eavesdropping on the other person's conversation with the experimenter may create a second (theoretically undesirable) source of motivation in addition to the evaluation anxiety which exists over all conditions. When overhearing the other person reveal his personal *dislike* toward the subject, voyeuristic guilt may be induced in the subject because he must assume he is violating the privacy of the other. However, when that person is saying nice things about the subject, then it is more likely he would say the same things to him directly, or that he would not be upset to learn that he had been intentionally overheard. If this is true, then when the evaluation switches from negative to positive there is a reduction in both sources of motivation, guilt as well as evaluation anxiety, resulting in a marked increase in liking for the person whose behavior is so drive-reducing.

3) If a negative evaluation hurts in proportion to how much the subject has been positively attracted to the evaluator previously, then a good dependent measure of interpersonal attraction should be how much one is hurt by the first negative evaluation.

4) Why should a person who dislikes you but is discerning be so highly liked as these data indicate? It must be that there is an expectation that if the evaluator is discerning, he will come around to discover your positive features in future interactions. However, this should hold only for people whose self-esteem is high, since they

think well of themselves and believe others will too if given adequate evaluation time, and if they are discerning. But for low self-esteem subjects, a discerning-disapproving evaluator already knows what there is to know about them. Thus the prediction would be that high self-esteem subjects will like the Discerning-Dislike evaluator more than will the low self-esteem subjects, and the effect will be reversed for the Discerning-Like evaluator. On the other hand, if our dependent measure is the desire for more social contact and not merely liking, then this line of reasoning yields a lovely non-obvious prediction. The low self-esteem person will want to avoid the Discerning-Like evaluator because future contact will only undo this initial impression, which can't last since such a subject "knows" that he doesn't deserve to be really liked and thought well of.

5) Aronson's law of marital infidelity has two aspects worth serious consideration. First, consistently positive evaluation of one spouse by another leads to a lukewarm marriage because there is adaptation to the evaluation and no obvious improvement in evaluation, which leads to the perception of the other as undiscerning. Therefore, marriage counselors ought to recommend programmed dips in evaluation followed immediately by strong positive evaluations. The second part of this law of marital infidelity is that friends, relatives, and spouses become less effective reinforcement dispensers over time than are strangers. However, friends et al. come to serve a different interpersonal function; they become a source of constant social support, a maintenance of the individual's ties with others in the absence of evaluation anxiety. They may not be able to provide the same excitement, fascination, and flattery as strangers who have the capacity to make the individual feel unique, special, and individuated, but with one's close acquaintances, the individual feels comfortable, can relax, can see his values, aspirations, and flaws reflected in his similarity with them and can enjoy feeling undifferentiated. Every person wants the latter most of the time, but requires the former some of the time.

Relevant to this discussion is a recent experiment Norman Miller and I conducted to test Schachter's generalization that misery loves miserable company. High school students made to be fearful were given a choice to await the feared experience either alone or (depending on the condition) with a person of similar personality but in a dissimilar emotional state, or one in the same state but with a different personality. What do these alternatives offer the fearful person? Someone who is usually similar to you but hasn't experienced this emotional condition provides a baseline control for how much you have been changed or been affected by the experience. The degree to which someone who is usually dissimilar to you reacts emotionally in a manner similar to yours reveals the potency and generality of the arousal, and may provide guidelines for future action. Almost all subjects chose affiliation, the majority preferring the same personality other over the same-state other person.

The reader will undoubtedly find much more that is provocative in this paper, such as the consequences of repeatedly inconsistent or variable evaluations, especially for children.

It should be clear from these comments that my attempt to show that Elliot Aronson is less than perfect is designed to enable the reader to learn to like and appreciate him as I have.

# Motives in a Conceptual Analysis of Attitude-Related Behavior

STUART W. COOK

*University of Colorado*

I want to discuss with you a conceptual analysis I have been developing for the study of behavior toward members of disliked groups and indicate my present understanding of the place of motives in this analysis. By behavior toward disliked groups I shall mean what is ordinarily meant by such terms as *prejudiced behavior*, *discrimination*, *segregation*, *outgroup hostility*, *intergroup relations*, and so on. This is the attitude-related behavior to which my title refers. Persons interested in this type of social behavior will usually characterize their work as concerned with attitude and attitude change. I am no exception. Like others, I often employ the term *attitude theory* to describe my work and might well have used it in my title. However, attitude, like motive, is a construct inferred from behavior, and in this presentation I should like to explore the advantages of looking at both constructs in the context of a broader behavioral analysis.

Before describing the research I have in mind and the framework for studying it, let me comment briefly on the question of theoretical strategy in social psychology. Most social psychological theories, as you know, focus on single explanatory processes. Such theories feature a key hypothetical explanatory concept and utilize this concept in the explanation of any instance of social behavior to which it appears relevant. You will recognize these examples: social comparison theory, social evaluation theory, adaptation level theory, comparison level theory, reference group theory, and, most prominent of all, cognitive dissonance theory. Let me refer to these as process theories. Taken together they represent one of two distinct theoretical strategies—and, to date, certainly the more successful one.

The second strategy focuses not on a key explanatory concept or process but on a recurring pattern of events. A familiar example of it in social psychology is persuasive communication. This pattern of events is usually described like this: A source emits a message; the message is transmitted through some communication channel to a recipient; the recipient, who may or may not be in the presence of others, reacts in some way to the message. In everyday life, this pattern recurs repeatedly, with many variations in the source, in the message, in the channel medium, in the personal attributes of the recipient, in the social environment of the recipient, and in the recipient's reactions.

The social psychologist trying to build a theory for such a pattern of events has no expectation that he will find a single explanatory process to be sufficient. To the contrary, he formulates multiple working hypotheses about processes, anticipating that some aspects of the event pattern will be explained in one way and some in another. Let me refer to these theories as event theories.

Needless to say, the two theoretical strategies—or, if you prefer, research styles—have the same ultimate objectives and should be regarded as complementary. My point in noting the distinction is to indicate that what I shall present falls clearly in the event theory category. The recurring pattern of events with which I am concerned is that which centers around unintended contact or personal experience with members of a disliked group and the reaction to this experience. In everyday life racial desegregation is an example of this pattern of events. If we draw a parallel to the events in persuasive communication we might say that the contact experience is parallel to the message and the member of the disliked group is parallel to the message source. The subject individual having the contact experience is parallel to the message recipient. Like the message recipient, his reaction to the message may be influenced by the presence of others. Since face-to-face contact is a constant in this event pattern, there is no parallel here to variation in the communication channel.

Since the task of event theory is to account for the various aspects of the event pattern, it is clear that we need a conceptual analysis of the pattern. That is, we need an interrelated set of concepts or variables which, taken together, describe the components of the phenomenon with which we are dealing. Accompanying this set of descriptive concepts or variables are hypotheses about relationships among them. As time goes on, the availability of verified hypotheses will suggest concepts about mediating processes. The latter, of course, are parallel to the theories of the process theory strategy. In event theory terminology, however, they combine with the descriptive variables and relationships among variables to constitute the theory of the event pattern.

The event theory approach has one major disadvantage. It makes limited use of its explanatory concepts. No premium is placed on exploring the generalizability of such ideas across many phenomena. On the other hand, it has a potential advantage of some importance. If the event pattern has been abstracted from significant natural events, then the utility of the theory for the understanding and control of these events should be high. Those of us who work with unintended contact and behavior toward members of disliked groups hope, as you might imagine, that such theory as we produce will prove applicable to the problems of racial desegregation.

## Background of Research

In the 1930s and 1940s a number of social scientists had begun to raise the question of the effect of personal association upon racial and religious attitudes. In several questionnaire studies investigators asked their respondents first to describe their own beliefs and feelings about a social group and then to report the nature and frequency of associations they had had with members of the group in question. Out of these studies came the suggestion that frequency of contact in itself was of little consequence. Favorable attitudes seemed to be associated rather with the nature of the contact, described usually in terms of equality of status or of a somewhat vaguer attribute of intimacy. During the same period several experimenters undertook to bring whites and Negroes together for short periods. They utilized for the purpose visiting lecturers in classrooms, meetings with Negro professionals, or joint recreational activities. For the most part, favorable outcomes were reported, although there were exceptions. This work, while suggestive, was, of course, open to various interpretations having to do with selective recall of experience congenial to current attitudes, self-selection for interracial activities on the part of the already favorable subjects, and so on.

In his 1946 presidential address to the Society for the Psychological Study of Social Issues, Theodore Newcomb suggested what he thought to be the most likely avenue to the reduction of intergroup hostility (Newcomb, 1947). He described it as the crossing of institutionalized barriers to communication with members of the other group, with the shared support of members of one's own group —or, to put it another way, association with outgroup members of status, education, etc., similar to one's own with the approval of significant persons from one's own group.

Following Newcomb's address, two influential reviews of intergroup relations appeared: one by Goodwin Watson, called *Action for Unity* (1947), and another by Robin Williams, called *The Reduction of Intergroup Tensions* (1947). Both reported that many practitioners in the field of intergroup relations believed that contact or personal association with the object of one's prejudice was likely to be more effective in changing behavior and attitudes than were such alternative experiences as exposure to correct information, persuasive communication, etc. But both also pointed out that neither everyday experience nor research uniformly supported this view, and raised questions stressing the need to consider the effects of different conditions of contact.

As the evidence accumulated on such matters as selective rejection of favorable communications regarding disliked groups, the boomerang effects of cartoons opposed to prejudice, and the self-selection involved in exposure of the already favorable to intergroup educational programs, I concluded, along with a number of colleagues, that personal contact might well prove to be a more potent influence than other experiences. Accordingly, we decided to focus our work, where possible, on the contact experience. We recognized that we should exclude the type of contact that had been sought out by the participant, since in such a case the effect of the experience on the individual's actions could not be separated from the effect of the favorable attitudes he had brought to the situation. For this reason we limited ourselves to contact which had *not* been intended by the participant and was, in this sense, involuntary.

We decided to look into interracial public housing as a possible setting for our research. Federally assisted public housing projects for low-income families were being constructed throughout the country. Some of them had both white and Negro tenants. The extensive demand for housing made it seem likely that in the case of such biracial projects we had an excellent instance of unintended contact. Some preliminary investigation supported this view; professional personnel in the housing field assured us that it was rare, if ever, that a tenant admitted to a project turned down his opportunity for any reason, including the knowledge of its interracial character.

We learned, however, that interracial housing projects did not all come in the same mold; among other things, they varied in what housing professionals called occupancy pattern. The Negroes might occupy one section of the projects with the whites in another, an arrangement which we later came to call *area segregation.* Or the Negroes might occupy one apartment building with the adjacent one being occupied by whites and the next one in line being occupied by Negroes, that is, a pattern of *building segregation* or, in housing slang, the checkerboard pattern. Finally, there could be found instances of complete integration with white and Negro tenants occupying adjacent apartments.

We decided to begin our work by comparing the two extremes, namely, area segregation and complete integration (Deutsch & Collins, 1951). Fortunately, we found what we needed—two area-segregated projects and two roughly comparable integrated projects—and emerged with clear-cut and striking findings. We found, as anticipated, that more neighborly or intimate contacts had, in fact, developed in the integrated projects than in the area-segregated ones. Also, white housewives in these projects reported with much greater frequency that they believed other white tenants approved of friendly relations with Negro tenants. And, when we examined the beliefs and feelings of the white housewives, we found that many more of the integrated project respondents than of the area-segregated ones showed favorable attitudes toward Negroes. An extensive study of the possibility that these differences might have existed prior to the public housing experience convinced us that this was highly unlikely. It would take too long to present this evidence to you today.

As we reflected on the differences between the two occupancy patterns, we realized that they involved at least two components. The first, and more obvious, was the fact that the integrated occupancy pattern led to Negro and white tenants living closer to each other than did the area-segregated—this was a proximity component. The second was that the two patterns might be interpreted by the tenants to symbolize different attitudes on the part of persons in authority as to what was proper and appropriate in race relations; the integrated might indicate approval of mixing, the area-segregated, disapproval—this was a social norm component. However, it was not possible to examine separately the effects of the two components because in the housing projects in this study they went completely together.

Such an examination did become feasible in a second housing study some time later (Wilner, Walkley, & Cook, 1955). In this second study, the segregated projects were building-segregated, i.e., checkerboard, rather than area-segregated, and only about 10 percent of the tenants in any of the projects were Negroes. Because of the relatively small proportion of Negro tenants it worked out that there were white tenants in the completely integrated projects who lived a great distance from any Negro family, and some who lived in apartments on the same floor of the same building. Similarly, in the building-segregated projects some white tenants lived in a building adjacent to one housing Negroes, while others lived in buildings some distance away. Given this range on the proximity variable within each of the two types of occupancy patterns, we were able to compare tenants within each type who differed in proximity but for whom the social norm implied by occupancy pattern was constant. The results supported the interpretation that proximity, taken alone, constituted an important *condition* for the development of friendly intergroup contact.

In this second study we were able to take still another step. As in the first study, we had collected evidence not only on the degree of intimacy of contacts, but also on the perception of approval or disapproval of interracial associations anticipated from other tenants. While these two variables were associated with one another, there was enough unrelated variation so that we could examine the relationship of each to favorableness of attitudes. While the picture was complex, there seemed little doubt that each variable was related to attitude change.

Meanwhile we had been involved in other studies of personal contact and had learned of still others. Some were raising questions about the effects of such contact. Others had introduced new qualifications limiting its potential significance. While I do not have time to review these in any detail, let me mention two studies of interracial housing which present a somewhat different picture than the one I have given to date.

Kramer (1951) conducted a study of white residents of five small contiguous residential areas in Chicago. In one area (Zone 1), Negro and white dwelling units were found in the same block. The Negroes had moved into this block relatively recently. The remaining four areas contained no Negro residents, and varied in distance from the Negro-white zone. Zone 2 (a strip three blocks wide) lay directly south of Zone 1; Zone 3 (also three blocks wide) was directly south of Zone 2, etc. On an attitude scale constructed for the study Kramer found the least prejudice in Zones 1 and 5—the zones where white residents lived *nearest to* and *farthest from* Negroes—and the most prejudice in the zones of intermediate proximity. He felt that a possible interpretation might be that those in the zone farthest from Negroes represented an "average" degree of prejudice—that is, the attitude of the typical Chicago resident not faced with the prospect of having Negro neighbors. According to this interpretation residents of the three intermediate zones may be thought of as having undergone an increase in prejudice as a consequence of feeling "threatened" by the impending closeness of Negroes. The actual experience of living in the same block as neighbors evidently reduced the anticipation fears and brought the attitudes of the white residents of Zone 1 back to—but not below—the "average" degree of prejudice shown in Zone 5.

With regard to salience of the racial issue, however, Kramer found a different pattern. There was a consistent linear relationship between proximity to Negroes and the likelihood of prejudiced statements being made spontaneously, those living close to Negroes being the *most* inclined to voice such statements. Data on education, age, religious background, and home ownership showed no significant differences between the zones which would suggest differences in initial attitudinal predispositions.

Winder conducted a similarly designed study (1952). He too chose neighborhoods in Chicago which were in varying degrees of proximity to an area into which Negroes had recently moved. Like Kramer, he reported, for the sample as a whole, least prejudice on the part of those *closest to* and *farthest from* the interracial area. Breaking down his sample in terms of socioeconomic groupings, however, he found that it was only in the middle-income group that residents in the area closest to Negroes showed less prejudice than those in the intermediate zones. The low-income whites in the area closest to Negroes were even more hostile than those in the intermediate zones. Winder concluded on the basis of interview responses that the hostility of the low-income white residents was based on competition for dwelling units in the midst of a severe housing shortage. These white residents felt—evidently on the basis of objective evidence—that owners of multiple dwellings were eager to force them out because higher rents could be demanded from Negroes (who were, of course, suffering even more severely from the housing shortage).

Without going into further detail I think you will see that we face the problem of abstracting conclusions from studies with superficially conflicting results. I emerged from such an effort with the conviction that I could identify five characteristics of unintended interracial contact which favored friendly social behavior and favorable attitude change. The *first* of these was that the setting or situation in which the contact occurred defined as equal the status of the participants from the two racial groups. This would be illustrated by the tenant status of the white and Negro residents in interracial public housing projects or by equivalent sales clerk status in a department store. The *second* was that the contact situation called for or encouraged a mutually interdependent relationship—

cooperation in the usual sense. The *third* was that the contact took place in a social climate in which the social norms of the immediate situation favored interracial association and equalitarian attitudes. The *fourth* was that the attributes of the Negroes with whom the contact occurred contradicted the prevailing stereotyped beliefs about them. *Fifth*, the setting was such as to promote personal or intimate association, that is, association of a sort which revealed enough detail about the Negro participant to encourage seeing him as an individual rather than only as a Negro.

While the ability to enumerate these aspects of unintended contact with some feeling of confidence about their significance represented a forward step, it nevertheless leaves us in a very unsatisfactory situation. While I think it would be possible to learn much more than we now know from controlled field studies of the type represented by the interracial housing studies, there are real problems involved. A major one is that it is very difficult to find instances of unintended interracial contact characterized by positive values of only one of the five key attributes. For example, situations involving mutual interdependence of Negro and white participants almost inherently favor the development of intimate personal contact. Hence the chances of evaluating the effect upon attitude change of any one of these components of the contact situation or even pairs of them is slight if not nonexistent. Yet, it is only with such knowledge that we can add to a theory of attitude-related behavior and attitude change and provide more precise guidance to social programs in this area.

## A Laboratory Study of Unintended Interracial Contact

For these reasons I decided to try to take the research into the laboratory. If this could be done, it would have two possible advantages. The first is that it would make it possible to put to test the adequacy of any given overall analysis of the results of the field studies. In other words, if one could put together a laboratory experience explicitly compounded of the hypothesized characteristics of change-producing situations, he could then make a rough check on his analysis by determining whether this constructed situation produced the expected attitude change. The second, and admittedly more problematical, advantage is that it might permit the independent manipulation of the separate components of the situation. If so, it would then be possible to have four of the components at a neutral or negative value with only one at the positive value presumed to lead to behavioral and attitudinal change.

I decided to use as a cover story for the experiment the setting of a part-time job for which the subject is employed.[1] On this job he works for two hours a day for twenty days in an interracial group. For reasons which will become clear, this is preceded by two periods of work where no Negroes are present. The subject never learns that he has been part of an experiment. To him the experience will remain a part-time job. Let me describe the experience first in chronological sequence as the subject experiences it. After this I will indicate the manner in which its five components are brought into play.

Subjects being used are students from several different colleges in Borderville, a city in the border South. They are recruited by way of their responses to a posted handbill or a newspaper advertisement offering part-time work "taking paper-and-pencil tests of attitudes and abilities for the Educational Testing Institute." Instructions in the advertisement lead them to a room in a building at Biltmore University where the Educational Testing Institute is conducting its local Borderville operations.

Here, over a ten-day period in four to six sessions of two to three hours each, potential subjects are tested for a total of twelve hours. Approximately four hours go to ability measures, four to measures of personality and needs, two to miscellaneous social and political attitudes, and two to attitudes toward Negroes. The latter are scattered throughout the test battery. The potential subjects take the tests in groups of ten to twenty. They are told in nontechnical terms about the problem of test-retest reliability and learn that, because of this problem, they will have an opportunity some weeks later to work for another twelve hours. This prepares them for the post-experimental measurement which I will tell you about later.

From this pool, a subject is selected in terms of two principle criteria: first, a strong anti-Negro attitude as reflected consistently

1. I carried out this study in collaboration with Shirley and Lawrence S. Wrightsman.

by three measuring instruments, and, second, availability for part-time work two hours daily for four weeks.

Some weeks after the testing comes to an end the subject selected receives a telephone call from a faculty member at St. George College in another part of town. The latter invites the student to apply for part-time work on a "group project" and describes briefly a simulated management task. This task, it is explained, is being tried out for a government agency as one of several being evaluated for the purpose of selecting and training small units which must work together under conditions of isolation such as exist at early-warning radar outposts.

There follow two days in which the subject is interviewed; tested, presumably for "suitability" for the job; receives some training in the management game; and is signed to a contract to work two hours a day for a month. It is important to note that payment of all salary is made dependent upon completion of the full month of work.

Before describing the events of the next twenty days, it will help if I give you a brief description of the management game. The task is to operate an imaginary railroad system composed of ten stations, six lines, and 500 freight cars of six different types. Successful operation involves learning how to maintain an appropriate distribution of these cars so that they are available when shipping orders are placed with the railroad. When the team receives requests to ship merchandise of specified types from one station to another, it makes decisions regarding the route to follow and the types of cars to use. These decisions are telephoned to the supervisor and his assistant working in another room. The latter maintain the fictional "computer" which furnishes the team the official records of dispersion of cars, profits earned, losses and penalties incurred, etc.

The three tasks to be done by the members of the team are: First, to decide which orders are to be filled, the kinds of cars to be used, and the route to be taken. Second, to keep track of the present and future availability of cars. This may involve initiating the redistribution of empty cars. This task requires close collaboration with the person doing the first task and may call for making joint decisions. Third, to keep account of earnings and costs. This task is carried out alone but on the basis of information supplied by the person sending orders.

The management task, as we use it, lasts for 40 periods. A period covers 20–30 minutes. Two such periods separated by a 30-minute break make up an experimental session. The break is explained to the subject as giving the supervisor and his assistant time to prepare materials for the second period.

On the second calendar day, as noted earlier, the subject receives preliminary training for one of the three jobs, namely, that of keeping track of the cars. On the third day he gathers for the first time with the other members of the management team—all strangers to him. One is white like himself. The other is Negro. Both are introduced as students from nearby colleges—which is true—and act as though they are as new to the situation as the subject. In fact, both are confederates—but not in the historical sense of the term.

The supervisor briefly reviews the task and mentions the team's opportunity to make additional "bonus" money by excelling the performance of prior teams. After answering questions (some asked purposely by the confederates) he presents the first day's shipping requests and retires to another room. Communication from the team, thereafter, is by telephone.

After 20 minutes the supervisor enters and the team decides whether it wishes to use (at a penalty) up to 10 minutes overtime. Next comes the 30-minute break. Food ordered at the beginning of the session is brought in by the supervisor, who then, together with his assistant, leaves the room. The team distributes its food and converses while eating. As I shall explain in a moment, this conversation is quite important to the experiment. Midway through the break, the Negro assistant to the supervisor, also a college student and an experimental confederate, returns from his "duties" to join the lunch and the conversation.

Later the supervisor enters, hands the team its second set of shipping requests and, together with his assistant, again retires from the room. At the end of each period the supervisor compares and reconciles accounts with the team's accountant and announces the official profit or loss. This supposedly concludes the group activity until the next session. However, each team member is required to perform individually a reading comprehension and delayed-recall memory task on 20 occasions. The explanation given is that this is necessary as part of the background information needed to interpret the team's performance on the management game. If the students' schedules permit, this individual task must be done immediately following the management game sessions. The schedule of the subject is known to permit this; the white confederate is selected so that his schedule also makes it possible. We arrange, however, that the Negro confederate report himself as having another obligation at this time. He indicates this in the subject's presence and arranges another time of day for his participation. This frees him to leave. The Negro assistant to the supervisor completes his duties and also leaves at this point.

The supervisor now brings into the room an article for the subject to read, and a different one for the white confederate. A reading time of five minutes is allowed. The articles are then removed. Ten minutes must elapse before questions on the articles may be answered. The white confederate and the subject spend this time in conversation. The nature of these conversations, which are guided by the confederate, will be explained later.

At intervals of three to four calendar days the team learns how its profits compare with those of an earlier team whom it must surpass to earn a bonus. While its fortunes vary from report to report, it is prearranged that the team finally wins out and earns the hoped-for extra money.

For the first 19 days of the team activity the overall procedure remains constant. Variation takes place only in the nature of the 30-minute food-break conversation, in the nature of the 10-minute conversation between the subject and the white confederate, and in the task assignments. I will tell you about the nature and purpose of this variation in a moment.

On the final day, the last half hour is devoted to a questionnaire filled out by each member of the team in a separate room. This is explained as a part of the procedure of evaluating the management task as a potential training task. Included are several open-end questions about the other team members; the questions do not mention race in any way. The answers to these questions give the subject an opportunity to give his reactions to the confederates; he may or may not mention race. These comments are *not* used as part of the evidence for attitude change. They serve only to indicate the degree of respect and liking the subject has developed for the particular Negro confederate. Characteristically, this turns out to be quite strong.

During the week following the final session, the subject is provided with an additional experience, which represents an attempt to encourage generalization from responses to the Negro confederates to responses to Negroes in general, and to desegregation policy beyond the job setting which the subject has experienced. The additional experience is made up of detailed interviews of two Negro college students. The subject is told that there are five candidates for the next tryout of the management game. It seems possible, he is told, that persons who have done well in the task could select others who might do well. As a test of this he is to interview each candidate and judge him on a number of attributes appropriate to success in the management game. He is given a partially structured interview guide to follow. Two of the five individuals interviewed are Negro.

Between one and three months after the part-time job at St. George College has come to an end, the subject receives a letter from the Educational Testing Institute. The letter reminds him of what he had been told during the initial testing period, namely, that there would be an opportunity later to serve as a paid subject for additional tests. It gives the time and place at Biltmore University where the Institute will administer its new test series. The subject retakes most of the original tests, including those measuring attitudes. A number of new tests are also introduced to add reality to the test development cover story.

Now let me indicate how I think these operations bring into play the five components around which the situation was constructed. The *first* is relative status within the situation. The Negro confederate is defined by the situation as being an equal member of the team. Status here is limited to its specific situational meaning. The broader community status of Negroes and whites in Borderville is quite disparate.

Built into the procedure is a rotation of team assignments, explained in terms of preparation for possible "sickness" among the crews of small isolated units. This further enhances the situational equality of the subject and the Negro confederate.

The *second* component is the nature of the interdependence

requirements of the situation. The requirements of the management game are such as to involve the subject in efforts to achieve a goal in common with the Negro participant. This leads to close interaction and mutual assistance, especially when the two are paired in the two assignments requiring collaboration. They share reverses as well as successes day by day for 20 days. Rotation of team assignments puts the subject in the position both of teaching the Negro confederate and being taught by him.

The *third* component is the extent of the Negro confederate's dissimilarity to commonly held stereotypes about Negroes in general. The Negro confederate is selected and presented throughout as being personable, able, ambitious, and self-respecting.

The *fourth* component is the extent of personal, intimate information about the Negro participant brought out in the interaction. This is introduced through the conversation of the confederates. The two Negro confederates bring into each food-break conversation facts about themselves, their histories, their future plans and aspirations, their families, etc., and such personal feelings as preferences, tastes, apprehensions, dislikes, disappointments, etc. Sometimes these are volunteered; sometimes they are evoked by planned questions from the white confederate. A frequency count is kept for each confederate of the personal information brought out in each of ten categories. This serves as a basis for controlling the personal information variable and roughly equating it from subject to subject.

The *final* component is the direction and strength of the situational norms toward interracial association and attitude. In the ten-minute conversation between the white confederate and the subject in the Negroes' absence, the former brings the conversation back to the lunch-break topic. In the context of what had been said there about race relations, he indicates his sympathy for the Negro confederates and his disapproval of segregation. He recalls related instances of desegregation, indicates his belief that these are on the increase and his approval of this fact. He is permissive toward expression of disagreement and reservations by the subject and discusses them with understanding. However, he is careful not to imply endorsement.

I will not take your time to detail the manner in which I plan to vary each component of this experience, since unfortunately this remains a matter for the future. However, to give you a general idea of what I had in mind, it should be relatively simple to substitute for the interdependent team task one which requires independent activity or one which requires competitive activity, and, moreover, this can be done without altering other features of the experience. Similarly, it will be possible to change the social norms which are established during the final ten-minute conversation between the subject and the white confederate. Continuing to use the technique of guided conversation, the white confederate could create a social norm favoring segregation by characterizing the Negro confederates as favorable exceptions to Negroes in general, by expressing the belief that they were hired because of the unavailability of white students, and by endorsing in other ways the continuation of segregation with respect to Negroes as a group.

The reason I have not gone on with my plans for an experimental analysis of this complex experience is that I am not yet satisfied with its impact on attitudes. Before explaining what I mean by this, let me describe for you the attitude change results to date.

Three measures were used. One of these, the Komorita Segregation Scale (Komorita, 1963), deals with desegregation policy, with an emphasis on school desegregation. It is made up of 67 items with which the respondent may indicate strong agreement to strong disagreement. A second is a social distance inventory, the Westie Summated Differences Scale (Westie, 1953), covering the following areas: residential desegregation, community leadership, personal relationships, and physical contact. The score is based on a comparison of acceptances of whites and Negroes of identical occupations. Four hundred and thirty-two ratings of acceptance are made. The third measure is a first-person sentence completion test of ten items developed by Getzels (Getzels & Walsh, 1958); these items test for reactions to a variety of experiences with Negroes.

We found the standard deviation for each of these three tests for an attitudinally heterogeneous group of students from the colleges of Borderville. We then expressed the amount of change for each subject on each of the three tests separately in standard scores. Finally, for each subject the average over the three tests was obtained.

Taking an average change of approximately one standard score for the three tests as a criterion, 8 of the 23 subjects (35%) worked with to date (all are girls) have undergone attitude change. (Seven of the eight exceeded an average score of 1.0, ranging from 1.1 to 2.9; one was just below this point at an average S.D. change of .84.) For a group of 23 students with equally antagonistic attitudes whom we used as controls, 2 (9%) approximated this level of change, achieving average change scores of .90 and .91 S.D. Among the experimental subjects there was one who approached an average change of one standard score (−.82) in the *unfriendly* direction; this was true for two of the control subjects (−.76 and −.73).

Let me attempt to give you a qualitative picture of the shifts in responses by three subjects illustrative of those whom I characterized as having undergone attitude change. The first had initially rejected the idea of having Negroes on her city council or heading her community chest drive. She balked at sharing restrooms and beauty parlors with them. She was averse to the idea that she might exchange social visits with Negroes or have them as dinner guests. All of these relationships she accepted at the time of the post-test.

The second had endorsed complete residential segregation but after the experiment said she would welcome Negroes in her part of town. She came to accept them in leadership positions from which earlier she wished to exclude them. She made the same change with respect to exchanging social visits with Negroes and sharing with them beauty parlors, restrooms, and dressing rooms in department stores.

The third subject made similar changes. She abandoned entirely her former endorsement of residential segregation, accepting Negroes as next-door neighbors. She moved entirely away from rejecting the idea of potential physical contact with Negroes in beauty parlors, restrooms and dressing rooms. She came to accept them as social visitors and dinner guests.

In one sense these are highly satisfactory results. While it is difficult to compare them directly with changes observed in desegregation outside the laboratory, I would say that the proportion and extent of change we have obtained is at least as great—and it must be remembered that we are accomplishing in 40 hours what is accomplished in the natural setting over a much longer time span.

On the basis of these results it would seem reasonable to conclude that for a sizable proportion of the college population of highly anti-

Negro, anti-desegregationist individuals, we know not only how to modify racial attitudes, but also how to make modifications of a sort which might be expected to have considerable practical meaning. This gives me some additional confidence that we have correctly analyzed the differences between those community settings in which unintended contact led to attitude change and those in which it did not.

However, in another sense, the results are quite unsatisfactory. We have no idea of why we fail when we do. It may be that some people are more resistant to attitude change by reason of attributes of their personal make-up. On the other hand, it may be that the non-changers are susceptible only to different experiences than those we provide them—or perhaps to different methods of presenting the same experiences. At any rate, two broad approaches to increasing the frequency of change seem possible. One of these is to modify the experimental procedure. This we have been doing, although I will not have time to describe the changes for you. To give you a single illustration, at one point we were having the white confederate support desegregation with the Negro confederate present. We came to suspect that the Negro's presence caused the subject to react defensively or in some other way to discount the confederate's remarks. This led to the procedure I described to you of reserving this type of conversation until the Negro confederate had left the scene.

The second approach would be to use selected subjects only; in other words, to screen out those persons with personalities that put them beyond the reach of the procedures in our experiment. The difficulty here is that we have not discovered how to do the necessary screening job. Only recently did we get a lead which may make it possible. Our lengthy test battery contained many group-administered tests of personality, interests, and opinions. A factor analysis made it possible for us to score respondents on a limited number of factor scores. One factor separates our changers and non-changers with only a single overlapping case. It is based on tests which can be best described as measuring positive attitudes toward people. Most of the scales measuring cynicism and anomie appear on this factor.

To a somewhat lesser extent, two other factors separate our changers and non-changers. One of these is responsiveness to social influence or the need for social approval. The other is low self-esteem or dissatisfaction with self as indicated by a discrepancy between description of self and description of self-ideal. Should these hold up with future subjects, we may develop enough confidence in them to screen potential subjects in advance.

Why have I not proceeded to the experimental analysis which, as I said earlier, was one of my objectives? Basically this is due to the small number of subjects and, as yet, low frequency of change. The fact that a month must be spent with each subject necessarily limits me to small numbers and will continue to do so unless extensive financial support becomes available. With small numbers of subjects, one is handicapped in evaluating the significance of small differences resulting from experimental treatments. One way to minimize this problem, although certainly not to solve it, is to start with a high rate of change in the basic condition, to which later variations will be compared. Through future modifications of either procedure or selection of subjects, I hope to reach a frequency of change of 75–80% before beginning experimental variations.

## A Conceptual Analysis

I shall now turn to the conceptual analysis of the problem area illustrated by the research I have described. As I proceed I shall point out the ways in which motives enter the analysis.

Let me say again that I think of the problem area as a recurring pattern of events which begins with the events that bring a person into unintended contact with a member or members of a disliked group, continues through the development of friendly or unfriendly behavior to such group members, and may culminate in change in social relationships and attitudes with other members of the group as well. The study that I have just been describing breaks into this sequence after contact has been established and interaction is beginning. For this reason I should like to begin with an illustration that covers the full range of events. One step in the analysis is to subdivide the pattern of events into manageable time stages. I will do this as I give the example. I will choose a Mr. White as my research subject and have him in contact with a Mr. Brown, a member of a nonwhite disliked group.

Mr. White had just been married and needed a job. During his military service he had had airplane traffic control experience. A position in this field becomes available at a local commercial airport. While inquiring about the position, White found that at least one or more of his group of co-workers would be nonwhite. Mr. White looked down on nonwhites, as did his friends and neighbors. After vacillating until the last moment, White took the position. He experienced relief and satisfaction at having a job, but at the same time felt discomfort and shame at working with nonwhites. I shall be referring to the events up to this point as the *pre-proximity stage* of the event pattern.

To continue with the illustration, Mr. White did the work on his new job speaking to a nonwhite co-worker, a Mr. Brown, only when the occasion demanded. Soon after beginning work, he inquired into the possibility of changing to another position at the airport and gave as his reason his dislike of working with nonwhites. His supervisor, who governed promotions and raises in the section in which White and Brown worked, explained to him that it was not the policy of the airport to make distinctions on this basis and told him he either would have to stay in his position or leave the organization. White considered quitting but decided against it because the job was well paying, and he needed money badly to support his new wife. By the time he had been on the job for a while, he had noticed that other co-workers were friendly to Mr. Brown. Sometime later during a coffee break a second white co-worker suggested a visit to inspect a new type of plane which had landed at the airport for the first time. Mr. Brown, the nonwhite, went along. In the course of their inspection of the new plane, White and Brown discussed the innovations it contained. Events from the pre-proximity stage up to this point I shall call the *proximity stage*

In the days which followed, White participated in other conversations in which Brown was involved. These conversations were like the first in that they dealt with events related to the business of the unit in which the two men worked. Sometime later someone within the section proposed the organization of a bowling team for competition against other airport units. Brown supported the proposal and joined the team. When the group turned to White, whom they knew to be a bowler, he joined also. Bowling on the same team involved efforts at mutual assistance among the team members, including White and Brown. It also involved partisan emotional backing for one another against opposing teams. Mr. White came to appreciate the value of Mr. Brown's work at the airport and his contribution to the bowling team. Also, he came to treat Mr. Brown in the same way as his other co-workers and told other friends he liked him. The events from the proximity stage up to this point I shall call the *interaction stage.*

As time went on Mr. White encountered the question of relations between whites and nonwhites in other settings. When asked by his friends what he thought of whites and nonwhites working together he said he approved. When asked why, he said he thought nonwhites were just as good workers as whites. When Negroes came to a political meeting he attended he introduced himself. Events such as these make up the *post-interaction stage.*

## Time Stages in a Conceptual Analysis

Now let me review each of the four stages and describe each in somewhat greater detail. The first, the *pre-proximity stage*, covers the period in which the individual is still separated from the attitudinal object, the member of the group he dislikes. During this stage, environmental developments in conjunction with a variety of personal characteristics such as values and motives may bring him to take an action in apparent contradiction to his unfriendly attitude, namely, an action which brings him into proximity with the disliked person. In the illustration above, the availability of the job opportunity, in conjunction with Mr. White's economic need, was the occasion for his unwilling movement into the proximity situation. As a result of his action, the individual may experience a variety of consequences; these will include rewards and satisfactions associated with the inducement to take the action (e.g., a salary) as well as unpleasant affective reactions (e.g., discomfort at his increased nearness to the object of his dislike).

The *proximity stage*, you will remember, begins when Mr. White goes to work. The environment of this stage will include the characteristics of the focal social object (the member of the disliked group) and the role or position of this person in the proximity situation.

Some of these environmental features may, in association with the individual's motives and values, lead him to attempt to separate himself from nonwhites in the job setting. On the other hand, he will have an opportunity to observe the actions others take toward nonwhites and his work may lead to close observation of nonwhites' behavior. He will experience anticipations as to the consequences, both pleasant and unpleasant, associated with various actions on his part. As a result of some of these observations and anticipations, or as the result of unavoidable requirements of the situation, he may begin to interact with the members of nonwhite groups he at first avoided.

The third stage, the *interaction stage*, begins in the illustration with a conversation. Additional conversations and work associations develop with time. Sometimes, as in the bowling illustration, interactions develop that are not limited to the initial setting. One of the by-products of this interaction is to add new aspects to the environment which the subject individual experiences. For example, various aspects of the behavior and personal qualities of the nonwhite may be noticed. In addition, participation in the interaction may bring other consequences. For example, Mr. White may experience relief in acting in a manner approved by his supervisor and his white co-workers. At the same time, however, he may experience discomfort at being seen in close interaction with a nonwhite. His actions toward nonwhites in the situation may be such that one could infer his liking and admiration for them.

In the fourth, or *post-interaction stage*, we assume a further elaboration of the subject's environment, and especially of its attitude-relevant features. The subject meets new nonwhites and has new occasions on which to react to nonwhites as a class. If his actions now differ from what they were in the *pre-proximity stage* we may feel confident that he has changed in some way—in his racial attitudes, presumably. If they do not differ we are uncertain what to assume. Our subject may have changed but his new attitude may not be strong enough to counter the disapproval he anticipates from friends and neighbors should he act accordingly.

In concluding these comments about the time stages I should note again one matter to which I will return—that the cutting line between time stages is such that each terminates with significant developments in the subject's behavior. For example, the behavioral outcomes of stage 1, the pre-proximity stage, are those actions which bring the subject into the desegregated setting. In stage 2, the proximity stage, the behavioral outcomes are the interactions between white and nonwhite. In stage 3, the interaction stage, they are the feelings of liking and respect for nonwhites in the contact situation. In stage 4, the post-interaction stage, they are behavior and attitudes toward nonwhites in general.

## Components of the Conceptual Network

In addition to time stages the analysis has three additional features. The first—and the one to which I have given most attention—is a set of concepts for describing the components of the event pattern. Taken together, they form a conceptual network in terms of which to cumulate and organize knowledge about the research area. Such knowledge takes two forms and these represent the two remaining features of the analysis. One is verified empirical relationships among the descriptive concepts or variables. The other is explanatory processes in the form of hypothesized psychological events which organize and give meaning to the relationships among variables.

When I describe the first of these three features, the components of the conceptual network, I follow the familiar S-O-R, or stimulus-organism-response, pattern of looking at things. The broad categories in the analysis are shown in Fig. 1. Some of the concepts to be employed describe the environment or *situation* of the individual under study; these are discussed under *Situational Variables.* Others describe the individual himself; these are discussed under *Person Variables.* Still others describe the individual's reactions within the situation and outside it; they are labeled *Outcome Variables.*

However, certain variables overlap this three-way distinction. They are variables which arise from neither the person nor the situation but from an interaction of the person with others in the situation. I have called these *Interaction Variables.*

The concepts describing the environment are thought of in two groups. The first group refers to members of the disliked social group who are present and to features of the situation directly involving

| *S* Situational Variables | | Interaction Variables | *O* Person Variables | | | *R* Outcome Variables | |
|---|---|---|---|---|---|---|---|
| | Situational Characteristics | Situational Interactions | | Subject Attributes | | Behavior to Focal Attitude Object | Behavior to Attitude Class |
| | Focal<br>Contextual | | | | | | |

FIGURE 1

them. An example of the latter would be their status in the situation. I speak of such concepts as the *focal* environment to indicate their relation to the focal attitudinal object, that is, the nonwhites.

The remaining features of the situation I have called the *contextual* environment. Concepts describing the contextual environment refer to aspects of it which are independent of the attitudinal object, such as the presence of an authority figure who constitutes a source of reward or punishment.

This division of situational variables into focal and contextual carries implications also for the concepts considered under "Person Variables." Racial attitude is a person variable related to the focal aspects of the environment. However, a person variable such as a postulated approval motive would gain its relevance from a feature of the contextual environment. Such a feature might be a source of social approval present in the situation. More about this later.

Typically there is research background justifying each concept I shall mention. However, in order to save time for other aspects of the discussion, I shall not take time to review it. After I have presented the conceptual network I shall review some suggestions about relationships among concepts in the network and explanatory processes that give meaning to these relationships.

| *S*<br>Situational Variables | | Interaction Variables |
|---|---|---|
| Coupling and Guiding Events | Situational Characteristics | Situational Interactions |
| | *Focal—Nonwhite Persons*<br><br>Proportion of Nonwhite<br>Correspondence to Stereotype<br>Valued Traits<br>Similarity in Belief<br>Relative Soc.-econ.-Educ. Status<br>Relative Situational Status<br><br>*Contextual—Nonsocial*<br><br>*Contextual—Other White* | |

FIGURE 2

Let me begin with those *situational variables* related to the focal environment. These are shown in Fig. 2. Fig. 2 is taken from Fig. 1 but shows only the section of it that we need for this aspect of the analysis.

## I. Characteristics of the Focal Environment

The focal environment is made up of members of the disliked social group and features of the situation directly involving them. Hence, it will be described in two parts. The first will deal with characteristics of the nonwhite person or persons. These are discussed under the heading "Characteristics of the Focal Attitudinal Object." The second will deal with the situationally defined relationships between the nonwhite persons and other components of the situation. These are discussed under the heading "Situationally Defined Relationships between the Focal Attitudinal Object and other Components of the Situation."

### A. *Characteristics of the Focal Attitudinal Object*

Among the characteristics of the disliked person four have been emphasized: First is *the extent to which the individuals from the disliked group correspond to or differ from the commonly held stereotypes about the group*. For example, the general belief in the culture may be that members of the disliked group are unintelligent, lazy, and without ambition. The particular individuals of that group who are in the proximity situation may be of this sort or they may be intelligent, industrious, and ambitious; or they may present a range with some being one way and some another.

Second is *the extent to which the disliked group members manifest generally valued social traits*, such as friendliness, helpfulness, honesty. These are the traits which generally sum up to admiration and respect by others.

Third is *the extent to which the disliked group members are similar to the subject-individual in beliefs, attitudes, and values*. The subject may be conservative politically; the nonwhites may be conservative or liberal. The subject may be interested in world affairs, in baseball, in making money; the nonwhites may or may not share these interests.

Fourth is *the relative socioeconomic-educational status of the disliked group member.* Nonwhites in the situation may be higher than, equal to, or lower than the white subject in this respect.

### B. *Situationally Defined Relationships between the Focal Attitudinal Object and Other Components of the Situation*

I have listed two variables which fall in the class of situationally defined relationships between the disliked group members and other components of the situation.

One of these is *the relative status within the proximity situation of the subject-individual and members of the disliked group.* The positions to which the subject-individual and members of the disliked group are assigned within the proximity situation do not necessarily correspond to the pattern of their status relationships in the general society. In a given work situation, for example, members of one group may be present only in menial jobs, while members of the other group are in skilled or supervisory positions; in another work situation, members of the two groups may be doing the same kinds of jobs.

A second variable of this sort is *the proportion in which the disliked group is represented in the situation.* This may range from an insignificant proportion through a moderate number to a large majority.

## II. Subject Attributes Related to the Focal Attitudinal Object

Now let me shift for a moment to the *Person Variables* section of the overall outline (Fig. 3).

As I have already noted, it is convenient in this analysis to think of the subject attributes also in two parts: 1) those attributes for which some feature of the focal environment is the reference object, for example, a characteristic of the subject which might be expected to influence directly his relations with nonwhites; and 2) those attributes not so related, for example, needs and values of the subject which make him responsive to features of the situation other than nonwhites. At this point I will speak only of the first type of attribute. In this case the attribute in question is, of course, *racial attitude.*

| *O* Person Variables | | | |
|---|---|---|---|
| Situational Variables as Perceived | Subject Attributes | | Anticipated Consequences |
| | *Inferred Constructs* | *Observed Behavior* | |
| Perceived Stereotype<br>Perceived Dissimilarity | Racial Attitude | Verbal Statements<br>Overt Action<br>Ambiguous Stimuli<br>Judgment<br>Task Performance<br>Classification<br>Perception<br>Physiological | Discomfort in Racial Contact |

FIGURE 3

In Fig. 3 I have distinguished (under "Subject Attributes") between inferred constructs and observed behavior. If the construct is to be treated as a variable for which we estimate individual differences in strength among subjects, then such differences must be inferred from variation in observable behavior. Usually this behavior is a test of some sort. I have listed a number of types of behaviors from which attitude can be inferred, provided that we have adequate assurance that some other influence is not at work to determine the test scores. These behaviors range from verbal statements and overt actions to physiological responses.

In the concept of racial attitude, we first encounter in this analysis a motivelike construct. Of the two characteristics often attributed to motives, that is, energizing and directing, attitude clearly exhibits the second. The directing influence can be seen on both the stimulus input and the response output side. On the input side, attributes of the attitudinal object are misperceived and misinterpreted to accord with attitudinal expectations. On the output side, actions are taken either to avoid or to enhance association with the attitudinal object.

This directing characteristic of attitude is, in part, responsible for the column in Fig. 3 headed "Situational Variables as Perceived." It is a reminder of the familiar point that perceived environment and objective environment may differ. This point is of considerable importance in this analysis. Strong social attitudes are notable for influencing perception of the environment. An example is that anti-Negro whites perceive black strangers to have different beliefs from theirs (Byrne & Wong, 1962; Stein, Hardyck, & Smith, 1965). However, in the course of personal contact the perceived environment may become more veridical to the objective environment This suggests one of the avenues through which behavior in such situations may be modified.

The column in Fig. 3 labeled "Anticipated Consequences" is also related to the motivational characteristics of attitude. An attitude involves a specified class of objects and implies a tendency to approach or avoid such objects. These objects, or events associated with them, when experienced give rise to pleasant or unpleasant affective reactions. Expectancy of such reactions, which I have called *Anticipated Consequences*, becomes part of the pattern of determinants of attitude-related behavior.

## III. Characteristics of the Contextual Environment

Now let me complete the description of the situational variables (Fig. 4). I pointed out in discussing the focal environment that the focal attitudinal object and its situationally defined relationships are only a part of the environment of an individual in unintended proximity to someone from a disliked group. The disliked person is typically experienced in a context of activities and other persons. Some of these contextual features of the environment may become quite influential in governing the subject-individual's actions toward the disliked group member and may be equally influential in attitude change, should any occur.

The contextual features fall into two groups: those having to do with other whites and those describing nonsocial characteristics of the situation.

### A. *Situational Variables Involving Other Whites*

Prominent among the former is *the norms of the peer group with respect to beliefs about and association with members of the disliked group.* Members of the subject-individual's peer group may feel that association with nonwhites should be kept to the minimum required by

| S<br>Situational Variables | | Interaction Variables |
|---|---|---|
| Coupling and Guiding Events | Situational Characteristics | Situational Interactions |
| | *Focal—Nonwhite Person*<br><br>Proportion of Nonwhite<br>Correspondence to Stereotype<br>Valued Traits<br>Similarity in Belief<br>Relative Soc.-econ.-Educ. Status<br>Relative Situational Status<br><br>*Contextual—Nonsocial*<br><br>Acquaintance Potential<br>Physical Proximity<br>Interdependence Requirements<br><br>*Contextual—Other White*<br><br>Peer Norms<br>Valued Traits—Peers<br>Belief Similarity—Peers<br>Authority Norms | |
| Statements by Sources of Reward<br>Observation of Consequences<br>Observation of Source's Actions | Sources of Social Approval<br>Sources of Material Reward | |

FIGURE 4

the situation, or they may feel that greater association is acceptable or even desirable. The generally expressed "climate of opinion" on the part of other whites within the given situation may indicate positive, negative, or neutral feelings and beliefs about nonwhites; similarly, it may indicate approval, disapproval, or neutrality toward social interaction with nonwhites.

However, social norms originating with peers may or may not be influential for a given research subject. There seem to be two peer characteristics of potential importance in determining this. One of them is *the extent to which white peers in the situation are similar to the subject-individual in beliefs, attitudes, and values*. The second is *the extent to which the white peers manifest generally valued social traits*, that is, are persons likely to be admired and respected. Similar to peer group norms are *the norms of authorities in the situation with respect to the disliked group*. Those in power in the setting in which unintended contact takes place may hold expectations about appropriate attitudes and actions which differ from those of the subject's peers.

I have listed in this section of Fig. 4 two other aspects of the contextual environment which are somewhat different in character. These are *persons in the situation who represent potential sources of reward and gratification, on the one hand, or of deprivation and punishment on the other*. It is clear that these reward sources (such as Mr. White's supervisor in our illustration) in conjunction with attributes of the subject (Mr. White's economic need) often have an effect upon the subject-individual's actions toward the disliked group member. Presumably, the influence of such persons comes into play only in conjunction with associated needs and apprehensions characterizing the subject-individual; I will discuss such needs and apprehensions when I return in a moment to the "Person Variables" section of the outline.

The persons who represent potential sources of reward and punishment might be classified in a number of ways. I have chosen two categories that will serve to illustrate the possibilities. One of these is *sources of social approval or disapproval*. Any individual is sensitive to the approval or disapproval of certain other persons and groups. Which persons or groups have this quality depends upon the history of the individual. Common examples are religious authorities, social leaders, leaders of membership groups, etc.

A second is *sources of material reward and punishment*. Persons in the environment often control economic gain or loss, for example, an employer offering a promotion or threatening a discharge. On occasion the environment may present the possibility of imprisonment (in the person of a police officer) or of physical harm (as represented by a mob).

### Coupling and Guiding Events

These sources of gratification and punishment call attention to two classes of events which may occur in the situation. In the outline I have called them coupling and guiding events. They are necessary for the following reason. The presence in the situation of some potential source of gratification or punishment has no inherent relationship to the subject's actions toward the person from the disliked group. Something must happen to engage the source and the action. For example, in our illustration there was no relation between Mr. White's pay check and equalitarian behavior toward Mr. Brown *until* White's supervisor made a statement connecting the two. Thereafter, need for the money played a part in White's actions. A statement by a visiting leader of Mr. White's church proclaiming that religious beliefs of his church required friendly race relations would be another example.

I have listed three categories of coupling and guiding events. The first, which includes my two examples involving Mr. White, are *statements by accepted sources of social influence* regarding actions which should be taken toward the attitudinal object (Charters & Newcomb, 1952). Such statements might come from a respected judicial or legal authority, an admired political leader, a peer group leader, and so on.

A second category, differing only slightly from the first, is made up of *observed relationships between particular actions toward the disliked group member and various pleasant or unpleasant consequences.* An observation that persons who participate in recreational activities with nonwhites are thereafter avoided by their former friends offers a case in point.

I think of these first two categories as coupling events—that is, the event couples potential gratification or punishment to attitude-related behavior. The third category is different in that it consists of *guiding events.* Sometimes the association between action toward the attitudinal object and a particular source of satisfaction exists, but the *direction* of action which will result in the desired consequences is not clear. In such a case the subject-individual seeks action-guiding cues from the sources of gratification located in the proximity situation (Kohn & Williams, 1956). He might, for example, wait to see how members of a club to which he wishes to belong treated nonwhites.

B. *Situational Variables Involving Nonsocial Features of the Environment*

The remaining variables needed to describe the contact situation are related directly to neither the white nor the nonwhite participants. They refer instead to physical arrangements and activities which have consequences for behavior in the situation—and perhaps for changes in the research subject.

The first of these is *the physical proximity between white and nonwhite provided by the situation.* To illustrate, in a housing project nonwhites and whites may live as next-door neighbors having apartments within the same building; or they may live in separate buildings interspersed throughout the project; or they may live in separate sections of the project. Even in the absence of patterns such as this, which are set up on the basis of some policy decision, there may be variations in the physical distance or closeness between whites and nonwhites that are a function of the setting rather than of choice on the part of the participants.

The second of these variables is *the acquaintance potential of the situation.* This is the extent to which the situation provides opportunities for getting to know members of the other race as individuals. Sitting next to a nonwhite on a bus or in the theater or swimming at the same beach is not usually conducive to getting acquainted with him. Living next door to a nonwhite family, belonging to a small club that has both white and nonwhite members, or being on a team with both whites and nonwhites provides more opportunities for becoming acquainted with individuals of the other race.

A third variable of this type is *the interdependence requirements of the situation.* This is the extent to which the structure of the situation itself fosters cooperative activity. Membership on a team requires interdependent cooperative behavior if the team is to win; working as sales clerks in the same department in a store in which pay depends on the amount of sales and only the most successful clerk gets a bonus is likely to engender competitive behavior; an activity that is essentially individual, such as handicrafts, is neutral with respect to this variable.

## IV. Subject Attributes Related to the Contextual Environment

Now let me return to the "Person Variables" and consider relevant attributes of the research subject other than his racial attitude. I should note that what I say at this point, unlike what I have said earlier, has not been abstracted from the research literature on unintended racial contact. The studies in this area have typically not included data on subject attributes. You will recall my saying in the time stage analysis that with respect to outcome variables we would consider the subject's behavior at the end of each stage. Those at the end of the *proximity stage* are the white-nonwhite interactions which become part of the environment of the *interaction stage*. Those at the end of the *interaction stage* are his reactions to persons in the situation. Those in the *post-interaction stage* are reactions to nonwhites and to nonwhite symbols outside the setting. You may have recognized that these three sets of outcome variables are parallel to three we find in other areas of social psychological research. I have drawn on findings from these areas, which I shall identify in a moment, in developing a proposed list of subject attributes for the area I am analyzing.

Under "Interaction Variables" (Fig. 1), remember that we are dealing with the developing relations between nonwhites and a white whose negative racial attitude impels him to avoid these relations. In other research we refer to parallel phenomena by such names as compliance, conformity, or counter-attitudinal action. In studies under these headings investigators have examined the contribution of subject attributes to the criterion behavior. From their findings we can take one set of leads for this analysis.

Under "Outcome Variables" is the column headed "Behavior to the Focal Attitude Object"—that is, to members of the disliked group who are in the contact situation—the behaviors in which we are interested are such things as interpersonal ratings and sociometric choices. Similar phenomena have been studied under rubrics like social attraction, social choice, or interpersonal attraction. Here again the research on the contribution of subject attributes to behavior offers leads to potentially significant subject variables for this analysis.

The outcome variables labeled in Fig. 1 as "Behavior to the Attitude Class" deal with actions outside the situation toward newly encountered members of the disliked group or some symbol of the group. This is the type of behavior from which we are most comfortable in inferring attitude change. Hence, a look at attitude change research provides still another source of suggestions regarding significant subject attributes. Here I have in mind such attitude research programs as those on persuasive communication and the resolution of cognitive dissonance.

Partly from these various research areas and partly from inferences drawn directly from the research on racial contact, I have chosen a minimum list of concepts. These are shown in Fig. 5 in the

| *O* Person Variables | | | |
|---|---|---|---|
| Situational Variables as Perceived | Subject Attributes | | Anticipated Consequences |
| | *Inferred Constructs* | *Observed Behavior* | |
| Perceived Stereotype<br>Perceived Dissimilarity | Racial Attitude | Verbal Statements<br>Overt Action<br>Ambiguous Stimuli<br>Judgment<br>Task Performance<br>Classification<br>Perception<br>Physiological | Discomfort in Racial Contact |
| | Approval Motive | Social Desirability | Increased Approval |
| | Achievement Need | TAT | Inc. Sense of Achievement |
| | Affiliation Need | TAT | Social Support |
| | Economic Need | | Material Gain |
| | Self-Esteem | Trait Ratings: Q-Sort | |
| | Ego-Defense | "F" Sub-Scale; Ego Def. | |
| | Anxiety | Manifest Anxiety | |
| | Justice | Value Self-Rating | |
| | Religious Brotherhood | Value Self-Rating | |
| | Government by Law | Value Self-Rating | |
| | Concrete-Abstract | This-I-Believe | |
| | Complex-Simple | Role Rep. Test | |
| | Open-Closed | Dogmatism Scale | |

FIGURE 5

column "Subject Attributes." Opposite the concept name I have shown the observed behavior from which the construct is inferred.

A. *Needs and Motives*

The first four variables have been customarily labeled motives or needs. For the first of these, the *approval motive*, the strength of the variable is often inferred from scores on the Crowne-Marlowe Social Desirability test (Crowne & Marlowe, 1964).

Given certain situational characteristics, subjects with a strong need for approval might be expected to interact more readily with a disliked person than might one with a lesser need. Among such situational characteristics would be peer group norms supporting equalitarian interracial association. In addition, peer group members endorsing the norms in the situation must have characteristics that lead the subject to accept them as a reference group—that is, a source of approval. Among such characteristics are similarity to the subject's beliefs, interests, and attitudes and/or valued traits that lead to admiration and respect.

What I have just said referred to the interplay of the approval motive with situational factors in influencing the development of interaction between whites and nonwhites. These same factors might be expected to exert a similar influence on the development of social attraction by the subject for the nonwhite in the contact situation.

Rather than treat the three remaining need-concepts in such detail, let me simply enumerate them together with one or more of the situational variables with which they may be especially likely to interact.

The first is *affiliation need*. The strength of this variable is inferred from the Thematic Apperception Test (Murray, 1938) as well as from other instruments. Like the approval motive, it may be expected to interact with peer norms and peer attributes. Should cooperative interaction with the nonwhite come about, affiliation need should partially determine the influence of such interaction on the amount of social attraction the subject develops for the nonwhite.

Let me digress a moment to comment on one assumption about this and other motivelike variables. As I discuss them it will sound as though I assume that high need has more effect than moderate need and this, in turn, more than low need. It may happen, however, as seems to be the case with affiliation need, that moderate need produces the greater effect (Hardy, 1957; Byrne, 1962). You should remember that this may be true in relation to any of the subject attributes I shall mention.

The second is *need-achievement.* The Thematic Apperception Test is the usual basis for inferring the strength of the variable, but other tests of the need are also available. Here the interplay with the situation should be most evident in relation to its interdependence requirements and the competitive or cooperative interaction to which this gives rise. In particular, the strength of need-achievement in relation to successful cooperative interaction should influence liking for the nonwhite participant.

The third is *economic need.* Strength here is estimated from ratings, usually made by the experimenter. Here the interaction with situational variables is by way of the source of material reward, and as I have noted already, it is this type of motive in conjunction with an appropriate incentive in the situation that we assume brings the prejudiced subject into the contact setting and keeps him there during the proximity stage of the sequence of events.

B. *Personality Traits and Mechanisms*

The next three subject attributes are usually identified as personality traits or mechanisms.

The first is *self-esteem.* Strength here is inferred usually from self-ratings or Q-sorts of valued traits. The interplay of self-esteem with situational factors in inhibiting or facilitating participant interaction, for example, is assumed to parallel that for affiliation need. Low self-esteem may be a characteristic that magnifies the need-affiliation effect.

The second of the trait concepts is *anxiety.* Amount of chronic anxiety has been inferred from test scores (Miller Anxiety Scale, for example), as well as from self-ratings and projective techniques. Anxiety level can be expected to have complex interactions with situational variables and with other subject attributes (Marlowe & Gergen, 1968). For example, high anxiety in conjunction with negative racial attitude may tend to enhance avoidant behavior, in particular when the situational variable, proportion of nonwhites, is at a high value. By contrast, when anxiety level interacts with peer group norms and sources of social approval, high anxiety may contribute to enhancing white-nonwhite interaction and social attraction by the white for the nonwhite participant.

The third of the trait concepts, *ego-defense*, is of course usually labeled a dynamic mechanism. However, it is a trait in the sense that individual differences in amount or strength are always assumed. The strength of the trait may be inferred from scores on the ego-defense subscale of the F scale. As an example of the interplay of ego-defense level with situational factors, it may be that low ego-defense will enhance the belief changes that result from exposure to favorable characteristics of the nonwhite in the situation.

Before moving on to the two remaining groups of subject attributes I should take note of some similarities and differences between the two just reviewed. The motives in the first group and the traits in the second all seem to have been studied in essentially the same way. Given the existence of individual differences in either a motive or a trait, it has been assumed by the investigator that some behavioral outcome will either bring satisfaction or relieve discomfort. The difference appears to be only that for motives the environmental source or event is indicated more specifically in the motive name than it is in the trait name. The approval motive presumably names an attribute of the subject (or a state induced in him) to which approval from others is the appropriate environmental event. It follows that awareness of anticipated motive-related consequences which should follow from certain behaviors by the subject is a meaningful part of the pattern of determinants. Accordingly I have indicated this in the appropriate column in the outline.

The trait name, in contrast to the motive name, does not identify a satisfying or disturbing source or event. As a consequence, hypotheses about trait effects on behavior must involve more steps of inference. For the same reason awareness of anticipated consequences related to some trait-related goal state seems unlikely.

However, to repeat, I do not see that these differences have made a difference in the way motives and traits have been studied. Individual differences in chronic levels of both characteristics have been varied in essentially the same way. Moreover, differences in the temporary level of both types of characteristic have been induced through experimental manipulation. I am led by this to conclude that in an analysis like this one, motives, needs, personality traits, and dynamic mechanisms all serve in essentially the same way as motivelike constructs to help account for individual differences in behavioral and attitudinal outcomes.

C. *Values*

The third group of subject attributes are generally called values. They, too, have motivational aspects, but of a somewhat different character. The values I have listed are *justice*, *religious brotherhood*, and *government by law*. Their strength is inferred from ratings or rankings. One way of looking at values is that they describe conditions which their holders desire in some degree to exist. This desire to move toward a value or valued state closely parallels the customary use of need or motive concepts.

One might infer from this that persons who hold strongly to a value like *justice* might endorse actions and favor policies which seemed to increase justice. If some motive-coupling event makes it clear that certain actions and policies which the subject had not related to his values were in fact likely to advance them, he might be expected to perform these actions and support these policies where he had not done so before. Such a development might have quite unexpected consequences. It might, for example, lead our subject to enter interaction with disliked nonwhites. Or it might lead him to a new view of policies involving nonwhites. This has been referred to as the instrumental effect of attitudes (Smith, Bruner, & White, 1956; Katz, 1960). The term applies equally well, however, to actions taken in apparent service of a value.

The two other values listed, *religious brotherhood* and *government by law*, are included because they represent strong values often served by entering and remaining in desegregated situations. As such they play a part in maintaining the unintended contact in the course of which participant interaction may later develop.

D. *Cognitive Characteristics*

The final group of attributes are generally thought of as cognitive characteristics. Cognitive style, cognitive systems, and personality structure are other labels under which they have been studied.

The three I have listed are *concrete vs. abstract* cognitive organization, *complex vs. simple* cognitive structure and *open vs. closed* mind. The first of these is measured by the This-I-Believe test (Harvey, Hunt, & Schroeder, 1961), the second by the Role Rep test (Kelly, 1955), and the third by the Dogmatism scale (Rokeach, 1960). These attributes have in common the expectation that persons on the undesirable end of the continuum (concrete, simple, closed) are not receptive to new information. Often a proviso is attached that the information screened out will be in an area of high salience or importance to the subject.

When we look for probable interaction between these cognitive characteristics and situational variables, available research directs us to two conflicting possibilities. First, in unintended contact the focal environment supplies new counter-attitudinal information about nonwhites. This is particularly true if cooperative interaction and exchange of personal information has developed during the interaction stage. Here we may assume an interaction such that concrete-simple-closed subjects would process input of the new counter-attitudinal information less accurately and, hence, change less.

However, if other assumptions are made, an opposite outcome is possible. Let us suppose situational factors such as interdependence requirements and peer group norms are prominent and that the subject involved is characterized by moderate affiliation need and low self-esteem. From this pattern we would expect strong interaction of the cooperatively interdependent sort, accompanied by compelling registration of the new and favorable information about the nonwhites in the situation. Under these circumstances information input might be processed with sufficient accuracy by all subjects. However, those with concrete-simple-closed cognitive structure may be unable to entertain simultaneously the conflicting old and new information and hence change more quickly than their abstract-complex-open counterparts.

## V. Outcome Variables

What we have left to complete in the description of the components of the conceptual framework are the *Outcome Variables.* As I noted earlier we look at the subject's behavior at four different points in time. The first, at the end of the pre-proximity stage, is upon his entry into the contact situation. The second, at the end of the proximity stage, is at the initiation of situational interaction. The third, at the end of the interaction stage, is on the occasion of assessment of the subject's behavior toward nonwhites in the situation. The fourth is in the post-interaction stage; it consists of observations of behavior toward nonwhites and toward nonwhite symbols (pictures, labels, etc.) outside the situation. The first of these, the entry into the contact situation antedates the time stages I have been outlining. I shall begin therefore with the behavioral outcomes in stage 2.

A. *Interaction Variables*

The behavioral outcomes of stage 2 are the same variables I have earlier labeled "Interaction Variables" (Fig. 6). I did this, you remember, because they double as outcome and situational variables. While they describe the subject's behavior, they also describe experiences of the subject which help to determine later behavior.

Two dimensions of interaction stand out. The first of them is the degree and type of *interdependence*. At one end of this dimension is cooperation—complete interdependence with a common goal and a shared fate. At the midpoint of the dimension is complete independence. At the other extreme is competition—interdependence in the sense that if one wins the other loses. The interdependence aspect of interaction is closely related to a feature of the contextual environment, namely, the interdependence requirements of the situation. These may be such as to require given types of interaction or, conversely, to make any interaction difficult. Hence, any inference from the strength of the interaction to the strength of the subject's racial attitude should be made with care.

The second dimension of interaction is its degree of *intimacy*. This is largely a function of the nature of the conversation and information exchange that develops. The dimension ranges from personal and intimate to impersonal and public. A number of situational variables may facilitate intimacy of interaction. One of these is high acquaintance potential of the situation. Others are equality of

| *S* Situational Variables | | Interaction Variables |
|---|---|---|
| Coupling and Guiding Events | Situational Characteristics | Situational Interactions |
| | *Focal—Nonwhite Person* | |
| | Proportion of Nonwhite<br>Correspondence to Stereotype<br>Valued Traits<br>Similarity in Belief<br>Relative Soc.-econ.-Educ. Status<br>Relative Situational Status | |
| | *Contextual—Nonsocial* | |
| | Acquaintance Potential<br>Physical Proximity<br>Interdependence Requirements | Intimacy of Interaction<br>Interdependence of Interaction |
| | *Contextual—Other White* | |
| Statements by Sources of Reward<br>Observation of Consequences<br>Observation of Source's Actions | Peer Norms<br>Valued Traits—Peers<br>Belief Similarity—Peers<br>Authority Norms<br>Sources of Social Approval<br>Sources of Material Reward | |

FIGURE 6

situational status, equality of socioeconomic-educational status and similarity in beliefs and interests.

B. *Behavior toward the Focal-Attitudinal Object*

At the end of the interaction stage, if not earlier, it is likely that a systematic assessment will be made of the subject's behavior toward the members of the disliked group who are in the contact situation (Fig. 7). Such an assessment may occur on two dimensions: *attraction* and *esteem or respect.*

*Attraction* is a construct whose strength has been inferred from a variety of ratings and choices. Among the more frequently used are

| *R* Outcome Variables | | | |
|---|---|---|---|
| Behavior to Focal Attitude Object | | Behavior to Attitude Class | |
| *Inferred Construct* | *Observed Behavior* | *Inferred Construct* | *Observed Behavior* |
| Attraction | Rating of Liking<br>Rating to Share Activities<br>Choice as Group Member<br>Choice as Friend | Racial Attitude | Verbal Statements<br>Overt Action<br>Ambiguous Stimuli Judgment<br>Task Performance<br>Classification<br>Perception<br>Physiological |
| Esteem & Respect | Rating of Ability<br>Rating of Contribution<br>Rating of Leadership<br>Rating of Effort | | |

FIGURE 7

ratings of liking-disliking, ratings of desirability for sharing specified activities, choice as a group member, and choice as a friend (Lindzey & Byrne, 1968).

*Esteem and respect* has been inferred from still other ratings and choices. Among them are ratings of ability and competence, ratings of degree of contribution to a group task, choice as a member of a working group, ratings of leadership ability and potential, and ratings of industry and effort.

## C. *Behavior toward the Attitudinal Class*

In the post-interaction stage behavior toward members of the disliked group, or to symbols of the group, will occur outside the contact situation. From such behavior, change in social relations with nonwhites may be assessed and change in racial attitude inferred. The behaviors from which such inferences are usually drawn have already been pointed out in the earlier discussion of attitude as a subject attribute.

## Relationships and Explanatory Processes

This completes the description of the components of the conceptual network. Hopefully they constitute an effective selection of descriptive concepts in terms of which to cumulate and organize knowledge about the pattern of events in which we are interested. Such knowledge will take two forms: One will be relationships among situational, personal, and outcome variables. The other will be explanatory processes in the form of hypothesized psychological events which organize and give meaning to the relationships among variables. Needless to say, such explanatory processes also direct the continuing search for significant new variables and new relationships among variables.

In presenting the descriptive concepts I referred frequently to relationships we might expect to find among them. Additional detail about such relationships is unnecessary for the purpose of this analysis. However, I do wish to indicate the manner in which explanatory processes supplement the conceptual network. I will do this by reviewing briefly four different analyses of the course of events in unintended interracial contact. After giving each account, I shall describe the course of events a second time in terms of the variables and explanatory hypotheses of this conceptual analysis. I shall use Fig. 8 for this purpose.

### 1. *Reorganization of Beliefs, Restoration of Cognitive Balance, and Stimulus Generalization*

The first analysis begins at the point where a white who is in a contact situation against his will begins to get acquainted with nonwhites. He finds the ones he meets to be different from his expectations and changes his beliefs about them. His feelings change in line with his new beliefs. As time goes on, favorable beliefs and feelings spread to nonwhites in other settings and to nonwhites whom he does not know.

| *S* Situational Variables | | Interaction Variables | *O* Person Variables | | | *R* Outcome Variables | |
|---|---|---|---|---|---|---|---|
| Coupling & Guiding Events | Situational Character | Situational Interaction | Situational Variables as Perceived | Subject Attributes | Anticipated Consequences | Behavior to Focal Attitude Object | Behavior to Attitude Class |
| | Focal—*Nonwhite Person* | | | | | | |
| | Prop. Non-wh. | | | | | | |
| | Corres. Ster. | | Perc. Stereo. | | | | |
| | Valued Traits | | | | | | |
| | Belief Simil. | | Perc. Dissim. | Racial Attit. | Discomfort in Racial Cont. | Attraction | Racial Attit. |
| | Rel. Soc.-Ed. St. | | | | | | |
| | Rel. Sit. St. | | | | | | |
| | Contextual—*Nonsocial* | | | Approv. Motive | Inc. Approval | Est. & Respect | |
| | | | | Achiev. Need | Inc. Achiev. | | |
| | | | | Affil. Need | Soc. Support | | |
| | Acqu. Pot. | Intim./Intera. | | Economic Need | Material Gain | | |
| | Phys. Prox. | | | | | | |
| | Interd. Req. | Interd./Intera. | | Self-Esteem | | | |
| | | | | Ego-Defense | | | |
| | Contextual—*Other White* | | | Anxiety | | | |
| | | | | Justice | | | |
| | Peer Norms | | | Rel. Bro'hood | | | |
| | Val. Tr.—Peer | | | Gov't. by Law | | | |
| | Bel. Sim.—Peer | | | | | | |
| | Author. Norm | | | Concrete, Abstr. | | | |
| St. by Source | Source of Soc. Approval | | | Complex, Simple | | | |
| | | | | Open, Closed | | | |
| Obser. Conseq. | Source of Mat. Reward | | | | | | |
| Obser. Source | | | | | | | |

FIGURE 8

This account of how things go begins in the proximity stage. An unstated assumption is that some source of reward or approval in conjunction with some attribute of the subject brought him into the situation and is influencing him to remain. Once in the situation the subject observes either the lack of correspondence of the nonwhite to the commonly held stereotype or the similarity of the nonwhite to him in beliefs and interests, or both. During the proximity stage we might assume that the distorting effect of negative racial attitude prevailed and that consequently the nonwhites were perceived as conforming to the stereotype and being dissimilar in beliefs. We must assume, however, that eventually other situational factors lead to interaction of the subject with the nonwhites. If this interaction is sufficiently personal and intimate, it brings new information about the nonwhite's noncorrespondence to stereotype and his similarity in beliefs to bear on the subject with such force that a cognitive change occurs. This is a postulated explanatory process designated simply as a *reorganization of beliefs*. Underlying the process is assumed to be something like a need to know, to put things in order, to establish a manageable, understandable picture of reality. This has been identified by those who advocate the functionalist approach to attitude maintenance and change as a reflection of the knowledge or object appraisal function of attitude. According to this view, attitude, like other concepts, serves to reduce the limitless complexity about us to a limited number of internally consistent entities. If new information is extensive and sufficiently compelling, the conceptual entity embracing it may be altered.

At any rate, according to this account of things, the postulated reorganization of beliefs will mean that a set of derogatory beliefs toward nonwhites in the situation is replaced by a more favorable set. But liking for the nonwhites in the situation also changes. To explain this we postulate another process, this time a *restoration of cognitive balance* (Rosenberg, 1960). Favorable beliefs, summing to a new level of esteem and respect, do not coexist peacefully with negative feelings; a belief-affect imbalance is said to exist. The postulated restoration of balance happily changes affect in the favorable direction rather than reversing belief to its unfavorable early status.

Next in the course of events is the development of favorable actions and statements toward the attitude class in situations outside the contact setting. A third explanatory process is postulated to cover this step. This is *stimulus generalization.* It refers, of course, to the fact that stimulus cues such as skin color mediate the transfer of reactions developed to specific nonwhites to other members of the nonwhite attitude class.

2. *Affect Conditioning, Restoration of Cognitive Balance, and Stimulus Generalization*

The second analysis of the course of events begins with the subject engaged in interaction with the nonwhites in the situation. According to this view, he enjoys the cooperative interaction—in part, perhaps, because the outcomes of it bring rewards. He grows to like the nonwhites with whom he has been cooperating. Soon he develops favorable beliefs about them as well. Later the feelings of liking and respect spread to nonwhites outside the situation.

This course of events begins in the interaction stage. Developments prior to this have brought the subject into the proximity situation and influenced him to remain there. These same plus additional influences have been responsible for the initiation of his interaction with the nonwhites in the situation.

Interaction of the cooperative type is known to generate positive affect, particularly where outcomes of the interaction are successful and where the cooperation takes place under conditions of external threat. *Affect conditioning* is the explanatory process postulated to account for the attachment of this affect to the nonwhites who were present when it was generated.

In addition, according to this account, beliefs about the nonwhites in the situation also grow more favorable. For this development, *restoration of cognitive balance* is again called into play as an explanatory process. This time, fortunately for our story, belief yields to affect rather than vice versa.

As in the first analysis favorable beliefs and feelings about the disliked group were also observed outside the contact situation. As in that case, *stimulus generalization* is assumed to cover the step from positive views toward nonwhites in the situation to positive views toward those outside.

3. *Dissonance Reduction and Stimulus Generalization*

In the third account, the course of events begins with the entry of the subject into the contact situation. Before entering he vacillates for some time comparing his distaste for contact with nonwhites with the material and social rewards he anticipates from other sources in the situation. Once in the situation, he enters into interaction with the nonwhite participants. He develops both high esteem and a strong liking for them. Later he shows these same reactions to nonwhites in general in other settings.

This account of events begins with the initiation of the proximity stage. Negative racial attitude had led the subject to avoid the contact situation. Some contextual feature of that situation—perhaps a job opportunity—aroused in him a related economic motive. Entry into the situation thus came to have both positive and negative anticipated consequences—specifically, the expectation of satisfying an economic need as against the expectation of association with someone he thought he would dislike.

The outcome of this conflict was the entry into the situation—a counter-attitudinal act. We next assume that the counter-attitudinal act aroused dissonance. We postulate a process of *dissonance reduction* achieved by an act consistent with entering the distasteful setting, namely, by entering into interaction with the members of the disliked group (Brehm & Cohen, 1962).

However, if we assume that the negative racial attitude persists through this interaction, the interaction is yet a greater counter-attitudinal act. Additional dissonance should be aroused and additional dissonance reduction should be in order. This time we assume that the dissonance reduction is achieved by an increase in liking and esteem for the nonwhites in the situation. For the generalization of these changes to nonwhites outside the situation, *stimulus generalization* is again called into play.

4. *Social Reinforcement*

The fourth analysis begins with the subject in contact with his white peers in the situation. He respects these individuals and finds they share many of his beliefs and interests. He discovers gradually that they favor racial equality and believe in equalitarian associations with nonwhites. He enters the interactions with the nonwhites in the situation as they develop. Following these interactions he shows respect and liking for the nonwhites with whom he has been associating. Both respect and liking are also shown for nonwhites in other settings.

The initial steps in this analysis occur in the proximity stage. We begin with the point about the characteristics of the peer group. The peers in the situation possess valued traits and show beliefs and interests similar to those of the subject. The significance of this is that they become a source of social approval and arouse in the subject an approval motive.

At some point the subject learns that the peer norms in the situation support racial equality and endorse equalitarian interracial association. This is a motive-coupling event. It tells the subject what to do to satisfy his aroused approval motive, namely, to endorse racial equality and interact on friendly terms with the nonwhites in the situation. When the subject follows this lead and conforms to the peer group norms, he then receives peer group approval.

We hypothesize that the effect of this approval is to reinforce (with social incentives) equalitarian behavior and feelings toward nonwhites. We attribute to this explanatory process the observed equalitarian behavior shown later to other nonwhites.

*Summary of Explanatory Processes*

In these four illustrative accounts of a hypothesized course of events in unintended contact, we encounter the following explanatory processes: reorganization of beliefs, affect conditioning, restoration of cognitive balance, dissonance reduction, social reinforcement, and stimulus generalization. They will serve to illustrate how such explanatory processes supplement the network of descriptive concepts and the empirical relationships among them. With more illustrations the list would of course be longer.

Of the six explanatory processes listed, at least three are motivational in character. These are: reorganization of beliefs, restoration of cognitive balance, and dissonance reduction. Each of these three assumes a condition of inconsistency or incongruity or discrepancy which is discomforting and for which certain types of action or change offer relief.

A fourth of the six processes, social reinforcement, is motivational in a somewhat broader sense. Any one of several combinations of motives and incentives may be involved in the reinforcement process.

## MOTIVES IN THE CONCEPTUAL ANALYSIS: A SUMMARY

To conclude this analysis of unintended contact and behavior toward members of a disliked group, let me summarize the ways in which motives and motivelike constructs have been used in carrying it through. My overall impression is that in studying attitude-related behavior such as this we call upon such constructs frequently. I shall review the various uses of these constructs in the order they were encountered in the analysis.

### 1. *Social Attitude as a Motivelike Construct*

First, I noted that the construct of attitude toward members of a disliked group shows clearly one characteristic often attributed to motives, namely, that of "directing" behavior. This "directing" influence can be observed on both stimulus input and response output. On the input side we can observe the biasing influence of attitude on such functions as social perception, retention of information, interpretation of motives, and so on. This biasing effect is one of the facts that makes it advisable to distinguish in the conceptual analysis between objective characteristics of nonwhites in the contact situation, on the one hand, and their characteristics as perceived by the subject, on the other. On the output side are the actions taken to avoid or enhance association with the attitudinal object. These latter tendencies may be preceded by anticipated consequences, that is, expectancies of either unpleasant or pleasant experience if contact with the attitudinal object is in prospect.

### 2. *The Multiple Functions of Motives and Needs*

As we examined the interplay of motives and needs, on the one hand, with the contextual features of the contact situation, on the other, it became clear that these subject attributes contribute to determining several types of behavioral outcomes. A motive such as economic need may be an important determinant of entry into the contact situation. One like the approval motive may help speed up the initiation of interaction. Others like need-achievement and need-affiliation may, in conjunction with interaction experiences, determine the level of esteem and liking for nonwhites in the situation.

3. *Personality Traits as Motivelike Constructs*

Personality traits like self-esteem appear to interact with situational variables in essentially the same way as do motives and contribute to the same range of behavioral outcomes. The principle difference between motives and personality traits, as I used them in this analysis, seems to be that the rewarding or punishing agent or event is indicated more specifically in the motive name than in the trait name. Designating a motive, for example, as *approval* motive points rather explicitly to an environmental source of social approval as the relevant rewarding agent. By contrast, the environmental agent relevant to increased self-esteem is not so readily identifiable.

4. *Values as Motive Goal-States*

We noted that values may be thought of as conditions or goal-states which their holders desire to exist. How strongly a value is held or where it stands in a hierarchy of values may be taken as indicating how strongly the goal-state is desired—at least in relative terms. If we translate "desire" for the goal-state to "need" for it, the parallel to motive becomes clear. Take as an example the value of justice and consider a person for whom justice is a major value. We might say of such a person that an instance of blatant injustice aroused a need to increase justice. We might expect that actions or policies which seemed likely to increase justice would be endorsed by such a person. This has in fact been shown to be the case.

Like motives and personality traits, values may contribute to determining behavior at any one of the several time stages into which we break the event pattern. For example, if entry into a contact situation came to be seen as consistent with government by law, and this value was strongly held by a subject, that subject's entry should become more likely. Or if a religious leader stated that cooperative interaction with nonwhites was consistent with religious brotherhood and a subject held religious brotherhood as a strong value, his participation in such interaction should be more likely.

5. *Motivational Explanatory Processes*

Finally, we observed in the discussion of explanatory processes just completed that some of these processes are motivational in character. This is particularly true in the area of cognitive consistency where the impulsion to restore consistency, balance, or consonance is a familiar and widely accepted idea.

We may sum up by saying that motives and motivelike constructs enter a conceptual analysis of attitude-related behavior both as 1) explanatory processes and as 2) subject attributes in which individual differences may be observed. As subject attributes they range from motives and needs to such motivelike constructs as attitude, personality trait, and value. Such attributes interact with situational characteristics to determine outcome variables at each of several times stages in the analysis. These include entry into the proximity situation, initiation of interaction, development of esteem and liking for the nonwhites in the situation, and change of behavior and attitude toward nonwhites in general.

## REFERENCES

Brehm, J. W., & Cohen, A. R. *Explorations in cognitive dissonance.* New York: Wiley, 1962.

Byrne, D. Response to attitude similarity-dissimilarity as a function of affiliation need. *J. Person.*, 1962, **30**, 164–177.

Byrne, D., & Wong, T. J. Racial prejudice, interpersonal attraction and assumed dissimilarity of attitudes. *J. abnorm. soc. Psychol.*, 1962, **65**, 246–253.

Charters, W. W., Jr., & Newcomb, T. M. Some attitudinal effects of experimentally increased salience of a membership group. In Swanson, G. E., Newcomb, T. M., & Hartley, E. L. (Eds.), *Readings in social psychology.* New York: Henry Holt, 1952. Pp. 415–419.

Crowne, D. P., & Marlowe, D. *The approval motive: Studies in evaluative dependence.* New York: Wiley, 1964.

Deutsch, M., & Collins, Mary E. *Interracial housing: A psychological evaluation of a social experiment.* Minneapolis: University of Minnesota Press, 1951.

Getzels, J. W., & Walsh, J. The method of paired direct and projective questionnaires in the study of attitude structure and socialization. *Psychol. Monogr.*, 1958, **72**, no. 454.

Hardy, K. R. Determinants of conformity and attitude change. *J. abnorm. soc. Psychol.*, 1957, **54**, 289–294.

Harvey, O. J., Hunt, D., & Schroeder, H. *Conceptual systems and personality organization*. New York: Wiley, 1961.

Katz, D. The functional approach to the study of attitudes. *Public Opinion Quarterly*, 1960, **24**, 163–204.

Kelly, G. A. *The psychology of personal constructs*. New York: Norton, 1955.

Kohn, M., & Williams, R. M. Situational patterning in intergroup relations. *Amer. sociol. Rev.*, 1956, **21**, 164–174.

Komorita, S. S. Attitude content, intensity and the neutral point on a Likert scale. *J. soc. Psychol.*, 1963, **61**, 327–334.

Kramer, B. M. Residential contact as a determinant of attitudes toward Negroes. Unpublished Ph.D. dissertation, Harvard University, 1951.

Lindzey, G., & Byrne, D. Measurement of social choice and interpersonal attractiveness. In Lindzey, G., & Aronson, E. (Eds.), *The handbook of social psychology*. Reading: Addison-Wesley, 1968. Vol. II, pp. 452–525.

Marlowe, D., & Gergen, K. J. Personality and social interaction. In Lindzey, G., & Aronson, E. (Eds.), *The handbook of social psychology*. Reading: Addison-Wesley, 1968. Vol. II, pp. 590–666.

Murray, H. A. *Explorations in personality*. New York: Oxford University Press, 1938.

Newcomb, T. M. Autistic hostility and social reality. *Human Relations*, 1947, **1**, 69–86.

Rokeach, M. *The open and closed mind*. New York: Basic Books, 1960.

Rosenberg, M. J. An analysis of affective-cognitive consistency. In Hovland, C. I., & Rosenberg, M. J. (Eds.), *Attitude organization and change*. New Haven: Yale University Press, 1960. Pp. 15–64.

Smith, M. B., Bruner, J. S., & White, R. W. *Opinions and personality*. New York: Wiley, 1956.

Stein, D. D., Hardyck, J. A., & Smith, M. B. Race and belief: An open and shut case. *J. Person. soc. Psychol.*, 1965, **1**, 281–289.

Watson, G. *Action for unity*. New York: Harper, 1947.

Westie, F. R. A technique for the measurement of race attitudes. *Amer. sociol. Rev.*, 1953, **18**, 73–78.

Williams, R. M., Jr. *The reduction of intergroup tensions*. New York: Social Science Research Council, 1947.

Wilner, D. M., Walkley, Rosabelle P., & Cook, S. W. *Human relations in interracial housing: A study of the contact hypothesis*. Minneapolis: University of Minnesota Press, 1955.

Winder, A. E. White attitudes toward Negro-white interaction in an area of changing racial composition. *Amer. Psychol.*, 1952, **7**, 330–331 (abstract).

## COMMENTS

*Philip G. Zimbardo*

Social psychologists have been concerned with the antecedents and dynamics of prejudice for a long time. They ought to be in a position now to offer answers that are desperately needed to questions like, How can prejudice be reduced? How can people come to live together in harmony, responding to one another as individuals and not as subsets of a class to which there is a learned, generalized, stereotyped response? Stuart Cook's research can be viewed as either a repository for such answers, or as another instance of the futility experienced in actually trying to change prejudiced attitudes.

On the one hand, he offers us a descriptive model which interrelates virtually all of the variables which influence feelings of prejudice and prejudiced behavior. His model provides the starting point for many programs of attack on the components of this problem. The first step in utilizing it should be to annotate each conceptual variable with the prior research findings relevant to it. Then controlled laboratory research should study the many variables and relationships not yet investigated. Finally, Cook advocates a back-to-the-field, real-life testing of our laboratory findings.

His experimental findings may be taken as strong support for his equal-status contact hypothesis, since he demonstrates that the attitudes of extremely prejudiced people can be significantly changed (using a stringent criterion of one S.D.) in a relatively naturalistic work situation involving repeated interpersonal contact.

On the other hand, a pessimistic reading of his paper reveals that after this most ambitious, concentrated effort, involving a team of programmed confederates, establishing an independent testing center, 40 hours of interaction and theoretically ideal conditions, only 30 percent more change occurred than with untreated controls. Moreover, the very complexity of the model makes it unmanageable as presently stated, and the failure to indicate the relative importance of each component (by means of some weighted coefficient of importance) means that a behavior technologist has few guidelines as to where to begin any practical attitude change program.

But it may be that our current state of ignorance in psychology has resulted from our predilection for overly simplistic models, single-stage processes, and monotonic relationships. Perhaps Cook's model is the corrective we've needed in this area, and may be instructive of the way to proceed in other areas. Theoretical elegance loses its charm and appeal when it offers only explanation but not principles for control and modification of behavior.

Some more specific comments are:

1) The experimental situation employed involves both a high initiation fee, (testing, training, evaluation, and work) as well as a high exit fee, that is, subjects lose money if they drop out. According to the earlier study by Aronson and Mills, such subjects ought to increase their liking for the group, in this case, of their group partner. But if we rethink the implications of that study, is greater liking and self-deception all that is desired? If the group is not a good one, do you want uncritical loyalty to it? How will constructive change ever come about? Who will innovate and initiate change in the group, will it be the self-deceived high dissonance subjects? Albert Hirschman, Mark Synder and I are exploring these relationships between costs of group membership, liking for the group, and constructive or destructive behavior toward the group using a repeated exposure technique similar to that developed by Cook in his research. Our results may have a bearing upon the social conditions necessary for establishing groups which can effectively reduce prejudice.

2) Cook provides a valuable lead with his findings of systematic individual differences between changers and non-changers on several interpersonal traits. The relationships between these variables and social-environmental ones need to be made explicit and to be elaborated.

3) I cannot agree that dissonance is a useful conceptual tool to understand the results of this particular research because there is such a high degree of extrinsic justification for engaging in the discrepant behavior that it undercuts the perception of choice in the situation, thereby minimizing the perceived dissonance. When considering what happens to a prejudiced white who moves into an integrated housing project, we see that at the time of entry he has a need for inexpensive housing which justifies his discrepant behavior of living with blacks (thus little dissonance). As time elapses between

entry and interaction with blacks, general positive features of living in the project become more salient, and the initial prejudiced attitude which would have prevented living in such a project becomes less salient. Thus, as Daryl Bem has argued in connection with other dissonance research, there may not be dissonance between current behavior and initial attitude, because the latter is not cognitively salient. In fact, it might be argued that there would be more positive attitude change in line with the tolerant contact behavior if this act were seen as truly counter-attitudinal.

4) The use of the principle of stimulus generalization to explain transfer effects of changed attitudes involves some subtle and complex issues. Transfer should increase as cue distinctiveness does, with a high level of transfer over a narrow band width (i.e., to stimuli qualitatively similar to those in initial training). But as the initial stimulus is both highly visible and distinctive between classes but not within members of the same class (as in black/white skin color), then transfer effects ought to be more diffuse, a weaker effect over a flatter generalization gradient. The question is what kind of transfer is desired, how specific is the stimulus generalization expected: to all blacks, to only those of a certain skin color shading, to only those who look like the confederate, or confined only to the confederate who is perceived as an exception to the rule (the Lena Horne–Harry Belafonte effect)?

5) Finally, we arrive at the point where the thinking of Cook and Aronson converge with my own—the importance of the process of individuation for generating interpersonal attraction. There is no more effective technique for getting someone to like you than to break through the barrier of depersonalization, to induce in the other an individuated perception of you, while making him feel you are responding to his unique individuality. No one wants to be part of the ground all the time (even if it is an unchanging positive background of evaluation). The discerning other offers the possibility that he will discover what we believe is special in us. The prejudiced person uses verbal stereotypes to make himself inaccessible to new information about particular features of the stimulus complex, becomes less discerning, and minimizes the considerable psychological effort involved in being discriminating (type 1). "To encourage seeing him [the Negro] confederate as an individual

rather than only as a Negro," is clearly a necessary condition for prejudice reduction (perhaps its best criterion), and equal-status contact may be the best technique for changing the perception of the black from ground to figure. We might also ponder whether someone ought not to try the reverse procedure on black militant subjects to see if they can be made to differentiate among the varied manifestations of Mister Charley.

# The Human Choice: Individuation, Reason, and Order versus Deindividuation, Impulse, and Chaos

PHILIP G. ZIMBARDO

*Stanford University*

Control. That's what current psychology is all about. The use of powerful schedules of reinforcement, probing neurophysiological techniques, computer simulation, and the new behavior therapies (among other advances) enable psychologists to manipulate the responses of a wide range of research subjects in order to improve learning and discrimination; to arouse, rechannel, and satisfy drives; and to redirect abnormal or deviant behavior. It has, in fact, become the all-consuming task of most psychologists to learn how to bring behavior under stimulus control.

It is especially impressive to note (in any volume of the *Nebraska Symposium on Motivation*) the relative ease with which laboratory researchers can induce motives which have an immediate and often demonstrably pervasive effect on a vast array of response measures. On the other hand, one must reconcile this with the observation that in the "real world" people often show considerable tolerance (or unresponsiveness) to environmentally determined states of deprivation or arousal. To what extent is man at the mercy of environmental and physiological demand stimuli? Under what conditions is behavior *not* controlled by stimulus intensity, hours of deprivation, rumblings in the gut, or passion for success?

Laboratory studies of motivation and behavior control have typically been designed to render living organisms into passive subjects, who simply convert stimulus inputs into correlated response outputs. Of course, it is then possible to generalize laws of control across species. But such an approach neglects attention to the processes which characterize human behavior in its nonlaboratory manifestations; people have cognitions about the conditions associated with their entrance into, and acceptance of, deprivation and aversive states. When man exercises his volition, chooses to commit himself to a course of action, and accepts personal responsibility for its consequences, he distinguishes himself as unique among living creatures and calls into question our laws of behavioral control.

We have found in an extensive series of experiments (cf. Zimbardo, 1969) that the expected impact of drive stimuli on behavior can be altered by creating a set of conditions which make the subject active in initiating cognitive appraisal of the relationship between self, commitment, and the social and physical environment. This occurs where subjects are made aware of their volition in choosing to enter or to avoid a state known to be unpleasant, and where their commitment is supported by only minimal extrinsic justifications. When a person must directly confront the environment which his choice has created for him, then cognitive intervention destroys the isomorphic correspondence between stimulus level and reactivity. In the process of having to generate *intrinsic* justifications in order to make a discrepant commitment appear rational and consistent, man shifts the locus of control of his behavior from external stimuli to internal cognitive controls.

Our studies reveal that this cognitive control of motivation extends equally to biological drives (hunger, thirst, pain) and to social needs (achievement, approval, aggression). These effects are shown in subjective responses (attitudes, perceptions, judgments), behavioral reactions (learning, conditioning, memory, reaction time), consummatory behavior (eating, drinking), and even in physiological responses (release of free fatty acids in the blood, galvanic skin response). Since these studies emerged from a dissonance theory framework, it is not surprising that central to our analysis of the dynamics involved are consistency, commitment, and responsibility. However, these processes take on a slightly different appearance when used as basic ingredients in the human stew we hope to concoct in the present paper.

## Consistency, Rationality, and Responsibility

It is frequently necessary to strive for consistency because consistency between action and self-knowledge, between word and deed, are so prized in our culture that to be inconsistent is to be abnormal. If one's behavior is not comparable to that of people whom he uses for reference, then he must establish the rationality of his behavioral commitment. He must first convince his observing, critical self (who stands in for society) that his commitment follows *rationally* from an analysis of the stimulus conditions. It is irrational to expose oneself to a series of shocks previously experienced and known to be painful, especially when one is given little justification for doing so, as well as an explicit option to refuse (cf. Zimbardo, Cohen, Weisenberg, Dworkin, & Firestone, 1966). This psycho-logical self-deception induces motivational changes which lower the drive state to match the behavioral commitment.

The psychological homeostasis posited by such a consistency principle is not an end in itself, but rather a means toward minimizing dependency on the environment and maximizing control over it. This is achieved not by accepting the environment as given but by modifying it to effect a "rational" fit after the commitment. The response then comes to determine the nature of the stimulus, rather than the opposite. It has been said:

> On a more primitive, personal level consistency is a safeguard against chaos, it is the ordering aspect of rationality that is in constant struggle with the irrational forces within and outside the individual. Thus, consistency becomes a self-imposed principle in order for the individual to maintain a conception of himself as a normal member of society who, in behaving as others expect him to, gains their social recognition (the most potent of all reinforcers) as a rational decision-maker, whose decisions help him to control his environment. [Zimbardo, 1969, p. 280]

Volition, commitment, and responsibility fuse to form the core of one pole of the basic human choice[1] we shall be considering in this

1. Under Italian law, a woman was arrested recently (in Caserta, Italy) for keeping her boyfriend a prisoner for five months. She was charged with the rare crime of *plagio*—reducing somebody to psychological slavery by eliminating his faculties of choice, criticism, and will.

One way in which the Japanese avoid personal responsibility for their action

paper. The act of freely making a commitment for which one assumes responsibility *individuates* the decision-maker. By this readiness to enter into a contractual agreement which has consequences for which he must be liable, man sets himself in opposition to all those who refuse to act individually, and thus separates himself from tribal ties to undifferentiated (safer) group action.

If the reader will be indulgent enough to sustain another flight of rhetoric, we can say that one way of conceptualizing the research we have done on the cognitive control of motivation is in terms of freedom. Through utilizing cognitive controls (of virtually limitless potential) man gains freedom from the behavioral proscriptions imposed by his history, physiology, and ecology. Indeed, thinking and believing can make it so!

## All Control Be Damned

"The eyes of chaos shining through the veil of order."—R. Rolland

While we were myopically uncovering the many implications of this approach and were demonstrating in the laboratory the remarkably fine degree of control which man had at his disposal, all hell was breaking loose outside in the real world. All about us—from the mass media, from our everyday observations, from reliable anecdotes—the evidence overwhelmingly points to a very different conception of the human organism. Reason, premeditation, the acceptance of personal responsibility, the feeling of obligation, the rational defense of commitments, appear to be losing ground to an impulse-dominated hedonism bent on anarchy.

Perhaps after surveying a portion of this evidence thrust upon our sensibilities, we can draw some inferences about the processes involved which may help clarify the nature of the other, darker side of the Human Choice we are considering.

---

is through the use of the passive-causative verb tense. This linguistic device characterizes the speaker as having been made to do something by someone else or some external force, as in "I don't want to be made to drink too much tonight because I must drive." The American counterpart appears in the old song, "You made me love you, I didn't want to do it . . . ."

1. *Self-Destruction*

For each of the one thousand suicides committed every day, the UN's World Health Organization estimates (in its booklet *Prevention of Suicide*, 1968) that another seven attempts at self-destruction are unsuccessful. The means vary across countries—hanging in Nigeria, poison in Brazil, gas in Great Britain, guns for American men and asphyxiation for American women. There appear, however, to be some common causes which bridge national boundaries, notably social isolation from family or friends and a break with one's routine or habitual life pattern. Self-mutilation can also come under other guises, as seen in a report from two villages in Manila where hundreds of Filipinos "flogged themselves in processions behind masked men dragging crosses. They beat themselves until blood streamed down their backs" (*New York Times*, April 12, 1967). See also Mexico's *flagelantes* (*Look*, September 3, 1968). Young boys dying from sniffing hair spray in plastic bags and similar gruesome tales are constant reminders of how many of us are bent on self-destruction. (Cf. Schneidman, 1967.) One of the more extreme cases of a "mod" mode of destroying our bodies and minds was observed recently at the Haight-Ashbury Medical Clinic: A twenty-two-year-old boy had injected himself 37,000 times in the last four years with every conceivable drug he could put into his needle.

2. *Destruction of Others*

In America approximately 760,000 persons have been murdered by gunfire since the turn of the century. In 1967 alone there were (according to FBI statistics) 7,700 homicides with guns. This figure increased 16 percent in the first quarter of 1968, with rape up 19 percent and aggravated assault with a deadly weapon also soaring by 13 percent. Surveys across the nation reveal that only about 15 percent of murderers were strangers to their victims, two-thirds of the rape victims knew their attackers, and most victims of felonious assault were also acquainted with their assailants.

The public slaying of nationally known figures such as Medgar Evers, Martin Luther King, Malcolm X, John and Robert Kennedy, as well as Lee Harvey Oswald and George Lincoln Rockwell can be regarded as a catalyst for the recent flurry of mass murders by Charles Whitman (14 shot to death and 33 injured from his tower at the University of Texas), Richard Speck (8 nurses strangled and stabbed to death), and Robert Smith (5 women and 2 children arranged in a cartwheel formation and shot through the head). Although the nation is horrified by these crimes, nevertheless a Gallup poll of February, 1968, showed that 70 percent of the respondents wanted to continue bombing Vietnam in order to "improve our chances for meaningful peace talks."

Sometimes the murder is planned and systematic, as with Rio de Janeiro's "Death Squad" (a self-appointed group to help curb crime), which left their 150 victims in one month "bullet-ridden and tortured beyond recognition" (*San Francisco Chronicle*, January 28, 1969). In other cases, it is the result of an insignificant dispute over a parking space, a seat in a bar, or a lost wager, but more frequently it occurs for no apparent reason other than that one person wants to kill another—for the feel of it.

The hypocrisy which underscores this assault on humanity is seen in society's demand for revenge over one crime while ignoring a second and participating in a third. One cannot help but be horrified by the brutal rape-murder of young Ann Jiminez in San Francisco (*Chronicle*, December 26, 1968) witnessed by perhaps 25 other teenagers, who watched or participated in her being abused, sexually violated, kicked, and left to die in an alley with obscenities scrawled on her body with lipstick. The reason? She allegedly stole a friend's pair of motorcycle boots. The citizens of Zurich were likewise outraged at the merciless beating to death of a young girl by religious fanatics who claimed to be exorcising the devil from her (*Newsweek*, February 14, 1969). However, where was the concern for human values, for revenge, when the new superintendent of the Arkansas State Penitentiary discovered that torture and killing of prisoners (over 200 inmates reported "missing") had been a common occurrence (*New York Times*, January 28, 1968)? He was removed from the position, and the "politically delicate situation" was quickly covered up. A congressional hearing into abuse of prisoners was conducted by Senator Dodd (D-Conn.) early this year. The thousands of complaints which forced this inquiry were substantiated by numerous statements such as the following: "I have seen them [boys no more than 12 years old] raped with a blanket around their head to muffle screams, forced into prostitution, bought and sold and even used for security in a loan or gambling debt" (*San Francisco Chronicle*, March 29, 1969).

But how many of us can afford righteous indignation at any inhumane crime when we are told that at least 700 children are killed each year in the United States at the hands of their parents, and that up to 40,000 more youngsters suffer serious injury by beatings and tortures from their parents and siblings. In their somber appraisal of the "battered child syndrome," Helfer and Kempe (1968) report some of the reasons given by parents who were incited to murder their child: "baby was fussy," "cried too much," "soiled diapers," "would not eat," "drinking sibling's bottle," "needed love and attention." One survey reported in this volume makes it clear that there is a community conspiracy of silence against the abused child, since it is estimated that about 3 million adults personally knew families in which there was child abuse. Only rarely did this knowledge ever result in intervention of any kind.

We are now also witnessing a new use of an age-old destructive technique, the "Dear John" letter. Not only has there been an apparent increase in the incidence of these letters to American servicemen fighting in Vietnam (compared to the Second World War), but their format is also predictably different than in the past. Dr. Emanuel Tanay, who has been studying this problem, reports that "some [wives and girl friends] send photographs of themselves with other men in compromising positions. Some send tape recordings of intimate exchanges with another man." No longer is the blow softened by the guilt experienced by the women or by their feelings of empathy; rather there is resentment at being abandoned, unwillingness to delay gratification, and direct expression of hatred toward the perceived cause of their frustration.

### 3. *Riots and Mob Violence*

The past five years have witnessed an unprecedented eruption of mass action against the government, war, industries, and "the establishment" as it exists in colleges and elsewhere. According to a report prepared by the National Commission on the Causes and Prevention of Violence there have occurred during this time: 230 violent urban outbursts resulting in 191 deaths and 8,000 injuries, as well as millions of dollars in property damage; 370 civil rights demonstrations and 80 counter-demonstrations with more than a million participants; hundreds of seizures and destruction of university buildings with injury to students, faculty, and police; and a large number of antiwar marches and protests, some of which have resulted in widespread injuries to participants from counter-demonstrators.

We have witnessed "police riots" of the Tactical Squad called in during the night to evacuate student rebels from occupied buildings at Columbia University in the spring of 1968, and the savage abuse displayed by the police at last year's Democratic Convention in Chicago.

> The ones who actually got arrested seemed to have gotten caught up among the police, like a kind of human medicine ball, being shoved and knocked back and forth from one cop to the next with what was obviously *mounting* fury. And this was a phenomenon somewhat unexpected, which we were to observe consistently throughout the days of violence—that rage seemed to engender rage; the bloodier and more brutal the cops were, the more their fury increased.

This account by writer Terry Southern ("Grooving in Chicago," *Esquire*, November, 1968) squares with a statement by a group of University of California Admissions Office clerks who accused police of the bloody beating of students, staff, and reporters without provocation. Their letter (quoted in the *San Francisco Chronicle*, February 29, 1969) alleges that a student being beaten as he was dragged down the stairs, screamed, "'Please don't hit me any more! Won't someone help me?' . . . *The more he begged, the more they hit.*" It is also reminiscent of the account of an American sergeant who was part of an army intelligence unit interrogating (and torturing) Vietcong prisoners:

> First you strike to get mad, then you strike because you are mad, and in the end you strike because of the sheer pleasure of it. This is the gruesome aspect of it which has haunted me ever since I came back from Viet Nam. [*Toronto Star*, November 24, 1967]

Mob violence doesn't require confrontations between ideologies —it can, under the right circumstances, be triggered by almost any event. Recently a crowd of about 100 teenagers in New York, angered when a girl was hit by a light panel truck, assaulted the driver, overturned his truck, set it ablaze, and hurled bricks and bottles at firemen attempting to douse the fire. A false rumor that a friend had been beaten by white girls sent a group of 15 black girls on a rampage through Lincoln High School in San Francisco (*Chronicle*, February 27, 1969). "More than 300 persons were killed and about 500 injured in events that followed an unpopular ruling by the referee in a soccer match between Peru and Argentina" (*New York Times*, May 25, 1964). This tragedy was replayed last year when a stampede at a soccer stadium in Argentina killed 71 and injured 130 spectators (June 24, 1968).

4. *Loss of the Value of Life*

> A crowd of 200 students at the University of Oklahoma gathered to watch a mentally disturbed fellow student who threatened to jump from a tower. Their chanting of "Jump, jump" in unison and taunting of him may have contributed to his subsequent jump and death. [UPI release, September 23, 1967]

Several years prior to this incident, an Albany, New York, man was saved from a similar suicide leap by the coaxing of his seven-year-old nephew while onlookers jeered, "Jump! Jump! Jump!" Among the curious crowd of about 4,000 were people challenging him to jump, "C'mon, you're chicken," "You're yellow," and betting whether he would or not. Instructive is the comment by one well-dressed man, "I hope he jumps on this side. We couldn't see him if he jumped over there" (*New York Times*, April 14, 1964).

The value we place on human life is in part reflected in our attitudes and treatment of the aged and the dead. Recently at a home for the aged in San Francisco (Laguna Honda), one man died of a heart attack shortly after being taunted by a roving band of teenagers, while another elderly resident collapsed after being lassoed by them.

One of the commodities which our affluence has been able to purchase is nursing homes in which many American children can now dump their aged parents. We have about 30,000 institutions offering long-term care for the aged, and regardless of the quality of care they dispense, being sent to one "is rather like condemning old cars to the scrap heap" (according to Charles Boucher, senior medical officer in the British Ministry of Health). Gerontologists have pointed out that many of these "homes" can strip a person's will to live by enforcing inactivity (keeping the patients bedridden makes them easier to deal with and less of an insurance risk); over-sedating the patients (to control them); disregarding their privacy (since they are only objects to be managed); depriving them of small conveniences; and serving minimally adequate diets (only 94 cents per patient per day is the average food cost—according to probably overestimated figures supplied by the homes to welfare agencies). Finally, the newest insult to the patient's humanity is the notorious "life-care contract." By making the institution his life insurance beneficiary in return for guaranteed bed and board for the patient, an insidious situation is created in which "the unconscious resentment of a guest who is 'overdue' cannot fail to have its effect" (cf. R. E. Burger, "Who Cares for the Aged?," *Saturday Review*, January 25, 1969).

In Atlanta, Georgia, a mortician has built a *drive-in* mortuary. "The deceased will be lying in a lighted window, sort of tilted to the front so they can conveniently be seen," said the mortician. This way busy people "who just don't have the time . . . can drive by and just keep on going." Another feature of this innovation, according to its originator, is that "the people won't have to dress up to view the remains" (*San Francisco Chronicle*, March 14, 1968).

5. *Loss of Behavior Control*

When an individual or collection of individuals loses control of the mechanisms which regulate behavior and make responses sensitive to feedback, then any of these phenomena can become common occurrences:

a) A teenage boy was beaten nearly to death during a junior high school fraternity initiation. When the boy refused to cry—the signal which would have terminated his being pounded by the fists of his fraternity brothers—"they lost their heads" and beat him until he lost consciousness. His father did not press charges because he said the boys liked his son, they had no grudge against him, but merely "got carried away" (*New York Post*, April 7, 1964).

b) From time to time certain automobile drivers experience episodes of violence and use their car as a weapon against other cars and their drivers, "almost certainly contributing to a significant number of automobile crashes" (according to a government advisory committee report, *New York Times*, February 29, 1968).

c) A resident surgeon who had an argument with his girl friend, a woman physician working with him at Methodist Hospital in Brooklyn, stabbed her 25 to 30 times (*New York Times*, December 26, 1967). This uncontrolled aggression, and the inability to terminate it after a "reasonable" time, reminds one of Albert Camus' stranger, who unloads the full chamber of his gun into his Arab adversary because once he pulls the trigger it is easier to do it again and again than it is to stop.

Recently, as soon as Montreal's police left their jobs in a wage dispute, the reaction of the professional criminals was immediate and predictable—they knocked off ten banks in short order. What was unexpected was the "national disgrace" created by "just plain people" doing their own inner thing once formalized social controls were lifted. Roving groups of "citizens" smashed store windows, looted, set fires, disrupted traffic, and ran amok until finally reinhibited by the return of the police and the presence of the Canadian army (*Time*, October 20, 1969).

### The Times They Are A-changing

This brief chronicle of American life in the latter part of this decade represents, I believe, a fundamental change in the quality of individual and mass hostility, aggression, and inhumanity from what it has been in our lifetime. Less than ten years ago, Anatol Rapaport (1961) was able to state with authority, "The mob has disappeared from the American scene and has carried with it into seeming oblivion the phenomenon of overt mob violence" (pp. 50–51).

But our concern should not be limited to the new forms of violence. Much more is happening which, though less dramatic, is equally significant. Audiences of the Living Theater are stripping off their clothes and marching naked through staid, old, blue New

Haven. Wordy psychoanalysis is being pushed aside by encounter groups, implosive therapy, "touchies" and "feelies," and non-cognitive therapies. While the over-thirty crowd is getting divorced at a faster rate than ever before, getting turned on by topless and/or bottomless waitresses and public showings of pornographic films, their children are swinging in Free Sex League activities, becoming "groupies" (girls who sleep with all or most members of rock bands, cf. *Time*, February 28, 1969), entering communal marriages, and rapidly increasing the tide of illegitimate births and the cases of v.d. "Fly now, pay later" has become "Fly now, maybe later won't ever come, or if it does, you'll be too stoned to care."

What we are observing all about us, then, is a sudden change in the restraints which normally control the expression of our drives, impulses, and emotions. For better or for worse, we have here the emergence of a kind of freedom different from that made possible through use of the cognitive control mechanisms we described earlier. It is the freedom to act, to be spontaneous, to shed the straitjacket of cogitation, rumination, and excessive concern with "ought" and "should." Behavior is freed from obligations, liabilities, and the restrictions imposed by guilt, shame, and fear.

### *Dionysus Revisited?*

What we are setting up as protagonists are not simply Cognition and Action, but more basically the Forces of Individuation versus those of Deindividuation. These forces are hardly new to each other; their antagonism can be traced back through all recorded history, as an integral part of the myth and ritual of peoples everywhere.

If the reader recoils at the motiveless murders, senseless destruction, and uncontrolled mob violence we've just described, he might alter his sense of wisdom, justice, and propriety by considering Nietzsche's analysis of the similar Apollonian view of Dionysiac forces:

> In order to comprehend this total emancipation of all the symbolic powers, one must have reached the same measure of inner freedom those powers themselves were making manifest; which is to say that the votary of Dionysos could not be understood except by his own kind. It is not difficult to imagine the awed surprise with which the Apollonian Greek

> must have looked on him. And that surprise would be further increased as the latter realized, with a shudder, that all this was not so alien to him after all, that his Apollonian consciousness was but a thin veil hiding him from the whole Dionysiac realm. [P. 28]

Nietzsche goes on to note:

> Throughout the range of ancient civilization . . . we find evidence of Dionysiac celebrations. . . . The central concern of such celebrations was, almost universally, a complete sexual promiscuity overriding every form of established tribal law; all the savage urges of the mind were unleashed on those occasions until they reached that paroxysm of lust and cruelty which has always struck me as the "witches' cauldron" *par excellence*. [Pp. 25–26]
>
> Schopenhauer has described for us the tremendous awe which seizes man when he suddenly begins to doubt the cognitive modes of experience, in other words, when in a given instance the law of causation seems to suspend itself. If we add to this awe the glorious transport which arises in man, even from the very depths of nature, at the shattering of the *principium individuationis*, then we are in a position to apprehend the essence of Dionysiac rapture, whose closest analogy is furnished by physical intoxication. Dionysiac stirrings arise either through the influence of those narcotic potions of which all primitive races speak in their hymns, or through the powerful approach of spring, which penetrates with joy the whole frame of nature. So stirred, the individual forgets himself completely. [P. 22]

Mythically, deindividuation is the ageless life force, the cycle of nature, the blood ties, the tribe, the female principle, the irrational, the impulsive, the anonymous chorus, the vengeful furies. To be singular, to stand apart from other men, to aspire to Godhead, to honor social contracts and man-made commitments above family bonds, is to be individuated (as in Agamemnon's choice to sacrifice his daughter for his role as leader of men).

## The Psychology of Deindividuation

One might suppose that social scientists have long been concerned with a process which claims to underlie all human social organization and forms the very basis of human tragedy. Hardly. There appear to be only two experiments and one conceptual article explicitly dealing with these phenomena. Festinger, Pepitone, & Newcomb (1952) describe a state of affairs in which there is a "reduction in inner restraints" toward expression of counter-norm behavior when individuals are "submerged in a group." Their correlational study tends to show that groups in which there is more public expression of hostility toward parents (the experimental anti-social task response) are perceived by their members to be more attractive, and that these members notice less which others made specific negative remarks.

It took more than a decade before a second study was done by Singer, Brush, and Lublin (1965). They emphasize the loss of self-consciousness and the reduction in feelings of distinctiveness as essential to deindividuation. On the response side, this inferred construct should lead to engaging in a usually undesirable act and feeling greater attraction to the group which allows such behavior. Under manipulated conditions of identification (dressed in best clothes versus dressed in old clothes and baggy lab coats), differences in the use of obscene language were found. More groups given the Low Identifiability manipulation used obscenity than those given the High Identifiability treatment, and these groups were found to be more attractive.

Ziller's analysis (1964) of deindividuation centers more on the concepts of ego identity and individual assimilation into large organizations. Individuation is viewed as a subjective differentiation of self from other social objects in the field; "the greater the number of bits of information required to locate the person, the greater the degree of deindividuation" (p. 345). Ziller's proposal that "individuation is desirable within a supportive social climate, but deindividuation is sought as a defense against a threatening environment" (p. 344) certainly deserves to be put to empirical test, and will receive indirect support from our subsequent analysis of big-city vandalism.

Although Golding's *Lord of the Flies* is not a formal piece of social science research, it is perhaps the best available source of observations on and insights into the antecedents and range of consequences of deindividuation in emerging groups.[2]

2. Other fascinating aspects of the process of deindividuation and dehumanization (which will be treated later in this paper) can be found in the novels of Anthony Burgess (*A Clockwork Orange* [New York: Ballantine, 1965]), George Bataille (*The Story of the Eye* [North Hollywood, Calif.: Brandon House, 1968]),

## Deindividuation Unmasked

The remainder of this paper (which should be viewed only as a working paper in the process of developing a comprehensive model of deindividuation) will: a) define how the term *deindividuation* will be used; b) specify a set of antecedent variables and characteristic consequences; c) describe a series of laboratory experiments to test the validity of these distinctions; d) evaluate in field observations and in a simple field experiment conclusions derived from the laboratory studies; e) suggest new directions in which our research is headed; and f) distinguish dehumanization from deindividuation, as well as voluntary and involuntary forms of the latter.

Deindividuation is a complex, hypothesized process in which a series of antecedent social conditions lead to changes in perception of self and others, and thereby to a lowered threshold of normally restrained behavior. Under appropriate conditions what results is the "release" of behavior in violation of established norms of appropriateness.

Such conditions permit overt expression of antisocial behavior, characterized as selfish, greedy, power-seeking, hostile, lustful, and destructive. However, they also allow a range of "positive" behaviors which we normally do not express overtly, such as intense feelings of happiness or sorrow, and open love for others. Thus emotions and impulses usually under cognitive control are more likely to be expressed when the input conditions minimize self-observation and evaluation as well as concern over evaluation by others.

We may speak loosely of: conditions of deindividuation (conditions stimulating it), the feelings or state of deindividuation (the experiential aspect of the input variables together with the inferred subjective changes), and deindividuated behaviors (characterized by several specific output behaviors). Deindividuation refers to the entire process and only then becomes a unique psychological construct.

---

and Pauline Réage (*Story of O* [New York: Grove Press, 1967]). The interested reader is also referred to the classic study *The Crowd* by LeBon (New York: Ballantine, 1969; first published 1895) and Smelser's sociological *Theory of Collective Behavior* (New York: Free Press, 1962), and Canetti's *Crowds and Power* (New York: Viking Press, 1963).

The major variables in the process are summarized in the descriptive model outlined in Fig. 1. At this primitive stage in formulating a theory to organize our diverse set of observations and to guide our future data-gathering, this schematic model is but a starting point to focus attention on some relevant variables and testable relationships. For the present argument, it must suffice to elaborate only briefly upon the reasoning (and intuition) which generated this categorization. Before examining each antecedent and consequence of deindividuation, let us mention two models to account for the control mechanism of this process.

*A Social Learning or Energy-Form Core Mechanism*

Our starting point may be either a mundane motivational assumption or a farfetched symbolic-mythical one. The first states that many behaviors which would be inherently pleasurable to manifest are denied expression because they conflict with norms of social appropriateness. The affect associated with these inhibited behaviors mounts over time, but is held in check by a learned concern for how others would react to the expression of this behavior, as well as by the self-observing aspect of conscience. Conditions which minimize the use of these twin inhibitors—looking outward for normative controls and inward for internalized controls—should lead to disinhibition, or to a release of the presumably gratifying behavior. By definition, expression of such pleasurable behavior is self-reinforcing; therefore, once initiated, it should be self-maintaining and -perpetuating until a marked change occurs in the state of the organism or in environmental conditions.

Consider for a moment a very different core mechanism. Start by assuming that life represents the conversion of matter into energy; that initially this energy is undifferentiated and uncontrolled in its onset, direction, intensity, and terminal properties. Such a force is dangerous to the individual organism because it could be turned in on itself and become self-consuming and destructive. Likewise, it is dangerous for society because it makes every member potentially subject to the transient (demonic) impulses of all others. To contain this energy from destroying the substance which creates it or the environment which nourishes it, forms, structures, and

*Input Variables →*

A—Anonymity
B—Responsibility: shared, diffused, given up
C—Group size, activity
D—Altered temporal perspective: present expanded, future and past distanced
E—Arousal
F—Sensory input overload
G—Physical involvement in the act
H—Reliance upon noncognitive interactions and feedback
I—Novel or unstructured situation
J—Altered states of consciousness, drugs, alcohol, sleep, etc.

*Inferred Subjective Changes →*

Minimization of:
1. Self-observation-evaluation
2. Concern for social evaluation

↓

Weakening of controls based upon guilt, shame, fear, and commitment

↓

Lowered threshold for expressing inhibited behaviors

*Output Behaviors*

a. Behavior emitted is emotional, impulsive, irrational, regressive, with high intensity
b. Not under the controlling influence of usual external discriminative stimuli
c. Behavior is self-reinforcing and is intensified, amplified with repeated expressions of it
d. Difficult to terminate
e. Possible memory impairments; some amnesia for act
f. Perceptual distortion—insensitive to incidental stimuli and to relating actions to other actors
g. Hyper-responsiveness—"contagious plasticity" to behavior of proximal, active others
h. Unresponsiveness to distal reference groups
i. Greater liking for group or situation associated with "released" behavior
j. At extreme levels, the group dissolves as its members become autistic in their impulse gratification
k. Destruction of traditional forms and structures

FIGURE 1

Representation of the Deindividuation Process

institutionalized systems of control have evolved. The most basic of these is "ego identity"—the imposition of a unique form on this energy of nature which differentiates it, brings it into contact with social and physical reality. Although this reason-conferring form is essential for man to survive, evolve, and develop into the supremely intelligent being he is, nevertheless it is "as though nature were bemoaning the fact of her fragmentation, her decomposition into separate individuals" (Nietzsche, p. 27). In each of us, therefore, resides a fascination with the confrontation of natural energy and imposed human structure; an attraction toward the irrational and the impulsive; Caligula's arbitrary use of power; and a morbid curiosity about danger, destruction, and death. We admire the matador and intellectually want him to win, but our viscera side with the bull and emotionally we identify with the force of his untamed power.

We must then posit a "universal need" to shatter all formal controls, albeit temporarily, as occurs in every person through dreaming. This fact is the basis of society's institutionalization of revelous behavior—harvest festivals in agrarian societies and carnivals in religious ones—where an "unproductive waste of energy" is encouraged. Functionally, such festivals serve to siphon off destructive energy, prevent unpredictable individually initiated release of impulses, and enable the deindividuated reveler to experience both the pleasure of his revels and the satisfaction of becoming *reindividuated* following their termination. Since "ego identity" alone is not enough to thoroughly contain this energy, concepts of time, history, logic, law, and religion were developed to distill it further.

The human imposition of a temporal ordering on experienced events is the most interesting of these systems of control. Time can be thought of as a function of the ego which gives it a (spurious) continuity in the face of the timelessness of the unconscious and its instinctual demands.

> The concept of time is used among other methods as a defense against the too massive impact of the outer world. By breaking experience up into measured time units the mass of reality itself is broken into small bits which the eye can "taste." [Dooley, 1941]

Our insistence on preparing for the future makes our desires for immediate gratification seem infantile. The present becomes negated, according to Heidegger, since it is but "the no longer past and the not yet future." History and logic similarly force us to perceive continuity and rational consistency; legal systems impose future responsibility and liability, while religion denies the corporeal substance of this energy, except as sin to be obliterated. Behavior, then, usually succumbs to the control of these "cognitive" systems which guarantee the existence of self and society by fostering individuation.

*Component Analysis of Our Model*

Since such talk is upsetting to many psychologists, let us rather pursue the more reasonable assumptions underlying the deindividuation process that we outlined previously (Fig. 1). How can we generate spontaneous, impulsive behavior—behavior which is "unusual" in the individual's life experience? Or put more personally, can you remember a time when you were completely spontaneous, where action precluded thought and you experienced total freedom of expression? If so, what conditions surrounded this unlikely event?

The output behaviors described above should become more likely as the individual feels more *anonymous*. If others can't identify or single you out, they can't evaluate, criticize, judge, or punish you; thus, there need be no concern for social evaluation. Another type of anonymity derives from feeling alienated from others and from aspects of the self. Karl Marx distinguishes between estrangement from others (*Entfremdung*), loss of control over the products of one's labors (*Entaussurung*), and being made to feel one is only an object, a thing (*Verdinglichungen*). The loss of identifiability can be conferred by being "submerged in a crowd," disguised, masked, or dressed in a uniform like everyone else, or by darkness. Social conditions can also encourage anonymity, but we will hold our discussion of that until later. The most prevalent fantasy of children which illustrates the appeal of anonymity is wanting to be "the invisible man." That this loss of identifiability is also frightening can be seen from the ambivalent reaction of many children toward wearing masks or seeing other people in masks. Marcel Marceau's pantomime of a clown hopelessly struggling to remove his smiling mask is an eloquent expression of this ambivalence.

The *responsibility* one feels for the consequences of having engaged in antisocial behavior (here broadly defined) may be made insignificant by situations in which it is shared by others, by conditions which obscure the relationship between an action and its effects, or by a leader's willingness to assume all of it. The presence of others facilitates the first of these techniques. After the 1964 slaying of the civil rights workers (Schwerner, Chaney, and Goodman) in Mississippi, it is reported by Huie (1965) that the Klansmen passed the murder weapon from hand to hand, so that all shared equally the responsibility, or so that no one was individually responsible. Similarly, in modern electrocution chambers in American prisons there are often three executioners, each of whom pulls a switch simultaneously—only one of which is operative. In firing squads, one gun is loaded with blanks so that each man may believe he personally was not responsible. Compliance with the demands of a role limits perceived responsibility, as argued by Adolph Eichmann at his war crimes trial. Group and national leaders often trade assumption of responsibility for power: the masses yield their power to the fascist dictator in return for his willingness to relieve them of responsibility for many kinds of action. It is, of course, also likely that inadequate socialization can fail to develop a sense of responsibility in an individual, but we are here focusing primarily upon initially "responsible" persons.

Although the presence of a *group* (and its size) is an aid to member anonymity and shared responsibility, it can serve additional functions by providing models for action, generating physical activity which itself is arousing, or serving as a catalyst by triggering behavior in a given direction or toward a given object. It should be clear, however, that although deindividuation can be influenced by group phenomena, it is presented here as an intra-individual process. As such, it is also equally sensitive to the other antecedent variables and states outlined in Fig. 1 (items B through E).

Elicitation of any behavior at time $t_l$ should become more probable as the subject's *temporal perspective* is changed so that time $t_l$ is expanded and assumes greater significance than prior or subsequent time. Colloquially, such a person "lives for the moment," and his behavioral freedom is not trapped between past obligations and future accountings and liabilities.

A generalized state of *arousal* also increases the likelihood that gross, "agitated" behavior will be released, and that cues in the situation which might inhibit responding will not be noticed. Extreme arousal appears to be a necessary condition for achieving a true state of "ecstasy"—literally, a stepping out of one's self. In many societies, facilitative arousal techniques which have proved effective in inducing such states are institutionalized as preparatory rites for war, self-sacrifice, initiation, and rites of intensification.

The prototype of this preparatory arousal is, of course, the war dance (cf. Radcliffe-Brown, 1948, on the war dance of the Andaman Islanders). Loud repetitive music which is dominated by simple but powerful rhythms, group dancing for hours or days on end, singing, chanting, shouting, symbolic enactment of the anticipated confrontation with the enemy and with death, all merge to create a collective state of arousal which is then channeled into directions prescribed by tribal demands.

Preparatory arousal was also used in World War II by Japanese kamikaze pilots, whose individuation had to be sacrificed for the needs of the nation. Among cannibals, like the Cenis or certain Maori and Nigerian tribes, the activity of the ritual bonfire dance which precedes eating the flesh of another human being is always more prolonged and intense when the victim is to be eaten alive or uncooked (cf. Kilman, 1959, & Hogg, 1966). It is sometimes equally true that cannibalism facilitates arousal for war, just as the excitement of war facilitates battleground cannibalism.

Many cultures have rites which signify changes in status, where one's interaction with the society as a whole is to be intensified. Dance, physical torture, and exhaustion are the primary sources of preinitiation arousal, often for both the initiate and his initiators. Among the Buryats of Siberia, when a young girl is to be initiated as a shaman her seminude body is repeatedly massaged and stimulated and then "the older women bend over her and suck her breasts and belly with such force that blood spurts out" (Eliade, 1964). After additional arousal is achieved by all participants, the older women mix their blood with hers.

The end state which extreme facilitatory arousal may achieve is perhaps best illustrated by the rite of intensification in some districts of southern Nigeria when a boy is permitted to join the men in his first antelope hunt. The excitement becomes so great that he is able to lose self-awareness to the point that he has intercourse with the first antelope he kills while the corpse is still warm (Talbot, 1927).

Cognitive-verbal-intellectual activities are anathema to the spontaneous, behavioral release (disinhibition) we are talking about. Therefore, they must be overwhelmed by intense *sensory stimulation* (the psychedelic light-show phenomenon), or the person must get *absorbed in the action* itself—in the way that children do when playing certain games—where the only meaning of the act is inherent in its performance and lacks further implications or goals. Related to this, a *noncognitive feedback* system must be operative, which does not rely on memory, logic, or association. Rather, it is influenced directly by proprioceptive feedback from one's own action as well as the activity of coacting others. This feedback becomes an auxiliary input to a closed-loop system which results in a spiraling intensity whose terminal state cannot be predicted from knowledge of the initial boundary conditions (cf. J. Durkin's analysis of "encountering," Christie and Geis, 1969).

When one is in a *novel* or *unstructured situation*, behavior is less constrained by learned situation-bound cues. There is more opportunity to act than merely to continue to react, to project what is being experienced internally rather than to accept external physical and social reality as personal reality. When a lower-class neighborhood is razed and replaced with better public housing, an unfamiliar environment replaces the familiar one. Neighborhood cohesiveness with its controlling influences is lost when such a novel environment is created. Our voluntary geographical mobility also puts many Americans into unfamiliar living situations, making us a nation of strangers, separated from our families and from ties to people and places we think of as our own. The American Institute of Real Estate Appraisers reported at their annual (1969) meeting that the total tenant turnover in the San Francisco Bay Area was 81 percent, while it was 85 percent in the Los Angeles area. Another way of looking at our national rootlessness comes from a survey by Srole and his associates of mental health in Manhattan. Of 1,660 respondents living in the Yorkville section of New York City in 1954, two-thirds were not born there (36 percent foreign-born and 28 percent migrants from other cities).

Cognitive controls can be directly undermined by *altering states of consciousness*. Drugs like LSD and mescaline shatter the ordering principles imposed on thought and action by our learned perceptions. Agitated, acting-out, impulsive behavior is characteristic of chronic amphetamine users due to that drug's action as a behavioral stimulant. Under the influence of alcohol, reality testing decreases and is impaired. In sleep all mechanisms of censorship control are abandoned and in the "behavior of dreaming" there is an abrogation of chronicity, consistency, meaningful ordering, and arrangement, and also of social altruism, the golden rule, and the Ten Commandments.

*Deindividuated Behaviors*

Now we turn to what comes out at the other end. Deindividuation can claim uniqueness as a theoretical construct only if we can show that its occurrence is characterized by a pattern of behavior not shared equally by existing related concepts such as contagion, extreme aggression, disinhibition of specific responses, etc.

Virtually by definition, deindividuated behavior must have the property of being a high-intensity manifestation of behavior which observers would agree is emotional, impulsive, irrational, regressive, or atypical for the person in the given situation. But that is not enough. In addition, the behavior must not be under discriminative stimulus control. It must be unresponsive to features of the situation, the target, the victim, or the states of self which normally evoke a given level of response or a competing response. This is due to the combined effects of arousal, involvement in the act, and the direct pleasure derived from action-feedback, without regard for associated conditions which sanction or justify the action.

Under individuating circumstances, the individual is normally responsive to many sources of feedback. With deindividuating ones, however, there is a gating or screening effect in which the only source of feedback allowed into the system is affective-proprioceptive. It is not diluted or contaminated by other feedback channels, and therefore is more intense. Since such feedback is assumed to be pleasurable, a self-reinforcing amplification process is generated. Once begun, each subsequent response should have progressively shorter latencies, coupled with greater vigor.

Evidence for this phenomenon comes from three sources: the undersea-explorer Jacques Cousteau, black racer snakes, and John Lennon's new wife, Yoko Ono. One of the most terrifying of all sights, according to Cousteau, is the "dance of death" by sharks when they surround a passive victim. After a dozen or so killer sharks circled an injured baby whale for several hours with no sign of attack, suddenly one bit into its flesh. Within moments pandemonium broke loose; the sharks tore and ripped flesh, leaped over each other, attacked again and again until soon only blood and bones remained.

Jim Myers, a psychologist at Johns Hopkins University, reported a similar phenomenon in his study of the effects of length of food deprivation on the eating behavior of snakes. He has consistently observed that when snakes are placed in a cage with live mice, their initial attack latency is unrelated to length of deprivation. However, once they strike the first mouse, there is an almost linear decrease in latency of subsequent strikes until all or most (five or six) are killed. The attack itself appears to provide a self-excitation feedback which stimulates more attack.

Human animals exhibit similar behaviors, only one example of which will be offered here. Yoko Ono originated an audience-participation act called "Cut Piece." "She sat in her best dress and invited the audience to cut it up with a pair of scissors. At first, there was an awful silence. Then—well—it was terrible. Once they started, they couldn't stop. They went wild. She was left naked, of course" (art critic's report, *Look*, March 18, 1969).

That the behavior will be difficult to terminate follows from the previous discussion of its self-reinforcing aspect and its lack of control by external stimuli. This provides a direct test of the assumed loss of concern for social evaluation, since the behavior ought not to cease even when confronted by verbal instructions to do so from a prestigious, powerful source. However, it may be that when the deindividuated behavior is still at a relatively low level of intensity, as in a mob getting worked up, it is easy to stop it and disperse the "mindless" mob by firm, unequivocal reason-restoring action. On the other hand, at some point of intensity, any agent of termination will be intolerable, and will be attacked and destroyed by the deindividuated mass.

Before explaining why the other behaviors listed in Fig. 1 are possible correlates of a state of deindividuation, it may be valuable to some readers first to recast our thinking about the initial set of behaviors just described. Two concepts borrowed from operant conditioning appear to be particularly useful: drl (differential reinforcement for *low* rates of responding) and drh (differential reinforcement for *high* rates of responding). The drl schedule generates a very low rate of responding by reinforcing responses only after a given interresponse time (IRT). "Gradually, the differential reinforcement of IRT's brings responding under the control of the temporal stimuli present when a response is reinforced" (Reynolds, 1968). Stable drl performance eventually results because of the equilibrium between the opposing functions of reinforcement: reinforcing responses increases their rate, but reinforcing responses in the presence of stimuli associated with long IRTs decreases their rate.

This schedule is of interest to us because it is the basic social reinforcement schedule underlying most social interaction. To be socially appropriate, behavior must not be at a high rate of output, but spaced. There must not be too much (even of a good thing) all at once. The individual must learn to bide his time and not be effusive even in making responses which are affectively positive. He learns that responding must be paced and consistent, and also that time is a key variable which relates his behavior to certain events. If our time sense is altered by manipulating the input variables, and the feedback from the response is its own continually increasing reinforcement, then social behavior is no longer under drl control, and responding shifts to a drh schedule. Delay between response and reinforcement and between successive reinforcements becomes minimized, and thus immediate gratification, great activity, and physical involvement are "locked in" by virtue of the demanding response rate. As drl schedules typify individuated social behavior, drh schedules reflect deindividuated asocial behavior.

The reader may be wondering how such behavior is ever terminated, once initiated in the ways we have described and maintained by the processes postulated. Think back to the story mentioned earlier of the resident surgeon stabbing his girl friend over and over, 25 to 30 times, or Camus' Stranger repeatedly pulling the trigger of his gun. This behavior may be terminated by: a) a change in state of the person, such as fatigue or loss of consciousness; b) a marked change in state of the target object or victim, if there is one; or c) a total change in state of an instrument of action or of the environment, such as the gun being emptied. Following the act, amnesia or "blacking out" might occur as part of the termination sequence, or in reaction to the return of self and social awareness in the face of the action just completed (especially if it has been a very ego-alien one).

Arousal and emotion should reduce cue utilization as Easterbrook (1959) has shown (Simon Klevansky, Spencer Sherman, Alan Schiffenbauer, and I are currently studying this phenomenon across a variety of induced drives of high intensity). If one is not concerned with evaluating others or being evaluated by them, it follows that he ought to be unable to relate the deindividuated behaviors to specific participants in the action. This is the major conclusion of the study by Festinger, Pepitone, and Newcomb (1952), although it should be replicated.

Behavioral items g through j in Fig. 1 are relevant only when a group is present. The situation they describe is one in which deindividuation is not simply conforming behavior in response to perception of a new norm of what is acceptable. The presence of other actors stimulates contagious behavior which is not mediated by cognitive awareness of pressures toward group uniformity, but by sensory awareness of behaving others who are within one's personal distance space (as used by E. T. Hall, 1966). At the same time there is a total loss of conformity to relevant norms of any reference groups not physically present—this is the antisocial feature of the behavior.

If release of the behavior is pleasurable, then stimuli associated with it (such as the group itself) ought to become conditioned reinforcers and be perceived as more attractive. The concept of a group implies that individuals are interacting and influencing each other's behavior. However, attraction to the group and group interaction break down once the divergent feedback control has reached a high level, because then each member is in a sense autistically responding only to himself and his own actions, and all others cease to exist for him.

Before I present the research done to test some of these relationships, we cannot omit mention of the behavior that would be derived from the "Jungian primitive energy-form model" advanced earlier. Forms, structures, and institutions which represent order, reason, and individuality ought to be likely targets for destruction. And given enough time and high levels of deindividuation, formed entities should be rendered into a formless mass by people in a deindividuated state. We shall witness this phenomenon in a later section of this paper which deals with the ritual destruction of abandoned automobiles in New York City.

## Research Evidence

Starting with a model as complex and fuzzy as this one means that many different kinds of evidence must be collected in order to establish its psychological validity. Although we have only begun to test out its many relationships and implications, we can report the results of the following studies: several controlled laboratory experiments relating anonymity to aggression in American coeds and Belgian soldiers; field observations of vandalism and a bizarre field experiment on anonymity and car smashing; interviews and observations of people involved in destroying a traditional form; and, finally, pilot studies on hypnotically induced time distortion and emotional contagion.

### *Laboratory Experiment on Anonymity and Aggression*

In our first study, we combined several manipulations in order to maximize the probability of producing the inferred state of deindividuation. Anonymity was induced in half the subjects by making them unidentifiable, by never using their names, and by having the experimental task done in the dark. For the other subjects, their individuality and identifiability were emphasized throughout the study. In addition, all subjects were tested in groups which allowed them perception of shared responsibility for the antisocial behavior—delivering painful electric shocks to another girl.

We[3] predicted that these conditions of deindividuation should lead to greater levels of aggression (shock duration) than the

3. My undergraduate senior seminar at New York University (especially Barry and Myrna Schwartz) skillfully assisted in the execution of this research.

conditions of identifiability, and that this aggression would increase over trials only for the deindividuated group. In addition to this between-groups variable, there was a within-groups manipulation. If this aggression is hypothesized to be under the control of external discriminative stimuli, then differences between victims (which normally would justify differential treatment of them) should not have any effect on the shocking behavior of the subjects in the deindividuated condition, but it should have an effect on the others. Accordingly, one victim was portrayed as nice and the other as obnoxious, and correlations were computed between shock duration and perception of the victim's traits. Our hypothesis was that there would be a positive correlation for those in the Identifiability Condition (more shock as victim is more obnoxious, less as she is seen as nicer), but little or no correlation for those in the Deindividuated condition.

*Procedure.* The procedure to be briefly outlined should be coordinated with the sequential flow diagram presented in Fig. 2. When each girl in a group of four coeds from the introductory psychology class at New York University (Bronx) arrived at the laboratory, she was asked to put on a very large lab coat (size 44), and a hood over her head, and her name was never used. Thus, none of these subjects in the Deindividuation Condition (De-I) knew the identity of the other group members, nor could we tell them apart. In contrast, the subjects randomly assigned to the Identifiability Condition (I) were greeted by name and given big name tags to wear, while the importance of their unique reactions was emphasized by the instructions. Although they too were not previously acquainted with the other girls in their group, they could identify them.

The rationale for this manipulation (and the cover story for the experiment) centered around the assessment of the subjects' empathic response to strangers. Since this was such a subtle process, sensitive both to "demand characteristics" from E and biasing by the other Ss, the subjects' facial expressions had to be concealed from each other, and E could only have minimal interaction with them (the instructions were delivered via a tape recording). For the Identifiability Ss, the importance of their personal, individual response was stressed within a similar spiel.

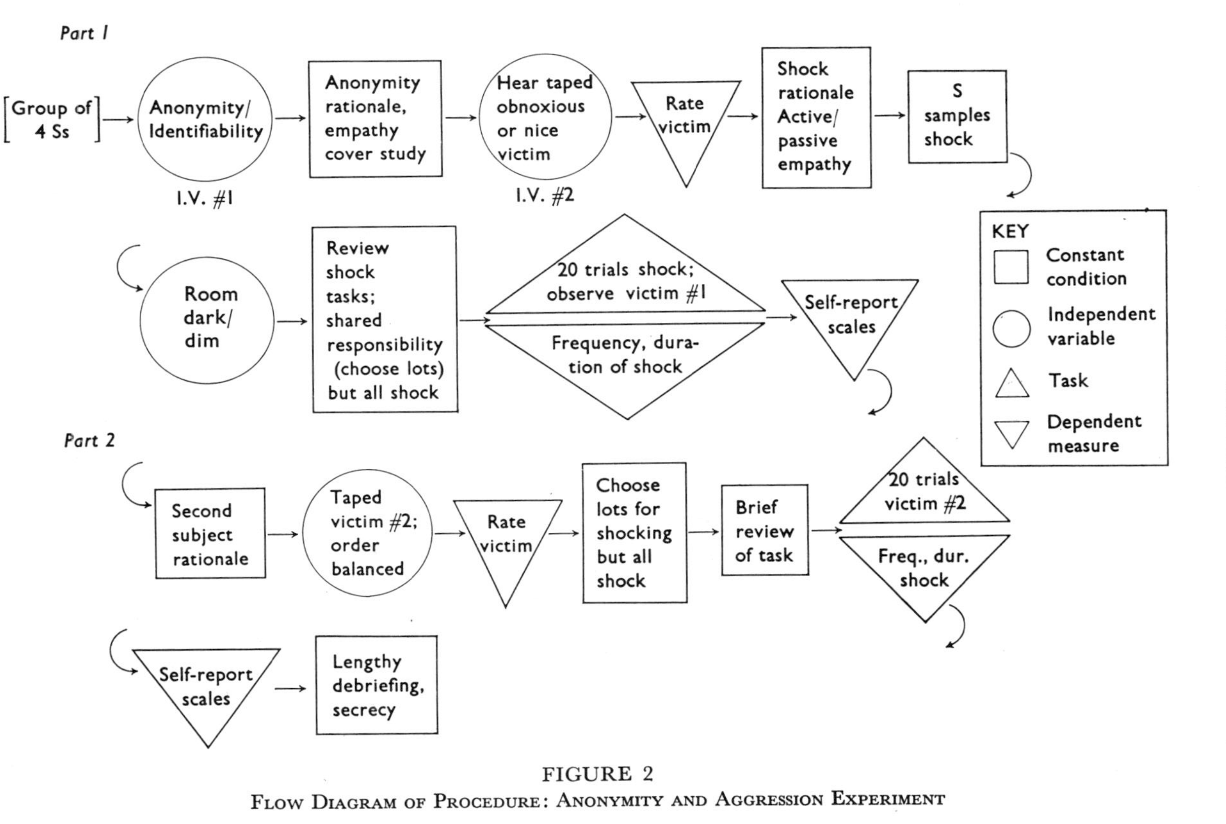


FIGURE 2
Flow Diagram of Procedure: Anonymity and Aggression Experiment

The subjects then heard a five-minute tape-recorded interview between me and the first of the future "victims" (see Fig. 3). Immediately afterwards they rated her honesty, sincerity, warmth, and genuineness. One of the tapes portrayed a nice, accepting, altruistic, sweet girl who wanted to work with retarded children and make money to help her fiance through medical school. The second "victim" (presented in part 2) was made to appear quite the opposite—obnoxious, self-centered, conceited, and critical. She was a transfer student who had to make money by modeling to pay for her Ivy League dates, since she couldn't stand either the Jewish boys or the girls at N.Y.U., and just had to get away as often as she could, etc. The order in which these victims were heard, and later "shocked," was counterbalanced across groups.

The rationale for delivering shock was as follows: We were allegedly studying whether empathy judgments differ when one is passively or actively involved with the target person ("actively involved" meant inducing reactions in this person directly). Since the girl supposedly was a paid subject going through a series of conditioning studies anyway, we could combine the two studies so that she would get only one series of shocks (since it was by delivering shock to her that our Ss would become "actively involved"). The Ss were led to believe that two of the four would shock, while the other two would merely observe, and then all of them would make empathy judgments. They chose lots, which were rigged so that each one of the four thought she and one other would deliver shock. They were separated into cubicles so that they could not see how the others reacted, thus keeping their behavior independent. Each S experienced a sample of the (strong) "typical" shock the victim would get, the room lights were turned off (De-I) or only dimmed (I), and the shock procedure was described. A signal light indicated when S had to depress her shock key while a second (green) light signaled that shock was being transmitted and would continue to be delivered as long as the key was held down (2.5 seconds maximum). S was to continue this procedure until told to stop.

The victim-subject was then viewed seated behind a one-way mirror talking with the E, who appeared to be giving her a verbal test (they could not be heard). Each time she was supposedly shocked by the Ss, the victim reacted with symptoms of extreme

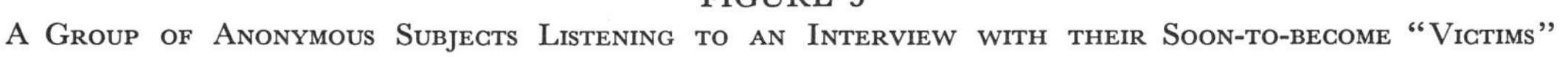

FIGURE 3

A Group of Anonymous Subjects Listening to an Interview with their Soon-to-become "Victims"

pain, writhing, twisting, and grimacing. The Ss believed that the shock would come on if either one of them held her finger down and would persist as long as either continued pressing the key, but that it would not be greater in intensity if both shocked at once. They also were led to believe that we could not tell which one of them had actually delivered the shock, since the two circuits had a single common terminal.

On each of 20 trials, we recorded whether shock was administered and for what duration. After the tenth trial, the victim reacted so strongly that her hand ripped out of the electrode strap. She rubbed her fingers, was strapped down again, and the Ss had 10 more trials to hurt her. This standard reaction divided the 20 trials into two blocks which could then be analyzed for change in aggressive response in the second as compared to the first half.

After completing some self-report scales (of estimated frequency of shocking, victim's reactions, and other bits of information) the Ss were told we would repeat the procedure in part 2 with a second empathy target. They heard her on tape, rated her traits, and chose new rigged lots for shocking the victim (of course, all Ss actually "shocked"). The task was reviewed, 20 more trials with a different "victim" took place, and after the self-report scales were completed, we terminated the study with a very thorough debriefing and appeal for maintaining experimental secrecy.

In order to minimize systematic response bias to any particular target-victim, 7 different girls, trained to emote pain, and unaware of whether they were nice or obnoxious, were seen as victims. Three different experimenters conducted the study, all task instructions were tape-recorded, the responses were automatically recorded on an Esterline-Angus recorder, and the coded data were analyzed without knowledge of the independent variable assignment of the 30 subjects.

*Results.* Deindividuating subjects in the way we did had a significant effect on their aggressive behavior. The total *duration* of shocking was twice as much for the De-I group (mean = .90 seconds) as for the I group (mean = .47 seconds). The overall difference graphically depicted in Fig. 4 is significant beyond the .01 level ($t = 2.89$). In addition, the De-I group gave a wider *range* of shock durations than

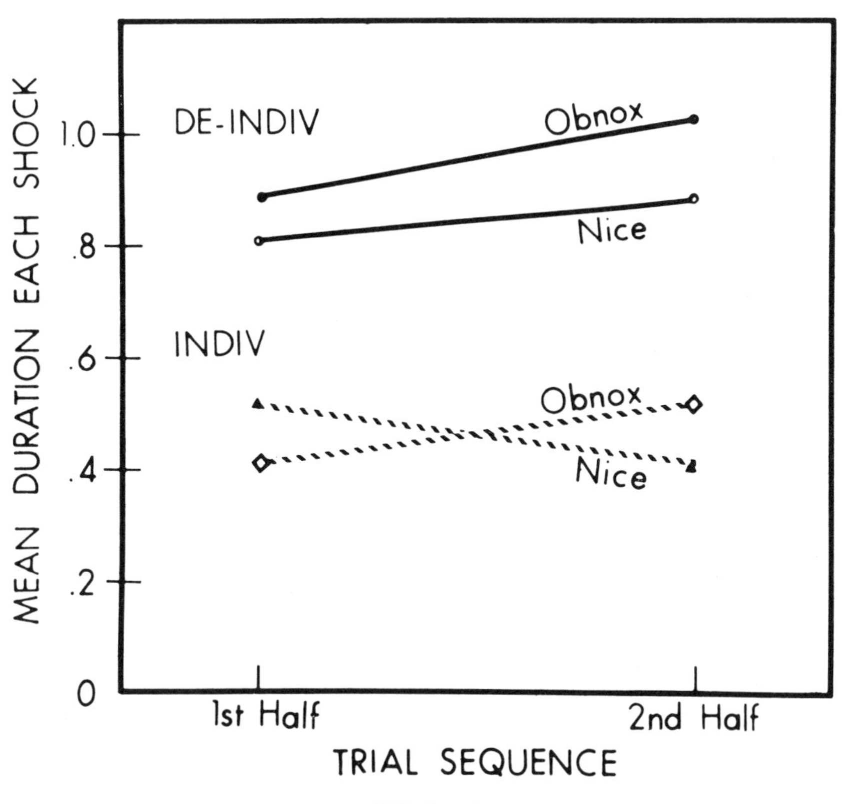


FIGURE 4
Aggression, Measured by Shock Duration, as a Function of the Deindividuation Treatment, Victim Characteristics, and Repeated Shock Trials

the I group—1.40 seconds compared to .91 (of a possible 2.50-seconds range; $t = 2.21$, $p < .05$). However, the equally shared responsibility and the experimental demand produced an equivalent compliance effect in both groups on *frequency* of shocks—a high average of 17 shocks in 20 trials across both conditions. Almost all Ss obeyed and pressed down the shock key when the signal appeared, but the De-I subjects continued the shock twice as long as did the I subjects. There was a greater increase in shock duration over trials (first 10 versus the second 10 trials) for the De-I than the I group, as predicted, but it is not statistically significant.

That the aggression of the I group was under the stimulus control of the victim's traits can be seen from two sources of data: First of all, they shocked the nice victim less and less over trials, but shocked the obnoxious victim more and more. Secondly, the correlation between their individual ratings of the victim's traits made prior to shocking, and the duration of shocking the victim (across both victims) is $+.67$ ($p < .02$). That the aggression of the De-I group is *unaffected* by these salient, dramatically different victim traits is shown by an identical pattern for both victims of increasing shocks over trials and a correlation of only $+.10$ between trait ratings and shock duration. These correlations are significantly different ($p < .05$, one tailed-directional prediction).

Supplementary data indicate that the two victims were perceived veridically, in line with our manipulation, such that there was no overlap in the rating distributions ($p < .001$). They were not differentially perceived by Ss in the two treatments, nor were the ratings affected by their order of presentation. There were no group differences in discrepancy between actual and estimated shock frequency, or in the desire to get to know better the other members of the group or the victim.

These results clearly supported two of our hypotheses relating anonymity, aggression intensity, and stimulus control of aggression. We were also encouraged by the trend of increasing aggression over repeated trials. It must be remembered that there was no prior aggression arousal or victim-instigated provocation to aggress. Under conditions specified as deindividuating, these sweet, normally mild-mannered college girls shocked another girl almost every time they had an opportunity to do so, sometimes for as long as they were allowed, and it did not matter whether or not that fellow student was a nice girl who didn't deserve to be hurt. In addition, there was no agent of coercion present to force the girls to act like killers (as in Milgram's obedience studies), and each girl knew that even if she didn't deliver shock, the experiment could carry on because the other subject might do so. It should be noted that these findings are in agreement with Milgram's (1965) analysis of the role of the variable of "remoteness-proximity" between victim and aggressor. Conditions which induce feelings of remoteness lead to lowered self-consciousness, less embarrassment, and reduced inhibitions about punishing the victim.

*A Pilot Study on Direct Aggression and Catharsis*

We used this same paradigm with another group of subjects, with one change: between victims one and two there was an interpolated activity of direct verbal and physical aggression by each S toward members of another group. This pilot study is presented because the techniques and the theoretical implications appear to be valuable.

Would aggression toward the second victim have been less than that toward the first if the Ss were allowed direct expression of aggression just before the second victim was presented? The procedure used was to ask the Ss' cooperation in a passive resistance training program I was starting. A racially and sexually mixed group of four students (accomplices) were allegedly in training to experience and learn passive resistance in the face of confrontation. The Ss heard me tell my trainees that they would be attacked by a group in the next room, and that they could not retaliate. They entered the laboratory and marched up and down carrying signs, as if they were picketing. The real Ss, anonymity guaranteed by their hoods, began to shout at them and were verbally abusive. Then they made signs: "Black + White = Dirty Grey," "Get Lost," etc. They tore away the signs of the resisters and began making paper balls with them and throwing them at their heads. Suddenly the resisters, who had thought this was all one big joke up to this time, locked arms and began singing protest songs in earnest. The hooded Ss blocked their path and forced them into a smaller and smaller space. Then a small anonymous girl got behind one of the male Ss and used him as a battering ram, shoving him into the resisters. The other hooded girl followed suit, using the second male as a weapon. Both girls cursed, shouted, pushed, and shoved; when they started to kick the resisters, I stopped the "interpolated activity" and thanked everyone for their participation. The accomplices left, stunned and shaken, while the deindividuated Ss returned to their individual cubicles and proceeded to shock the next victim slightly *more* than they had shocked the first. There was certainly no catharsis effect operating to limit their aggression, even when allowed this ten-minute period of rather intense prior expression of hostility and aggression. This general approach deserves further use—if brave, strong accomplices are available.

*Individuating the Belgian Army*

This preliminary success engendered enough (unwarranted) confidence in the universality of our model to lead us to attempt to replicate the first study with a noncollege male population from a European culture. One hundred and two soldiers of the Belgian Army stationed at Louvain were required (by the Minister of Defense)[4] to participate in this study. They were in their early twenties, had not (on the average) graduated from high school, and spoke only Flemish. We pretested the manipulations and translations on a sample of 54 subjects and then executed the final study using 8 groups composed of 6 Ss each.

In essential details the procedure was similar to that of the N.Y.U. study. The major improvements consisted of better methodological controls and measurements. Subject anonymity was again the major independent variable, while victim-type was changed to victim-identifiability, as the second factor studied in a 2 × 2 design.

*Procedure.* The soldiers came from the army base to the University of Louvain, waited in a group in the university canteen, and then were individually escorted into separate cubicles in the laboratory. A Belgian experimenter delivered the rationale and the tape-recorded instructions and controlled the technical phases of the study from a master console. The study was presented to the soldiers as being concerned with impression formation—how people judge the reactions and attributes of others under different conditions. Therefore, they would be asked to judge a stranger when they could see his facial reactions (identifiable victim) or where they could not (non-identifiable victim). It was alleged that because such interpersonal judgments can easily be biased by others, we wanted to minimize this bias by concealing the Ss' identity. We had half of the Ss wear

4. Actually, he was persuaded to assist the European Research Training Seminar in Experimental Social Psychology, directed by Josef Nuttin, Jr. The study was conducted under the auspices of the Seminar in the magnificent laboratory of Professor Nuttin with the assistance of superb graduate students: Jean-Claude Abric (France), Vera Bokorova (Czechoslovakia), Freddy Lange (Netherlands), Anna Potocka-Hoser (Poland), and Renee Honai and John Rysman (Belgium).

hoods (non-identifiable subject), while for the others we tried to increase their identity (identifiable subject) and emphasized that their judgments should be their own.

One of the conditions we were allegedly studying was where judgments follow a period of direct interaction between subject-judge and the person observed, in contrast to only passive exposure to him. Therefore, the Ss' task was to control the duration of electric shock the observed person would receive and then judge his reactions to a condition they helped create. The number of seconds a shock-key was depressed (three seconds maximum) was again the major dependent measure of aggression toward the victim. Each subject knew that the other subjects were also delivering shocks, but his response was independent since he could not see their reactions. All Ss believed that it was not possible for us to determine individual shock responses (thus, diffused responsibility).

The identifiability manipulation incorporated several different treatments. Non-identifiability, or loss of personal identity, was assumed to be created by having the subjects wear large hoods covering their heads (see Fig. 5), removing their name tags, never using their names during the experiment, keeping the laboratory under low illumination, and allowing the Ss to witness their non-identifiability and that of the other members of their group (whose backs were directly visible) on a closed-circuit TV. In contrast, identifiability was created by emphasizing the Ss' names and having them see the faces of the other group members on the closed-circuit TV. The Ss' feelings of "satisfaction" (being calm, at ease, cheerful, and relaxed) were measured after these treatments (but before they knew their task), and again after the shock trials.

For purposes of efficiency and control, the interaction observed by the Ss between the professor (P.G.Z.) and the student-victim was prerecorded on video tape. To make it believable, the Ss watched the closed-circuit TV monitor and saw the professor sampling the shock himself, and then administering a sample jolt of shock to each of them. They could see him pack up the equipment (both directly and on the monitor) and then walk out of their room into an adjacent room, where he again appeared on the TV monitor. However, the circuit had been switched over from closed-circuit to the video tape. Next they saw the target person being greeted, having

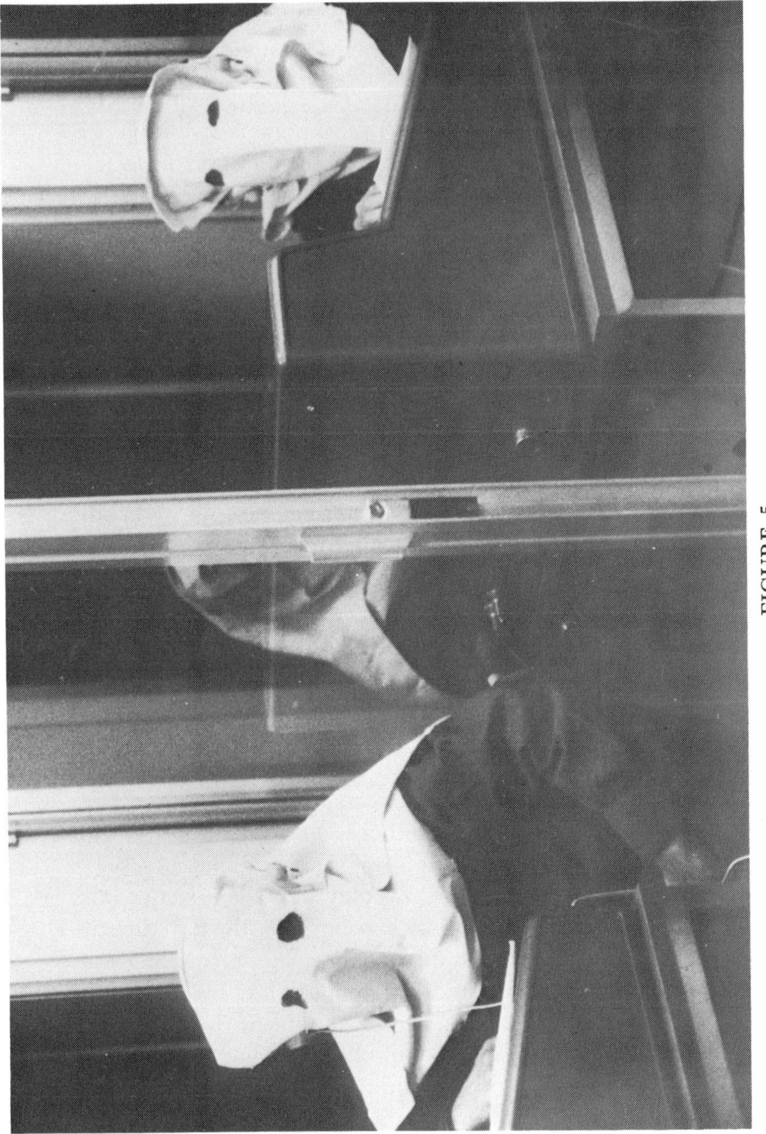

FIGURE 5
Hooded Belgian Soldiers, Not Very Deindividuated

electrodes attached, and then jumping, twisting, and shaking following each of the 20 receptions of shock which they delivered.

Following the shock trials, the Ss rated the victim's reactions, indicated again their satisfaction level, and responded to a series of TAT cards assumed to measure covert aggressivity. Assignment to experimental treatments was randomized across groups, and treatments were counterbalanced over time and sequence of testing.

*Results.* The results obviously should have shown most aggression where subject and victim were *not* identifiable, least aggression where they were, and intermediate levels in the mixed-treatment cells. Not so! Shock duration was *less* under either condition of anonymity—with the extreme cells significantly different: 1.35 sec. mean shock for Non-I subject and victim, compared to 2.04 sec. mean shock for the I subject and victim cell (Mann-Whitney U = 36.5, $p < .05$).

To make matters worse, shock duration increased over trials for Ss in the Identifiable Condition, but was constant for the Non-Identifiable Condition (though not significant). Fifteen percent more of the I Ss than the Non-I Ss delivered shock for the full duration allowed (i.e., they had to be stopped to allow the next trial to begin), while on 14 percent of the trials Non-I Ss refused to shock at all. The supposedly deindividuated subjects were behaving in a most individuated manner, while the reactions of the individuated subjects resembled those of our N.Y.U. deindividuated coeds. This last statement became even more valid when our questionnaire data revealed that the I Ss felt more "satisfied" after shocking the victim when they perceived him as most hurt and tense (the correlation was $+.45$, $p < .05$). There was no relationship for the Non-I group on these self-report measures.

However, our failure to conceptualize adequately the subjects' phenomenology for this unusual experience was made apparent by two additional sources of data. Immediately after the anonymity manipulation, the Ss in the Non-Identifiable Condition described themselves as significantly less satisfied and more uneasy on the four scale items than those given the Identifiability manipulation ($t = 2.33$, $p < .05$). Putting on the hoods, as well as the rest of the operations, made them anxious even before they knew they had to administer shock. But why? To the question, Would you like to be in a group or individual experiment the next time you are asked to participate?, many of the Ss who had been hooded said they wanted to be with a group and *not alone again.* Remember, they could see that there were five others seated in adjacent seats, and were physically part of a group.

Subjects came to our study as soldiers in uniforms, and they were already as indistinguishable to us as we in our white lab coat uniforms were to them. Ziller notes (1964) that a deindividuated perception is shown by use of categorical responses to individuals (such as "he's a soldier"). We did, in fact, view them simply as the next group of army subjects to be tested. They came in a uniformed group and waited together for this new experience. But consider what our anonymity manipulations accomplished. They isolated each soldier from his buddies (he couldn't even be sure they were his buddies), took away his name tag, and thrust him into a scientific laboratory, where he saw himself on television—in a hood. Our supplementary evidence would lead us to conjecture that our conceptual treatment labels did not correspond to the psychological reality of the subjects. The Identifiable Ss were still relatively deindividuated, while the Non-Identifible Ss were made to feel self-conscious, suspicious, and anxious. We had inadvertently taken a natural situation with built-in anonymity and destroyed it with the too literal translation of our previous anonymity induction.

Before describing how this post hoc explanation was validated, I might add one further bit of evidence against the aggression-catharsis notion. The correlation found here between shock duration and subsequent aggression themas on the TAT was +.60 ($p < .01$). Across all groups, those who were most overtly aggressive were still most aggressive in their fantasy.

*Alone in a Hood at N.Y.U.*

If the anonymity manipulation made the soldiers feel self-conscious and isolated, which, in turn, inhibited aggression, then the same outcome should result when these *specific* operations are used on isolated subjects. Being the only person wearing a hood in an experimental setting should create the same subjective feelings of self-centered concern. The subject feels salient, as though he "sticks out like a sore thumb." While he is not identifiable as a particular individual X, he is still singular and unique.

Using subjects from the same population at N.Y.U. as in the original study, we repeated the initial experiment with 16 girls. Again, half were randomly assigned to the Non-Identifiable Condition and half to the Identifiable one, with victim characteristics manipulated within both groups. The only difference between this and the first study was that the subjects were being tested individually, rather than in groups.

To make the experimental rationale similar to the other study, the subject was informed, after having waited for the other group member to arrive, that the girl couldn't make it and had been rescheduled for later. The solution we[5] proposed to the subject was that she would be the "active empathizer." We would video-tape the shocked subject's reactions, and then the other subject, when she came, could be the "passive empathizer" by judging these taped reactions. Everything else in the procedure was the same as before.

*Results:* The Non-I, alone girls were *less* aggressive on every measure than the I-alone girls, and much less so than the initial group of Non-I-group girls:

1. They gave shocks of only a third as long duration as the I-alone Ss—total mean seconds, 10.8 vs. 27.8 ($t = 2.79$, $p < .02$).
2. They refused to comply with the experimental demand to shock on 21 of the 40 trials (20 for each of two victims), while the average number of no-shock trials was only 5.4 for the I-alone group ($t = 2.80$, $p < .02$).
3. The average duration of each shock that they did give was significantly smaller than the I-alone group ($t = 2.19$, $p < .05$).
4. However, as expected, the manipulation of victim characteristics was equally successful for both treatments, with the obnoxious victim being perceived as significantly less warm, sincere, genuine, sensitive, and empathic ($p < .01$).

5. I was ably assisted by Harriet Kay, James Thomas, Alice Ross, Sharon Gurwitz, and Ned Anscheutz—all graduate students at Columbia University.

A summary comparison of the effects of the anonymity manipulation in the group and alone conditions for the aggression measures is presented in Table 1.

TABLE 1
AGGRESSION AS A FUNCTION OF ANONYMITY IN GROUP VERSUS ALONE CONDITIONS

| | Social Condition | |
|---|---|---|
| *Measure* | *Group* | *Alone* |
| 1. Shock duration | Non-Identifiable > Identifiable; $p < .001$ | Identifiable > Non-Identifiable; $p < .02$ |
| 2. Shock frequency | No difference; equally high | Identifiable > Non-Identifiable; $p < .02$ |
| 3. Range of shocks given | Non-Identifiable > Identifiable; $p < .05$ | No difference; equally narrow |
| 4. Change in shock duration over trials related to victim characteristics | (a) Identifiable: obnoxious victim shocked more, nice victim shocked less ($p$ = ns) | Identifiable: both victims shocked less ($p < .002$) |
| | (b) Non-Identifiable: both victims shocked more, regardless of traits ($p$ = ns) | Non-Identifiable: both victims shocked less ($p < .02$) |

Spontaneous comments of the subjects during the experiment and in the debriefing phase point up the degree to which the alone conditions emphasized their feelings of individuation.

$S_1$: "I feel so mean."

$S_2$: "Oh, that was awful."

$S_3$: (After receiving instructions and sample shock) "So it's not *my* responsibility, is it? I don't like the idea of shocking someone." (After having shocked, "I feel very cruel.")

$S_4$: (On learning during debriefing that the victim was not really hurt) "I'm glad the shock was mild. I felt horrible inflicting pain."

Other Ss also said they didn't like being in the study or that they thought the shocks were not hurting the victim very much. A few of the girls in the group-identifiability condition reacted similarly, but none of those in the group-anonymity condition expressed any such concerns.

Thus we have learned that the same operations may yield divergent effects depending upon the presence or absence of others.

Deindividuated behaviors are more likely to be released when loss of personal identity occurs in a group setting than when the individual has no group support and is made to feel self-conscious by obvious cues of difference from those observing him. Furthermore, where anonymity operations conceal the identity of the members of a natural group from each other, the individual feels isolated from his friends and cut off from this source of social support. Our future research will have to be more sensitive to the complex matrix of interactions between these variables.

*Criticism of Laboratory Research on "Loss of Control"*

In retrospect, it is surprising that we were able to demonstrate effects of the magnitude which we did in fact obtain, because our experimental methodology was often working against eliciting the phenomena we wanted to observe. The situation and tasks were all very structured, intellectual, and cognitive. To obtain a precise dependent measure, we recorded shock duration in a series of fixed duration trials. However, fixed, discrete trials impose constraints on the "release" of any behavior and make spontaneous, impulsive behavior impossible. Moreover, the aggression was not direct, but mediated (i.e., there was no immediate noncognitive feedback, such as one gets from punching another person in the face, smashing a window with a hammer, etc.). Because we wanted to study *individual* behavior in a social context rather than group behavior, no group interaction was allowed. Thus, we cut off all potential for "behavioral contagion" (the major concept linking individual processes of deindividuation to mass action, as occurs in riots and orgies), (cf. Wheeler, 1966). The omnipresence of a rational, responsible member of the establishment (the experimenter) also probably had an inhibiting effect upon impulsive aggression. Finally, the subject was put into a compliance dilemma, since not to shock violated the task demand of the experiment.

One could get around some of the criticisms with simple changes in the paradigm employed, but the knotty problem is to obtain a sensitive, reliable, and valid dependent measure which is not inherently static and anchored to onset and offset cues. This might be accomplished, for example, by giving subjects a measured supply of ammunition (paper clips, rubber bands, peas in a pea shooter, etc.) which they could fire at a target at their own rate, the dependent measure being the amount of the supply remaining. Or they could be given objects to destroy or a "Bobo clown" to punch.

*A Pilot Study Measuring Patterns of Aggression*

We devised a technique for our next study which would get closer to free responding, but would still give us an ongoing record of S's discrete responses and the pattern of responding over trials. The subject is asked to distract a target person from an experimental task by pressing one of three buttons, each of which controls one type of distractor (electric shock, white noise, or intense light). One of the three keys must always be pressed (thus continuous responding), but which one and for how long is determined by S's preference. By providing S with prior information about how upsetting each type of distractor is to the target person, we can then differentiate intention to hurt the subject from compliance with task demands. Moreover, it may prove true that from an analysis of the sequential pattern of responding we could observe the S's guilt reactions to having been maximally aggressive, that is, after S delivers the worst distractor, guilt would motivate switching to the mildest distractor. An analysis of the total proportion of time that S delivers the most, moderate, and least punishing stimulus to the victim yields the four major pattern types described in Table 2.

At this point, all we can use to support such an expectation is the data from a pilot study (using coeds from Barnard College) which revealed that an experimental manipulation did yield two different response patterns for Identifiable and Non-Identifiable subjects.

A brief overview of the study is sufficient for presenting this data. The major operation of deindividuation was the manipulation of the S's knowledge that the victim could identify what the S had done to her. Half the Ss were led to believe the victim would know only what the total group's reaction was (Non-Identifiability), while the other Ss saw a control panel which would display to the victim the names[6] of the Ss who were administering each type of distraction throughout the study.

6. The individuating effect of names in a situation like this was first observed during the Second World War. It is reported that Nazi SS guards were more

Each S first experienced the three types of unpleasant stimuli which they were later to use in distracting the "stooge-subject" during a mirror-tracing task. In addition, they learned how that "subject" rated each of the distractors. The Ss, tested in groups of three, were not made anonymous in any way other than through the manipulation which varied the victim's knowledge of their complicity. The feedback they received from their response consisted of programmed buzzer beeps allegedly signaling that the victim had made an error on the task (presumably caused by the distractors).

TABLE 2

FOUR BASIC PATTERNS OF AGGRESSIVE RESPONDING

(Rank order of amount of time each of these upsetting stimuli is delivered to a victim where 1.0 = most time spent)

| | Rating of Painfulness of Stimuli | | |
|---|---|---|---|
| | *Most Painful* | *Moderate* | *Least Painful* |
| 1. Rational compliance to E's demands and victim's pain | 2.5 | 1.0 | 2.5 |
| 2. Guilt reaction to occasions of having been maximally hostile | 1.5 | 3.0 | 1.5 |
| 3. Maximum hostility—deindividuated release of aggression | 1.0 | 2.0 | 3.0 |
| 4. Either: extreme concern for victim or reaction against strong hostile impulses | 3.0 | 2.0 | 1.0 |

We expected that the individuated Ss would generate a response pattern similar to the first one in Table 2 as a way of being rationally responsive to both victim and experimenter needs. Indeed, this is what was found for those I Ss (n = 17) who felt that the victim would know their names; they spent most of their time (40 percent) delivering the intermediate level, while the most painful stimulus was used 32 percent, and the least painful 28 percent of the time.

The pattern anticipated for the deindividuated Ss should certainly not be this compromise reaction, and ought not to be the

lenient to prisoners at the Auschwitz concentration camp after Radio Free Europe in Great Britain broadcast their names, which the Polish Underground had smuggled out of the country in 1944.

guilt pattern. A powerful manipulation ought to generate pattern three, namely, most use of the painful alternative and least use of the weakest one. However, arousal of aggressive impulses without adequately lowering controls could also produce a paradoxical opposite reaction. This is certainly not a satisfactory distinction, since such a reaction cannot be differentiated (without finer micro-analyses) from a nonaggressive concern for the victim. For the present, however, we will have to tolerate such looseness. The data support the weak form of our[7] argument—that the deindividuation manipulation would produce different response patterns. The typical response of this Non-I group (n = 14) who felt the victim couldn't single them out, was to spend the largest proportion of time (44 percent) delivering the least noxious stimulus and the least time (25 percent) delivering the most noxious—a pattern four reaction.

Again, we do not want to make much of this difference, except to suggest that it invites further exploration into the many problems of manipulation and measurement necessarily present in studying the process of deindividuation under experimentally valid conditions.

## Anonymity and Destruction in the Real World

Now we must return to our starting point in the real world to demonstrate that the aggression observed under our contrived laboratory conditions of anonymity or unidentifiability is really a genuine phenomenon of the human condition. It should follow, from what we have described thus far, that where social conditions of life destroy individual identity by making people feel anonymous, then what will follow is the deindividuated types of behaviors outlined previously. Assaultive aggression, senseless acts of destruction, motiveless murders, great expenditure of energy and effort directed toward shattering traditional forms and institutionalized structures become our dependent variables. Vandalism is the prototype of this behavior and represents a social problem which will soon reach

7. Lucy Friedman, Alice Ross, and Sharon Gurwitz contributed their creativity and industry to every phase of the development of this study. My analysis of this and other aspects of the deindividuation process especially benefited from the intellectual stimulation generated by Judith Rodin, Irv Piliavan, James Thomas, and Lee Ross.

epidemic proportions. How serious is the problem now? Can it be understood in terms of our analysis of deindividuation?

*Vandalism*

The extent and intensity of the mindless, wanton destruction of property and the expenditure of effort on the part of vandals may be extracted from the following sampling of individual cases and summary statistics. Following a Halloween celebration (October 31, 1967), a mob of teenagers began overturning gravestones in Montefiore Cemetery in Queens, New York, and throwing rocks at passing cars. Public School 26 in Brooklyn was broken into 15 times and 700 panels of glass broken in a two-month period (April to June, 1968). The principal reported that vandals threw library books and catalog cards all over the floor and covered them with glue. Vandalism was also a major problem at the recent New York World's Fair. The Ford Company's cars, which conveyed visitors into a Disney-designed "past" and "future," were also reminders of the reality of the present. The exhibit supervisor remarked that vandals "tear things apart. They carve up the upholstery and pull some of the components out of the dash board. One Thunderbird came back with every wire ripped out."

"God is dead" may be a provocative intellectual issue of debate for theologians, but for kids in the Southeast Bronx (my primal neighborhood), its truth is reflected much more concretely; within a recent six-month period, 47 Christian churches and 20 synagogues were vandalized. One of them was the Netzach Israel Synagogue, where children broke the Torah scrolls, ripped curtains and prayer books, splashed paint on the walls, threw rocks through the stained-glass window, and finally tore the Star of David down from the roof. Anti-Semitism? That assumes motivation and purpose. The rector of the famed St. Mark's in the Bowery Episcopalian Church has threatened to close it down unless similar acts of theft and vandalism in his church are halted. During the past year the church has been broken into about a dozen times and graves in the adjoining churchyard have been desecrated.

While major cities provide a conducive setting for the appearance of vandalism, it is by no means solely an urban phenomenon. In

Union Township, New Jersey, roving vandals damaged more than 250 autos parked on streets (March 21, 1968) by ramming them and breaking their windows. Across the country in Richmond, California, a small city near San Francisco, vandals stormed through six schools one weekend (February 25, 1969) causing $30,000 worth of damage. Equipment and furniture were overturned, windows were smashed, food was thrown on the floor and ink squirted on the walls and on library books. Vandals recently destroyed an irreplaceable arbor of beautiful trees in San Francisco's Golden Gate Park, to the puzzlement of all who couldn't understand why anyone would commit such a senseless act.

The incidence of vandalism can be appreciated by reference to the following statistics obtained from the relevant public and private agencies in a single city—New York City.

a) *Schools:* In 1967 there were 202,712 window panes broken (replacement cost over $1 million); there were 2,359 unlawful entries (causing $787,000 damage); there were 199 fires (costing $154,000 in destruction, but not including the loss of one entire school, P.S. 5 in Queens). The January, 1968, bulletin of the Board of Education's Division of Maintenance, noting that these figures do not include costs from defaced desks, walls, fixtures, etc., concludes, "It is almost impossible to estimate the costs of these items, but it is a huge amount." Even without a complete accounting of the havoc wrought on the free public education system in New York City, the bulletin indicates that the nearly $2 million cost of repairs in 1967 was up 21 percent from 1966, and preliminary 1969 reports reveal that the vandalism has continued its spiraling rise.

b) *Public Transportation:* Well over $100,000 was spent in 1967 to repair the damage caused by vandals to buses and subways.

c) *Public Parks:* The $650,000 damage to benches, rest rooms, playgrounds, lights, trees, and fences in 1967 represented an increase of more than 11 percent from the previous year, and it, too, continues to climb. In Brooklyn alone, there were 35 fires set in park buildings, mostly comfort stations.

d) *Public Telephones:* The convenience provided by the city's 100,000 pay phones is rapidly being undermined by hordes of vandals who wreck an average of 35,000 of them *monthly*. At least 25 percent of the sidewalk phones are out of service all the time, and it is a rarity to find a subway station phone in operation. Recently I tried 15 phone booths in the Times Square Station before I could find one whose metal-encased wires were not severed, dial ripped off, mouthpiece dismantled, change slots clogged, or money containers ripped out. The New York Telephone Company estimates that last year it lost nearly $1 million in stolen coins and spent another $4 million to repair vandalized phones.

e) *Automobiles:* The Sanitation Department reports that over 31,500 abandoned cars had to be removed from New York's streets last year (an increase of 5,000 from the previous year). These are cars which either had been stolen or were abandoned by their owners because they were no longer in good running condition. What is interesting is that most of them are stripped of usable parts and then battered and smashed almost beyond recognition. During the past several years I have been systematically observing this new phenomenon of ritual destruction of the automobile—the symbol of America's affluence, technology, and mobility, as well as the symbol of its owner's independence, status, and (according to motivation researchers) sexual fantasies. In a single day, on a 20-mile route from my home in Brooklyn to the campus of New York University in the Bronx, I recorded 218 such vandalized cars.

Repeated observations of the transformation of a typical car lead me to conclude that there are six distinct stages involved. First, the car must provide some "releaser" stimuli to call attention to itself, such as lack of license plates, hood or trunk open, or a tire removed. However, there are also less obvious cues, such as a flat tire not repaired within a day or two, or simply a car which has not been moved from one place for several days. In a city that is always on the go, anything static must be dead, and it becomes public domain if no one calls for the body. Older boys and men are attracted by the lure of usable or salable parts, and so the car is stripped of all items of possible value. Either late in this stage or after it is completed (depending on implicit neighborhood norms), younger children begin to smash the front and rear windows. Then all easily broken, ripped, or bent parts are attacked. Next, the remainder of the car is smashed with rocks, pipes, and hammers. Sometimes it is set on fire, and sometimes even the body metal is torn off. Finally, and most ignominiously, the last stage in the metamorphosis occurs when

FIGURE 6

A Stage Six Corvette Convertible—Becoming a Vandalized Refuse Container

people in the neighborhood (and even Sanitation Department clean-up men) use it as a big garbage can, dumping their refuse into it (see Fig. 6).

*A Field Experiment on "Auto-Shaping"*

In order to observe in a more systematic fashion who are the vandals and what are the conditions associated with their acts of vandalism, Scott Fraser and I bought a car and left it on a street across from the Bronx campus of New York University, where it was observed continuously for 64 hours. At the same time, we repeated this procedure in Palo Alto, California, on a street near the Stanford University campus. The license plates of both cars were removed and the hoods opened to provide the necessary releaser signals.

What happened in New York was unbelievable! Within ten minutes the 1959 Oldsmobile received its first auto strippers—a father, mother, and eight-year-old son. The mother appeared to be a lookout, while the son aided the father's search of the trunk, glove compartment, and motor. He handed his father the tools necessary to remove the battery and radiator. Total time of destructive contact: seven minutes.

> By the end of the first 26 hours, a steady parade of vandals had removed the battery, radiator, air cleaner, radio antenna, windshield wipers, right-hand-side chrome strip, hubcaps, a set of jumper cables, a gas can, a can of car wax, and the left rear tire (the other tires were too worn to be interesting). Nine hours later, random destruction began when two laughing teenagers tore off the rearview mirror and began throwing it at the headlights and front windshield. Eventually, five eight-year-olds claimed the car as their private playground, crawling in and out of it and smashing the windows. One of the last visitors was a middle-aged man in a camel's hair coat and matching hat, pushing a baby in a carriage. He stopped, rummaged through the trunk, took out an unidentifiable part, put it in the baby carriage and wheeled off. [As reported in *Time* magazine, February 28, 1969]

In less than three days what remained was a battered, useless hulk of metal, the result of 23 incidents of destructive contact. The vandalism was almost always observed by one or more other passersby, who occasionally stopped to chat with the looters. Most

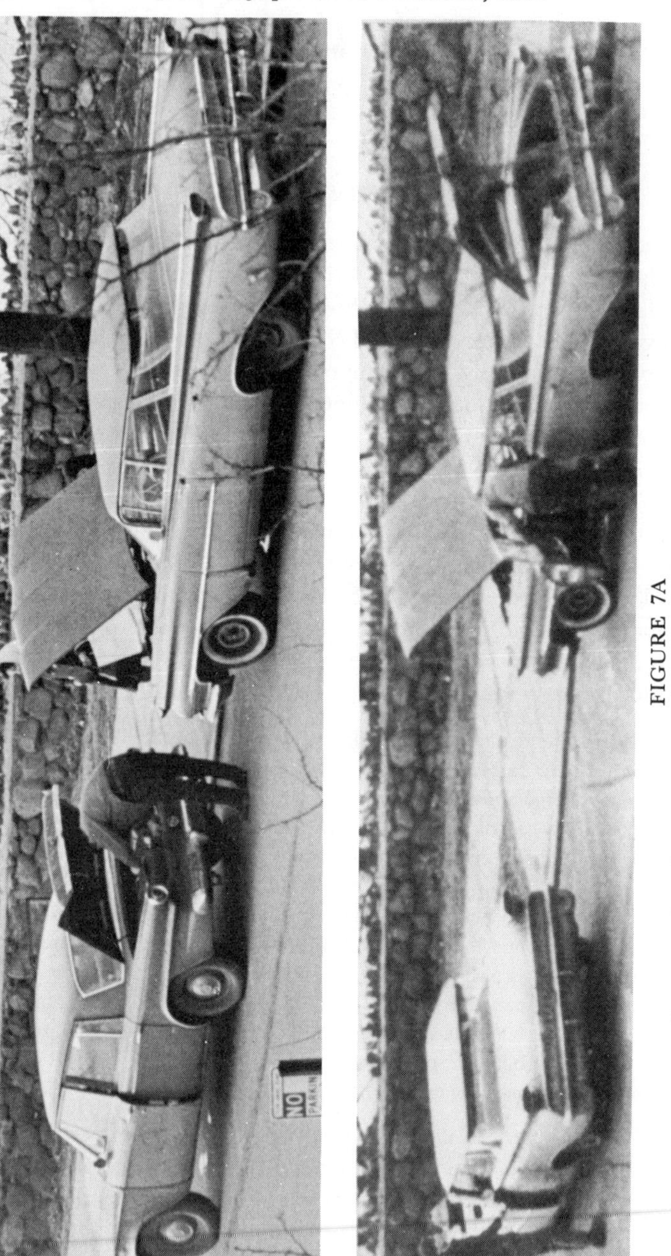

FIGURE 7A

Stripping Our Abandoned Car Before Destroying It (in New York City)

FIGURE 7B

VANDALIZING THE ABANDONED CAR—FUN AND GAMES FOR CHILDREN, FAMILIES, AND OBSERVERS

The same destructive phenomena have been witnessed in subsequent observations of planted cars by other investigators in Milan and Paris.

of the destruction was done in the daylight hours and not at night (as we had anticipated), and the adults' stealing clearly preceded the window-breaking, tire-slashing fun of the youngsters. The adults were all well-dressed, clean-cut whites who would under other circumstances be mistaken for mature, responsible citizens demanding more law and order. The one optimistic note to emerge from this study is that the number of people who came into contact with the car but did not steal or damage it was twice as large as the number of actual vandals.

In startling contrast, the Palo Alto car not only emerged untouched, but when it began to rain, one passerby lowered the hood so that the motor would not get wet!

### *Vandalism Is Alive, Though Sleeping, in Stanford*

Next, this car was abandoned on the Stanford University campus for over a week without incident. It was obvious that the releaser cues which were sufficient in New York were not adequate here. I expected that vandalism needed to be primed where it did not occur with a higher "natural" frequency. To do so, two of my graduate students (Mike Bond and Ebbe Ebbesen) and I decided to provide a better model for destruction by taking a sledge hammer to the car ourselves and then seeing if others would follow suit.

Several observations are noteworthy. First of all, there is considerable reluctance to take that first blow, to smash through the windshields and initiate the destruction of a form. But it feels so good after the first smack that the next one comes more easily, with more force, and feels even better. Although everyone knew the sequence was being filmed, the students got carried away temporarily. Once one person had begun to wield the sledge hammer, it was difficult to get him to stop and pass it to the next pair of eager hands. Finally they all attacked simultaneously. One student jumped on the roof and began stomping it in, two were pulling the door from its hinges, another hammered away at the hood and motor, while the last one broke all the glass he could find (see Fig. 8). They later reported that feeling the metal or glass give way under the force of their blows was stimulating and pleasurable. Observers of this action, who were shouting out to hit it harder and to smash it, finally joined

FIGURE 8
"HIT IT AGAIN, HARDER, HARDER!" THE AWAKENING OF DARK IMPULSES AT STANFORD UNIVERSITY

in and turned the car completely over on its back, whacking at the underside. There seemed little hope to expect spontaneous vandalism of this car since it was already wrecked so badly. However, that night at 12:30 A.M. three young men with pipes and bars began pounding away at the carcass so intensely that dormitory residents (a block away) shouted out for them to stop.

We might conclude from these preliminary studies that to *initiate* such acts of destructive vandalism, the necessary ingredients are the acquired feelings of anonymity provided by the life in a city like New York, along with some minimal releaser cues. Where social anonymity is not a "given" of one's everyday life, it is necessary to have more extreme releaser cues, more explicit models for destruction and aggression, and physical anonymity—a large crowd or the darkness of the night. A heightened state of preparatory general arousal would serve to make the action go, with less direct priming. To maintain and intensify the action, the ideal conditions occur where the physical act is a gross one involving a great deal of energy, thus producing considerable noncognitive feedback. It is pleasurable to behave at a purely sensual, physical, unthinking level —regardless of whether the act is making love or making war.

It is only proper to conclude this section with two final, recently gathered anecdotes. 1) A tank, which was part of an army convoy traveling through the Bronx, developed trouble and had to be left in the street while a mechanic was dispatched. He arrived a few hours later to find it totally stripped of all removable parts (which earned it the *Esquire* Dubious Prize of the Year, 1968). 2) A motorist pulled his car off a highway in Queens, New York, to fix a flat tire. He jacked his car up and, while removing the flat tire, was startled to see his hood being opened and a stranger starting to pull out the battery. The stranger tried to mollify his assumed car-stripping colleague by telling him, "Take it easy, buddy, you can have the tires; all I want is the battery!"

What is being destroyed here is not simply a car, but the basic fabric of social norms which must regulate all communal life. The horrible scene from *Zorba the Greek* in which the old townswomen begin to strip the home of the dying Bubbalina before she is yet dead is symbolically enacted many times every day in cities like New York where young and old, poor and affluent strip, steal, and vandalize cars, schools, churches, and almost all symbols of social order.

It is for the sociologist to discover the specific roots of this induced anonymity,[8] but Hall (1966) sees the type of behaviors we have discussed as one consequence of squeezing man into too small a space and limiting his personal distance (the study of proxemics).

> The animal studies also teach us that crowding per se is neither good nor bad, but rather that overstimulation and disruptions of social relationships as a consequence of overlapping personal distances lead to population collapse. [P. 175]

## Living for the Moment, for the Kicks Now

One approach to studying the psychological process of deindividuation involves isolating theoretically relevant antecedent conditions and observing their effects, while a second approach starts with dramatic natural occurrences of the behavior and then traces back their causes. Our current research is utilizing both strategies—the first one to study the consequences of hypnotically induced alterations of time perspective, and the second to discover the psychological causes of the violent behavior attributed to "speed freaks," chronic amphetamine users.

### *Time Out of Time*

Our model predicts that impulsive behavior is more likely to occur if a "here and now" time orientation is adopted, one which attenuates the controls imposed by past concerns, guilt, and commitments as well as by future anxieties and responsibilities. Aaronson (1967) has been using hypnosis as a technique to induce altered time sense. Simply suggesting to trained hypnotic subjects that their present will be expanded was sufficient to create marked changes in mood and behavior. As a subject under the skillful training of Dr. Paul Sacerdote, I experienced the "expanded present"

8. One social indicator of urban anonymity is the failure of people living in tenement houses to display their name on their mailbox, at their downstairs doorbell, or on their door. In a survey I conducted of 100 tenements, the apartments of only 24 percent of the occupants could be located from their name plates on the ground-floor bells or mailboxes.

suggestion as a state filled with sensations, simultaneous awareness of all one's senses, physical well-being, and a desire to run, jump, play, or do anything, but not sit still. My thoughts and perceptions were focused only on things in my immediate sensory field. Everything else seemed not to matter much, or else seemed too far away to merit any attention.

At Stanford, Gary Marshall, Christina Maslach, and I are currently working on this exciting phenomenon with a group of a dozen hypnotic subjects (drawn from my introductory psychology course). The subjective reactions I had were experienced similarly by all of our subjects. One girl reported she felt so good that she wanted to scream and shout, and then began to do so. Soon the other two subjects in her group were doing likewise. In another group, the eruptive laughter and joking of one "expanded present" subject infected a second one, and they went on in near hysteria for 15 minutes until stopped. When one boy got angry over not finding a name in a phone book (he was told he would not be able to), he began ripping out the pages in the book. The other subjects immediately followed suit with phone books we provided them. Suddenly pages were flying everywhere. In minutes the books were ripped to shreds, and paper missiles were fired at each other and at the researchers until we (somewhat frightened at this loss of control) gave the instruction to return immediately to a deep level of hypnotic relaxation. This is clearly a beautiful technique for studying emotional and behavioral contagion, and we are now working on developing appropriate tasks and response measures, as well as delineating the necessary control groups and procedures.

One of our "expanded present" female subjects has already provided us with a provocative lead into the relationship between time sense, physical identity, and responsibility.

> I'm melted. I am so thin, I cover practically everything. In fact, I am sort of falling into everything because I am so thin, and I can hear all the little things vibrating, and I can taste all the different things, like wood and the carpet, and the floor and the chairs. I really can't see any more, though, I mean it's all different colors, but it's so big you can hardly see it, everything is very confusing, but I've just sort of melted into everything. . . . I'm unresponsible! . . . I'm everything! I can keep going. . . . I'm not a thing anymore, I'm everything so I can't do

anything. There's nobody there, nobody who says to me, "Hey, Everything, you have to do this."

### *"Acid" Blows Minds, But "Speed" Kills Society*

We need look no further than the innumerable drug subcultures of our nation to find the embodiment of acting upon impulses for immediate gratification—the total immersion in the moment, in today's trip, in the high in the sky. However, it is only recently that violence and the senseless crimes mentioned in the introduction to this paper have become part of the drug scene. This change is most obvious in San Francisco's Haight-Ashbury district, where there have been 17 murders in a recent two-month period, innumerable assaults, muggings, rapes, torture orgies, and other crimes of violence. The director of the free medical clinic there, Dr. David Smith,[9] is convinced that the change from a "flower-peace" culture to one of violence can be traced to a transition from use of LSD ("acid") to methamphetamines ("speed"). The pseudoreligious, self-analytic, creative, transcendental, nonviolent "acid heads" have been replaced by a new generation of young, white, middle-class teenagers and adults who become hyperactive, irrational, paranoid, and violent. These are the reactions caused by excessive reliance upon speed. After the initial exhilaration of the injected speed and the well-being of the ride up comes an acute anxiety reaction on the ride down. To avoid this, speed users go on a speed "ride," "shooting up" again and again, up to ten times a day for several days, or in some cases a week or two. "Speed freaks" develop paranoid reactions (maybe as a side effect of prolonged sleep deprivation) which make them suspicious of and hostile toward everyone. The combination of agitation, anxiety, irritability, and paranoia experienced in the threatening environment of such a subculture makes violence a common, prepotent reaction to any type of real or imagined provocation.

David Smith, Christina Maslach, and I are in the process of designing collaborative field and laboratory studies to study systematically the relation between the use of speed and aggression.

9. See Smith, D. E. "Changing drug patterns in the Haight-Ashbury." *California Medicine*, February 1969 (In press).

We hope to be able to differentiate the functional significance of the hyperactivity, the paranoid reaction, and the increase in sense of time rate upon impulsive behavior, both aggressive and non-aggressive. Related to our earlier discussion of time-rate schedules of responding is the conjecture that maybe it is the sudden drug-induced shift from the usual drl schedule to a drh schedule which accounts for the loss of control over socially responsive behavioral output. How much of the variance in impulsive-hostile behavior can be accounted for by such a change in timing, relative to the effects of hyperactivity and suspicion? We hope to answer questions like these which have both theoretical value and obvious social relevance.

## A Different Face of Deindividuation: Dehumanization

We have just been talking about youths in desperate trouble—begging, stealing, and prostituting for drug money; living in fear of hepatitis, the police, and the underworld—as "speed freaks" or "acid heads." The mere use of such categorical labeling makes it difficult for you to empathize with the person, the human being who is just like you, huddled in a mass behind such labels. To exterminate Jews, the Nazis did not have to become deindividuated in the sense in which we have used the concept; they merely had to dehumanize their victims. By perceiving them as inferior forms of animal life, they could destroy them just as you would crush a mosquito, an ant, or even a harmless spider. Similarly, KKK lynch mobs in the South often posed for pictures next to the "strange fruit" of their labor, obviously not seeking anonymity (see Fig. 9).

This phenomenon is even more pervasive than its kindred spirit of deindividuation. There are four classes of situations which lead most people to treat others as if they were not human beings, as if they had no personal identity. Once that perception is adopted, there is no limit to the outrage one man can bring against his former "fellow man."

1) Dehumanization is more probable whenever a numerically large, continuous flow of people has to be managed efficiently and "processed." In such cases people get IBMized (a cause of the first Berkeley student riots), get stuffed into crowded subways by New York and Tokyo Transit employees hired as "packers," don't

FIGURE 9

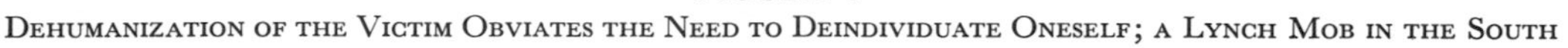

Dehumanization of the Victim Obviates the Need to Deindividuate Oneself; a Lynch Mob in the South

get listened to at the welfare bureau when they have justified complaints, etc. We plan to study the development of cynicism and loss of empathy among idealistic college students working in welfare in urban ghettos, as well as to employ an analogue of the phenomenon in a laboratory manipulation.

2) The "institutional sergeant" syndrome emerges when the individual is exposed to others (e.g., the mental patient, the mother on welfare) whose plight arouses extreme empathy. After repeated exposure, with improvement slow or not apparent, the individual feels helpless to effect any change and views such people as emotional burdens, to be serviced without personal involvement. Mental patients at New Jersey's largest asylum in Trenton were recently discovered being used in a prostitution ring run by the psychiatric attendants. Women and even little girls were smuggled out of the hospital for prostitution and sexual abuse. The attendants received ten dollars for each set-up; the patients got a piece of candy.

3) Special training in dehumanization is required when an individual is called upon to perform a role which violates a social taboo. Surgeons represent the best illustration of this principle. Even though their goal is desirable, in practice they are violating the integrity of the human body. To be effective, they must learn to perceive not a person under their scalpel, but an organ or part. Their language clues us into this immediately, as illustrated in a recent medical report of a clinic patient which stated, "The *body* awoke approximately 18 hours later and complained of hunger and depression."

Another form of this dehumanization is the rigidly prescribed role which the doctor forces upon the patient. Recently when I was being given emergency treatment for an eye laceration, the resident surgeon abruptly terminated his conversation with me as soon as I lay down on the operating table. Although I had had no sedative or anesthesia, he acted as if I were no longer conscious, directing all his questions to a friend of mine—questions such as, What's his name?, What occupation is he in?, Is he a real doctor?, etc. As I lay there, these two men were speaking about me as if I were not there at all. The moment I got off the table and was no longer a cut to be stitched, the surgeon resumed his conversation with me, and existence was conferred upon me again.

How do medical schools train their students to be emotionally inoculated to cutting up their first cadaver? Would more students be unable to do so if they began with the face or eyes—where it is harder to deny the humanity of the object being operated upon? What characterizes medical students who do become eye surgeons or pathologists and coroners? How do gynecologists learn to inhibit their sexual arousal? We will also study issues like these in our future research, as well as what techniques are most effective in training soldiers to kill.

4) When a person wants to engage in a behavior solely for self-gratification and doesn't want to take into consideration the mutual needs of the other interacting person, he can best achieve that end by dehumanizing the other. Prostitution flourishes precisely because it satisfies this aspect of absorption in self-gratification to the exclusion of giving of the self to another, or recognizing anything but the temporary instrumental function the other serves. Payment to a prostitute (especially by married men who are not sexually deprived) is for the privilege of dehumanizing her, which enables the buyer to indulge his fantasies without the constraints normally imposed by awareness of the woman's feelings of shame, or of future contact. This response is not limited to such men, but is part of the way most men learn to perceive almost all women. Women who are ugly are "beasts" or "dogs," promiscuous ones are "pigs," fertile ones are "cows." Or the part comes to stand for the whole person, as witnessed by expressions such as "a piece of ass." In short, the dehumanization of women by men is the only way many of them can come to react to women at a sexual level at all. They must render them into objects, perceiving them as little more than semen receptacles. Romance individuates, lust deindividuates.

But men do not have an exclusive on this process, nor is it limited to sexual expression. Most readers surely can fill in other areas of application personally known to them.

## Deindividuation: Imposed or Chosen

Control—it is perfectly obvious—they have brought this whole mass of human beings to the point where they are one, out of their skulls, one psyche, and they have utter control over them—but they don't know

> what in the hell to do with it, they haven't the first idea, and they will lose it . . . suddenly GHHHHHHWOOOOOOOOOWWWWWWW, it is like the whole thing has snapped, and the whole front section of the arena becomes a writhing, seething mass of little girls waving their arms in the air, this mass of pink arms, it is all you can see, it is like a single colonial animal with a thousand waving pink tentacles;—vibrating poison madness and filling the universe with the teeny agony torn out of them . . . it is *one being*. They have been transformed into one being. [Tom Wolfe's description of the teeny-boppers' reaction to the Beatles' appearance at the Cow Palace, San Francisco, 1966, in *The Electric Kool-Aid Acid Test* (New York: Farrar, Straus, Giroux, 1968), p. 205]

Before concluding this paper, we must distinguish between social situations which appear to have some of the characteristics of deindividuation but may either result in antisocial behavior, with a loss of control, or extreme conformity to social norms and even altruistic behavior. Two variables may explain much of the seeming confusion which arises when we think of orgies, the Mardi Gras, riots, the behavior of uniformed priests and nuns, the conformity of soldiers, etc., as all being instances of deindividuation. In the $2 \times 2$ matrix in Table 3, the locus of deindividuation (internally generated needs versus ones externally imposed by another person or group) is orthogonal to the degree of voluntary exposure to group situations where anonymity, shared responsibility, and other deindividuating operations are likely to be experienced.

An individual may have high choice to enter the group, the decision being voluntary, rational, premeditated, and with certain outcomes anticipated. Or the decision may be a low-choice one, where entry into the group is involuntary or forced by circumstance. The locus of the need to become deindividuated may be internal, as when the individual uses the situation to satisfy his own needs which, to the extent that they are exclusively self-satisfying, must be antisocial. On the other hand, a deindividuation-like process may become institutionalized and used as a technique for achieving the leader's or group's goals. Here idiosyncrasy must give way to conformity, and whether the end is antisocial or not depends upon the norms of the group.

1) *High Choice: Internal Locus*—The individual chooses to enter a group or situation that holds promise of fulfilling his needs for

TABLE 3

EXAMPLES OF SOCIAL PHENOMENA IN WHICH THE CHOICE OF ENTERING A GROUP OR SITUATION AND THE LOCUS OF NEEDS FOR ANONYMITY RESULT IN DIFFERENT TYPES OF CONFORMITY AND DEINDIVIDUATION

| | | Entry Choice | | |
|---|---|---|---|---|
| | | *High: Voluntary* | *Low: Voluntary* | |
| Locus of Needs | *Internally Generated* | Mardi Gras, Vandalism 1 | 2 Behavioral contagion, Riots, Gang rape | Norms of social appropriateness are violated |
| | *Externally Imposed* | 3 Volunteer Army, Taking Holy Orders, Formal Dress Ball | 4 Conscripted Army, Prisoners | Consequences may be either prosocial or antisocial |

expressing impulsive or taboo behavior. Leaders are not necessary, nor is it required that identifiability be reduced to in-group members, but only to outsiders.

2) *Low Choice: Internal Locus*—By chance or necessity, individuals find themselves in a situation in which their personal needs can be expressed and where there is no superordinate group goal to which such individual needs must be subjugated. Here a small minority can effectively steer a large group. This cell comes closest to what we have been talking about as deindividuation.

3) *High Choice: External Locus*—Externally imposed processes of deindividuation may also occur in groups which are voluntarily chosen. However, here the individual joins the group not for the purpose of being deindividuated, but rather because he values some norm of the group. For such a person, the demand of the group to minimize individual differences is not a major consideration. He recognizes that personal anonymity is a means rather than an end. In this manner, the priest assists in the deindividuation process demanded by his order because he recognizes it as a device for achieving the denial of egocentricity, which leads to the goal of freeing him from worldly preoccupations.

4) *Low Choice: External Locus*—Where group membership is involuntary, as in a conscripted army, loss of individuality is induced by rigid requirements of dress and behavior and by severe penalties for nonconformity. Although within such a group individuals may maintain singularity, their actions as a collective, identifiable unit demand the loss of each member's individuality in the eyes of the out-group.

The use of a distinctive uniform is a characteristic method for getting people to conform; the uniform becomes the visible symbol of that abstraction, the group, in which individuality is dissolved. In *Mein Kampf*, Hitler describes in detail this method of gaining control over usually unpredictable masses: dress them alike and variability in their behavior will be eliminated. When the American GI's in Charlie Company entered the Vietnamese village of Song My (or "Pinkville") on March 16, 1968, they proceeded to commit such atrocities that American eyewitnesses couldn't believe what they were seeing. Some soldiers "went crazy" and slaughtered wounded villagers, women and children. Others murdered perhaps hundreds of civilians in "business-like" fashion, firing M-79 grenade launchers as well as machine-gunning clumps of "gooks." Most of Charlie Company did kill... "everyone in the village, animals, and everything" (*San Francisco Examiner-Chronicle*, November 23, 1969).

In religious orders, monks, nuns, and priests are required to wear a habit. Dressing alike also encourages behavioral conformity to a code of group behavior, yet obviously, such behavior is not antisocial in the sense in which we usually employ this term. However, if we examine this group behavior we find that it is antisocial in a different, very special sense. The priest denies the impulses of his material nature; he takes himself out of the material flow of life (to the preservation of which society is dedicated) and enters a "community of souls." His dress and the code of behavior of the group to which he belongs are designed to help free him from his individuation.

In all of these examples, uniformity of appearance results in the perception by out-group members of a distinctive group within which individual members are not differentiated. The in-group member forgoes individual recognition from the out-group to achieve the greater recognition that accrues to him from his membership in the group. Although members may have personal identity within the group, the group's strength and impact depend upon the members' belief that all of them are equally valid representatives of the group's norms. Since the group gains in its power to the extent that its members sacrifice their individuation to the distinction of the group as a whole, it must demand from its members extreme conformity to its norms. To preserve its collective identity, the group can allow no individual deviation.

## Conclusions

Although we have covered a lot of ground in this paper, we have only treated this complex problem at a rather superficial level. Nevertheless, it becomes apparent that the human choice we have been considering is fundamental to understanding a wide range of human behavior. The study of deindividuation links social psychology not only to other social sciences but to the basic themes in Western literature, mythology, and religion. The model rather crudely outlined here is but a heuristic device for generating further ideas and pointing to relationships and areas of inquiry with which psychologists have not before been concerned. It needs to be refined, and much research must be done to firm it up or expose its inadequacies.

At the level where social scientists become involved with social issues, our discussion of deindividuation leads to the following suggestions. Police must be retrained to cope with the emergence of the "new" kind of crime and criminal depicted in this paper. The policeman must be individuated in the perception of those he must deal with, and must feel so, in order for him to maintain his individual integrity (they should wear their names on their uniforms as athletes do). Also, the current theory of ever increasing deterrents against crime (more police patrols, search and seizure, aggressive police action) is based upon outmoded concepts of the criminal. When a dehumanized person has become an object, then it may be that the only means he can use to get anyone to take him seriously and respond to him in an individuated way is through violence. A knife at someone's throat forces the victim to acknowledge the power of the attacker and his control. In one sense, violence and destruction transform a passive, controlled object into an active, controlling person. When driven to the wall by forces of deindividuation, the individual must assert his own force or become indistinguishable from the wall. Conditions which foster deindividuation make each of us a potential assassin.

We might also venture the suggestion that what is wrong with American society is that currently it neither promotes individuation nor allows for deindividuation. There are a myriad of social forces which make anonymity prevalent while diminishing individual uniqueness, singularity, and personal pride. At the same time, there is a breakdown of tribal communal ties, as well as a weakening of the extended family due to our extreme geographical mobility. The concurrent breakdown of the nuclear family through divorce results in a loss of being related to the soil or the blood cycle of nature—the primitive (positive) deindividuated experience. What we will begin to see more and more is young people attempting to regain these lost ties through new forms of group marriages and communal families.

Viewed in another sense, what is wrong is that there are no institutionalized forms of release of antisocial impulses within a prescribed time period and other boundary conditions. Individuals who normally live controlled lives need such revels so that they can experience both the pleasure derived directly from such expression and the greater pleasure of becoming *reindividuated* following a period of abandon or running amok.

Although on special occasions the society must provide such opportunity for release, at all other times we must insist on greater individuation in all aspects of our lives.[10] For example, we should not give up our names for more efficient numbers, and should resist urban planning which nurtures sterile, drab sameness and wipes out neighborhoods where people are recognized by others and are concerned about the social evaluation of those others.

Furthermore, there must be provision for socialization training in which mild forms of aggression can be expressed. Megargee (1966) has found that the problem with extremely assaultive criminal offenders is not that they are uncontrolled, impulsive types. To the contrary, they are so over-controlled that they can never allow any release of aggression. Anything which threatens or breaks down this rigid control system can lead to unimagined acts of violence in response to minimal direct provocation. Many of the mass murders and senseless homicides which we examined earlier developed from just such a background.

In the eternal struggle between order and chaos, we openly hope for individuation to triumph, but secretly plot mutiny with the forces within, drawn by the irresistible lure of deindividuation.

> Even as on an immense, raging sea, assailed by huge wave crests, a

10. An intriguing experimental situation involves placing a person in a small group in which the other members are all accomplices of the researcher. Their task and the experimental procedure are designed to deny the individual any uniqueness. They wear masks which look like him, their voices are changed to be like his, they mimic his speech, gestures, posture, habits. They role play having identical attitudes, values, and goals. In short, there is nothing he is that they are not. Will this similarity be pleasing? Or will it motivate the person to demonstrate what he believes is unique about himself? But suppose he shows his cards and they also share that trait, ability, or whatever; then maybe it's better to keep it concealed and as long as *he* knows he has it, it's enough. Or is it? This raises the provocative question, What keeps you from becoming someone else, or someone else from becoming you?

man sits in a little rowboat trusting his frail craft, so, amidst the furious torments of this world, the individual sits tranquilly, supported by the *principium individuationis* and relying on it.

—Schopenhauer

## REFERENCES


Aaronson, B. S. Hypnotic alterations of space and time. Presented at International Conference on Hypnosis: Drugs and Psi Induction, 1967.

Christie, R., & Geis, F. L. *Studies in Machiavellianism.* New York: Academic Press, 1969.

Dooley, L. The concept of time in defense of ego integrity. *Psychiatry,* 1941, **4**, 13–23.

Easterbrook, J. A. The effect of emotion on cue utilization and the organization of behavior. *Psychol. Rev.,* 1959, **66**, 183–201.

Eliade, M. *Shamanism: Archaic techniques of ecstasy.* New York: Princeton Univ. Press, 1964.

Festinger, L., Pepitone, A., & Newcomb, T. Some consequences of deindividuation in a group. *J. abnorm. soc. Psychol.,* 1952, **47**, 382–389.

Golding, W. *Lord of the flies.* New York: Capricorn Books, 1959.

Hall, E. T. *Hidden dimensions.* New York: Doubleday, 1966.

Helfer, R. E., & Kemper, C. H. *The battered child.* Chicago: Univ. of Chicago Press, 1968.

Hogg, G. *Cannibalism and human sacrifice.* New York: N.Y. Citadel Press, 1966.

Huie, W. B. *Three lives for Mississippi.* New York: WCC Books, 1965.

Kilman, E. *Cannibal coast.* Texas: Naylor, 1959.

Megargee, E. I. Undercontrolled and overcontrolled personality types in extreme anti-social aggression. *Psychol. Monogr.,* 1966, **80**, Whole No. 11.

Milgram, S. Some conditions of obedience and disobedience to authority. In I. D. Steiner and M. Fishbein (Eds.), *Current studies in social psychology.* New York: Holt, Rinehart, Winston, 1965, pp. 243–262.

Nietzsche, F. *The birth of tragedy.* New York: Doubleday, 1956.

Radcliffe-Brown, A. R. *The Andaman Islanders.* Illinois: Humanities Press, 1948.

Rapaport, A. *Fights, games, and debates.* Ann Arbor: Univ. of Michigan Press, 1961.

Reynolds, G. *A primer of operant conditioning.* Glenview, Ill.: Scott, Foresman, 1968.

Schneidman, E. S. (Ed.) *Essays in self-destruction.* New York: Science House, 1967.

Singer, J. E., Brush, C. A., & Lublin, S. C. Some aspects of deindividuation: identification and conformity. *J. exp. soc. Psychol.,* 1965, **1**, 356–378.

Srole, L., Langner, T. S., Michael, S. T., Opler, M., & Rennie, T. A. *Mental health in the metropolis: The midtown Manhattan study.* New York: McGraw Hill, 1962.

Talbot, J. *Some Nigerian fertility rites.* Oxford: Oxford Univ. Press, 1927.

Wheeler, L. Toward a theory of behavioral contagion. *Psychol. Bull.*, 1966, **73**, 179–192.

Ziller, R. C. Individuation and socialization. *Human Relations*, 1964, **17**, 341–360.

Zimbardo, P. G. *The cognitive control of motivation.* Glenview, Ill.: Scott, Foresman, 1969.

Zimbardo, P. G., Cohen, A. R., Weisenberg, M., Dworkin, L., & Firestone, I. Control of pain motivation by cognitive dissonance. *Science*, 1966, **151**, 217–219.

# The Nebraska Symposium on Motivation: An Overview

RUBEN ARDILA

The purpose of this article is to present a panoramic view of the Nebraska Symposium on Motivation and a cumulative index of the papers read during the first seventeen years of the Symposium. Articles will be classified in four categories, and the origins of the Symposium will be presented.

The Nebraska Symposium on Motivation began in 1953, financed through a training grant of the U.S. National Institute of Mental Health, and sponsored by the Department of Psychology of the University of Nebraska (Lincoln, Nebraska, U.S.A.). The topic of motivation was chosen because of its importance in contemporary psychology and its relevance to practically all branches of the discipline. On January 15 and 16, 1953, J. S. Brown, H. F. Harlow, and L. J. Postman delivered the first papers; on March 26 and 27, V. Nowlis, T. M. Newcomb, and O. H. Mowrer delivered theirs.

The Symposium was edited by Marshall R. Jones from 1953 to 1963, and by David Levine from 1964 to 1967. The 1968 volume was edited by William J. Arnold due to the temporary absence of Dr. Levine from the Department of Psychology of the University of Nebraska. The 1969 volume is edited by William J. Arnold and David Levine, and the editors of the 1970 volume will be William J. Arnold and Monte M. Page.

Currently the Symposium meets twice a year, in the spring and in the fall. At each session three speakers present their papers and each participant comments on the papers given by the other participants. Those comments are occasionally published, and generally they constitute a valuable summary of the papers and a critical evaluation of them.

In the spring of 1968 the first psychologist from overseas, Heinz Heckhausen, from the Psychologisches Institut, Ruhr-Universität, Bochum, Germany, took part in the Symposium. He added to the international outlook of the meeting, although, as a matter of fact, the Symposium was already very well known in many parts of the world.

The papers read at the Symposium are published by the University of Nebraska Press. These published volumes provide a convenient way for scholars to keep abreast of recent work in the area of motivation. No one volume can hope to be comprehensive, nor is it intended to be; but the entire series has some claim to be representative of theory and research in the broad field of motivational psychology.

One of the basic problems has been how to conceptualize motivation. The concept has somewhat different connotations for different psychologists; there is no agreement on exactly what should be included within the concept. The question of whether or not we even need the concept, whether or not it explains anything that cannot be explained by other concepts, has been raised on several occasions. The participants have usually clarified their own definitions and explained the way in which they used the term.

Ernest Hilgard (1963), in his contribution to the well-known Project A of the American Psychological Association, examined the possibility of dividing motivational psychology into several classes. With that aim he reviewed the contents of the published volumes of the Nebraska Symposium on Motivation from 1953 to 1956. He assumed that participation in such a symposium placed social pressure on the participant to relate his ideas to those who express similar viewpoints, or to pay attention to viewpoints that appear antagonistic to his own.

Hilgard classified the participants in the Symposium into four groups. I would like to take this frame of reference for the classification of all the Nebraska Symposium participants and their work, although there are other possibilities (Madsen, 1968). Including that of 1969, there are 17 volumes of the Symposium available. These include 100 papers (actually it should be 102 papers, but two of them have not been published, although they were presented orally). In order to given an idea of the classification, the following list will present a sample of the authors in each group.

I. Learning Theory and Experimentation: Harlow, Nissen, Solomon, Estes, Spence.

II. Biological and Physiological Orientation: Beach, Olds, Malmo, Schneirla, Lindsley.

III. Learning and Personality Orientation: Littman, Whiting, Osgood, Wittenborn.

IV. Personality and Social Psychology: Cattell, Festinger, Maslow, Newcomb, Pettigrew.

Table 1 presents a categorization of the 100 papers of the Nebraska Symposium according to their orientation. I am classifying papers, not authors, although the results would be almost the same if the categorization were based on workers and not on the works.

TABLE 1

ORIENTATION OF THE PAPERS PRESENTED AT THE NEBRASKA SYMPOSIUM ON MOTIVATION FROM 1953 TO 1969 (17 VOLUMES)

| Orientation | Number |
|---|---|
| Learning Theory and Experimentation | 34 |
| Biological and Phsyiological Orientation | 20 |
| Learning and Personality Orientation | 15 |
| Personality and Social Psychology | 31 |
| Total | 100 |

Two things may be inferred from this table: first, probably the fact that learning theory and experimentation balances with the orientation toward personality and social psychology can be considered as a reflection of the current state of affairs in the field, although editorial policy is of necessity also involved; second, very few nonpsychologists have taken part in the Symposium. In actuality, only one anthropologist, one sociologist, one zoologist, one physiologist, and one psychiatrist have presented papers, and all of them are very psychologically oriented.

In closing, I present a chronological and an alphabetical list of participants in the Nebraska Symposium on Motivation since its beginning. I hope these lists will be useful to those interested in the Symposium.

## REFERENCES

Arnold, W. J. (Ed.), *Nebraska symposium on motivation.* Lincoln: University of Nebraska Press, 1968.

Hilgard, E. R. Motivation in learning theory. In Koch, S. (Ed.), *Psychology: A study of a science.* Vol. 5. New York: McGraw Hill, 1963. Pp. 253–284.

Jones, M. R. (Ed.), *Nebraska symposium on motivation.* Lincoln: University of Nebraska Press, 1953, 1954, 1955, 1956, 1957, 1958, 1959, 1960, 1961, 1962, 1963.

Levine, D. (Ed.), *Nebraska symposium on motivation.* Lincoln: University of Nebraska Press, 1964, 1965, 1966, 1967.

Madsen, K. B. *Theories of motivation.* 4th ed. Copenhagen, Denmark: Munksgaard, 1968.

# Chronological List of Contents of the Nebraska Symposia on Motivation

1953 (Vol. 1)

Brown, J. S. Problems presented by the concept of acquired drive, pp. 1–21.
Harlow, H. F. Motivation as a factor in new responses, pp. 24–48.
Postman, L. J. The experimental analysis of motivational factors in perception, pp. 59–108.
Nowlis, V. The development and modification of motivational systems in personality, pp. 114–138.
Newcomb, T. M. Motivation in social behavior, pp. 139–162.
Mowrer, O. H. Motivation and neurosis, pp. 162–184.

1954 (Vol. 2)

Farber, I. E. Anxiety as a drive state, pp. 1–45.
Atkinson, J. W. Exploration using imaginative thought to assess the strength of human motives, pp. 56–111.
Ritchie, B. F. A logical and experimental analysis of the laws of motivation, pp. 121–176.
Festinger, L. Motivation leading to social behavior, pp. 191–218.
Klein, G. S. Need and regulation, pp. 224–274.
Nissen, H. W. The nature of the drive as innate determinant of behavioral organization, pp. 281–320.

1955 (Vol. 3)

Maslow, A. Deficiency motivation and growth motivation, pp. 1–30.
McClelland, D. C. Some social consequences of achievement motivation, pp. 41–64.

Olds, J. Physiological mechanisms of reward, pp. 73–138.
Peak, H. Attitude and motivation, pp. 149–188.
Young, P. T. The role of hedonic processes in motivation, pp. 193–237.
Rotter, J. B. The role of the psychological situation in determining the direction of human behavior, pp. 245–268.

1956 (Vol. 4)

Beach, F. A. Characteristics of masculine "sex drive," pp. 1–31.
Koch, S. Behavior as "intrinsically" regulated: Work notes towards a pre-theory of phenomena called "motivational," pp. 42–86.
Marx, M. H. Some relations between frustration and drive, pp. 92–130.
Miller, D. R., & Swanson, G. E. The study of conflict, pp. 137–173.
Seward, J. P. A neurological approach to motivation, pp. 180–208.
Solomon, R. L., & Brush, E. S. Experimentally derived conceptions of anxiety and aversion, pp. 212–305.

1957 (Vol. 5)

Morgan, C. T. Physiological mechanisms of motivation, pp. 1–35.
Lindsley, D. B. Psychophysiology and motivation, pp. 44–104.
Rodnick, E. H., & Garmezy, N. An experimental approach to the study of motivation in schizophrenia, pp. 109–183.
Wittenborn, J. R. Inferring the strength of drive, pp. 191–258.
Sears, P. S. Problems in the investigation of achievement and self-esteem motivation, pp. 265–338.
Osgood, C. E. Motivational dynamics of language behavior, pp. 348–423.

1958 (Vol. 6)

Bolles, R. C. The usefulness of the drive concept, pp. 1–32.
Estes, W. K. Stimulus-response theory of drive, pp. 35–68.
Spence, K. W. Behavior theory and selective learning, pp. 73–107.
Littman, R. A. Motives, history and causes, pp. 114–168.
Eriksen, C. W. Unconscious processes, pp. 169–226.
Malmo, R. B. Measurement of drive: An unsolved problem in psychology, pp. 229–265.

1959 (Vol. 7)

Schneirla, T. C. An evolutionary and developmental theory of biphasic processes underlying approach and withdrawal, pp. 1–41.

Hess, E. The relationship between imprinting and motivation, pp. 44–77.

Cattell, R. B. The dynamic calculus: Concepts and crucial experiments, pp. 84–133.

Levin, H., & Baldwin, A. L. Pride and shame in children, pp. 138–173.

Whiting, J. W. M. Sorcery, sin, and the superego. A cross-cultural study of some mechanisms of social control, pp. 174–194.

Janis, I. L. Motivational factors in the resolution of decisional conflicts, pp. 198–231.

1960 (Vol. 8)

Barker, R. G. Ecology and motivation, pp. 1–48.

Taylor, D. W. Toward an informational processing theory of motivation, pp. 51–78.

Toman, W. On the periodicity of motivation, pp. 80–94.

White, R. W. Competence and the psychosexual stages of development, pp. 97–140.

Heider, F. The Gestalt theory of motivation, pp. 145–171.

Rapaport, D. On the psychoanalytic theory of motivation, pp. 173–247.

1961 (Vol. 9)

Falk, J. L. The behavioral regulation of water-electrolyte balance, pp. 1–32.

Teitelbaum, P. Disturbances in feeding and drinking behavior after hypothalamic lesions, pp. 39–64.

Pfaffmann, C. The sensory and motivating properties of the sense of taste, pp. 71–108.

McKeachie, W. J. Motivation, teaching methods, and college learning, pp. 111–141.

Sarason, S. B. The contents of human problem solving, pp. 147–174.
Birch, D. A motivational interpretation of extinction, pp. 179–197.

1962 (Vol. 10)

Vinacke, W. E. Motivation as a complex problem, pp. 1–45.
Brehm, J. W. Motivational effects of cognitive dissonance, pp. 51–76.
Kelly, G. A. Europe's matrix of decision, pp. 83–122.
Epstein, S. The measurement of drive and conflict in humans: Theory and experiment, pp. 127–205.
Bandura, A. Social learning through imitation, pp. 211–268.
Deutsch, M. Cooperation and trust: Some theoretical notes, pp. 275–318.

1963 (Vol. 11)

Rogers, C. R. Actualizing tendency in relation to "motives" and to consciousness, pp. 1–24.
Sears, R. R. Dependency motivation, pp. 25–64.
Miller, N. E. Some reflections on the law of effect produce a new alternative to drive reduction, pp. 65–112.
Pribram, K. H. Reinforcement revisited: A structural view, pp. 113–160.
Magoun, H. W. Central neural inhibition, pp. 161–196.

1964 (Vol. 12)

Hilgard, E. R. The motivational relevance of hypnosis, pp. 1–43.
Walker, E. L. Psychological complexity as a basis for a theory of motivation and choice, pp. 47–94.
Logan, F. A. The free behavior situation, pp. 99–128.
Edwards, A. L. The assessment of human motives by means of personality scales, pp. 135–162.
Mandler, G. The interruption of behavior, pp. 163–220.
Schachter, S., & Latané, B. Crime, cognition, and the autonomic nervous system, pp. 221–272.

1965 (Vol. 13)

Kendler, H. H. Motivation and behavior, pp. 1–24.

Leeper, R. W. Some needed developments in the motivational theory of emotions, pp. 25–122.
Premack, D. Reinforcement theory, pp. 123–179.
Hunt, J. McV. Intrinsic motivation and its role in psychological development, pp. 189–282.
Campbell, D. T. Ethnocentric and other altruistic motives, pp. 283–312.
Guilford, J. P. Motivation in an informational psychology, pp. 313–334.

1966 (Vol. 14)

Holt, R. R. Measuring libidinal and aggressive motives and their controls by means of the Rorschach test, pp. 1–48.
Burke, C. J. Linear models for Pavlovian conditioning, pp. 49–66.
Masling, J. Role-related behavior of the subject and psychologist and its effects upon psychological data, pp. 67–104.
Dethier, V. G. Insects and the concept of motivation, pp. 105–136.
Helson, H. Some problems in motivation from the point of view of the theory of adaptation level, pp. 137–182.
Malamud, W. The concept of motivation in psychiatric practice, pp. 183–200.

1967 (Vol. 15)

Berlyne, D. E. Arousal and reinforcement, pp. 1–110.
Scott, J. P. The development of social motivation, pp. 111–132.
Katz, I. The socialization of academic motivation in minority group children, pp. 133–191.
Kelley, H. H. Attribution theory in social psychology, pp. 192–240.
Pettigrew, T. F. Social evaluation theory: Convergences and applications, pp. 241–318.

1968 (Vol. 16)

Grossman, S. P. The physiological basis of specific and nonspecific motivational processes, pp. 1–46.
McClearn, G. E. Genetics and motivation of the mouse, pp. 47–84.

Levine, S. Hormones and conditioning, pp. 85–102.
Heckhausen, H. Achievement motive research: Current problems and some contributions towards a general theory of motivation, pp. 103–174.
Lazarus, R. S. Emotions and adaptation: Conceptual and empirical relations, pp. 175–270.
Aronfreed, J. Aversive control of socialization, pp. 271–320.

1969 (Vol. 17)

Bindra, D. The interrelated mechanisms of reinforcement and motivation, and the nature of their influence on response, pp. 1–33.
Wike, E. L. Secondary reinforcement: Some research and theoretical issues, pp. 39–82.
Black, R. W. Incentive motivation and the parameters of reward in instrumental conditioning, pp. 85–137.
Aronson, E. Some antecedents of interpersonal attraction, pp. 143–173.
Cook, S. W. Motives in a conceptual analysis of attitude-related behavior, pp. 179–231.
Zimbardo, Philip H. The human choice: Individuation, reason, and order versus deindividuation, impulse, and chaos, pp. 237–307.

# Alphabetical List of Contents of the Nebraska Symposia on Motivation by Author


Aronfreed, J. Aversive control of socialization. 1968, **16**, 271–320.

Aronson, E. Some antecedents of interpersonal attraction. 1969, **17**, 143–173.

Atkinson, J. W. Exploration using imaginative thought to assess the strength of human motives. 1954, **2**, 56–111.

Bandura, A. Social learning through imitation. 1962, **10**, 211–268.

Barker, R. G. Ecology and motivation. 1959, **8**, 1–48.

Beach, F. A. Characteristics of masculine "sex drive." 1956, **4**, 1–31.

Berlyne, D. E. Arousal and reinforcement. 1967, **15**, 1–110.

Bindra, D. The interrelated mechanisms of reinforcement and motivation, and the nature of their influence on response. 1969, **17**, 1–33.

Birch, D. A motivational interpretation of extinction. 1961, **9**, 179–197.

Black, R. W. Incentive motivation and the parameters of reward in instrumental conditioning. 1969, **17**, 85–137.

Bolles, R. C. The usefulness of the drive concept. 1958, **6**, 1–32.

Brehm, J. W. Motivational effects of cognitive dissonance. 1962, **10**, 51–76.

Brown, J. S. Problems presented by the concept of acquired drive. 1953, **1**, 1–21.

Burke, C. J. Linear models for Pavlovian conditioning. 1966, **14**, 49–66.

Campbell, D. T. Ethnocentric and other altruistic motives. 1965, **13**, 283–312.

Cattell, R. B. The dynamic calculus: Concepts and crucial experiments. 1959, **7**, 84–133.

Cook, S. W. Motives in a conceptual analysis of attitude-related behavior. 1969, **17**, 179–231.

Dethier, V. G. Insects and the concept of motivation. 1966, **14**, 105–136.

Deutsch, M. Cooperation and trust: Some theoretical notes. 1962, **10**, 275–318.

Edwards, A. L. The assessment of human motives by means of personality scales. 1964, **12**, 135–162.

Epstein, S. The measurement of drive and conflict in humans: Theory and experiment. 1962, **10**, 127–205.

Eriksen, C. W. Unconscious processes. 1958, **6**, 169–226.

Estes, W. K. Stimulus-response theory of drive. 1958, **6**, 35–68.

Falk, J. L. The behavioral regulation of water-electrolyte balance. 1961, **9**, 1–32.

Farber, I. E. Anxiety as a drive state. 1954, **2**, 1–45.

Festinger, L. Motivation leading to social behavior. 1954, **2**, 191–218.

Grossman, S. P. The physiological basis of specific and non-specific motivational processes. 1968, **16**, 1–46.

Guilford, J. P. Motivation in an informational psychology. 1965, **13**, 313–334.

Harlow, H. F. Motivation as a factor in new responses. 1953, **1**, 24–48.

Heckhausen, H. Achievement motive research: Current problems and some contributions towards a general theory of motivation. 1968, **16**, 103–174.

Heider, F. The Gestalt theory of motivation. 1960, **8**, 145–171.

Helson, H. Some problems in motivation from the point of view of the theory of adaptation level. 1966, **14**, 137–182.

Hess, E. The relationship between imprinting and motivation. 1959, **7**, 44–77.

Hilgard, E. R. The motivational relevance of hypnosis. 1964, **12**, 1–43.

Holt, R. R. Measuring libidinal and aggressive motives and their controls by means of the Rorschach test. 1966, **14**, 1–48.

Hunt, J. McV. Intrinsic motivation and its role in psychological development. 1965, **13**, 189–282.

Janis, I. L. Motivational factors in the resolution of decisional conflicts. 1959, **7**, 198–231.
Katz, I. The socialization of academic motivation in minority group children. 1967, **15**, 133–191.
Kelley, H. H. Attribution theory in social psychology. 1967, **15**, 192–240.
Kelly, G. A. Europe's matrix of decision. 1962, **10**, 83–122.
Kendler, H. H. Motivation and behavior. 1965, **13**, 1–24.
Klein, G. S. Need and regulation. 1954, **2**, 224–274.
Koch, S. Behavior as "intrinsically" regulated: Work notes towards a pre-theory of phenomena called "motivational." 1956, **4**, 42–86.
Lazarus, R. S. Emotions and adaptation: Conceptual and empirical relations. 1968, **16**, 175–270.
Leeper, R. W. Some needed developments in the motivational theory of emotions. 1965, **13**, 25–122.
Levin, H., & Baldwin, A. L. Pride and shame in children. 1959, **7**, 138–173.
Levine, S. Hormones and conditioning. 1968, **16**, 85–102.
Lindsley, D. B. Psychophysiology and motivation. 1957, **5**, 44–104.
Littman, R. A. Motives, history and causes. 1958, **6**, 114–168.
Logan, F. A. The free behavior situation. 1964, **12**, 99–128.
McClearn, G. E. Genetics and motivation of the mouse. 1968, **16**, 47–84.
McClelland, D. C. Some social consequences of achievement motivation. 1955, **3**, 41–64.
McKeachie, W. J. Motivation, teaching methods, and college learning. 1961, **9**, 111–141.
Magoun, H. W. Central neural inhibition. 1963, **11**, 161–196.
Malamud, W. The concept of motivation in psychiatric practice. 1966, **14**, 183–200.
Malmo, R. B. Measurement of drive: An unsolved problem in psychology. 1958, **6**, 229–265.
Mandler, G. The interruption of behavior. 1964, **12**, 163–220.
Marx, M. H. Some relations between frustration and drive. 1956, **4**, 92–130.
Masling, J. Role-related behavior of the subject and psychologist and its effects upon psychological data. 1966, **14**, 67–104.

Maslow, A. Deficiency motivation and growth motivation. 1955, **3**, 1–30.

Miller, D. R., & Swanson, G. E. The study of conflict. 1956, **4**, 137–173.

Miller, N. E. Some reflections on the law of effect produce a new alternative to drive reduction. 1963, **11**, 65–112.

Morgan, C. T. Physiological mechanisms of motivation. 1957, **5**, 1–35.

Mowrer, O. H. Motivation and neurosis. 1953, **1**, 162–184.

Newcomb, T. M. Motivation in social behavior. 1953, **1**, 139–162.

Nissen, H. W. The nature of the drive as innate determinant of behavioral organization. 1954, **2**, 281–320.

Nowlis, V. The development and modification of motivational systems in personality. 1953, **1**, 114–138.

Olds, J. Physiological mechanisms of reward. 1955, **3**, 73–138.

Osgood, C. E. Motivational dynamics of language behavior. 1957, **5**, 348–423.

Peak, H. Attitude and motivation. 1955, **3**, 149–188.

Pettigrew, T. F. Social evaluation theory: Convergences and applications. 1967, **15**, 241–318.

Pfaffman, C. The sensory and motivating properties of the sense of taste. 1961, **9**, 71–108.

Postman, L. J. The experimental analysis of motivational factors in perception. 1953, **1**, 59–108.

Premack, D. Reinforcement theory. 1965, **13**, 123–179.

Pribram, K. H. Reinforcement revisited: A structural view. 1963, **11**, 113–160.

Rapaport, D. On the psychoanalytic theory of motivation. 1960, **8**, 173–247.

Ritchie, B. F. A logical and experimental analysis of the laws of motivation. 1954, **2**, 121–176.

Rodnick, E. H., & Garmezy, N. An experimental approach to the study of motivation in schizophrenia. 1957, **5**, 109–183.

Rogers, C. R. Actualizing tendency in relation to "motives" and to consciousness. 1963, **11**, 1–24.

Rotter, J. B. The role of the psychological situation in determining the direction of human behavior. 1955, **3**, 245–268.

Sarason, S. B. The contents of human problem solving. 1961, **9**, 147–174.

Schachter, S., & Latané, B. Crime, cognition, and the autonomic nervous system. 1964, **12**, 221–272.

Schneirla, T. C. An evolutionary and developmental theory of biphasic processes underlying approach and withdrawal. 1959, **7**, 1–41.

Scott, J. P. The development of social motivation. 1967, **15**, 111–132.

Sears, P. S. Problems in the investigation of achievement and self-esteem motivation. 1957, **5**, 265–338.

Sears, R. R. Dependency motivation. 1963, **11**, 25–64.

Seward, J. P. A neurological approach to motivation. 1956, **4**, 180–208.

Solomon, R. L., & Brush, E. S. Experimentally derived conceptions of anxiety and aversion. 1956, **4**, 212–305.

Spence, K. W. Behavior theory and selective learning. 1958, **6**, 73–107.

Taylor, D. W. Toward an informational processing theory of motivation. 1960, **8**, 51–78.

Teitelbaum, P. Disturbances in feeding and drinking behavior after hypothalamic lesions. 1961, **9**, 39–64.

Toman, W. On the periodicity of motivation. 1960, **8**, 80–94.

Vinacke, W. E. Motivation as a complex problem. 1962, **10**, 1–45.

Walker, E. L. Psychological complexity as a basis for a theory of motivation and choice. 1964, **12**, 47–94.

White R. W. Competence and the psychosexual stages of development. 1960, **8**, 97–140.

Whiting, J. W. M. Sorcery, sin, and the superego. A cross-cultural study of some mechanisms of social control. 1959, **7**, 174–194.

Wike, E. L. Secondary reinforcement: Some research and theoretical issues. 1969, **17**, 39–82.

Wittenborn, J. R. Inferring the strength of drive. 1957, **5**, 191–258.

Young, P. T. The role of hedonic processes in motivation. 1955, **3**, 193–237.

Zimbardo, P. H. The human choice: Individuation, reason, and order versus deindividuation, impulse, and chaos. 1969, **17**, 237–307.

# *Indexes*

# Subject Index

Ability and interpersonal attraction, *see* Attraction, interpersonal
Achievement need, *see* Need
Action and cognition, 248
Affiliation, *see* Need
Aggression and shock duration, 269; *see also* Anonymity and aggression
"Aggression sites," 19
Alcohol, *see* Drug subcultures
American Psychological Association, 42, 310
Amsel-Roussel double-alley study, 46
Analysis, conceptual, *see* Behavior toward members of disliked groups
Anger, 14, 51
Anonymity and aggression,
  in laboratory conditions, 263–282
  in the real world, 282–293, 304
Anonymity and destruction, *see* Anonymity and aggression
Anxiety, *see* Attraction, interpersonal; Behavior toward members of disliked groups
"Apparent Reinforcement Value" (ARV), 88, 131, 132, 140
Appetitive conditioning, *see* Reinforcement
Approach and withdrawal, 23
Approval, *see* Need
Arousal and emotion, 262
ARV, *see* "Apparent Reinforcement Value"
Attitude change, 179, 194–197; *see also* Behavior toward members of disliked groups
Attitude-related behavior, 179–230
Attitude toward members of a disliked group, *see* Behavior toward members of disliked groups
Attraction, interpersonal, ix, 143–173
  anxiety and, 155–156, 159, 161
  being liked and, 144
  complementarity of need systems and, 144
  gain-loss theory of, x, 150–172
  high ability and, 144, 147–149
  "mini-theories" of, 150, 166, 174
  physical beauty and, 160–161, 167
  pleasant characteristics and behavior and, 144
  propinquity and, 143
  reward cost theory of, x, 150–172
  similarity of personal traits and, 144
  similarity of values and beliefs and, 143
Automobiles, abandoned, *see* Destruction of abandoned automobiles
"Auto shaping," 29
  a field experiment on, 287

Barnard College, 280
Beauty, *see* Attraction, interpersonal
*Behavior of Organisms, The*, 52
Behavior toward members of disliked groups,
  anxiety and, 215

cognitive characteristics and, 217–218, 224
ego-defense and, 216
interaction variables, 201, 202, 208, 212, 219
outcome variables, 201, 202, 212, 218–222
person variables, 201, 202, 205–207, 211–218, 229
situational variables, 201, 202, 204–205, 207–211
sources of gratification and, 209, 210, 224
stimulus generalization in, 222, 225–226
values and, 217
*See also* Disliked groups, members of; Racial desegregation
Being liked, and interpersonal attraction, *see* Attraction, interpersonal
Belgian army, 272–276
Berkeley student riots, 296
Brain sites involved in motivation, *see* Motivation
Broad response tendencies, 19

Catharsis, 271
Central motive state, 12, 16, 19; *see also* Motivation
Children, battered, 243
Choice, human, 237–307
Civil rights workers, slaying of, 256
Cognition, 238, 240
Cognitive control, *see* Control, cognitive
Cognitive factors, 18, 36
Columbia University, 244
Commitment, 238
Conceptual analysis, *see* Behavior toward members of disliked groups
"Conceptual paradox" of $S^r$ and frustration, 55
Conditioned incentive stimuli, 16
Consistency, 238, 239–240, 255
Consummatory activity, 93, 124–131, 238
Control,
cognitive, 238, 240, 255
external, 238
in psychology, 237
internal, 238, 270
loss of, 246–247, 279, 294
*See also* Order
Curare, conditioning under, 8

"Danger" signals, 55
Dehumanization, 296–299, 304; *see also* Deindividuation; Individuation
Deindividuation, 237, 248, 249, 251, 306, *see also* Individuation
"Demand characteristics" of experiments, 264
Destruction of abandoned automobiles, at Stanford University, 290–292
in New York City, 263, 285–290, 292
in Palo Alto, California, 287
Destruction of others, 241–243
Differential reinforcement of low rates (DRL), 45
Dionysus, 248–249
Disliked groups, members of,
contact with, 182, 183–187, 197, 199
hostility toward, 182
motives toward, 170, 180, 197
*See also* Behavior toward members of disliked groups; Racial desegregation
Dissonance theory, 238
Drive reduction, *see* Drives; Reinforcement; Reward
Drives,
hunger, 10, 11
pain, 11
physiological processes and, 11–16
primary, 39
secondary, 39
sexual, 10
thirst, 10, 12, 16
Drug subcultures, 295–296

"Ego identity," 254
Event theory, xi, 180–181, 197–199; *see also* Social Psychology, strategy in
"Expectancy," 18
Experiments on "response substitution," 3
Exploration, 8, 20
Extinction, 75, 83
  and frustration, *see* Frustration
  resistance to, 83

Factor analysis, 196
Fear, 14, 51
Feedback, *see* Sensory feedback
Fractional antedating goal reaction, viii, 40, 42, 51
Free Sex League, 248
Frustration, viii, 40, 42, 46, 53, 55
  and extinction, 56–63
  fractional anticipatory, 46
Gain-loss theory of interpersonal attraction, *see* Attraction, interpersonal
Goal-directed behavior, 4, 8

Habit, 8
Homeostasis, psychological, 239
Homicides, 241
Hope, 50, 51
Hunger drive, *see* Drives
Hypnosis, 293–295, 306

Incentive motivation, vii, 11, 25, 85, 101, 131
Incentives, 5, 9, 85, 133
Individuation, 237, 240, 248, 250, 272, 304, 305
Inhibited behaviors, 252, 253, 255
Instrumental conditioning, 3, 85
Interaction variables, *see* Behavior toward members of disliked groups
Intergroup relations, *see* Behavior toward members of disliked groups; Disliked groups, members of
Internal control, *see* Control, internal
Intracranial stimulation, 6, 7, 19, 31, 91

Japanese and personal responsibility, 240
*Journal of the Experimental Analysis of Behavior*, 53
Joy, 14
Jungian primitive energy-form model, 263

Ku Klux Klan (KKK), 296

Laboratory studies,
  of motivation, 237
  of unintended interracial contact, 187–197, 232
Laws of behavior control, 238
Learning and motivation, *see* Motivation, learned sources of
"Learning without responding," 3, 34
Levels of aggression, *see* Anonymity and aggression
Living for the moment, 256, 293; *see also* Time
*Lord of the Flies*, 250
Loss of behavior control, *see* Control, loss of
Loss of the value of life, 245–246
Love, 14
LSD, *see* Drug subcultures

Mechanisms of reinforcement, *see* Reinforcement
Methamphetamines, 295
Metronome, 4, 6
"Mini-theories," *see* Attraction, interpersonal
Mob violence, *see* Riots and mob violence
Motivation,
  and drive, 9–11
  and reinforcement, 1–33
  Bindra's model of, 22
  brain sites involved in, 8, 28
  central motive state in, 12–14
  conditions affecting, 10

learned sources of, 39
secondary, 15
*See also* Laboratory studies, of motivation
Motivational psychology, 310
Motives toward members of disliked groups, *see* Behavior toward members of disliked groups; Disliked groups, members of; Motivation

National Institute of Mental Health, xii
*Nebraska Symposium on Motivation,* 171, 237, 309–323
Need,
achievement, 170, 213, 215, 229, 238
affiliation, 213, 214, 215, 229
approval, 213, 214, 229, 238
biological, 238
economic, 213, 215
social, 238
to shatter formal controls, 254
Neuropsychological mechanisms, 1
New York City, *see* Destruction of abandoned automobiles, in New York City
New York University, 263, 264, 266, 272, 276
Notterman-Block hypothesis, 54

Obedience studies, 270
Order, 237, 254, 305; *see also* Control
Outcome variables, *see* Behavior toward members of disliked groups

Palo Alto, *see* Destruction of abandoned automobiles, in Palo Alto, California
Parameters of Reward, *see* Reward, parameters of
"Police riots," 244
*Principles of Behavior*, 42
Propinquity and interpersonal attraction, *see* Attraction, interpersonal
Psychology, motivational, *see* Motivational psychology

Racial desegregation, 180, 183, 185–187, 196; *see also* Disliked groups, members of
Rationality, 239–240
Rats,
blocked at different distances from the goal box, 55
in restraining cages, 5
"Reconditioning hypothesis," viii, 75–77, 83; *see also* Reinforcement, secondary
Reinforcement,
as a change in performance, 87
as a hypothetical change within the organism, 87
as an empirical principle, 86
as a set of operations, 86
as primary factor of motivation, 4
as special case of motivation, 1–33
associative interpretations of, 95–96
brain sites involved in, 8, 28
definitions of, 85–88
incentive interpretations of, 95, 97–99, 100
mechanisms of, 94–99, 131
partial, 83
primary, 43, 73, 83
schedules of, 45, 69–74, 237, 261
secondary, vii, 15, 39–82
Reinforcing events, 3, 5, 24
Relief, 51
Religious orders, 303
Response determination, 18–30
Response instigation, 1–30
Response reinforcement, 1, 3, 8, 30
Responsibility, 238, 239–240, 255, 256
Reward,
anticipation of, 46
delay of, 48
drive-reduction factors in, 94
magnitude of, 103–124, 131, 133

mechanisms of, *see* Reinforcement, mechanisms of
omission of, 48
parameters of, 85–134
primary, 39, 100
response factors in, 91, 94, 99
secondary, 39
sources of, ix, 40, 90, 94, 99, 106, 133, 138
stimulus factors in, 90, 99
theories of, 89–100
Riots and mob violence, 243–245

Schedules of reinforcement, *see* Reinforcement, schedules of
Secondary reinforcers, 44, 75, 83; *see also* Reinforcement, secondary
Self-destruction, 241
Sensory feedback, 12
Sexual drive, *see* Drives, sexual
Similarity of values and interpersonal attraction, *see* Attraction, interpersonal
Situational variables in attitude change, *see* Attitude change; Behavior toward members of disliked groups
Social psychology, strategy in, 179–181
Society for the Psychological Study of Social Issues, 182
Sources of reward, *see* Reward, sources of
$S^r$, *see* Reinforcement, secondary
Stanford University, *see* Destruction of abandoned automobiles, at Stanford University
Stimulus control, *see* Control
Suicide, *see* Self-destruction

TAT, *see* Thematic Apperception Test
Thematic Apperception Test, 276
Theories of reward, *see* Reward, theories of
Thirst drive, *see* Drives, thirst
Time, 261, 293–296
Training animals, 5

Unintended interracial contact, *see* Laboratory studies, of unintended interracial contact
University of Louvain, 272
University of Oklahoma, 245
University of Texas, 242

Vandalism, 283–293

Work-inhibition theory, 43
World Health Organization, 241

*Zorba the Greek*, 292

# Author Index

Aaronson, B. S., 293, 306
Amsel, A., 46, 51, 77
Arnold, W. J., 309, 312
Aronfreed, J., 318, 319
Aronson, E., 143, 145, 148, 151, 157, 158, 159, 161, 165, 167, 169, 174, 177, 318, 319
Atkinson, J. W., 313, 319
Azrin, N. H., 54, 77

Baldwin, A. L., 315, 321
Bales, R. F., 147, 171
Bandura, A., 316, 319
Barker, R. G., 315, 319
Beach, F. A., 314, 319
Bell, L., 169, 172
Bergum, B. O., 62, 78
Berlyne, D. E., 91, 134, 317, 319
Bindra, D., vii, 1, 4, 5, 9, 11, 31, 34, 83, 132, 318, 319
Birch, D. A., 316, 319
Black, R. W., viii, 11, 31, 34, 85, 91, 98, 101, 103, 104, 106, 109, 114, 115, 132, 134, 138, 318, 319
Block, A. H., 53, 80
Bolles, R. C., 9, 31, 63–68, 75, 314, 319
Bower, G. H., 47, 79, 114, 134
Brehm, J. W., 316, 319
Brown, J. S., 309, 313, 319
Brown, P. L., 29, 31
Brush, E. S., 314, 323
Bugelsky, R., 55, 58, 65, 78
Burke, C. J., 317, 319
Butter, C. M., 8, 31
Byrne, D., 144, 145, 162, 171, 215, 230

Cammin, W. B., 120–122, 134
Campbell, D. T., 317, 319
Campbell, J. F., 6, 31
Camus, A., 247, 261
Capaldi, E. J., 78, 115, 134
Cattell, R. B., 315, 320
Chambliss, D. J., 58, 82
Chase, T., 170
Christopher, S. M., 8, 31
Cilluffo, A. F., 126–129, 134
Clore, G. L., 162, 173
Collins, M. E., 183, 230
Cook, S. W., x, xi, 179, 184, 231, 232, 233, 234, 318, 320
Crespi, L. P., 114, 135

Deaux, E. B., 45, 78
Dethier, V. G., 317, 320
Deutsch, M., 183, 230, 316, 320
Dollard, J., 15, 31
Dooley, L., 254, 306

Edwards, A. L., 316, 320
Egger, M. D., 58, 78
Elstad, P. A., 103, 104, 106, 107, 109, 110, 112, 135, 140
Epstein, S., 316, 320
Eriksen, C. W., 314, 320
Estes, W. K., 314, 320

Faber, I. E., 313, 320
Falk, J. L., 315, 320
Ferster, C. B., 70, 78
Festinger, L., 143, 172, 249, 262, 306, 313, 320

Fischman, P., 129, 131, 135
Floyd, J. M. K., 170, 172
Fowler, R. L., 122–124, 135

Garmezy, N., 314, 322
Getzels, J. W., 194, 231
Glickman, S. E., 93, 133, 135
Grossman, S. P., 317, 320
Guilford, J. P., 317, 320
Guthrie, E. R., 95, 135

Harlow, H. F., 39, 309, 313, 320
Harvey, O. J., 168, 172, 218, 231
Heckhausen, H., 310, 318, 320
Heider, F., 315, 320
Helfer, R. E., 243, 306
Helson, H., 317, 320
Hess, E., 315, 320
Hiers, J. M., 115–120, 135
Hilgard, E. R., 47, 79, 310, 316, 320
Hill, W. F., 47, 79
Hollander, E. P., 147, 172
Holt, R. R., 317, 320
Homans, G., 144, 172
Hull, C. L., 4, 11, 24, 31, 32, 36, 40, 41, 42, 88, 96, 135
Hunt, J. McV., 317, 320

Janis, I. L., 315, 321
Jenkins, H. M., 29, 31
Jones, E. E., 169, 172
Jones, M. R., 309, 312

Katz, I., 317, 321
Kelleher, R. T., 57, 65, 68–70, 76, 79
Keller, F. S., 40, 52
Kelley, H. H., 317, 321
Kelly, G. A., 316, 321
Kendall, P., 143, 172
Kendler, H. H., 316, 321
Klein, G. S., 313, 321
Koch, S., 314, 321
Komorita, S. S., 194, 231
Kraeling, D., 45, 79
Kramer, B. M., 185, 231

Lambert, W. W., 55, 80
Landy, D., 165, 172
Lashley, K. S., 3, 32
Latané, B., 316, 323
Lazarus, R. S., 318, 321
Leeper, R. W., 317, 321
Levin, H., 315, 321
Levine, D., vii, 309, 312
Levine, S., 318, 321
Linder, D., 151, 157, 158, 171
Lindsley, D. B., 314, 321
Littman, R. A., 314, 321
Logan, F. A., 41, 52, 80, 316, 321
Longstreth, L. E., 55, 57–63, 66, 80
Lott, D. F., 55–57, 80

McClearn, G. E., 317, 321
McClelland, D. C., 313, 321
McKeachie, W. J., 315, 321
Madsen, K. B., 310, 312
Magoun, H. W., 316, 321
Malamud, W., 317, 321
Malmo, R. B., 314, 321
Mandler, G., 316, 321
Marx, K., 255
Marx, M. H., 314, 321
Masling, J., 317, 321
Maslow, A., 313, 322
Mendelson, J., 11, 20, 28, 31
Mettee, D., 166, 172
Milgram, S., 270, 306
Miller, D. R., 314, 322
Miller, N. E., 15, 23, 31, 32, 58, 78, 80, 92, 93, 99, 316, 322
Mills, J., 160, 172
Morgan, C. T., 12, 32, 35, 314, 322
Mowrer, O. H., 18, 32, 35, 50–52, 74, 309, 313, 322

Newcomb, T. M., 143, 172, 182, 210, 231, 250, 262, 306, 309, 313, 322
Nietzsche, F., 248–249, 254, 306
Nissen, H. W., 11, 32, 313, 322
Notterman, J. M., 53, 80
Nowlis, V., 309, 313, 322
Nuttin, J., 272

Olds, J., 314, 322
Osgood, C. E., 314, 322

Page, M. M., 309
Palfai, T., 4, 31
Patten, R. L., 45, 78
Peak, H., 314, 322
Pepitone, A., 249, 262, 306
Pettigrew, T. F., 317, 322
Pfaffmann, C., 315, 322
Postman, L. J., 309, 313, 322
Premack, D., 93, 108, 136, 138, 317, 322
Pribram, K. H., 316, 322

Rapaport, A., 247, 306
Rapaport, D., 315, 322
Ray, E., 155, 173
Rescorla, R. A., 24, 32, 45, 80
Reynolds, G., 261, 306
Ritchie, B. F., 313, 322
Rodnick, E. H., 314, 322
Rogers, C. R., 316, 322
Rosenberg, M. J., 224, 231
Rotter, J. B., 314, 322

Saltzman, I. J., 56, 66, 81
Sarason, S. B., 316, 322
Schachter, S., 143, 146, 172, 176, 316, 323
Schneidman, E. S., 241, 306
Schneirla, T. C., 23, 32, 315, 323
Schoenfeld, W. N., 40, 52
Schopenhauer, A., 249, 306
Schuster, S. D., 162, 173
Scott, J. P., 317, 323
Sears, P. S., 314, 323
Sears, R. R., 316, 323
Seward, J. P., 11, 18, 32, 101, 136, 314, 323
Shapiro, D., 144, 173
Sheffield, F. D., 48–50, 81, 91, 98, 136
Sidowski, J., 58, 82
Sigall, H., 159, 162–165, 167, 169, 173
Singer, J. E., 250, 306
Skinner, B. F., 52–55, 70, 78, 81, 89
Solomon, R. L., 3, 8, 33, 55, 80, 314, 323
Spence, K. W., 11, 18, 24, 33, 43, 97, 107, 137, 324, 323
Spinoza, B., 155, 173
Stapert, J. C., 162, 173
Swanson, G. E., 314, 322

Taylor, D. W., 315, 323
Teitelbaum, P., 315, 323
Thibaut, J., 144, 173
Thorndike, E. L., 48, 95, 137
Tolman, E. C., 18, 33
Toman, W., 315, 323
Turner, L. H., 3, 8, 33

Vinacke, W. E., 316, 323
Walker, E. L., 316, 323
Walkley, R. P., 184, 231
Walters, R. H., 155, 173
Watson, G., 182, 231
Westie, F. R., 194, 231
White, R. T., 65
White, R. W., 39, 156, 173, 315, 323
Whiting, J. W., 315, 323
Wike, E. L., viii, 34, 39, 47, 56, 66, 68, 71, 82, 83, 124, 138, 318, 323
Williams, R., 182, 231
Wilner, D. M., 184, 231
Winch, R. F., 144, 173
Winder, A. E., 186, 231
Wittenborn, J. R., 314, 323
Worchel, P., 162, 173
Wrightsman, L. S., 188
Wrightsman, S., 188
Wyckoff, L. B., 58, 82

Young, P. T., 133, 137, 314, 323

Ziller, R. C., 250, 276, 307
Zimbardo, P. G., xii, 174, 232, 237, 238, 239, 318, 323
Zimmerman, D. W., 67, 74, 82
Zimmerman, J., 68, 71, 82